KNOWLEDGE, BELIEF, AND OPINION

KNOWLEDGE, BELIEF AND OPINION

By JOHN LAIRD, M.A.

ARCHON BOOKS
1972

Library of Congress Cataloging in Publication Data

Laird, John, 1887–1946.
　Knowledge, belief, and opinion.

　　Original ed. issued in series: The Century philosphy
series.
　　Bibliography: p.
　　1. Knowledge, Theory of. 2. Belief and doubt. I. Title
BD161.L3　1972　　　　　　　121　　　　　　　72-6560
ISBN 0-208-01215-X

Printed in the United States of America

PREFACE

This preface is written because I have to make, and am glad to make, certain acknowledgments.

While I was engaged in writing the present book, I accepted the onerous privilege of composing a presidential address for the Aristotelian Society, and it seemed to me, rightly or wrongly, that the best I could give them was connected with the work with which my mind was full. I therefore dealt, in a briefer way than here, with the general subject of the opening chapters of this book. When the same phrasing seemed appropriate to both enterprises, I did not usually attempt to alter it.

I have learnt so much from so many of my contemporaries that I am afraid I should not begin to express obligations of this order. For I wish this preface to be short. Perhaps I may say, however, that, in my own judgment, I owe more to the writings of Mr. G. E. Moore than to the works of any other of my contemporaries. And I may add that, among the masters in the history of philosophy, I have a predilection for the works of David Hume. The latter fact, I think, is pretty evident in the succeeding pages.

With insignificant exceptions, the writing of the book was completed in the autumn of 1929, and I have decided, with some reluctance but with more relief, to avoid all reference, even by way of footnotes, to any more recent philosophical works.

JOHN LAIRD.

CONTENTS

CONTENTS

PAGE

§ 4. TIME AND CONTEXT 203

§ 4. TIME AND CONTEXT 203
§ 5. THE IDENTITY OF PROPOSITIONS 206
§ 6. UNIVERSALS 208
§ 7. RELATIONAL PROPERTIES 212
§ 8. THE LAW OF CONTRADICTION 214
§ 9. THE LAW OF EXCLUDED MIDDLE 216
§ 10. GENERAL CONCERNING THE LAWS OF THOUGHT 217

CHAPTER IX OF INFERENTIAL CERTAINTY 220

§ 1. INFERENCE AND TRUTH 220
§ 2. IMMEDIATE INFERENCE 221
§ 3. MEDIATE INFERENCE 225
§ 4. EXTENSION OF THE TRADITIONAL SYLLOGISM 231

CHAPTER X THE CERTAINTIES OF ARITHMETIC AND GEOMETRY . . . 234

§ 1. PRELIMINARY 234
§ 2. THE NATURE OF NUMBER 235
§ 3. THE APPLICATION OF NUMBER TO FACT 237
§ 4. COUNTING 239
§ 5. A CONSPECTUS OF MODERN MATHEMATICAL IDEALS OF PROOF . 240
§ 6. GEOMETRY 245

CHAPTER XI OF CERTAINTY IN ETHICS 251

§ 1. GENERAL 251
§ 2. VARIETIES OF INTUITIONISM IN ETHICS 252
§ 3. PARTICULAR INTUITIONISM 252
§ 4. GENERAL INTUITIONISM 255
§ 5. FORMAL INTUITIONISM 260
§ 6. RIGHT AND GOOD 265
§ 7. INTUITIONS INTO VALUE 266

CHAPTER XII OF SENSITIVE CERTAINTY 269

§ 1. EXPLANATORY 269
§ 2. THE CERTAINTY OF SENSA 270
§ 3. THE MOMENTARY SENSUM 274
§ 4. DOUBTS CONCERNING SENSA 278
§ 5. THE TESTIMONY OF THE SENSES 282

CHAPTER XIII OF MNEMIC CERTAINTY, WITH SOME REMARKS CONCERNING HISTORY 292

§ 1. THE DESCRIPTION OF MNEMIC PHENOMENA 292
§ 2. REPRODUCTION VERSUS RE-INSPECTION 294
§ 3. THE SPECIOUS PAST AND THE SPECIOUS PRESENT 297
§ 4. THE PLACE OF MEMORY-IMAGES 299
§ 5. AN ALTERNATIVE THEORY 302
§ 6. THE COGENCY OF MEMORY-EVIDENCE 304
§ 7. SOME REMARKS CONCERNING HISTORY 307

CONTENTS

Book I

THE SCOPE OF THE INQUIRY

KNOWLEDGE, BELIEF, AND OPINION

CHAPTER I

INTRODUCTORY

§ 1. COGITATION

IT is my intention, in this essay, to examine the nature and the mutual relations of knowledge, belief, and opinion, or, in other words, to attempt the survey of what is usually and (I think) correctly described as the cogitative part of our nature. The puzzling features in this inquiry, as the history of philosophical speculation abundantly shows, are of high theoretical interest to many minds at many times, and so much in the subject is unsolved, if not insoluble, that no apology is needed, or should be expected, from any one who sets out, once again, upon a very ancient adventure. Indeed, it is important for every student of.philosophy to perambulate, and even to lose his way, in this familiar territory, provided always that he has a purpose in his wanderings and cultivates the art of losing his way methodically.

To be sure, there are certain psychophobiacs among us who maintain, or aver that they maintain, that there is nothing cogitative in human nature at all. What is called, or miscalled, cogitation, they say is only a habit of speech—that is to say a laryngeal trick of the human animal that leads the animal to emit recurrent noises. And so they themselves emit and reiterate their own meaningless noises. With these psychophobiacs we have here no concern.

In other words, we accept the fact tersely described by Spinoza in the second axiom of the second part of his *Ethics* —the fact that *homo cogitat*. Our object is to endeavor in some measure to understand the fact together with its implications, its functions, and its conditions.

3

We wish, in short, to accept the fact, but not to accept it uncritically. And the criticism is likely to be a long and intricate affair. In the end, we may be impelled towards the belief that the cogitative spirit, without spiritual pride, must, from self-respect, take pride in its spiritual autonomy. On the other hand, we may have to conclude, like the disillusioned and dying Hotspur, that

> "thought's the slave of life, and life time's fool;
> And time, that takes survey of all the world,
> Must have a stop."

The end of this adventure being hidden, there is no sense in preliminary surmises concerning it. What is clear at the moment is simply that human beings actually do think.

§ 2. EPISTEMOLOGY

Granting, however, that cogitations exist, it is necessary to grant, in addition, that they are examinable: supposing, that is, that a critical inquiry into them can be undertaken with any reasonable prospect of success. And such an inquiry is epistemology, or the self-criticism of our cogitative faculties. For it is plain that nothing except cogitation is able to examine our cogitations in the way required. Are we then entitled to assume that epistemology itself is possible, that the cogitative part of our being can really examine itself with any serious expectation of discovering the truth about its own nature?

According to several contemporary authors, the present age is wiser than former ages, at any rate in certain important particulars. It has learned to avoid *some* egregious mistakes; and one of these mistakes is the former reliance upon epistemology. Epistemology, we are informed, has become a plain anachronism. We have witnessed its decline, and should celebrate its obsequies, with due decorum if possible, but not without relief.

Since I am writing an epistemological essay, I am bound, of course, to deny that the door should be banged and bolted in this truculent fashion; but, for the rest, I am entitled to ask the reader to wait and see. Let it be granted that epistemology is on its trial, and even that every epistemological adventure is suspect from the start. The important point at the moment is that it should be given a chance. Let it be heard before it is struck down.

I propose, therefore, to smooth the way towards obtaining this very moderate initial concession, by endeavoring to show that some of the more serious objections currently advanced against the possibility of *any* epistemology are only objections against a certain type of assumption in epistemology.

According to the objectors, a full-blooded, or a blue-blooded, epistemologist is a person who believes that cogitation should examine its own powers and capacities *before* examining or conjecturing anything apprehended by means of cogitation. First test your bridge, and then you may know what traffic it is able to bear. Know your own mind, before you begin to ask what is or is not conformable to your mind. Such is the general sense of Kant's quotation from Persius: "Tecum habita, et noris quam sit tibi curta supellex."

This (the objector goes on) is pedigree epistemology—epistemology in earnest about itself. Yet the objector also avers that a mongrel or less resolute epistemology is forced to make assumptions equally illegitimate if not quite so objectionable. The moderate epistemologist may not assert that the mind must be known *before* anything else can be known, but at the least he must hold that the mind is a knowable thing, among other things. In fact, however, (the objector tells us) even if minds are somehow examinable, they are not examinable *in this way*. The mind is *not* a thing among other things. It cannot be directly inspected. It cannot be conquered, or even approached, by a direct frontal attack. On the contrary, we have to infer the potencies and the aptitudes of mind (if haply we can ever draw such inferences) at the end, not at the beginning, of any intelligible philosophical exploration. It is fact and science that tell us what we can do in the cogitative way. First clear up your facts, and your minds will look after themselves. Study things, reality, matter of fact, and mind (you will discover) slips easily and naturally into its proper place. To use the vernacular, epistemology has attempted to grasp (it cannot really grasp) the wrong end of the stick; and it is the business of any sane philosophy to grasp the right end of the stick firmly and from the outset.

Without attempting to debate this large topic at all fully at the moment, I shall have done enough for present purposes, I think, if I point out that epistemologists are not compelled to make either of the assumptions that are censured so severely in the objections stated above.

Firstly, then, we must concede, and indeed must strenuously insist, that there is no possibility of studying cogitations *in vacuo*. Even if they could conceivably exist quite alone, they are never, in our experience, discernible quite alone. On the contrary, we are acquainted with them only when they are performing their cogitative function, that is to say when we are cogitating, or excogitating, objects by means of them. Nevertheless, since it seems plain that objects may exist without being thought about, it is hard to deny that *something* supervenes when cogitation takes place; and this something, whether or not it occurs in isolation, may well be studied and may well repay study. It is conceivable, even, that we might learn what our cogitative faculties are fitted for, and where they fail us, by analyzing the nature of their employment. Such was Locke's opinion, and Kant's also. On the other hand, it is quite unnecessary to put our trust, at the outset, in this or in any other epistemological dogma. Epistemology is legitimate, and may be essential, even, if Locke and Kant were mistaken in holding this particular opinion.

Secondly, when we maintain that we may examine our cogitative faculties as well as simply employ them, nothing at all is said about the nature of this self-examination. It may well be true that the thinking part of us is not a thing among other things, and that, in itself, it is neither a thing nor a part of a thing. The examination, consequently, may have to adopt methods quite dissimilar from those that are appropriate to the examination of "things." It is part of our inquiry whether any such fundamental difference exists, or has only been falsely supposed to exist by certain notable but bemused philosophers; and there is no need for us to begin by prejudging this cardinal issue.

What must now be observed is, quite simply, that the examination of human cogitative powers may be entirely possible for mankind even if selves, and the cogitative parts of selves, have a unique status in the realm of existence and have to be assessed by quite special devices.

§ 3. KNOWLEDGE AND COGITATIONS

I have said that knowledge, belief, and opinion are species of cogitation, this last being the most general and the least question-begging word I could think of in order to indicate my meaning.

In saying so, however, I am fully aware that all important philosophical terms are to some extent question-begging, and particularly so in the present instance. Thus Hume maintained that belief belonged to the sensitive rather than to the cogitative part of our nature. Samuel Butler maintained that knowledge, in the fundamental sense of unquestioning and unquestioned assurance, was non-cogitative because it was strictly unconscious. And Cook Wilson held that it was a grave error to attempt to bring such utterly different processes as knowledge and opinion under any general caption.

These problems will occupy us in the sequel, along with many others. It seems expedient, however, to glance at some aspects of some of them in the present place.

If by "cogitation" we mean "thinking," it seems plain that in certain uses of ordinary language there is a decided contrast between "thinking" and "knowing." The word "thinking" suggests that we are pondering over something of which we make a question, whereas, when we "know," we are surely quite certain of what we know. Therefore, according to Cook Wilson, it is always a flat contradiction to say "I think I know," and it is always a mistake to regard "thinking" and "knowing" as co-ordinate species of the common genus "cogitation."

No doubt, there are certain loose and vulgar senses of "knowledge" in which there is no such contradiction. Thus we sometimes say we "know" something when we mean only that we could remember it, or perhaps that we could repeat it at will. In this sense there is no contradiction in saying "I think I know Gray's *Elegy*," for the statement means only "I am of opinion that I could repeat the poem correctly if I tried." Similarly, and more generally, if by "knowledge" we mean only the bare potency of understanding something not actually contemplated at the moment (e.g. a demonstration in geometry or in formal logic), we can say "I think I know" without contradicting ourselves in any way; for all we are saying is that we believe we could grasp the point with complete comprehension and with utter clarity if we gave our attention to it.

It is otherwise, however, if we are dealing with immediate present contemplation, whether by way of present memory or in any other way that (in the general view) is stamped with the certainty of full knowledge. Therefore we must concede that if "knowledge" implies certainty, and if "thinking" implies uncertainty, "knowledge" and "thinking" are very different indeed, and are only to be ranked in a common genus if, despite this difference, there are marked similarities in the kind of process that each of them essentially is.

I think there are very marked similarities of this order, and I doubt whether the presence or absence of possible questioning is truly so very important. The fundamental point, I think, is what can *abide* our questioning, not simply what remains unquestioned. But it is too early to debate so serious a matter; and therefore I propose to deal briefly with another aspect of this affair. This second aspect arises directly from the implications contained in the alleged contradiction "I think I know."

If "I think I know" is a contradiction, on the ground that I cannot entertain any doubts about my own certainty, is it therefore to be inferred that, as Spinoza said,[1] any one who knows also knows that he knows? Is not "knowing that we know" more complicated than simple knowing? Is it not a knowing of our knowing as well as a knowing of what we know?

Suppose, for example, that some interrogator (let us say, a detective in the story-books) asks us kindly to distinguish between what we *know* and what we only think, and suppose that the detective, not being a professional epistemologist, means by

[1] *Ethics*, II, xliii.

"knowledge" what we call "common knowledge." In that case it is assumed that any one who, as we say, "sees" a burglar in a good light and "sees him again" at an identification parade, knows for certain that he has seen one and the same person on the two occasions. Skeptical doubts about the general unreliability of memory, or about the relation of multiple personality to personal identity, do not enter the heads either of the interrogator or of the person interrogated. Both accept the premise that certain facts and events can be known with complete certainty, but both are very well aware that there is a very notable difference between what we clearly see, clearly remember, and the like, on the one hand, and what we are apt to surmise or think likely on the other hand. In the ordinary way of conversation we might expect others to accept our surmises as well as our "knowledge"; but not on a serious occasion when sterner standards are admittedly required.

Nevertheless, when a witness is asked to be careful, to be *sure* that he really does remember that he actually noticed that so and so was in the room when the clock conveniently struck nine, he is really being asked to perform rather a delicate operation. It is assumed that "seeing" implies knowing, but the witness is asked whether he is sure that he saw. Yet in general, when a man sees, he does not raise the question whether he is seeing or no. He interrogates himself on the point only when he has reason to suspect a trick or has otherwise to be on his guard. And in that case he may be genuinely puzzled. Did he really see the rabbits coming out of the hat at a conjuring show, or did he only think he saw them doing so? If he saw them coming out of the hat, he knows (according to the standards of "common" knowledge) that they really did come out of the hat. But did he see them coming out of the hat?

In general, therefore, it would appear that men may and do know many things without so much as considering whether they know them or not, and in that case they can hardly be said to know that they know. Accordingly, we can not assent quite literally to Spinoza's statement. "Knowing that we know" seems to be a secondary operation directed upon primary knowing, and the primary operation may occur without the secondary. On the other hand it may be argued that if, instead of "knowing," we speak of certainty, then the primary fact of certainty is the whole fact in the case. Is it not redundant and foolishly extravagant to speak of any one's certainty about being certain? Is there not just one fact in the case, the fact that he *is* certain? And if this be the truth, what are we to do about it?

Should we say that, in all cases of knowledge strictly so-called, any one who knows *would* know that he knows, *if* he considered the question whether he was knowing or not?

It seems difficult to answer this question. The operation of considering one's knowledge is frequently strained and unnatural, although it may become a species of second nature among epistemologists, that is to say among those who busy themselves, not with knowing in its primary employment by first intention, but with the secondary and more complicated question of *evidence* or of knowing that we know. Thus if the plain man, or the plain woman, were asked to give reasons for their certainty, it is highly improbable that they could give such reasons with any approach to technical accuracy, or at all in the way that trained epistemologists would rightly demand from one another. The best these plain people could do would be to indicate more or less clearly that they possessed the sort of acquaintance with certain matters that epistemologists, as a result of their own inquiries, might admit to be authentic knowledge.

Yet if this authentic knowledge is really (as some maintain) self-certifying and self-evidential, it might be held that all who possess such knowledge really do know that they know, whether or not they are capable of expressing their knowledge or of explaining it to other people. Those who are vulgar and ill-trained according to philosophical standards may be timid, evasive, careless, overbold, or actually speechless when they attempt to expound the evidential worth of their own evidence; and yet, in a sense, they may really, although inarticulately or misarticulately, know that they know. They may know that they know *until they are asked to give a reason.* And it is not altogether impossible that, in certain cases, human knowledge, even of the most vulgar kind, may be so utterly intelligible and so translucent in itself that puzzles can scarcely arise unless darkness is

artificially introduced by some mistaken endeavor to explain
these pellucid clarities in terms of something else—something
that does not clarify.

§ 4. EVIDENCE, SELF-EVIDENCE, AND CERTAINTY

We have started a hare, and, as a contemporary author neatly
says, "doubtless a pregnant hare." In other words, as soon as
we begin to debate concerning evidence, knowledge, and certainty, we find half a dozen questions to deal with instead of
a single one. Let us then briefly consider a few of these insistent
questions.

(a). It seems plain that knowledge is rather *evidence* than
simple vidence, seeing, or inspection. It is *in*sight rather than
mere sight. And this distinction appears to persist when such
terms as vision, seeing, or inspection are extended in such a way
as to include all primary apprehension of any sort whatsoever.
Of this more anon.

(b). The passage from vidence to evidence itself implies a
transition to something scarcely distinguishable from epistemology. What we ask, when we ask for evidence, is whether facts
or other entities apprehended in a certain way carry with them
a definite probative force. We demand a writ of *certiorari.* It
is true that this function is frequently ascribed to logic. According to J. S. Mill, "Logic is the science of proof or evidence."
It may be doubted, however, whether logic, so defined, is really
distinct from epistemology, and the two seem to cling together
very affectionately in Mill's pages. In so far as he distinguished
them, he did so by an arbitrary limitation of the meaning of
the term "evidence." "Evidence" he said referred to inference
and to inference only; [2] and therefore he sometimes maintained
that logic "in a direct way at least . . . had nothing to do
. . . with the original data, or ultimate premises of our knowledge, with their number or nature, the mode in which they are
obtained, or the tests by which they may be distinguished." [3]
Mill did not, however, renounce all consideration of these matters in his *Logic.* Had he done so his work would have been far
less valuable than it is.

[2] *System of Logic,* Introduction, § 4.   [3] *Ibid.*

(c). The statement that authentic knowledge may be self-certified and self-evidential probably presents serious difficulty to several readers. When Spinoza said [4] that truth supplied its own criterion—*veritas norma sui et falsi*—he was saying what, in some sense, finds very general agreement. If knowledge chokes you, what can you drink? Is there anything except (true) knowledge that can conceivably correct (mistaken attempts at) knowledge? To pass from this, however (as Spinoza meant to do) to the species of epistemological pluralism that relies on *several* self-evident truths or axioms, is a further step that seems clearly preposterous to many. According to this other point of view there can be no genuine knowledge short of the whole, or at any rate short of a highly integrated system of knowledge.

Let me say then at once that in referring to the possible self-evidence of knowledge I am trying to speak with the utmost innocence, and am endeavoring to refrain from any *arrière pensée* concerning the debate between a more or less) monistic view of epistemology and a (more or less) pluralistic doctrine in that science. In other words, I am saying nothing about the minimum girth or rotundity of "knowledge," and am not inquiring, at present, how much any one must have in his mind if he can truly be said to know anything at all. For all I have said, the light of self-evidence may not be able to shine even in the feeblest way unless it is reflected over a pretty wide area; and its illuminating power may presuppose many other conditions. I am only pointing out the apparent possibility of the phenomenon.

(d). Some preliminary explanation concerning the term "certainty" seems manifestly to be required. In one sense of the word we are certain whenever we are *sure;* and we *are* sure whenever we know anything. On the other hand, if mere psychological assurance or conviction were all that were meant, it would be obvious that the certainty of knowledge implies a great deal more than mere psychological conviction. For we can be *assured* when we can not pretend to *know;* and we may cherish the deepest convictions without a tittle of evidence, or against the evidence, or on very bad evidence, or from emotional or

[4] *Ethics,* II, xliii, Schol.

other causes that could not conceivably be considered adequate reasons.

The certainty of genuine knowledge, therefore, if it exists, must be *evidential* certainty, not any sort of assurance (however complete) acquired in any sort of way. The fact that we attain assurance is not enough for knowledge. What is equally important is how we attain it. And this important circumstance clearly distinguishes genuine knowledge from mere belief.

§ 5. BELIEF IN RELATION TO ASSURANCE

It should be remarked at the outset that there is a certain diversity in the popular usage of the term Belief. "Is this the train for St. Andrews?" "I believe so." Any one who received this answer would correctly infer that his informant *did not know*, and would be inclined to look for a porter or some other person who did know. Negatively, indeed, there is, or should be, general agreement. The man who *only* believes, *does not know*. To that extent belief and knowledge are always opposed. On the other hand there is genuine divergence of usage concerning the important point whether belief does or does not connote assurance.

In the example given above, it is clear that a guarded answer is being given in which assurance is not implied or intended. Yet belief, so far from being incompatible with full assurance, is frequently understood to imply that condition. An obvious example is to be found in the creeds of the church. The man who asserts his belief in God and in the life everlasting intends to assert his invincible conviction; and although there have been disputes on the point, there is a very general tendency among theologians to agree with Calvin in holding that it was a pernicious doctrine of some of the schoolmen to maintain that there is no stronger evidence in this matter than mere moral conjecture,[4] or that opinion and persuasion could suffice.[5] To be sure, it had to be admitted that the believer was often tortured by doubt and anxiety regarding these articles of his belief. To have denied this would have been to run counter to the whole course of Christian experience. Despite the difficulties, however, Cal-

---

[4] *Institutes*, III, ii, 38.   [5] *Ibid.*, III, ii, 1.

vin, Melanchthon, and other Protestants invariably affirmed that man's occasional lapses (due to his blindness and perverseness) did not, and could not, overcome the believer's unwavering assurance in the essentials of his faith.

Belief or assent therefore, is not inconsistent with full and unquestioning assent. It is only inconsistent with the kind of certainty implied in knowledge. Among Protestant theologians, at all events, it is not the orthodox opinion that those who believe—although (in certain senses) they can not know—therefore admit any element of risk or adventure in their believing. To quote Calvin again, the believer "is contented with the assurance that, however poor we may be in regard to present comforts, God will never fail us. Our chief security lies in the expectation of future life, which is placed beyond doubt by the word of God." [6]

Such a view would be difficult or untenable only if men never gave their assent except to sufficient logical evidence, and it is plain that they do assent very often indeed without any approach to full logical sufficiency.

§ 6. "Thinking," Belief, and Opinion

As we have seen, "thinking" in certain of its senses is opposed to knowledge; and it would almost universally be agreed that knowledge and opinion are fundamentally opposed. For if a man *knows* he does *not* opine.

Is there, then, any similar contrast between belief, of the one part, and either thinking or opinion, of the other part?

When we speak of "thinking" we sometimes understand the word in a very general sense, meaning by it any awareness or apprehension that is in some degree characterized or accompanied by the pallid rays of speculative or intellectual contemplation. In this general sense "thinking" need not hold itself aloof from knowledge, or from belief, or from opinion. If, on the other hand, "thinking" is taken to imply doubt and questioning —if it is, indeed, an active intellectual effort to dispel doubt and to resolve some question—it seems clearly to be opposed both to knowledge and to such belief as is full conviction.

[6] *Institutes*, III, ii, 28.

Admittedly, there is an important complication to be noted in this matter. There is a manifest distinction between questioning (i.e. doubting or disputing) a fact and raising questions *about* it. Consequently, it is entirely possible, and indeed quite usual, to raise questions of evidence, whether speculative or practical, concerning matters about which we do not entertain the slightest doubt. We do not question so-and-so's innocence, but we wonder how the fact of his innocence could be proved. Christian theologians of the orthodox cast do not doubt the existence of God or the divinity of His Son; and yet it is their business to examine, and frequently to question, the ontological and other arguments that seek to demonstrate God's existence, or the Sabellian heresy that sought to show that Christ is but a specialized function of the Godhead. In short, when we contrast "thinking" with assurance, we must be careful to note what precisely is questioned or challenged in the "thinking."

Nevertheless, since it seems impossible to think or deliberate about anything without *thereby* questioning or doubting some relevant aspect of it (at least tentatively and experimentally), it would appear that "thinking," in this sense, is somehow or somewhere opposed to conviction. We have now to ask whether any similar relation exists between conviction and opinion.

In ordinary language, the word opinion is used to signify a weak and dubious assent that is not only not knowledge, but is also far less pronounced than belief. In this sense, opinion is frequently so weak that few would be prepared to act or even to bet upon it; and it is plain that most men are ready and willing to act upon their beliefs. Still, there are grounds for wondering whether this linguistic distinction is not, occasionally at any rate, strained and arbitrary. After all, an opinion, even if it is but surmise, is an assent, and, what is more, a summary and a conclusion according to the presumption of evidence. There seems to be no essential reason why such conclusions should necessarily fall short of conviction, or why a strong (and particularly an unchallenged) opinion should be distinguishable from express belief. Any opinion may indeed be questionable on logical grounds, but those who entertain the opinion need not in fact question it at all.

For this reason, a number of authors deny that there is any essential difference between belief and opinion. Thus Cardinal Newman, dealing with what he called "credence," had "opinions and professed facts" [7] singly in mind, the assent to them being "of an otiose and passive character." [8] "The friends or strangers," he said, "whom we fall in with in the course of the day, the conversations or discussions to which we are parties, the newspapers, the light reading of the season, our recreations, our rambles in the country, our foreign tours, all pour their contributions of intellectual matter into the storehouses of our memory; and though much may be lost, much is retained." [9] "These various teachings," he went on to say, "shallow though they be, are of a breadth which secures us against those *lacunæ* of knowledge which are apt to befall the professed student, and keep us up to the mark in literature, in the arts, in history, and in public matters. They give us in great measure our morality, our politics, our social code, our art of life. They supply the elements of public opinion, the watchwords of patriotism, the standards of thought and action; they are our mutual understandings, our channels of sympathy, our means of co-operation, and the bond of our civil union." [10]

§ 7. TRUTH

Knowledge must be true knowledge, that is to say it is impossible to *know* what is false, or to know in any mistaken way.

It is, however, possible to believe falsely; and even if our beliefs are true in fact, they do not, in consequence, become identical with knowledge. If a man believes in May of some year that a particular horse will win the Derby in June of that year, his belief, as the event may prove, may be true in fact. But it could not conceivably be identified with knowledge.

What holds of belief in this respect holds also of opinion.

§ 8. FURTHER CONCERNING ASSURANCE AND CERTAINTY

In § 4 of this preliminary discussion, and elsewhere in it, we have had occasion to consider the relations between psychological

---

[7] *An Essay in Aid of a Grammar of Assent*, p. 50.
[8] *Ibid.*, p. 51.
[9] *Ibid.*
[10] *Ibid.*, p. 52.

or subjective conviction, on the one hand, and evidential certainty, on the other; and further consideration of the point seems advisable.

Beyond dispute, there is a strong affinity and a clear connection between the two. In both, there is absence of doubt and of the suspense that goes along with doubt. Where action is relevant, both involve readiness to act. Both imply confidence, security, and a certain stability of soul. Again, if either our convictions or our certainties are challenged by some one else, our emotional response seems in principle identical. Either we are scornful, bewildered, or angry, as when some one disputes the evidence of our own senses or something we clearly remember —there is nothing more vexatious than this—or our security is such that we do not have the slightest interest in anything any other person may think about the matter. The last of these conditions is that in which mystics now find themselves, when they have tasted and seen the verities of religion. It is to be noted, however, that the mystics have become accustomed to finding this difference between themselves and their fellows. Their earlier reaction towards doubters came nearer to scorn, or anger, or contempt.

Despite these weighty similarities, however, it need not be forthwith concluded that intellectual or cogitative certainty is wholly indistinguishable from emotional assurance,[11] instinctive practical conviction, beliefs whose security rests upon lazy passivity or drowsy ignorance, and the like. If this were so, the obvious inference would be that steadiness and acquiescence are all that certainty means, and that such steadiness or acquiescence may come about in very different ways—from ignorance, from the emotions, and also as the result of active intelligent scrutiny. It is unusual, however, to find this sharp separation between causes and effects in psychological affairs. What we normally find is a pattern or Gestalt in which all the relevant factors are visibly intermingled, and the certainty of knowledge bears the stamp of its origin.

In short, evidential assurance is different from other assur-

---

[11] Even if, in some sense, we are prepared to accept Columella's statement: "In universa vita pretiosissimum est intelligere quemque nescire se quod nesciat."

ance, and it is unfortunate that the same term, "certainty," should so frequently be used to describe such different conditions as indolent, stubborn credence; passionate prepossession; and intellectually certified insight. There would be some gain in clearness, therefore, if we abolished the ambiguous term, "certainty," and spoke instead of certified or self-certified insight, when this was what we meant. But it would be awkward and pedantic to persevere at all times with this language.

§ 9. Belief and Faith

In the English language "belief" and "faith" are in many ways regarded as interchangeable terms. "If ye have *faith,* and doubt not . . ." we read in *Matthew* xxi, 21. The next verse continues: "and all things, whatsoever ye shall ask in prayer, *believing,* ye shall receive." There is no relevant difference in the Greek.

On the other hand, it is abundantly plain that a cogitative assent or persuasion can not be all that is meant by "faith" in these passages, although such assent or persuasion is *one* of the things that are implied in them. The faith of the gospels and of St. Paul is a *fides heroica et mirifica*—a wonder-working faith that lays hold upon God and upon salvation unto eternity. It is not simply belief in the reality of these things. For as St. James said, "The devils also believe." [12]

Like many of the authorities, we might attempt to distinguish between *fides* and *fiducia,* and we might mean by the latter term the entire attitude of soul that goes along with the acceptance of the Christian faith—its serenity, loyalty, trust, and confidence, its sure and certain hope, its power and exaltation, and, as many think, its persistent tendency to bear fruit in good works. Even so, however, the former term *fides* can scarcely mean less than the full acceptance and possession of God and of Christ unto salvation and unto the remission of sins; and this is a fact (if fact it be) so much greater and so much more powerful than mere belief that it seems to annul and devour any important distinction between *fides* and *fiducia.* For if *fides* be the definitive act whereby we enter into possession of the

[12] *James,* II, 19.

way of salvation, it implies, subjectively, that a man's whole will and his whole life are possessed by his faith, and, objectively, that God has taken hold of him as well as he of God. What more could be meant by *fiducia?*

Regarded from another aspect, the same conclusion appears to emerge. Among latter-day Protestant theologians—although there are significant indications of a tendency to revert to a more inclusive and a more ancient point of view—it has been the custom to lay almost exclusive emphasis upon the subjective or psychological point of view. Nevertheless, it is *the* faith with which Christianity has to do, not any kind of loyalty or trust in some nobler order of things than the natural powers of secular man. *Fides* is therefore soteriological and communal as well as a piece of private psychology. It is union with the divine power that works redemption and abolishes death. It is membership in a definite spiritual community, the Church. Because of this, the mere fact of belonging to the Church, and of acknowledging Christ's suzerainty over a definite social (as well as a definite other-worldly) organization, is itself an aspect of faith, however external and legalistic such an aspect may be. And obedience to the Church and to the Scriptures is another aspect of the same thing—even when such obedience is largely nominal. This latter is external *fiducia*—faithfulness of a legal, but not necessarily of an unreal, sort.

Accordingly, *fides* and *fiducia* tend to coalesce, both when they are regarded internally as psychological attitudes and when they are regarded externally as acceptance of, and submission to, some *regula fidei*, or rule of salvation. The same tendency towards coalescence would have to be observed if, in some way, we tried to distinguish between the true or more spiritual believers in the Church, and those who are simply members of the ecclesiastical institution.

§ 10. PROBABILITY

If knowledge connotes certainty, the question at once arises whether there is any logical way of dealing with uncertainties, or whether in all such instances we have to fall back upon blind guesswork The importance of this question can scarcely be rated too highly. What we call prudence in the ordinary affairs of life is principally concerned with the attempt to guide our actions *reasonably* in relation to future contingencies that can be foreseen in part only; and all the sciences called inductive, as opposed to those that are said to be fully demonstrative, have, in the end, to face the same logical difficulty.

The problem is stated very fairly, although very briefly, in the justly celebrated "Introduction" to Bishop Butler's *Analogy of Religion.* Indeed, it has never been stated better. "Probable evidence," we read there, "is essentially distinguished from demonstrative by this, that it admits of degrees; and of all variety of them, from the highest moral certainty, to the very lowest presumption. . . . That which chiefly constitutes probability is expressed in the word likely, *i.e.* like some truth (verisimile), or true event; like it, in itself, in its evidence, in some more or fewer of its circumstances." It affords "grounds for an expectation," sometimes "without any doubt of it"; although "probable evidence, in its very nature, affords but an imperfect kind of information; and is to be considered as relative only to beings of limited capacities. For nothing which is the possible object of knowledge, whether past, present, or future, can be probable to an infinite intelligence since it cannot but be discerned absolutely as it is in itself, certainly true, or certainly false. But to us, probability is the very guide of life."

These problems of verisimilitude, Butler went on to say, belong to the subject of logic, although they constitute "a part of that subject which has not yet been thoroughly considered." For himself, he did not attempt to determine "how far the extent, compass and force of analogical reasoning can be reduced to general heads and rules; and the whole be formed into a system." On the other hand, he expressly affirmed that the matter was logical—an affair of reasonable evidence in all its degrees. The subject had been neglected by those (like Locke) best qualified to treat of it. Yet "this does not hinder but that we may be, as we unquestionably are, assured, that analogy is of weight, in various degrees, towards determining our judgment, and our practice."

Despite these profound and very explicit statements, an older fashion of thought long continued to prevail, at any rate among the better-known philosophers. According to this view, science and knowledge were the same thing, and logic was concerned only with the demonstrations of fully accredited science. Hence (science and knowledge being always quite certain when they existed at all), there is no science, no knowledge, and no logic in regard to anything in the least degree uncertain, or in regard to anything that, in the least degree, has to be discerned *per speculum in œnigmate*. In all such matters there is nothing but belief and opinion, and, in the last resort, nothing but *irrational*, illogical opinion—mere animal faith, or an unintelligible instinct. Estimates of probability measure "impressions of certainty," that is to say, they measure a series of unreasoning and unreasonable impacts in the way of persuasion. They belong, in the end, to the sensitive or emotional, not to the cogitative parts of our nature.

So Hume and many others. Reid was one of the few who expressly maintained the contrary.[13]

The monstrous conclusion that follows from this order of opinion, viz., that where complete certainty is absent, nothing approaching good evidence can be obtained, and in detail that there is no better reason for supposing that Queen Anne is dead than for supposing she is still alive, or for believing that fire is more likely to hurt us than vaseline is, was disguised to some extent by those who spoke in this vein. In the end, however, it *was* their view, and it is a fair statement of any doctrine of credence that relies ultimately upon mere animal faith.

One of our principal problems, therefore, is to consider whether Bishop Butler was right. Can there be *good* evidence that is *not conclusive?* May there be *reasonable* beliefs and opinions that are not quite certain knowledge, or have we to choose between a slender thread of certainty on the one hand, and thick, specious, brittle ropes of sand upon the other?

[13] E. g., *Intellectual Powers*, Essay VI, Chap. v.

Chapter II

ON CERTAIN HISTORICAL MATTERS

§ 1. Preliminary

A mere glance at the history of European philosophy is sufficient to show that the problem of the validity and of the scope of knowledge, together with its relations to opinion and, in general, to assent, has received a degree of attention accorded to very few others. Students of Plato, for example, are very well aware how salient such questions were to the mind of the greatest of the Greeks. Students of Christian dogma are similarly aware of the way in which the more reflective among the Fathers and among the Schoolmen immersed themselves in these inquiries. In the eighteenth century, that Age of Enlightenment, or *Aufklärung*, the reasonableness of beliefs or conjectures was always regarded as the essential point to be examined in connection with such beliefs, the one thing that could not, without absurdity, be left unanswered. In Kant's famous triad of questions, What may I know? What ought I to do? What may I hope? the second and third questions were investigated in the light of the answer to the first. In proceeding so, Kant, although he inaugurated much, also caught and hardened the common spirit and fluid essence of many centuries of inquiry.

On the whole, however, it seems wiser to concentrate attention upon one particular epoch in the philosophical discussion of such questions than to attempt a more expansive survey and run the risk of a very diluted conclusion. Here, even more than in most philosophical debates, it is essential to remember famous men and the way in which they have taught us to formulate and to discuss these perennial problems. But with so much from which to choose it is better to look for the systematic articulation of such ideas than to be content with something vaguer and more general. Indeed, it will repay us, I think, if within the selected epoch we choose a few outstanding and interconnected theories, and decline, in fear of aimlessness, to attempt to deal with very many.

The most suitable epoch for treating in this way is (speaking with rough chronology) the European philosophy of the eighteenth century, and the theories most deserving of attention are, in the main, those of Locke, of Hume, and of Kant.

To be sure, other authors in this or in some other century might be treated, so far as their individual merits are concerned, with equal, or with almost equal, appropriateness. Again, these particular authors have been discussed so often and, on the whole, with such adequacy, that it would be a mistake to expect any advance in the treatment of any of them taken singly. And thirdly, there is a specious if not wholly convincing air about the objection that dead philosophies should not be preserved beyond reason, like the Kings of Portugal in Lisbon. Might it not be better, for example, to go to the nineteenth century when men, preoccupied with the problems of religious faith, might be expected to have evolved some tolerable answer to these perplexities? Might it not be profitable to consult Mansel or Clifford or Lotze rather than Hume or Kant? And is it so certain, after all, that the twentieth century, distracted as it was so early in its course, has not something authentic to tell us—something more readily understandable to our ears than the fading accents of remote philosophers?

Without denying that there is force in these objections, I propose, for the time being, to ignore them. If it were necessary to make a reply, it might be sufficient to point out that the present age is, upon the whole, liker the eighteenth century in its general intellectual outlook than it is like the nineteenth, or, at any rate, the later nineteenth, and that it should be helped in its endeavor to consolidate its recovery of something that the later nineteenth century came near to losing. Such a statement, I think, could be made very plausible indeed by referring to the spirit both of eighteenth century science and of eighteenth century literature, and by comparing these two with contemporary science and literature. It is unnecessary to press the point, however, since it is sufficient for our purposes here to show that the questions we are now debating underwent a prolonged and most active scrutiny during the period we are about to consider. The caliber of the philosophers we are to examine in this chapter is beyond dispute, and the nature of the relevant questions, as we understand them, does not seem to have altered very appreciably. If it has altered, it has altered, in the main, because of what they did and of what they showed.

To put the point otherwise, there is a real danger of forgetting what we owe to these philosophers. To judge from much that is said nowadays, one would suppose that the whole eighteenth century movement in philosophy is now a spent force, having begun, it is true, as a bright, swiftly-flowing river, but tending, as it advanced, to lose itself in sandy, futile shallows, and in the end disappearing in certain dank and marshy places not greatly distant from Königsberg. May it not be maintained that Kant's philosophy—for it was he, of course, who lived in Königsberg—smothered the hopes that the earlier part of the century had cherished so fondly? And therefore that the movement as a whole is a warning and not an encouragement?

Even if this were so, it might be excellent policy on our part to discover wherein the warning consists. I do not think, however, that in reality it is so. On the contrary, I think that one of the wisest things we can do to-day is to ask what answers we should give to Locke's questions in the light of modern science and opinion. It is because I think so that I am writing this book. And Locke, Hume, and Kant, in this matter, form a trio so compact that it would be trebly absurd to stop short at an examination of Locke alone.

Undoubtedly, in certain ways, Hume was rather contemptuous of Locke, and Kant was frankly contemptuous of him. Yet these things should not stay us. The opening sections of the exordium to Hume's *Treatise* are amply sufficient to show how closely Hume, in reality, was following in Locke's footsteps, and a young man's arrogance should not conceal the fact. Hume and others in his generation had assimilated Locke's philosophy so completely that it did not occur to them to thank him. Instead, they prided themselves, beyond reason, upon clarifying some few of the things they thought he had left obscure. And Kant's references to Locke (there is nothing contemptuous about his references to Hume) do not evince any profound study of the earlier philosopher in detail.

Accordingly, the connection between Locke and Hume on the one hand, and between Kant and Hume on the other hand, is very close indeed, and I intend to show that the connection, in substance, between Kant's attitude and Locke's is also pretty close—so close, indeed, in certain respects, that the differences are the more significant. From this point of view, it is no great matter whether Kant himself thought so or not. Kant was not a Locke-philologist; and it is plain from his references to Locke that when he wrote his *Critique* he had missed or had forgotten much that we need not forget.

§ 2. The Empirical Standpoint

According to a prevalent view, slightly disguised and occasionally qualified by the more cautious historians, but upon the whole regarded both as orthodox and as true, Locke was essentially an empiricist who failed to be a complete empiricist only because, being a pioneer and more candid than sharp-witted in his cast of mind, he had not fully grasped what empiricism was and whither it led him. Hume, it is further contended, whose wits were very sharp indeed, perceived that the essence of empiricism was neither more nor less than presentationism, that is to say, that—baseless conjecture apart—nothing can be claimed to be a known existent except sense-impressions, passions, or, in other words, presentations, while nothing is even conceivable except these presentations and such echoes of them as modern psychologists call "images" and Hume called "ideas." Kant thereupon, we are told, "answered" Hume, giving an answer that different commentators interpret differently, but which most of them (not quite all) declare to be a proper and sufficient answer.

If this historical picture were true we might say that, according to strict empiricism, there is no knowledge except sense-knowledge and no imagination worth calling such except a species of mimicry and recapitulation of sense-perception; that, as Hume saw, "sensitive knowledge" is not really knowledge, but the mere existence of sense impressions that carry a feeling of conviction along with them when they are present and (perhaps) when they are very firmly remembered; and so that empiricism becomes skepticism, or the sexton of knowledge. Kant, however, revived the corpse that Hume had pronounced extinct and set it on its feet again, although he left it in a very chastened mood with repeated warnings against renewing its old bad ways.

A more accurate study of these authors casts the gravest doubt upon this over-clear but favorite picture.

As Mr. Gibson has recently shown, and as Locke's *Essay* sufficiently attests in detail, the question that Locke set himself to answer is the question quite sufficiently indicated in his Introduction to his *Essay*, and answered, to the best of his power, in the fourth book of that work. Locke's purpose, as he tells us, was "to enquire into the original, certainty and extent of human *knowledge* together with the grounds and degrees of belief and opinion."[1] Properly speaking, Locke's answer to this essential question was delayed until he came to the fourth book. But he did attempt to answer it. Knowledge, he there tells us, occurs wherever we perceive the connection of and agreement, or disagreement and repugnancy of, any of our ideas.[2] In this alone it consists; and anything short of this, while it may be very good fancy, excellent guessing, or even a settled belief and assurance, is not *knowledge*.

Locke's intention therefore—and he executed his plan not inadequately—was to discriminate, in an effective and thoroughgoing way, between knowledge and what is not knowledge. He concluded finally that we have an intuitive knowledge of our own existence and a demonstrative knowledge of God's existence, of mathematical demonstrations, and of certain ethical demonstrations concerning the nature of rectitude. Some of this "knowledge," we may agree, is doubtfully conformable with that "agreement of ideas" Locke defined as "knowledge"; yet in these parts of his answer, at any rate, Locke is a complete rationalist. It is otherwise, to be sure, with "sensitive knowledge," the only other species of knowledge he admitted to exist; and Locke in a

[1] *Essay*, Introduction, § 2.   [2] *Ibid.*, IV, i, § 2.

way admitted the theoretical inconsistency. "Sensitive knowledge," he said, "deserved the name of knowledge"; [3] and he suggested unconvincingly, with the aid of some irrelevant and would-be humorous *argumenta ad homines*, that it was absurd to think otherwise. Apart from this notable slip, however, it is quite clear what his doctrine was. "I think I have shown," he said, *"wherein it is that certainty, real certainty, consists."* In other words, he thought he had shown what genuine knowledge was, and what it was not.

This is not the language of an empiricist *manqué*, or of an empiricist slightly bewildered. It is the language of a rationalist; indeed, Locke, in a strong, and even in a prepotent part of him, was a rationalist after the order of Descartes, who himself was no Melchizedek, without father, without mother, and without descent.

§ 3. RATIONALISM

At an early stage in his *Regulæ ad Directionem Ingenii* Descartes wrote: "Omnis scientia est cognito certa et evidens." [4] What Descartes here called "scientia" is what Locke called "knowledge," or again, *"real* certainty." And it is plain that Locke understood the general point precisely as Descartes understood it Descarte's view was that anything not absolutely certain had to be banished from true science. There is no mishitting about certainty. Anything that is not a hit is just a miss. And probability is not certainty. It is not knowledge. It is not science. What is more, Descartes taught, as Locke also did, that much that was generally taken for knowledge, or for science, was actually spurious. Although a Catholic, Descartes made it his business to expose the pretensions of dogma and of authority so far as he dared, not because such views were necessarily false, but because they lacked the demonstrable logical basis that, *if they were science*, they clearly ought to possess. And lastly, giving the cue to Locke, or at any rate speaking as Locke was wont to speak half a century afterwards, Descartes affirmed that in the common affairs of life it was necessary and salutary to dispense with knowledge, to rely upon (unscientific) probability, and to trust our senses *beyond their evidence,* on the general ground that Heaven had given them to us to guide our actions. Nevertheless, Locke differed profoundly from Descartes.

§ 4. "KNOWLEDGE" and "JUDGMENT" IN LOCKE'S THEORY

In the result, the difference is very plain indeed. Locke, without challenging the Cartesian ideal of rational knowledge, found knowledge to be possible in a much more restricted sphere than Descartes did and was forced, on that account, greatly to enlarge the sphere of what he called "judgment" or probability. "The mind," he said, "sometimes exercises this judgment out of necessity, where demonstrative proofs and certain knowledge are not to be had; sometimes out of laziness, unskilfulness or haste even where demonstrative and certain proofs are to be had." [5] Making full allowance, however, for the existence of the latter alternative, the cumulative effect of Locke's argument was to show that demonstrative proof and certain knowledge were not to be had in many, very many, regions where Cartesians held they had attained or could attain knowledge. Particularly in physics, Locke held, we can attain only "experimental knowledge"—that is to say (in the large), physics is *not* science in the Cartesian sense.

The considerations that induced Locke to arrive at this conclusion are connected with the interpretation he put upon his "new way of ideas," although even there he did not consider himself an innovator. "The new way of ideas and the old way of speaking intelligibly" he thought were one and the same.[6] Again, as Reid stoutly maintained, there are historical grounds for believing that Locke's "new way of ideas" is derived from Cartesianism. Despite any similarities, however, it is apparent that there are also great differences *with respect to a rationalistic philosophy.* The more one reads Descartes, the more one is convinced that, in the end, he was bound to maintain that the human mind, strictly speaking, consists wholly of "reason," that is to say, of rational intellect and rational will, and consequently that passions, sensations, and images are but semi-mental, a mixture of mind and matter somehow aroused in connection with

[5] *Essay,* IV, xiv, § 3.   [6] Second Letter to Stillingfleet.

the pineal gland, with the consequence that we could never know what might conceivably be truly scientific until we had *separated* the rational mind and its works from any semi-mental amalgam. For Descartes, the very being of science and of knowledge depended upon the metaphysics of mind and body.

In this crucial respect, Locke's rationalism was not at all of the Cartesian pattern. On the contrary, he maintained that the essence or substantial nature both of mind and of body is quite unknown to us. The rationality of mind is never a phenomenon or apparition. All we have in experience is a phenomenal mind composed of what we observe introspectively when we take notice of such operations as perceiving, willing, remembering, and the like. Again, these operations are performed upon sensations or sensible appearances. Therefore appearances are the only entities concerning which we can possibly have any knowledge, although we can attenuate them by abstraction and thicken them by composition.

Principally for this reason, Locke's inquiry into the "understanding" takes a different turn from what might have been expected. In the main, he did not inquire into the understanding but into its ideas. While officially a thoroughgoing epistemologist, debating the scope and limitations of our faculties and examining the understanding *first* in order to infer its limitations, he preferred, in practice, to infer what the understanding can do from the character of the ideas upon which it operates. Indeed, it was through a palpable inconsistency that he persuaded himself and his readers that he was dealing with the understanding as a faculty at all.

The nature of this inconsistency may be set forth as follows: The main part of Locke's examination of the "understanding" is an inventory of its ideas. Even "knowledge," according to his account of it, depends upon discovering the connection between "ideas." The nature of these ideas, however, is not in any way deduced from the nature of the understanding. There is nothing in the bare powers of the understanding to show what "ideas" may, or could not, confront it. Any ideas that turn up in the course of experience do actually confront it; and that is all Locke has to say upon the point. Hence, this first and chief part of his discussion, the inventory of *ideas*, is only an examination of the *understanding* if the ideas belong to the understanding. And Locke, on the surface at least, carefully refrained from saying that they did. According to him, ideas are the direct and immediate *objects* of the understanding. If so, they are naturally regarded, in modern terminology, as "neutral entities" and Locke, up to a point, encouraged this view of them by refusing to discuss their physiological causes and by declining to stray into some other by-paths of the mind-body problem.[7]

Despite this, Locke, in a host of places, did assume that ideas of sensation are caused by, and essentially represent, external physical objects, with the inevitable consequence that many of his contemporaries, and perhaps Locke himself, took such "ideas" to be either mental modifications caused by impact between minds and physical corpuscles or, in the alternative, "species," forms, films, or tenuous essences of a material sort that were somehow transported into the mind's presence-chamber and became visible because they were so near. Yet Locke had no business, on his own premises, to assume anything of the kind. It was his duty to justify all such assumptions if he needed them for his theory; and he never did so.

Hence the result that, although nominally dealing with the human understanding, Locke dealt, for the most part, with something else, viz. with its ideas. In this, his doctrine of knowledge differed profoundly from the doctrine of the rationalists; and although Locke did not dream of denying either the possibility or the reality of "knowledge" in the straitest sense of "knowledge," his doctrine that all "knowledge" had to be shown in some visible dependency or connection of visible ideas led him inevitably to deny the existence of such "knowledge" where there was no visible connection to be discerned.

The most notable instance of such denial in Locke's pages is his (qualified) denial of a knowledge of substance, and particularly physical substance—those "parcels of matter" with which common sense, and the science of physics, seemed to be concerned. Locke admitted, indeed (without any obvious consistency), that the "obscure" idea of substance was always

[7] *Essay*, Introduction, § 2.

present in the plain man's idea of a thing.[8] But if substance is a dummy that we *have* to suppose, it is never, he thought, a visible support or substratum. We cannot perceive the thinghood of a chair in the same way as we can perceive the faded brown in the mahogany. The immediate visible reality of the chair seems rather of the sort that present-day Cambridge philosophers call a slab or slice of *sensa*. And physics, in the end, is based upon the observations of our senses. If, therefore, the testimony of our senses, beyond an immediately visible and momentary glimpse of shape or of color, is hopelessly dark, our "knowledge" of *permanent* physical substances is equally dark. In short, it is not knowledge, but faith, judgment, and probability. In the same way, the conjunction of substantial properties, e.g. the yellowness of gold or the heaviness of lead, is a union that obtrudes itself experimentally in repeated experience, but does not seem to show any essential or rational connection. White gold, or pink gold, does not seem contrary to reason. It simply does not turn up. Something better in the way of argument, Locke held, is needed if such "experimental knowledge" is to be transformed into intelligible science.

Obviously, substance was not the only part of natural knowledge that (if Locke had been right) was subject to the same type of criticism. There is also, at least, the notion of cause, with which Locke dealt very perfunctorily indeed. Again, if so much that was usually considered "knowledge" turned out to be only "judgment," the indubitably rationalistic parts of Locke's philosophy might have required a degree of revision that would have appalled their author. Again, Locke did not consistently follow the usual tenor of his usual thoughts. Even regarding substance, he suggested that there might be "real essences" from which we might "glean whole sheaves" of physical knowledge by the traditional method of logical deduction.[9] On the whole, however, despite his inconsistencies and hesitations, Locke may be said to have maintained that, if natural knowledge is only a function of the apprehension of momentary sensa, it can seldom, if ever, be *scientia* in the Cartesian sense. In our acquaintance with nature, knowledge is squeezed out until it becomes a sort of

[8] *Ibid.*, II, xxiii, 3. [9] *Cf. Essay,* IV, vi, § 11.

sapless pulp. "Judgment," probability, and experimental guess-work take its place.

§ 5. HUME'S DOCTRINE OF "KNOWLEDGE"

Book I of Hume's *Treatise* deals with the human understanding, and the central portion of it (Part III) is concerned, like Locke's *Essay*, with the problem of the relations between "knowledge" and "probability."

The usual accounts of Hume's philosophy lay stress, firstly, upon his empiricism, and secondly, upon the skepticism that is held to be implicit in the empiricism and clearly perceived by Hume to be so. Another numerically smaller but more recent set of expositors emphasizes Hume's "naturalism." A third party assert, with Mr. Russell, that Hume was "one of the very few philosophers not concerned to establish any positive conclusions" [10] although he "refused to feel the usual certainties."

There is probably a good deal to be said in favor of all three of these interpretations. They are exclusive only when they are ossified. But let us attempt to see what Hume's actual position, in outline, essentially was.

If Hume had been an empiricist *à outrance*, that is to say, a skeptical empiricist, he would have attempted to demolish the pretensions of reason and of logic altogether, and this, in the main, is not what we find him doing. True, he admits that there are grounds for being skeptical about reason; and he does tell us that "reason is nothing but a wonderful and unintelligible instinct in our souls" [11] and also that "knowledge resolves itself into probability, and becomes at last of the same nature with that evidence which we employ in common life." [12] His grounds for these culminating assertions, however, are admittedly somewhat slender, and it is even unlikely that they convinced him. He thought he could echo Montaigne's *Que sçais-je?* even with respect to chains of formal demonstration, owing to the difficulty the human intelligence finds in keeping so many links of the chain clearly in the memory without error; and he concluded, illogically as it happened, that if a certain allowance

---

[10] *An Outline of Philosophy*, p. 258.   [12] *Ibid.*, p. 181.
[11] *Treatise* (Selby Bigge's Activ.), p. 179.

were made for a possible error in each step, the cumulative tally of such allowances would eventually reduce the evidence of demonstrations to nothing at all.[13] Again he made the point that in some of the best evidenced demonstrations, particularly in mathematics, the difficulties of the infinite warn us against any overweening confidence.

On the other hand, on the very page on which we find him saying that "knowledge" degenerates into "probability" we also read that "knowledge and probability are of such contrary and disagreeing natures, that they cannot well run insensibly into each other, and that because they will not divide, but must be either entirely present, or entirely absent."[14] This is at least an admission that knowledge, logic, and reason are not in principle absurd or a mere fetish. And on the whole we must conclude that Hume did not deny the possibility of all "knowledge," interpreting that term in the Cartesian sense of utter and complete intelligibility. What he held, in effect, was that the sphere of such "knowledge" ought to be contracted even more resolutely than in Locke's philosophy, and that the sphere of mere belief, probability, or "judgment" should be proportionately enlarged.

Let us look at the question from another angle.

Hume held, as Locke had held, that "knowledge," if there *is* any knowledge, must be the apprehension of a clear and indefeasible agreement between "ideas." In other words, it must be the apprehension of a transparently connective relation between ideas. The framework of Hume's exposition, therefore, is a classification of philosophical relations.[15]

"Ideas," in this sense, are logical characters or conceptions, and a concept, of course, is precisely what it is, and unchanging. (To say that a concept changes is an imprecise way of stating that we have abandoned one concept and accepted another.) Hence there can only be knowledge if an invariant relation is perceptible between unchanging concepts. Yet many philosophers (Hume says) have claimed to have *knowledge* in cases in which the concepts evidently must change. Take, for example, the so-called "identity" of "things." The sapling, let us say, becomes an oak. This means that "it" must be characterized by different

[13] *Ibid.*, p. 182.   [14] *Ibid.*, p. 181.   [15] *Ibid.*, pp. 69 *sqq.*

concepts; for the properties possessed by the sapling are notably different in many respects from the properties possessed by the oak. Or take causation. An ivory chessman, we may suppose, has been pushed across a chessboard, but it still remains the same red ivory chessman. Its defining properties, in this instance, have not altered, but its position has altered; and the causation of the difference in position implies a difference in *some* of the relevant descriptive concepts in this case.

Hence, causal relations and the relation of substantial identity are not invariant relations of unchanging concepts-and therefore must be excluded from "knowledge" in the strict sense. Hume, going further, asserted that all "matter of fact" is similarly excluded from "knowledge" proper. In other words, he held, as Aristotle had held of ἐπιστήμη , that "science" must deal with what is invariable and eternal.[16]

Strictly speaking, it does not follow from this that all invariant relations between unchanging ideas are, in Kant's language, "analytical" or, in Locke's language, "trifling." [17] In other words, it need not follow that the mind, when it compares two concepts, perceives a necessary relation between them only if the two concepts are literally identical or if the one is visibly contained in the other, as the conception of shape is visibly contained in the conception of extended body. The relation might be what Kant called "synthetic" and Locke called "instructive"; and Hume's readiness to admit (on the whole) the scientific character or, in short, the knowledge, of "abstract reasoning concerning quantity or number" (which he was not inclined to "commit to the flames" [18]) may be taken to be evidence that he did not wholly intend to restrict the domain of reason, logic, and knowledge to tautologies and to mere analytical statements.

On the other hand, to say the least, he came very near to affirming this position. "Reason alone," he said, "can never give rise to any original idea." [19] In the case of "relations of ideas," "the contrary is always inconceivable," whereas, in matters of fact, "the contrary is always possible." [20] These statements, by

[16] E.g. *Nicomachean Ethics*, 1139 b.   [19] *Treatise*, p. 157.
[17] *Essay*, IV, viii.   [20] *Enquiry*, p. 25.
[18] *Enquiry*, p. 165.

themselves, would not settle the question of Hume's meaning in this important matter. But if the crucial statements in the Appendix to the *Treatise* are taken to govern his entire philosophy, the conclusion must be that Hume, except in so far as he was inconsistent, did maintain that the office of reason, science, and knowledge, although real, was only "trifling." This crucial passage runs, "There are two principles, which I cannot render consistent; nor is it in my power to renounce either of them, viz. that all our distinct perceptions are distinct existences, and that the mind never perceives any real connexion among distinct existences." [21]

§ 6. Skepticism and Naturalism in Hume's Philosophy

As appears from the foregoing statement, Hume clearly reduced the province of "knowledge" to very exiguous dimensions, and may have intended to leave nothing but analytical propositions within the tiny province that remained. Accordingly, if by skepticism is meant the belief that what usually passes for knowledge is not knowledge at all, Hume, for the most part at least, *was* a skeptic; and in this sense of the word he emphasized his skepticism regarding the whole of our supposed knowledge, (scientific or vulgar), concerning nature, the real existence of a continuing world, or "matter of fact" on any extended view.

If, on the other hand, we mean by a "skeptic" an incorrigible doubter, it is not at all necessary to conclude that Hume either was or should have been a doubter, even concerning "matter of fact." True, he himself told us that he was a doubter when he speculated in his study, but that he was not a doubter when he played backgammon, conversed, and was merry with his friends.[22] He said this, however, in a rather self-conscious, foppish, and dilettante passage, very little consistent with the march of his argument; and we may neglect the inconsistency. Ultimately we may take his argument to be that *if* belief and judgment ought to depend solely upon logic and rational demonstration, *then* he, and everybody else, *ought to be* doubters regarding all the important affairs of life. In fact, however, he declared, belief need not have any such origin. For nature, "by an absolute and un-

ⁿ *Treatise*, p. 636.   ²² *Ibid.*, p. 269.

controllable necessity, has determined us to judge as well as to breathe and feel." [23]

This is Hume's "naturalism." Let us now consider its outlines.

Hume's general intention was to introduce the experimental method of reasoning into moral subjects,[24] to be a second Newton in the realm of humanism, and to do for human nature what Newton, by acclamation, had done for physical nature. The cardinal point in this experimental method—the very thumbscrews of what Reid later called Hume's articles of inquisition—was the doctrine of pure phenomenalism. According to this view the mind consists, or is a "heap," of presentations or appearances, and nothing is even conceivable, in the remotest degree, except these presentations or appearances, including the derivative forms of presentation that arise during some process of habituation, "custom," or repetition. Hume called the fundamental or primary appearances "impressions," and he called their derivatives "ideas." The essence of the view was that anything not derived by custom from impressions, and not itself an impression, was utterly spurious and at the best an empty sound.

There can be little doubt that Hume adopted this view at a very early age. In a remarkable "letter to a physician" discovered and printed by his biographer, Hume, when a mere youth, and suffering from a nervous crisis induced by the ferment of his bold discoveries, declared that when he was "about eighteen years of age, there seemed to be opened up to him a new scene of thought, which transported him beyond measure, and made him, with an ardour natural to young men, throw up every other pleasure or business to apply entirely to it." [25] While the nature of the discovery is described generally in the letter as the doctrine that the clue to all human achievement is to be found in

---

[23] *Ibid.*, p. 183.

[24] The subtitle to the *Treatise*. In a certain sense Kant also claimed that he himself had followed the "experimental method," and explained the point in a series of footnotes to the Preface to the second edition of the *Critique of Pure Reason*. In these passages, Kant maintained that *his* experiments were with conceptions and rational principles, not physical objects; that he employed logical analysis instead of chemical reduction; and so forth; indeed, generally, that the grand Critical experiment was an experiment into the application of reason to sense experience.

[25] Burton's *Life and Correspondence of David Hume*, Vol. I, p. 117.

human nature, it can hardly be supposed that this, in itself, was what so transported Hume. For it was a commoplace of the age, as may be seen, for example, from the essentially imitative work of such a writer as George Turnbull [26] who had been a student at Edinburgh University some few years before Hume (at the age of about fourteen) had studied there. Hume must therefore be supposed to have hit upon some definite clue for interpreting human nature, and such a clue can hardly have been other than what we now call his presentationism.

In any case, Hume adhered to his presentationism from his first published words on philosophy to his last, with notable consequences to the present subject. First, he says, we have actual present impressions. Belief or assent always attends them. They strike upon the mind with such force that we always reckon them as realities. Secondly, we have the repetition of such impressions in the memory; and here again, belief or assent is an inseparable companion.[27] Impressions, and impressions repeated in memory, together form a "system"; however, the mind "stops not here," but forms a further system "which it likewise dignifies with the title of *realities*." [28] This further system is what is commonly meant by "belief" or "judgment" or "probability," and it is the result of custom or habitual association.

" 'Tis this latter principle," Hume declared, "which peoples the world, and brings us acquainted with such existences, as by their removal in time and place, lie beyond the reach of the senses and memory." [28] In other words, what each of us calls a world— and our "worlds" in this sense are obviously an authentic and a "natural" growth—is always something vaster than what we perceive at any moment, together with what we specifically remember. We believe that fire burns and that bread nourishes, not merely in the sense that the fire in front of us is burning and that the few camp-fires and other conflagrations we happen to remember *did* burn, but in the sense that fire burns anywhere in the course of nature, in Peru, in China, in Sirius, and in Betelgeuse, whether or not we chance to have noticed it doing so.

---

[26] See the Preface and the Introduction of Turnbull's *Principles of Moral Philosophy*.
[27] *Treatise*, p. 86.　　　　　[28] *Ibid.*, p. 108.

"All this," Hume said, "and everything else, which I believe, are nothing but ideas; though by their force and settled order, arising from custom . . . they distinguish themselves from the other ideas which are merely the offspring of the imagination." [29]

Such, then, is the province of belief. It is obviously a very extensive province. And the nature of belief or judgment, according to the theory, is thoroughly non-rational. Belief occurs when expectations due to custom and anchored upon the realities of waking life come to us with a degree of inevitableness barely to be distinguished from the vivacity of an actual sense-impression. We look at the sun, are dazzled, and turn away. That is action based upon perception. It is not a reaction to knowledge but a natural reflex. And belief, which is just as unreasoning and just as "natural" as perception, has the same relation to our actions. Because of the look of the bridge, we decide to cross it. We can not be said to *know* that it will bear our (perhaps considerable) weight. An enemy may have sawed the pillars across and be awaiting our disaster. But, from the look of it, we so very firmly expect it to support us that, without any reflection, we trust ourselves to it by an extension of the same natural instinct as we follow when we act according to the promptings of perception.

Such, in greater detail, was Hume's "naturalism." It was *very* natural. Yet, in an odd way, he endeavored to limit this naturalism. In the first place, he pointed out, perhaps correctly, that not every habit, custom, or association was sufficient to generate belief. He held, in fact, that association by resemblance or contiguity did not normally do so, although it tended in this direction, and in exceptional cases (e.g. idolatry, or the way in which liars cheat themselves by coming to believe in their own fictions) may achieve quite genuine conviction. This, as we have said, may pass for true psychology, but when Hume, in the second place, went on to argue, so to say, that there is a difference between good beliefs (or experimental *proofs*) and bad ones, it is scarcely possible to follow him and also to be content with his simple naturalism and his strong propensity to conceive certain ideas strongly. If all belief is non-rational, sensitive, and

[29] *Treatise.*

not cogitative, what is the point of arguing, as Hume argued in effect, that certain superstitious beliefs are negligible because absurd, and that sound beliefs follow certain rules for judging causes and effects? [30] (These rules, incidentally, anticipate Mill's Experimental Methods, and, from a logical standpoint, are even superior to Mill's in certain particulars.)

What Hume here endeavored to do, and what, on his premises, he could never succeed in doing, was to limit his account of belief to good horse-sense, and to the refinements of horse-sense that we call experimental or natural science. Persons with a scientific training do not in fact believe all their associations, at any rate in their own scientific province; but this is irrelevant if there is, in reality, no such thing as sound logical evidence in the experimental sciences. Again, there may be a certain importance in distinguishing, as Hume does, between associations that are "permanent and irresistible," [31] and those which do not have the same general efficacy however stubborn they may be in particular cases; and there may be a certain affinity (as we have said) between horse-sense and the traditions of the experimental sciences. Mere horse-sense and laboratory investigations, however, are not the same; and neither of them is a more authentic instance of belief than the credulity of the ancients concerning "miracles," [32] or than the superstitions of eminent men of science concerning politics.

Let us turn, however, to the broader philosophy of Hume's "naturalism." As he correctly declared, the great bulk of what ordinary people call their "knowledge" concerns "matter of fact," and, when interpreted in any extended way, revolves round the two conceptions of thinghood and of cause and effect. According to Hume, these conceptions are invariably misapplied by all the rationalists, and by all who regard such conceptions as descriptive of anything really knowable.[33] In reality, he held, there are no substances in nature, and there are no mysterious bonds or necessary efficacies in nature. There is only, *in us*, a strong propensity to expect in a certain way. We believe in

[30] *Ibid.*, pp. 177 *sqq.*
[31] *Ibid.*, p. 225.
[32] *Enquiry,* Chap. x.
[33] *Treatise*, p. 162.

the existence of bodies, but when we examine the evidence we perceive that "body" is only a name for a typical smoothness of association.[34] Thus we say we see the same room, or desk, or carpet again. This is not accurate. Such perceptions are thoroughly interrupted and unstable; but the resemblance between these interrupted impressions is so convincing that we cheat ourselves into the belief that we have been steadily engaged in observing a continuing entity. And so we put something of ourselves into nature, quite illegitimately, and seldom seek to take it back. Similarly in the instance of causation which, as all the world knows, was Hume's chosen ground for deploying his arguments. According to him, there are no causes in nature. What happens is that the repetition of similar sequences of fact comes to be felt with a characteristic sense of familiarity and to be expected with utter confidence. This is an impression of reflection,[35] i.e. a mere mental feeling. And so, again, we put our own feelings into nature and forget to take them back again.

In short, the wheel, as nearly as possible, had turned full cycle. According to Descartes, complete rational certainty was the whole of what is rational. Locke agreed; but was constrained to show that the domain of rationality is therefore pretty narrow, and the domain of faith and assurance, in contrast, very wide. Hume also agreed and, with Locke's example to help him, circumscribed the sphere of "knowledge" or of "science" so very effectively as to make "science" little more than a phantom. By contrast, he continued the good work of extending the domain of natural but non-rational belief and endeavored to explain, with great elaboration, precisely how this extensive province of belief and, indeed, "all probable reasoning" could be consistently, if irreverently, regarded as "a species of sensation." [36] On the other hand, he did not go quite far enough, according to his own declared principles. For he jibed at regarding *any* superstitious association as a genuine belief, and attempted, vainly, to show that probable reasoning, properly regarded, was a very creditable species of sensation that followed a special type of association conformable to experimental rules.

[34] *Ibid.*, p. 204.　　　　　　　　　[36] *Ibid.*, p. 103.
[35] *Ibid.*, p. 165,

§ 7. BELIEF IN RELIGION: LOCKE AND HUME

Although the tide of the argument in Locke's *Essay*, and in Hume's *Treatise* and *Enquiry*, is charged, and even surcharged, with the wreckage of pretensions to *knowledge* in affairs of experimental science and of common life, it is not therefore to be inferred that either of these authors was oblivious of, or uninterested in, the connections between this aspect of their theory of human nature and the vast ocean of cosmogony and religious credence. On the contrary, there is indisputable evidence of the keen interest felt by each of them in these ampler regions; and there is a certain plausibility, at least, in supposing that the larger purview was operative in both of them even when they were dealing, *ex professo*, with something narrower.

In Locke's case, the thing seems quite apparent. He was a political as well as a philosophical publicist, in an age in which politics and religion were not disjoined, but in which, on the contrary, the main problem, in England and elsewhere, was to prevent priest and presbyter, papist and puritan from making life hateful and unlivable. Locke pled for toleration, except to certain groups like atheists, in whose case "promises, covenants and oaths, which are the bonds of human society, can have no hold." [37] And he held that toleration was *reasonable*. "The toleration of those that differ from others in matters of religion," he said, "is so agreeable to the gospel of Jesus Christ, *and to the genuine reason of mankind*, that it seems monstrous for men to be so blind, as not to perceive the necessity and advantage of it, in so clear a light." [38] Again he declared, "Speculative opinions, and articles of faith, as they are called, which are required only to be believed, cannot be imposed on any church by the law of the land; for it is absurd that things should be enjoined by laws, which are not in men's power to perform; and to believe this or that to be true, does not depend upon our will." [39] Locke was also the author of *The Reasonableness of Christianity*.

In Campbell Fraser's edition of Locke's *Essay* evidence is given in support of the view that the *Essay* itself grew out of a

---

[37] Locke's *Works*, 1801, Vol. VI, p. 47.
[38] *Ibid.*, p. 9. [39] *Ibid.*, pp. 39 *sq.*

private discussion concerning "the principles of morality and revealed religion"; [40] and although the chapters in the *Essay* upon "Faith and Reason" and upon "Enthusiasm," while in conformity with the general tenor of the argument, are a sort of addendum to it, there is no real difficulty in believing that Locke, although his argument had led him into regions very remote, retained a lively remembrance of its starting point. In any case, the general character of Locke's attitude towards the faith of religious men is readily understandable. He strongly asserted the right, and ultimately the necessity, of individual judgment, but he was principally concerned to show how far it was reasonable, firstly, to rely on unaided reason, and, secondly, for reason to submit to revelation.

Locke therefore rejected "enthusiasm" "which, laying by reason, would set up revelation without it." [41] "*Credo, quia impossible est*," he said, "might, in a good man, pass for a sally of zeal; but would prove a very ill rule for men to choose their opinions or religion by." [42] In short, "reason is natural revelation" by natural faculties and "revelation is natural reason enlarged by a new set of discoveries communicated by God immediately." [43]

Therefore (as Mr. S. P. Lamprecht has recently shown), [44] it was necessary for Locke to reject both the doctrine of so many Protestant confessions and what he regarded as the extravagant claims made for "reason" by the Cambridge Platonists and others among his contemporaries. He could not believe, on the one hand, in the statement of the Formula of Concord: "The understanding and reason of man in spiritual things are wholly blind, and can understand nothing by their proper powers." On the other hand, while conceding to the Cambridge Platonists that reason was the candle of the Lord, he could not assent to their views concerning the luminosity of the candle. Our powers in this matter, while genuine and even considerable, are also greatly dark. They have to be won by the exercise and improvement of our native faculties and do not serve to ease the lazy

---

[40] *Essay*, pp. xvi *sq.*
[41] *Ibid.*, IV, xix, § 3.
[42] *Ibid.*, IV, xviii, § 11.
[43] *Ibid.*, IV, xix, § 4.
[44] *Philosophical Review*, November, 1926, and March, 1927.

from the pains of search or to stop the inquiry of the doubtful. And, in the end, they are but fitted to our state of mediocrity and of probationership, sufficient for the knowledge of God and our duty and not at all negligible as a guide to happiness. More in detail, Locke held that the written word of God supplemented natural revelation, although we had to exercise our natural reason in order to determine whether or no the word came from God. Yet, as might be expected, natural reason tended to supplant all else in his cogitations. The two great divisions of his creed were ultimately "the knowledge of God, maker of all things, and a clear knowledge of our duty." [45] In *The Reasonableness of Christianity*, the point that is stressed is not so much the necessity of supernatural revelation, as the justification of its efficacy in the life of the common man and the services it has done in the past.

"It is at least a surer and shorter way [we read] to the apprehensions of the vulgar, and mass of mankind, that one manifestly sent from God, and coming with visible authority from him, should, as a king and lawmaker, tell them their duties; and require their obedience; than leave it to the long and sometimes intricate deductions of reason, to be made out to them." [46]

Again, he says:

"He that travels the roads now, applauds his own strength and legs that have carried him so far in such a scantling of time; and ascribes all to his own vigour; little considering how much he owes to their pains, who cleared the woods, drained the bogs, built the bridges, and made the ways passable; without which he might have toiled much with little progress. A great many things which we have been bred up in the belief of, from our cradles (and are notions grown familiar, and, as it were, natural to us, under the gospel), we take for unquestionable, obvious truths, and easily demonstrable; without considering how long we might have been in doubt or ignorance of them, had revelation been silent. And many are beholden to revelation, who do not acknowledge it." [47]

It is much more difficult to speak with confidence about Hume's attitude to these fundamental questions. Obviously, they must have been present to his mind from a very early period, and there is a certain romantic plausibility about Mr. Hendel's

[45] *Works*, Vol. VII, p. 138.   [47] *Ibid.*, p. 145.
[46] *Ibid.*, p. 139.

conjecture that *"the* problem, for Hume, was to explain the world-order," [48] that it had been *the* problem for him all his life, and that the posthumous *Dialogues concerning Natural Religion* (which, as it happens, are too slavish an imitation of Cicero's *De Natura Deorum* for the highest literary art) are the fulfilment, at long last, of Hume's boyish zeal in the study of Cicero, interpreted partly through the spectacles of Bayle.

These romantic conjectures are of little philosophical moment, although there is more substance in them than in much philosophical gossip. The serious historical puzzle is what Hume himself intended to convey. Was Philo, in the *Dialogues*, none other than David Hume? Was he meant to be identical with David Hume at the time of the publication of the *Treatise* and of the *Enquiries?* If so, is the concluding sentence of the *Dialogues*, with its assertion that Cleanthes, the upholder of the argument from design, "approached nearer to the truth" than the skeptical Philo, to be taken as an indication that Hume, in his later years, was inclined to abandon his earlier views, and to accept the prevalent deism of the eighteenth century, although without any marked conviction? And had Hume ever been utterly skeptical concerning deism?

Hume left us guessing on these important matters, but something at least may be learned both from the care Hume took in his instructions for the posthumous publication of the *Dialogues* and from the fact that Adam Smith, his literary executor, declined to accept Hume's instructions, so that the book reverted to Hume's ordinary executors (with instructions, by the will, to publish forthwith) and even then did not appear for some years after Hume's death.

From the first of these circumstances we may infer that Hume took a serious concern in the book, and may perhaps conjecture that he wished, from the grave, to propound a great enigma in highly polished prose. From the second circumstance we may reasonably conclude the tenability of an interesting theory recently propounded by Mr. Wildon Carr. Mr. Carr says, "We shall not be wrong, I think, if we see in Adam Smith's concern for his friend's reputation the clear indication that at that time

[48] *Studies in the Philosophy of David Hume,* p. 29,

scepticism in regard to natural religion was far more shocking than scepticism in regard to revelation."⁴⁹ To doubt the manifest existence of Intelligible Design in the universe *was* inexpressibly shocking to Hume's contemporaries. It denied any reasonableness in anything.

To be sure, Hume had shown, or had professed to show, in the *Treatise* and elsewhere, that there is, strictly speaking, no *reason* in any causal inference. The obvious conclusion, therefore, was that there could be no reason in the inference to an Intelligent Cause, or Designer, of the universe. It was one thing, however, to state a principle that implied this conclusion, quite another thing to enforce the conclusion, and particularly to enforce it in the manner Philo chose. "If I am still to remain in utter ignorance of causes," he said, "and can absolutely give an explication of nothing, I shall never esteem it any advantage, to shove off for a moment a difficulty which, you acknowledge, must immediately, in its full force, recur upon me."⁵⁰ The troublesome thing about Philo was the way in which he elaborated the full force of the difficulty.

Even if, although ultimately in a quandary, we could in a sense *prove* certain instances of causal efficacy from experience, how, he asked, would the circumstance help us in natural religion? "When you go one step beyond the mundane system, you only excite an inquisitive humour, which it is impossible ever to satisfy."⁵¹ And that was not all.

Like effects, Hume conceded for the sake of argument, prove like causes. We have experience, however, only of finite mundane effects. How, then, overleaping all experience, can we infer the existence of an infinite, other-worldly cause? And if we infer, not an infinite cause, but a cause proportionate, and only just proportionate, to its effects, where do we stand? "Many worlds might have been botched and bungled throughout an eternity, ere this system was struck out: much labour lost: many fruitless trials made: and a slow, but continued improvement carried on during infinite ages in the art of world-making." Several deities might have combined in contriving and framing a world,

---

⁴⁹ *The Unique Status of Man,* p. 97.   ⁵¹ *Ibid.*
⁵⁰ Dialogue IV,

And if the world "sometime arose from something like design" it might have been "only the first rude essay of some infant deity, who afterwards abandoned it, ashamed of his lame performance" or "the production of old age and dotage in some superannuated deity." [52]

Statements in this vein were intended to be shocking, and seem very well adapted to their purpose. And what Cleanthes called the "whimsies" of the seventh dialogue, if not quite so shocking, were scarcely likely to induce philosophical apathy.

"We have no *data*," cried Philo, "to establish any system of cosmogony. Our experience, so imperfect in itself, and so limited both in extent and duration, can afford us no probable conjecture concerning the whole of things. But if we must needs fix on some hypothesis . . . does not a plant or an animal, which springs from vegetation or generation, bear a stronger resemblance to the world, than does any artificial machine, which arises from reason and design?"

"These words, *generation, reason,* mark only certain powers and energies in nature, whose effects are known, but whose essence is incomprehensible; and one of these principles, more than the other, has no privilege for being made a standard to the whole of nature. . . . In this little corner of the world alone, there are four principles, *Reason, Instinct, Generation, Vegetation,* which are similar to each other, and are the causes of similar effects. . . . The effects of these principles are all known to us from experience: But the principles themselves, and their manner of operation, are totally unknown: Nor is it less intelligible, or less conformable to experience to say, that the world arose by vegetation from a seed shed by another world, than to say that it arose from a divine reason or contrivance, according to the sense in which Cleanthes understands it."

If the jesting Hume meant to bequeath the greatest possible enigma to the world, it is not beyond the bounds of possibility that he should have described what he took to be the profoundest part of his thought as "whimsies that may puzzle, but never can convince." At any rate, these statements are his "naturalism" quite naked. They described the Life Force blindly procreative.

§ 8. GENERAL CONCERNING KANT

Regarding the central theme we are engaged in discussing in this chapter, Kant's conclusion was that he had abolished (a certain kind of) knowledge to make room for (a certain kind of)

---

[52] Dialogue V.

belief. We have therefore to consider the manner in which he sought to establish this conclusion.

By nature and by training Kant was what the Germans call a *Metaphysiker;* that is to say, his fundamental bent was towards an inquiry into the supersensible regarded as the timeless, invisible, and rational ground of all that exists.

This view in the eighteenth century, although it had undergone important modifications, may be regarded, without essential error, as the lineal descendant of the scholastic position that theology was the Queen of the Sciences. A few quotations from Harnack's *History of Dogma* will indicate sufficiently what the scholastics meant.

"Scholasticism is simply nothing but scientific thought." [53] "Hence it is useless to direct one's ingenuity to answering the question as to what *kind* of science presents itself in Scholasticism; we have simply rather to inquire into the condition under which scientific thought was placed at that time. Scholasticism is science applied to religion . . . science setting out from the axiom that all things are to be understood from theology, that all things must therefore be traced back to theology." [54] "The Church conceived itself at that time as *spiritual* power, as the power of the supersensuous over the sensuous; the subject of science was the supersensuous; science was therefore challenged by this revival. But even the science which revels in the transcendental, and which readily attaches itself to revelation, cannot deny its character as *science.*" [55] What is of importance here is only this, that the observation of the *external* world was extremely imperfect, that, in a word, natural science and the science of history, did not exist, the reason being that we know how to observe spirit, but not how to observe things of sense." [56]

The tradition in which Kant was bred, although Protestant and strongly tinctured with Leibniz's philosophy, was, at bottom, not dissimilar from this; and Kant himself used Baumgarten's textbooks when he taught at Königsberg. Now there can be no doubt concerning what Baumgarten meant by "knowledge" or concerning Baumgarten's assertion that we possess knowledge of the *mundus intelligibilis*, the supersensible world. On the first point Baumgarten's view was that knowledge is "scientia" in the Cartesian sense. As he tersely said: "Scientia est certa deductio

[53] English translation, Vol. VI, p. 23.   [55] *Ibid.,* p. 32.
[54] *Ibid.,* pp. 25 *sq.*   [56] *Ibid.,* p. 24.

ex certis.[57] And Baumgarten held, like every other *Metaphysiker* whose philosophy was derived, at various removes, from the great Leibniz, that metaphysics *was* the science of the *mundus intelligibilis.*

The success of metaphysics, thus regarded, is, of course, quite another matter; and Leibniz, at least, had questioned its success in his own day.

"The art of proving metaphysical propositions, in any view [Leibniz said] demands extreme precautions and a greater precision even than those required in mathematics. The reason is that when we are dealing with numbers and the figures and ideas that depend on them, our mind is in possession of an Ariadne's thread to guide it, namely, imagination and the example; this, moreover, gives it the means of control which arithmeticians call proofs, and which quickly lead us to expose paralogisms. In ordinary metaphysics, on the other hand, we have no such aids, and we have to make rigorous reasoning supply their place. And although many well-intentioned philosophers have held out to us the promise of metaphysical demonstration, they turn out for the most part to be self-deception. In fact, we possess very few and very rare metaphysical demonstrations worthy of the name." [58]

Although, as he thought, we possessed very few such demonstrations, Leibniz did not deny that we possessed some. And he believed he had added to their number. Again the Leibnizians, Wolff, Baumgarten, and others, codified and elaborated many such demonstrations in the proper textbook style, and were generally believed, in Germany, to have succeeded in their enterprise.

It is generally agreed among the expositors of Kant that in his precritical period, i.e. before the year 1772 or thereabouts when the ideas later put forward in the *Critique of Pure Reason* took hold of him, he did not definitely renounce this order of opinion, although, particularly in the *Nova Dilucidatio* (1770), he reached the conclusion that our knowledge of what is spatial or temporal must be of a fundamentally different order from the pure intelligibility of the science of the supersensible. In or about the year 1772, however, as the celebrated *Letter to Marcus Herz* and other evidence show, Kant reached a standpoint that

[57] *Philosophia generalis,* § 21.
[58] Mr. Wildon Carr's translation (*Leibniz,* p. 30) from a paper published by Foucher de Careil called "Animadversiones ad Weigelium."

forced him to deny that there can be any complete and perfect *science* of the *mundus intelligibilis* at all. He did not cease to believe that there *was* a supersensible world, or that the supersensible world was the foundation of the sensible. In these matters he remained a *Metaphysiker* to the end. But he held that the territory of high metaphysics could not be invaded in the old-fashioned way. It was the object of rational belief, and compelled such belief in all speculative minds. A knowledge or science of it, however, in the strict sense of these terms, was forever impossible.

§ 9. METAPHYSICS AS A SCIENCE

In general, if with some inadequacy, we may describe Kant's line of thought somewhat as follows. There is at least one science that every one of good understanding is bound to accept as such. This is pure mathematics. In addition to pure mathematics, there is also pure physics. For the essentials of physics are completely demonstrable and deal with *principiata e principiis*. True, there have been certain philosophers who possessed excellent understandings and yet were skeptical concerning the foundation of physics. Hume, for example, showed this skepticism when he maintained that the causes of physics were not different in principle from the strong, uncritical expectations of common life. According to Kant, however, it is possible to vindicate the principle of "causality," the conservation of "substance," and other such fundamental principles in the science of physics. Hume's denial of causality, if the principle of the denial were pursued with extreme logical rigor, would also involve the ruin of pure mathematics. And Kant declared, not altogether accurately, that Hume's good understanding would have saved him from this absurdity.

Of other sciences, there was, in strictness, none. Biology, for example, was not a science. It was guesswork, not the orderly treatment of *principiata e principiis*. For natural law is physical law, and physical law is Newtonian mechanics. Still less can geology, history, psychology, and the like be regarded as authentic sciences yielding perfect knowledge and necessary truth. Kant's problem, therefore, was whether there could be a science of the supersensible in the same sense as there is a science of pure mathematics or of pure physics, and, if not, whether there can be a science of the supersensible at all.

We may state his fundamental contentions in the following way:

A science of metaphysics, if there were one, would have to be derived wholly from pure reason. But pure reason is pure logic, and pure logic is analytical, an affair of dissecting concepts. What is merely analytical, however, is necessarily sterile. It can only divide and subdivide any given conception, and can neither show that the conception applies to real existence or that it implies any consequence other than its own specific character and meaning.

If mathematics and physics were analytical sciences, they would consist of trivialities and tautologies, and constructive thinking in them would be entirely impossible. In fact, however, so far from being exercises in logic-chopping, they are the generators of a universe of demonstrable interconnections. They are therefore synthetical, not analytical, and yet they are also rational and *a priori*. For they demonstrate with invincible necessity as mere experience can never do.

The problem therefore is (1) how are synthetic propositions *a priori* possible, and (2) are there any synthetic propositions *a priori* in metaphysics, or, indeed, anywhere except in mathematics and in physics?

According to Kant, sense-experience is evidently synthetical—indeed, he regarded the point as so plain that no question should be made of it. He also maintained that sensation is evidence of real existence, and that without sensation there can be no such evidence. It is no mere game with logical counters. Again, sense-experience obviously yields various associative conjunctions and integrations. There are, as we may say, natural connections which, even if they are non-rational are at least not analytical.

Experience for Kant, therefore (i.e. sense-experience) *is* synthetical, and is *not*, as such, *a priori*. But scientific experience in mathematics and in physics is both synthetical and *a priori*. Obviously, therefore, Kant held that the synthetical character of sense-experience is, in these sciences, somehow adopted by and assimilated with their *a priori* character.

Before attempting to explore this solution in greater detail, it is expedient to call attention to the properties that, as Kant habitually supposed, "reason" must possess. As Mr. Metzger points out,[59] "rational" for Kant was (a) the opposite of contingent or merely factual. The rational was the intelligible, that whose fundamental nature evinces necessary connection. (b) The rational was that which proceeded from, or was generated by, the faculty of understanding and intellect. It was pure spontaneity, not anything passive and *given* in sense-experience. (c) Occasionally, and in a manifestly subordinate sense, Kant regarded the rational as the deducible, and therefore opposed it to everything intuitive even when the intuition was self-evident.

On the whole, Kant was mainly concerned with reason in the second of these senses. For he believed that the second sense governed and determined the first. He could not see any meaning in supposing that reason could adapt itself to anything outside reason. Instead of being *ectypal,* or constrained by some outside pattern, reason must, he thought, be *archetypal* and produce its fruits from its own substance. Hence Kant's general conception of what pure reason had to do if it did anything at all. (Kant also assimilated the third sense of reason to the second, however, precisely because he held these matters not to be intuitive but to require an elaborate "deduction" or vindication.)

His question therefore was, "How can reason of itself produce a necessary connection, and vindicate its handiwork?" Part of his answer, as we have seen, was that, by itself alone, it would be analytic only. The rest of the answer is that it may generate a synthetic connection in some alliance with sensibility. This is the doctrine of the two "roots" of scientific knowledge.

It is obvious that if these two roots of reason and sense are of essentially different orders and opposed in their fundamental principle, they can not become a united organism, and Kant's entire philosophy, in one of its aspects, may be regarded as a

---

[59] *Der Gegenstand der Erkenntnis (Jahrbuch der Philosophie)*, Vol. VII, pp. 722 *sq.* note.

series of artifices for uniting what are not truly unifiable. Granting the initial and insoluble dilemma, however, Kant was able to soften the discrepancy between the two roots in several ways, partly by a doctrine of logical forms, partly by a doctrine of schemata, and partly by a doctrine that he called "symbolic anthropomorphism." The two former of these devices concern us now. The third will concern us shortly.

If reason were "empty logical form" and if sensations were formless "stuff" or "matter," it seems clear that the two together do not exhaust the ingredients of human cogitative capacity. For space and time are not formless heaps of amorphous sensory stuff. And yet they are not mere reason. Kant's solution, therefore, is that space and time are mediating forms. While not pure reason or bare logic, they are congruent with reason because they really are pure forms. And although these forms are empty (mental) receptacles in themselves (supposing that we could speak of them in themselves), they necessarily and inevitably *inform* any sensory stuff that we apprehend. Hence the alliance that actually exists in mathematics, which is formal and yet synthetic and applicable to reality. In Kant's doctrine of the schemata, again, we have a variant of this doctrine and an improvement upon it. The forms of space and time there appear rather as patterns of synthesis than as innate mental receptacles, unless, indeed, we take Kant to have meant that there are schemata as well as forms of space and time, and so that there is a double set of intermediaries.

In physical science, again, according to Kant, what happens is that we bring certain rational principles of interpretation to bear upon our subject-matter, and we have the same right to do so as we have in mathematics, provided that we do not attempt to deal scientifically with anything (e.g. color) that is not quite simply and quite rigorously spatio-temporal. Thus, so Kant held, the logical principle of subject, in the subject-predicate relation, although, in simple logic, sterile because merely analytical, is fitted to become the physical principle of substance when it incorporates sense-experience into a permanent spatial world-order, and even guarantees the existence of a fixed quantum of physical substance in nature. (It does so, of course, *quâ* a principle of unity in the organization of our experience, not in relation to "nature," if that term were misunderstood and regarded as non-experiential.) Again, the logical principle of ground and consequent, although empty in an analytical sense, is susceptible of a certain kind of synthesis in our scientific experience. In the organized (mental) world of science, it becomes the necessitated phenomenal sequence of cause and effect. In other words, the fundamental principles of physics are logical principles *schematized* and applied to sensory material.

What, then, of the traditional "science" of metaphysics, of our alleged "knowledge" of the supersensible in the traditional domains, God, Freedom, Immortality? According to Kant, reason, in these domains, can be but analytical; and therefore, in so far as it seeks *knowledge* or *science*, is condemned to triviality. All metaphysicians are solemnly suspended from their functions until they answer the question, "How are synthetic propositions *a priori* possible?" When they answer the question, they must perceive at once that, *except in the interpretation of sense*, reason is only analytical, and is therefore doomed to sterility. In the genuine sciences, where we have necessary and certain knowledge, reason spells out phenomena according to its rules, being able to apply these rules because the mind is in its own house and is concerned with its own sensory representations; and being able to apply the rules *with necessity* because these domestic arrangements are necessarily in conformity with the pure forms of space and time.

In short, Kant maintained, there are no sciences except mathematics and physics; and there is no knowledge except scientific knowledge. Metaphysics can not be a science according to this pattern. Metaphysicians can not spell out phenomena as physicists do because, in their case, there are no appropriate phenomena to spell. They are not dealing, and they do not think they are dealing with phenomena, but with the supersensible. Hence there is no such thing as a science of metaphysics.

§ 10. The Regulative Use of Reason

It is evident, therefore, that Kant interpreted "knowledge" differently both from Locke and from Hume, and also (partly as a consequence) fixed the boundaries of "knowledge and real certainty" in a different place from these earlier authors. In the earlier view there was an implicit assumption that knowledge (unless of mere particulars) can not result from sense experience. For the latter yields at the best only "experimental knowledge" which, being interpreted, is animal faith and probable conjecture. Kant held, on the contrary, that there could be no considerable knowledge unless sense and understanding worked in unison, and that there *was* real knowledge when this unity occurred in certain enumerable ways. Much that Hume and even Locke would have called "probability" Kant, after reinterpreting, called "knowledge"; and he would have denied that Locke and even Hume were entitled to reckon as "knowledge" much that they did so reckon.

He agreed with Locke and Hume, however, in holding that vulgar or infrascientific opinions and inferences about what we call the world must be sharply distinguished from "knowledge," and that it is impossible and stupid to seek to defend the rationality of these vulgar inferences. Although he called such inferences "judgements of perception," [60] he explained them as being phenomena of private association. And there is, properly speaking, no place in his system for reasonable, although admittedly inconclusive, scientific conjecture. "We might as well think of grounding geometry or arithmetic upon conjecture," [61] he said; or, in other words, be content with scientific slops.

Similarly, he could have had no sympathy with the familar modern view that metaphysical (or theological) systems must ultimately be regarded as large speculative hypotheses, necessarily comprehensive and, for the rest, only probable or only plausible. "Nothing can be more absurd," he declared, "than in Metaphysic, a philosophy from pure reason, to think of grounding our judgments upon probability and conjecture. Everything that is to be cognized *a priori*, is thereby announced as apodeictically certain, and must therefore be proved in this way." [62]

Nevertheless, Kant strongly averred that it was our duty, as rational beings, not to be content with knowledge (i.e. with

[60] *Prolegomena to Metaphysics*, Mahaffy's Translation, pp. 53 *sqq.*
[61] *Ibid.*, p. 140.   [62] *Ibid.*

demonstrable natural science) but to press on towards metaphysics. Natural science itself, he said in effect, should seek something more than *mere* science, although not directly for scientific purposes. It is very poor science to be merely scientific, although it is very bad science to attempt to use super-scientific explanations as scientific hypotheses.

One of the technical ways in which Kant conveyed this doctrine is his distinction between the constitutive (or scientific) use of reason and its regulative employment. What Kant called the Ideas of Reason—we might rather say, its Ideals—comprise the totality of all things, their necessary being, their dependence upon some supersensible ground, their ultimate origin. These matters are beyond the purview of mathematics and they are beyond the purview of physics. The ground of all succession and of all time, for instance, should never be confused with any rule of succession *within time*, and is therefore quite incapable of being known as a natural cause. Nevertheless, it is in the interest of natural science itself to press towards totality, even if it can be demonstrated (as Kant thought he had demonstrated in his antinomies) [63] that such totality is unattainable by scientific means.

If this be true of the sciences, it is still more obviously true of metaphysics. Man is not only a scientific animal. He is also a metaphysical animal. And the rational part of him has the need, the thirst, and the insistent disposition to search eagerly for ultimate truth. This is no blind, mysterious instinct, as Philo thought, no trick of the imagination or illusion of the Life Force, no timid reliance upon traditional authority. The thinking part of us, just because it is, so very thoroughly, our *thinking* part, has a definite and a single orientation towards these Ideas of Reason. It may not attain scientific certainty, but there is nothing arbitrary about the form that its eternal quest assumes.

§ 11. Symbolic Anthropomorphism

Any such doctrine seems legitimate, or, at any rate, not indefensible. In ultimate matters, the truth may well be that there is no satisfaction but in proceeding, and even if a Kantian is

* *Critique of Pure Reason*, Dialectic, Book II, Ch. ii,

bound to lack full satisfaction from his reason, this relative disappointment may be *toto genere* different from the sense of treachery and vacuity that would arise from proceeding in any other direction.

The same, however, can not be said for all the ways in which Kant stated his culminating point of view. His celebrated doctrine of *Als Ob*—reason's great *As If*—may indeed be put in so many ways that we may be doubtful what precisely it comes to. But his doctrine of symbolic anthropomorphism seems to express his contention in a way for which paradox is far too mild a word.

To illustrate in Kant's favorite way. Of all the speculative arguments for the existence of God, the Argument from Design, Kant declared, was by all odds far the strongest. Yet it was not conclusive, and it *was* anthropomorphic—Hume's term in the *Dialogues,* by the way. It is an application, on a cosmic scale, of the magnified human attribute of purpose; and purpose, according to Kant was not even a scientific concept. Nature is mechanical; although Kant also said, without obvious consistency, that we *know* that mere mechanical causes *could not* produce a single blade of living grass.[64]

Yet Kant drew the amazing conclusion that, *although* design was an unscientific and anthropomorphic notion and not to be ascribed to God or to the whole, nevertheless we can not help thinking of the universe in this way.[65] If this statement meant only that we can not prevent our imaginations from indulging in some such species of picture-thinking, Kant's contention might pass, although, *ex hypothesi,* we *are* capable of correcting our imagination by severe thought. Kant's argument, however, appears to apply to our reason, not to our pictorial fancies; and in that case it can not surely be true that we are bound as rational creatures to impute cosmic design although we also know, on grounds of severe logic, that it is utterly fallacious to do so.

[64] *Critique of Judgment,* Bernard's Translation, pp. 312 *sq.*
[65] *Ibid.,* pp. 292 *sqq.*

§ 12. MORAL BELIEF

In the main, however, we must conclude that, when Kant "abolished knowledge to make room for belief," he meant to abolish the pseudo-science of the supersensible and to make room for a justifiable assurance in the righteousness of the cosmos. This fundamental thought took various turns in his pages. Sometimes he argued only (for example, concerning immortality) that speculative proofs on the subject had never affected mankind at all closely, and that the moral aspects of the question were the only important ones. Sometimes his thought turned to the question of value. The only unconditional value is the good will which is purely rational; and the only justifying reason why anything should exist at all is, quite precisely, its value.[66] Sometimes, indeed usually, his argument was that moral action assures us of the fact of freedom, that is to say, of the fact that the rational or supersensible part of us need not be coerced or necessarily determined by the pressure of the natural or sensory side of us, and therefore that the practical or moral reason tells us something that the speculative or scientific reason may accept but does not tell us. Speculatively, Kant held, the question of freedom, in the sense of determination by the supersensible, has to be left entirely open. We know that supersensible (and therefore timeless) causes are not *scientific* causes; for scientific causes are only regular successions in time. But this is no proof, one way or the other, concerning the ultimate question whether the whole temporal order has a supersensible, non-temporal ground. Here natural science, and any philosophy that takes account of natural science *only*, must remain forever mute. Ethical science, however, informs us that such determination does take place, although it forbids us to use this information for particular scientific purposes regarding physical nature.

Finally, the thing is sometimes described as a matter of rational faith, and we are told that "faith (absolutely so called) is trust in the attainment of a design, the promotion of which is a duty, but the possibility of the fulfilment of which (and consequently also that of the only conditions of it thinkable by us) is not to be *comprehended* by us." [67]

[66] *Ibid.*, p. 372.　　　　[67] *Ibid.*, p. 410.

Chapter III

THE PLACE OF EPISTEMOLOGY IN PHILOSOPHY

§ 1. General

In § 2 of Chapter I of this Book, we dealt with epistemology *eo nomine,* and the history given in Chapter II was, in very large part, an epistemological narrative. It seems advisable now to discuss the nature of epistemology rather more fully than heretofore, and particularly the relation of epistemological to other philosophical questions. For obvious reasons, this discussion should, if possible, grow out of the story unfolded in the last chapter. The eighteenth century was manifestly the great era of epistemological study. As a preliminary, however, it may save, not waste, time if we consider, once again, what epistemology means.

There is need for a systematic study of epistemology precisely in proportion as there is need for philosophers to ask epistemic questions; and epistemology is an independent philosophical discipline, precisely in proportion as epistemic questions are distinctive and independent questions.

What, then, is an epistemic question?

The term "epistemic" is due to Mr. Johnson, and he states his position thus: Instead of employing the overworked and ambiguous contrast between subjective and objective, he says, we would do better to accept the antithesis between *epistemic* and *constitutive.*[1] The Kantian term "constitutive" "points to the constitution of such an object of thought-construction as the proposition treated independently of this or that thinker."[2] The term "epistemic," on the other hand, calls attention to the thought attitudes of individual thinkers, who pass judgment, at definite times, upon constitutive propositions, accepting or rejecting them, consciously believing them, consciously doubting

[1] *Logic,* Part I, p. 2.   [2] *Ibid.,* p. 3.

or questioning them, consciously disbelieving them. Even "the fundamental adjectives true and false," Mr. Johnson continues,[18] ". . . derive their significance from the fact that the proposition is not so to speak a self-subsistent entity, but only a factor in the concrete act of judgement." [3]

Very likely, this decided contrast between epistemic and constitutive is itself a little too Kantian to be other than question-begging. The status of what Mr. Johnson calls "constitutive" may itself involve acute epistemological (and therefore epistemic) problems, in which case it would be advisable to use the word "epistemic" somewhat more widely than Mr. Johnson does. And I propose to do so.

Nevertheless, the way in which Mr. Johnson approaches this subject is the natural way of approaching it. To say, "This is so," is not obviously epistemic. To ask, "How do I know that this is so?" or "What right have I to assume, or conjecture, or believe, that this is so?" is very obviously epistemic. It is difficult, indeed impossible, to see how serious philosophers can avoid raising questions of the latter type; and if they can not avoid considering such questions, they can not consistently dissociate themselves from epistemology. What is more, the study of epistemology must have a certain independence and distinctiveness, although it also may not be "self-subsistent."

§ 2. FURTHER CONCERNING LOCKE AND KANT

Returning now to our historical avenue of approach, we may make an appreciable advance by recollecting and, at the same time, elaborating the contrast between Locke and Kant.

The fourth paragraph of the Introduction to Locke's *Essay* runs as follows:

"If by this enquiry into the nature of the understanding, I can discover the powers thereof: how far they reach: to what things they are in any degree proportionate: and where they fail us, I suppose it may be of use to prevail with the busy mind of man to be more cautious in meddling with things exceeding its comprehension; to stop when it is at the utmost extent of its tether; and to sit down in a quiet ignorance of those things which, upon examination, are found to be

[3] *Ibid.*

beyond the reach of our capacities. We should not then perhaps be
so forward out of an affectation of an universal knowledge, to raise
questions, and perplex ourselves and others with disputes about things
to which our understandings are not suited; and of which we cannot
frame in our minds any clear or distinct perceptions, or whereof
(as it has perhaps too often happened) we have not any notions at
all. If we can find out how far the understanding can extend its view;
how far it has faculties to attain certainty; and in what cases it can
only judge and guess we may learn to content ourselves with what
is attainable by us in this state."

The program so expressed is, pretty obviously, very similar
indeed to Kant's. Examine the length of your line, from hand to
plummet, before you begin to take any soundings. Be wise
enough to expect nothing at all from your soundings when you
take them in mid-ocean. Is not this program the very marrow
of epistemology?

The answer is that it may be so, but that Locke and Kant
interpreted a fundamentally similar program according to such
very different preconceptions that, in the result, each of them
conceived and expounded a significantly dissimilar epistemology.
Their agreement is too often forgotten and their differences
overstressed. But the differences were undoubtedly very marked.

For Locke, in essentials, the understanding was an instrument
to see by. To vary the metaphor of the line and the plummet,
it was a lantern or a candle whose office was to illuminate
our path. Hence, Locke might have concluded, and, as we have
seen, very frequently did conclude, that we can observe things
only as they reveal themselves (or cloud themselves) by candle-
light. He also might have concluded, and consistently did conclude, that it is absurd to regard the ordinary standard candle
of the ordinary human intelligence as if it were a kind of
angelic candle, like the cepheid stars of twentieth-century astronomy. But, in principle, whatever he may sometimes have
said, there was never the slightest occasion for him to infer
that the candle produced its surroundings, or that it was obviously better suited for revealing itself or other similar candles
than for revealing anything else.

To drop metaphor, Locke gave us in essence an inspective view
of the understanding. Its primary office, according to him, was

to discern and compare. No doubt he also accorded it other powers, and he is completely misunderstood by those commentators who represent him as holding that the understanding is either entirely or essentially passive. No doubt, again, he was not always consistent with regard to his inspective view of knowledge, and many modern writers are of opinion that the inspective view, consistently followed, is capable both of persuasive and of far-reaching development. Quintessentially, however, Locke's doctrine was that the understanding is adapted to the discernment of certain facts, and of these only, together with the contrasts, similitudes, and relations of such facts.

Kant's doctrine, quite on the contrary, was fundamentally non-inspective. As Mr. Metzger has recently shown with great skill,[4] Kant held, up to the end, the view he succinctly expressed in his *Dreams of a Ghost-seer.* "In reality," this passage ran, "all kinds of concepts must be drawn from the inner activity of our spirit as from their source. External things may very well contain the condition under which they are assimilated according to this or the other kind, but cannot supply the essential energy required for their actual apprehension."

In this crucial respect, Kant's epistemology is in the forefront of his philosophy precisely *because* Kant was a *Metaphysiker.* His convictions concerning the epistemic functions of reason may or may not have been strengthened (as Mr. Metzger suggests) by the publication in 1765 of a posthumous essay of Leibniz's in which the *a priori* is said to be a law of coördination. "Opus est interno mentis principio, per quod varia illa secundum stabiles et innatas leges speciem quandam induant." In any case, Kant's attitude was unwavering. The things of reason can not be outside our rational faculty, but, on the contrary, must be the constructions of that faculty. That and that only is intelligible which is produced by reason and has its source in reason. The supersensible is not outside us; for we, in the invisible but essential part of us, *are* the supersensible itself. *Therefore,* the study of productive, creative reason *must* come first in any sane philosophy, and the product of reason, which is science and knowledge, must be deduced from the char-

[4] *Der Gegenstand der Erkenntnis,* p. 722.

acter and operations of reason, that is to say, from the mind. If it should transpire—and Kant, as we have seen, held that it did transpire—that natural science can not be deduced from *mere* reason, it is at any rate not deduced from inspection, still less from inspection of what is foreign. What happens is that our reason assimilates representations that may indeed have a foreign origin, but are themselves mental and conformable to the governing, integrating, and coördinating powers of the true mind, that is to say, of the reason. They are the *usus realis* of reason, and they can be nothing less. Nor need we falter if it also transpires that this *usus realis* of reason in natural science is the only way of obtaining genuine science and demonstrable knowledge.

Here, then is a signal contrast between Kant's view and Locke's; and the consequences for epistemology are very notable. Kant's view compelled him (although we must concede that Kant was not unwilling) to deduce the nature of the known and of the knowable from its authentic source in the rational soul. His principal difficulty was that we know the effects of reason much better than we know reason itself. There was no such compulsion in Locke's case, and no such difficulty. On the contrary, Locke inferred, and was entitled to infer, the nature of our "line" (or understanding) from the "soundings" in which, as he thought, success had empirically been obtained. The understanding itself, which ostensibly came first in his pages, really came last.

§ 3. THE EPISTEMOLOGICAL ARGUMENT FROM HUMAN NATURE

Other lines of argument than Kant's, however, and very different ones, may be adduced to prove the priority of epistemology in the philosophical disciplines. An interesting example of such an argument was given by Hume in the Introduction to his *Treatise*, the burden of which is: Epistemology must come first and should be based upon observation and experiment. Hence my system.

" 'Tis evident," Hume declared, "that all the sciences have a relation, greater or less to human nature; and that however wide any of them may seem to run from it, they still return back by one passage or another. Even *Mathematics, Natural Philosophy, and Natural Religion,* are in some measure dependent on the science of MAN; since they lie under the cognizance of men, and are judged of by their powers and faculties. 'Tis impossible to tell what changes and improvements we might make in these sciences were we thoroughly acquainted with the extent and force of human understanding, and could explain the nature of the ideas we employ, and of the operations we perform in our reasonings. . . ."

"If therefore the sciences of Mathematics, Natural Philosophy, and Natural Religion, have such a dependence on the knowledge of man, what may be expected in the other sciences, whose connexion with human nature is more close and intimate?"[5]

He proceeded to cite Logic, Morals, Criticism, and Politics as examples and went on:

"Here then is the only expedient from which we can hope for success in our philosophical researches, to leave the tedious lingering method, which we have hitherto followed, and instead of taking now and then a castle or village on the frontier, to march up directly to the capital or centre of these sciences, to human nature itself; which being once masters of, we may every where else hope for an easy victory. From this station we may extend our conquests over all those sciences, which more intimately concern human life, and may afterwards proceed at leisure to discover more fully those, which are the objects of pure curiosity. There is no question of importance whose decision is not compriz'd in the science of man; and there is none, which can be decided with any certainty, before we become acquainted with that science. In pretending therefore to explain the principles of human nature, we in effect propose a compleat system of the sciences, built on a foundation almost entirely new, and the only one upon which they can stand with any security."[6]

In one form or another, this point of view is very common indeed, whether or not it lays claim to novelty.

Thus, commenting upon the doctrines of Auguste Comte (and including certain *obiter dicta* concerning Herbert Spencer), J. S. Mill wrote:

"The proper meaning of philosophy we take to be, what, in the main, the ancients understood by it—the scientific knowledge of Man, as an intellectual, moral, and social being. Since his intellectual faculties include his knowing faculty, the science of Man includes everything that man can know, so far as regards his mode of knowing it: in other words, the whole doctrine of the conditions of human knowledge. The philosophy of a science thus comes to mean the science itself, considered not as to its results, the truths which it ascertains, but as

[5] *Treatise,* p. xix.　　　[6] *Ibid.,* p. xx.

to the processes by which the mind attains them, the marks by which it recognizes them, and the co-ordinating and methodizing of them with a view to the greatest clearness of conception and the fullest and readiest availability for use; in one word, the logic of the science."[7]

There could scarcely be a more explicit or a more intransigeant expression of this point of view. And the same perspective seems prominent in contemporary philosophy.

Indeed, it seems clear that arguments based upon the so-called egocentric predicament in cogitation, or upon the cerebrocentric, anthropocentric, or sociocentric predicaments, have a pronounced similarity in principle to these contentions of Hume, or Mill, or others. The argument from the egocentric predicament states, for example, that Cicero must always be the center of Cicero's world; hence that Cicero's world must be assumed to be markedly Ciceronian; hence, that if we knew Cicero's nature we should also be able to deduce the nature of the Ciceronian world; and that we could not do so otherwise. The other arguments are identical in principle. *For* Cicero *read* Cicero's brain, or Cicero's society, or the humanity that is in Cicero. Such is their modification, or interpretation, of the egocentric doctrine.

§ 4. Faculties and Their Functions

Keeping in the main to the English, and more empirical, line of development, let us try to examine its general principle. We know (or guess or divine), it is said, by means of our faculties, and consequently can not know (or guess or divine) anything beyond the reach of those faculties. Hence, we should first examine our faculties and, having discovered, on the one hand, their powers, and on the other hand, their limitations, we can, in Hume's phrase, sit down contented, or according to the metaphor that Locke suggested, browse, like captive goats, within the ambit of our tethers, being assured that these tethers are irremovable and inexpansible.

Obviously, the question resolves itself into the problem whether in any sense it is either possible or necessary to examine our faculties *first*, and thereafter to infer what may be known or conjectured by means of them; and we have already discussed

[7] *Auguste Comte and Positivism*, p. 53.

this problem very briefly in Chapter I, § 2. Something more, however, should now be said about the argument.

In many arguments of this type a good deal of play is made with the suggestion that the "understanding" or any other so-called human faculty is the instrument with which we know or believe, and that any practical man tests his tools, or asks for a guarantee that they have been tested, before he begins to use them. Similarly, it is said, practical men do not use their tools for purposes to which such tools are plainly unfitted. They do not attempt to fell trees with a meat-saw, or to saw granite with saws that are admirably suited for cutting timber.

Analogies, however, are, usually dangerous and are always an oblique form of argument. It is, therefore, entirely possible that our faculties are a very special kind of instrument, whose properties are not to be confused with those of any other kind of instrument, or again that, although instruments, they are not *merely* instruments. What is more, even if the analogy held good, it may well be doubted whether it proves what it is purporting to prove. Naval engineers presumably do a good deal of testing before a ship is launched, and still more before she puts out to sea on her maiden trip. Even so, however, the testing of her material is a testing of the material *itself;* and the ultimate test is what the ship *herself* will do. The ship is finally tested when she is doing the work of a full-grown ship, and no test of the ship-in-herself before she began to move and to float could conceivably be regarded as sufficient. Similarly of her material before she was built. The material is tested when at work.

Taking the ship, then, to be an instrument for transporting men and goods, it seems plain that some instruments, at least, are tested in the performance of their function, and can not be tested properly when they are doing nothing, with their hands, so to say, in their pockets. It is possible, therefore, that this may be the proper analogy concerning knowledge, understanding, and other mental faculties. And if we can only test our faculties when they are at work, we can not also test them before they set to work, but can only test them in proportion as we discover what they do, which is quite a different thing.

When all is said, a "faculty" is only a capacity or a power; and there is always a puzzle when we begin to ask what a power or capacity is when it is not being exercised. To choose the old example, what precisely is the difference between saint and sinner when both are asleep?

Let us grant, however, that the word "capacity" does mean something. If the good man, say Andrew, is something when asleep, and if the bad man, say Judas, is also something when asleep, then of the something called the sleeping Andrew it is possible to say that it (or he) will be, or will probably be, a faithful disciple when awake, while of the something called the sleeping Judas it is possible to say that it (or he) will be, or will probably be, a traitor when awake. At the same time, to put the point mildly, it would be very inexpedient to examine Andrew asleep, or Judas asleep, if we wanted to discover which of them had a faithful, and which of them had a treacherous, character. Even if they really have quite different characters in their sleep, it might not be possible for us to discover the difference until we came to consider their waking, conscious, and responsible actions.

Is the same not true of our cogitative, sensory, and other faculties? How can we test, for example, the accuracy of a man's visual faculties except by noting the accuracy with which he discriminates objects by the use of his eyes? We may infer, no doubt, from certain tests that he can see as well as other people, and, therefore, that he would be capable of seeing a rhinoceros at a considerable distance, although he never saw a rhinoceros in his life before. The reason for this inference, however, depends upon the things other people, like unto him in the relevant capacity, have seen under given conditions. The reason is not that sight can be tested before anything is seen at all.

And so in other cases. The faculty of sympathy can only be tested in proportion as we find men actually sympathizing with their fellows. The faculty of addition is only to be tested by the accurate reckoning of sums. And similarly of the limitations of faculty. So-and-so, we say, could not read the time on a clock about a mile away. Like Mr. Samuel Weller, he has *only* eyes, and so "his wision's limited." But suppose he became hyperæsthetic, by hypnotic means or otherwise. In that case he might well see the clock at more than a mile's distance. To be sure, he could never see it a hundred miles away. Yet his customary limitations, the occasional abrogation of these customary limitations, and his final limitations seem all to be deducible from his practice in one and the same way.

In short, our former conclusion must clearly be sustained. There is no such thing as the examination of faculties *in vacuo*, or, in that sense, *before* they operate. It may well be contended, however, that no one ever seriously meant that our faculties could be so examined, although some have said it and others have not been at all careful to show that they did not mean it. Even Kant, as we have seen, probably found his central difficulty in the fact that he had to examine reason in its fruits and not in itself, unless, indeed, in certain parts of his ethical theory. He "deduced" the categories from their *usus realis* in geometry and in Newtonian physics.

Therefore, it may still be contended that the study of our faculties *in their employment* evinces a manifest priority and hegemony either of "reason" or of some other facultative *prius*. And similarly it may be contended that the inverse relation or, in other words, the inherent limitations of intellectual or other capacity, may also be discovered from the faculties in use. If our intellectual powers are, say, macroscopic and also microscopic, but never ultramicroscopic, what is to prevent us, as sensible men, from accepting the limitation, without any other experience (or non-experience) than comes from appreciating the nature of intellect in use? Why should we not say that the intellect is unfitted for the study of ultimate being, in the same way, and for the same reasons in principle, as we say that the human eye can not discern wave-lengths (let us say those of X-rays) that are of an order ten thousand times more minute than the wave-lengths of light?

In this further and more serious contention, there seem to be three principal points to consider. These are (1) the connection between the limitations of this or the other human faculty and the limitations of all human faculty; (2) the question whether the intellect is, in principle, invincible; and (3) the relation between the questions so raised and the priority of our cogitative faculties in an epistemological sense. I shall deal with these three points *seriatim*.

§ 5. SPECIAL AND GENERAL FACULTIES

(1) It seems as certain as anything can be that some, at least, of our faculties are adapted to quite special functions and can not overpass these functions. Thus memory seems to be restricted to this or to that in the past of which we have had previous personal experience. It follows, accordingly, that if we apprehend some past event, say the murder of Julius Cæsar, of which we could not conceivably have been actual spectators, we can not have the sort of acquaintance with this event that we have with the events that we remember. Similarly we can not, through our sense of sight, penetrate beneath the surfaces of things, although if we had other senses, like Voltaire's Micromégas, we might well be equipped with a portable and ancestrally inherited X-ray apparatus. Similarly, it is not to be expected that the keenest-nosed bloodhound could pick up a scent five centuries old, or recognize his master's trousers by their odor if the bloodhound is in Surrey and the master is in Peru, although some olfactory wireless apparatus, or its like, might easily enable the dog to do so. In other words, there are limits to what the keenest senses can discern, even in a condition of hyperæsthesia. Similarly none of us can actually feel another man's toothache, or have the particular acquaintance with another man's psyche that most of us believe we have, in self-acquaintance, with our own psyche.

In general, therefore, it seems possible to say, with very small fear of devastating criticism, that, while we may be acquainted with some things in a sensory way, and with other things in an introspective way, there are certain things with which we can only be acquainted, if at all, in an intellectual way. Therefore, since there is nothing approaching identity between the intellectual and the sensory views in cases in which we have *both* sensory *and* intellectual acquaintance, there must be some limitations to intellectual as well as to sensory faculty. And similarly of the relation of intellect to introspection.

The assertion of Spinoza [8] and of certain other mystics to the effect that there is something lacking in merely general knowledge, even when it is demonstrative and there is nothing false in it, may be regarded as further evidence towards the same conclusion. To grant this, however, is not the end of the story. As Mill said: "There is no appeal from the human faculties generally; but there is an appeal from one human faculty to another"; [9] and Mill went on to argue that we can check the testimony of the senses or of introspection with those of the logical judgment, and reciprocally. In any case, the limitations of this or the other faculty need not be taken to imply any limitation of all our faculties conjointly.

On the other hand, no serious attempt has ever been made to argue in this vein without somewhere asserting or implying that there is some kind of hierarchy in our faculties, and it is rare if logic and intellect are not placed at, or near, the top of the hierarchy. In other words, the preëminence, if not the invincibility, of intellect is closely akin to most such arguments.

§ 6. The Invincibility of Intellect

(2) One of the most telling expositions of the principle I am anxious to discuss in this connection comes from the pen of Mr. Stout. I quote it in some fullness:

"It seems to me the most arbitrary dogmatism," Mr. Stout says, "for anyone to attempt to determine *a priori* what is and what is not capable of being known. If we consider the concept of knowledge in general, apart from the special circumstances of this or that individual knower, there is no reason why it should not be co-extensive with all being. There is nothing to confine it to this or that part of the universe, or to anything short of the whole in its unity and in its detail. That things are known is as much an inexplicable fact as that they exist. To ask how anything can be known is like asking how anything can exist. Both are wonderful facts, but it is no use wondering at them. We must take them as we find them. When therefore we turn to consider finite individuals, we must assume that their knowledge is limited, not because it is knowledge, but because they are finite. The problem is not—How can I know anything? But rather "How is it that I do not know everything?" What is to be accounted for is not knowledge, but ignorance, and error, and beliefs that may or may not be true." [10]

[8] In his account of *scientia intuitiva*, *Ethics*, Part V.
[9] *System of Logic*, III, xxi, § 1.   [10] *Mind*, N.S., No. 124, p. 393.

Mr. Stout goes on to speak of ignorance as "diluted knowledge."

In this passage, the term "knowledge" must be understood with the greatest possible latitude. Mr. Stout can not be speaking of "knowledge" in the sense in which knowledge is opposed to belief, thinking and opinion; and his argument can scarcely be restricted to, say, "intellectual knowledge," where such "knowledge" is contrasted with mystical possession on the one hand or with sensitive acquaintance upon the other hand. In terms of his argument every species of apprehension, and also every species of misapprehension, must be reckoned as "knowledge," although in very many cases such "knowledge" is either very much "diluted" or otherwise most appreciably modified.

This being granted, the claims Mr. Stout puts forward seem to contain two principal assertions, viz. (a) that there is never any point in attempting to go behind the fact of "knowledge" (in this wide sense), or in exploring the supposed origin of "knowledge" in something that is not "knowledge"; and (b) that knowledge is, in principle, invincible, omnicompetent, and all-embracing, although finite knowers may, no doubt, exhibit their limitations (or their finitude) in their cogitative as well as in their other employments.

Let us, then, examine these assertions.

(a) The first assertion is one which many philosophers utterly decline to swallow and which a still greater throng of philosophers is totally unable to digest. Even if the term "knowledge" be interpreted with very great latitude (these philosophers say in effect), it should not be robbed of every vestige of its actual meaning. "Knowledge" implies some degree, at least, of conscious apprehension; and consciousness, so far from being something to be taken for granted, inevitable, ineluctable, and invincible, is, on the contrary, very obviously a natural growth that in all probability has arisen from non-cogitative origins, and, naturalistically regarded, may even be taken to be a roving and almost casual mutant, with nothing more inevitable about its existence than the unexplained biological fact that cows assimilate iron in the hemoglobin of their blood and that crabs, in a parallel way, assimilate copper. It is *now* inevitable for cows to employ iron in this way, but, for all we know, some of their remote ancestors might have selected copper. And similarly, although it is now inevitable for human beings to *know*, their remote ancestors might have chosen some other kind of adaptation. In short, according to those arguments, we *must* go behind knowledge, if we do not wilfully shut our eyes to its natural or genetic conditions.

Again, it is the business of "knowledge" (is it not?) to achieve some conformity to fact or to "agree with its object"; and how can this happen (some say) unless knowledge is "like" its object, or unless some cosmic conditions ensure the conformity on both sides, either, on a creationist and pre-evolutionary view, by a preëstablished harmony, or, according to the evolutionary doctrine, by an acquired harmony gradually constructed and enforced in the type of process generally described by the phrase "Natural Selection"? And in that case is it not also apparent that knowledge is no more invincible or perfect than anything else that is rough-hewed by the rude divinity of natural selection? All such natural tools, although they are effective enough to survive, are nothing like perfect, for all are incredibly wasteful and contingent upon the *status quo ante* in nature for the time being. Mr. Stout's magnificent assertions, therefore, are assertions (it is said) that simply *can not* be accepted.

Despite the plausibility and even the truth of these contentions, however, it seems to me that Mr. Stout is entirely right in this part of his doctrine, and that those who dissent from him are entirely wrong. For what Mr. Stout calls "knowledge" is something that exists; and its reality (which is necessarily legislative or normative) is no more to be disputed than the reality of any other authentic piece of being. To say that it has *come to be* what it is, is an interesting fact of history concerning which various conjectures may be entertained and in regard to which (let us hope) certain true and relevant genetic considerations are discoverable. Supposing, however, that it *was* not always what it now is (or that, at one time, it had no existence at all), this circumstance is no proof that it *is* not what it now is; and any one who, on the strength of some theories or discoveries concerning its origin, dogmatically asserts that it should therefore abdicate its essential claims and pretensions, is thereby assuming, quite unwarrantably, that its claims are only kite-flying and its pretensions mere pretense. No one has any business to say so; and no clear-thinking person can, properly speaking, consider so.

From this point of view, there *is* a sense in which knowledge must be final; or, if not "knowledge" in the widest possible sense, then some function of "knowledge," or, as Mill suggested, the total impact of "knowledge." Even if we know, on evidence, that our ape-like, or, for that matter, our savage ancestors, must have been incapable of appreciating, or even of conceiving, certain types of evidence, *we*, by the mere fact of knowing the same, must ourselves be capable of conceiving and, in some measure, of appreciating them. And any theory put forward concerning the origin of knowledge, its possible conformity with fact, and the like, claims itself to be a piece of knowledge and must argue its claim at the bar of knowledge.

In short, if we try to condemn our knowledgeable capacity we have to do so in terms of our knowing. In McTaggart's skilful parody of Sir John Eliot's famous phrase concerning parliaments, "None ever went about to break logic, but in the end logic broke him." [11] In the wide sense of "knowing" here in evidence there can be no escape from this predicament. The merest conjecture concerning the reliability or non-reliability of "knowledge," together with all nasty aspersions upon its pedigree, are themselves, in this sense, pieces of "knowing," and the same is true of all arguments concerning error. If we "know" that "knowledge" is vulnerable, being given to straying in paths not straight, falling into pits, and surrendering to footpads, this piece of "knowledge" about "knowledge" is itself "knowledge."

(b) On the other hand, Mr. Stout's view that knowledge is, in principle, omnicompetent and also invincible seems much more disputable. No doubt, Mr. Stout's concessions concerning the "dilution" of our knowledge in respect of our finitude "dilute" his own doctrine a great deal. There is not very much resemblance, in the end, between Mr. Stout's rather watery "knowledge" and the robust omnicompetence of Hegel's Absolute Idea, or Absolute Spirit. On the other hand, the whole principle of

[11] *Studies in Hegelian Cosmology*, p. 292.

diluting knowledge, with finitude as a provisional explanation of the dilution, seems greatly suspect. Is it a foreign liquid or a neutral cogitative liquid that does the diluting? If so, what is the liquid? And is cogitation, or knowledge, in all its varied potency, a single essence that *could* be so diluted? Why should it be more reasonable, in principle, to take ideal knowledge first, and subsequently endeavor to explain any falling away from the ideal? Is the ideal heaven-sent, and the problem of backsliding, like the problem of evil, an eternal mystery? The fact of knowledge, upon which Mr. Stout relies, is the fact that we do know some things; and there is also the fact that we do not know other things. Why, then, should he object, in principle, to a simple acceptance of both sets of facts. Is his argument not rather like saying that, because surgical capacity for removing tonsils and appendices is "in principle unlimited," therefore what has to be explained is why any one on earth should be left with his appendix or with his tonsils?

More in detail:

(i) If the stress of the argument concerns logical or intellectual "knowledge," it is quite possible, as we have seen, to know intellectually that we have *only* intellectual knowledge. We have, for example, intellectual but not visual knowledge of the other side of the moon, intellectual but not memory knowledge about the length of Cleopatra's nose, and so forth. Even if visual or memory knowledge is governed, in certain ways, by intellectual knowledge, there is *more* in visual or in memory acquaintance than intellect can itself supply; and in this sense intellect is not omnicompetent. There is no contradiction in saying that we know intellectually that we do not have some other kind of knowledge, or that, in addition to the other kinds of knowledge we know we possess, there are yet others that we do not possess at all, e.g. a knowledge of the future comparable to our direct acquaintance with the past in memory, or a visual acquaintance with "colors" beyond the spectrum, or some other of the thousand and one conceivable modes of sense-acquaintance that we do not possess at all.

(ii) Certainly, such arguments do not touch what may be called the *intellectual* omnicompetence of the intellect. They do not show that anything is beyond intellectual reach. Yet other considerations yield at least a certain limitation even to this principle. Thus, supposing that we can define and understand the governing principle of some infinite series, it would not follow that we could be literally acquainted, all at once or at any time, with each of the infinite constituents of the infinite series; and this would be true whether or not the members of the series were or were not pure intelligibles (as numbers, for example, have sometimes been held to be). Again, we could not enumerate the members of such a series in half a million lifetimes; and therefore could not have, in this case, the sort of intellectual acquaintance with the individual members that is yielded by the intellectual operation of counting.

(iii) It may reasonably be asked whether there is not something more of faith than of sight (or of insight), in any assertion concerning the intellect's omnicompetence, in the vehement denial of any hiatus anywhere between knowing and being, or in an assurance (like Mr. Einstein's) in a "fundamental reliance on the uniformity of the secrets of natural law and their accessibility to the speculative intellect." [12] Are not such ideals only heuristic and regulative, as Kant said they were?

And what of our finitude? We are not compelled to assume, at any rate on grounds of simple logic, that there are any knowers except finite knowers, or that when anything is known, it is a recovery, or Platonic reminiscence, of something that has been eternally known in some ideal knowledge. Pretty obviously, Mr. Stout does not mean to imply anything of the kind; and certainly he does not actually assert it. He is saying only that there are no imbecilities of thought, but, on the contrary, that we are in authentic possession of a faculty that, according to its nature, is in principle omnicompetent, and have only to explain why we grow tired, or depend upon biassed and very partial sources for our cogitations. The passage from a human to a superhuman intellect is not the passage to anything different. It is but an extension and magnification of the powers we ourselves possess.

[12] "The New Field Theory" (Second Article), *The Times* (London), February 5, 1929.

Insight into the character of human intellect shows that this must be so. Its finitude is irrelevant to its authenticity.

This latter principle, I think, is probable, but it seems rash to say that the many philosophers and theologians who have denied it were talking nonsense. As has been said so very often in these pages, our intellects, like any other faculty, are only powers. Grant, then, that our powers give us genuine insight into certain matters. Grant also that the sphere of such insight may be greatly extended, without any essential alteration in the relevant power. Is it therefore to be inferred that a wide extension of the powers of the intellect in these accredited directions is a proof of its indefinite extensibility in all directions? And if there is no proof of this, is the assumption one that must inevitably be made?

§ 7. FURTHER CONCERNING EPISTEMOLOGICAL PRIORITY

(3) We come now to the third question mentioned at the close of § 4 of this chapter.

In considering it, we may take for granted two of the conclusions at which we have provisionally arrived. These are, firstly, that if there is any logical priority in the study of our faculties as distinguished from the direct study of being (i.e. of ontology) such priority cannot imply either the advisability or the possibility of studying the faculties in themselves apart from their employment, but must be elicited from any insight we may gain from our understanding of the faculties in their use. Secondly, that in this matter of logical or metaphysical priority it seems necessary to concede that our cogitative faculties form some sort of hierarchy. If sense-acquaintance, for instance, must be capable of being justified at the bar of intellect while intellect need not plead before sense-acquaintance as its judge, intellect, in this crucial respect, is to be regarded as superordinate and sense-acquaintance as subordinate.

If we do not simply assume, as Kant appears to have assumed, that reason or intellect is by nature superior to any other faculty, being something divine and not of earth—a view which in principle does not seem more defensible than the Aristotelian astronomy according to which the heavenly bodies were of a different and more perfect substance than our Earth—the relevant arguments seem to reduce themselves, in the main, to two classes, viz. either (a) that our minds are more easily known by us than anything else or (b) that they must be better known to us than anything else. These two classes of argument, while frequently allied, are not necessarily identical. It is quite conceivable, for instance that some entity X, might be more easily, although more superficially, apprehended in one way, and apprehended with greater difficulty, but more profoundly, in some other way. Indeed, regarding material things, it is very usual to find arguments of this kind. Thus, most of the Cartesians appear to have held that the natural and the easiest drift of our thoughts was towards a superficial acquaintance with the physical world, but that, in thoughts more profound, we know ourselves far, far better than anything else. Malebranche, indeed, was a notable exception; [13] but, being an exception, he was not typical.

(a) Concerning the first of these points, the main argument is that the task of enumerating and examining our faculties is at any rate manageable, for our faculties are comparatively few and are obviously exhaustible. The vast ocean of being, on the other hand, is utterly inexhaustible.

Obviously, this view might readily be challenged on certain assumptions. It is, for example, opposed to the spirit of the Coherence View of Truth, or, as we might say, to Contextual Monism; for the contextual monists, e.g. the late Dr. Bosanquet, assert that everything with which we are acquainted is relative to its context, and consequently that such acquaintance is provisional and indeed misacquaintance in any context short of the whole. In brief, we can not apprehend anything truly unless we apprehend everything completely. Granting, however, that acquaintance with a limited object may nevertheless be accurate, or, with Dr. Schiller and other critics of contextual monism, that a makeshift or provisional knowledge is all the knowledge we ever get, we should still have to concede *something* at least to the argument with which we are now concerned.

It might be, and should be, objected, of course, that Kant,

[13] *Recherche de la vérité*, Book III, Part II, Ch. 7.

Hume, and others were mistaken in supposing that it was comparatively easy to obtain a complete and final inventory of the powers of the mind, although it was always impossible to obtain a complete and final inventory of all existence. How could we rightly deny that some new type of object, some fresh adventure of the mind in its knowing, might reveal mental capacities hitherto undreamed of? The mystics frequently inform the rationalists that rationalistic inventories are always incomplete, although they admit that such inventories may well be as nearly complete as rationalists could make them. Why *must* these mystics be mistaken? And might there not be supermysticism of this species *in infinitum?*

Nevertheless, I think we ought to give a qualified assent to the argument. It *is* easier to make a fairly accurate chart of the mind's principal capacities in the way of knowing than to map out all existence with any approach towards the same degree of completeness. On the other hand, it is always a delicate question how far such charts are charts *of the mind.* Logical relationships, for instance, while they indicate certain capacities of the mind, are also general properties which all existence must contain. So far as they go, therefore, they are quite as truly charts of being (or ontological maps) as they are charts of the mind.

(b) Let us pass, in the next place, to arguments that purport to prove that the mind either must be, or should be, better known than anything else.

These arguments are so many and so various that an exhaustive treament of them is not to be expected. On the other hand, it may be possible to enumerate some of the more distinctive among such arguments and, with luck, to broach a good many questions of some general interest. Accordingly, I shall make the attempt and shall deal with the following arguments: (1) the argument from mental atmosphere, (ii) the argument from similarity, (iii) the argument from proximity, (iv) the argument from the nature of appearance, (v) the argument from mental activity, (vi) the high priori argument from the nature of reason.

(i) The argument from mental atmosphere is usually a form of the contextual argument (not necessarily of the monistic variety), and is to the effect that whatever we are acquainted with is dominated by the fringe or the aura of our mental experience or attitude. This contention, obviously, is closely akin to the arguments previously mentioned concerning the ego-centric, anthropocentric or sociocentric predicaments, and there is no considerable advantage in attempting to separate them. If the ego is not mental, what in the world is mental? And it is at least specious to argue that we can no more forgo our egoity in any cogitation than leap out of our skins. In this case the argument takes a very personal turn. It is each man's mental atmosphere, associations, and memories that are in question. The anthropocentric or sociocentric arguments are, in appearance at least, less definitely personal. Indeed, unless each of us is supposed to be swallowed up in some group-mind, these arguments must to some extent be impersonal. The mental atmosphere they invoke must be at least as impersonal as that of a bank, or of a city's corporation, or of a political party. Such groups can be very impersonal indeed when their members choose.

Since the logic of all three arguments, however, is substantially the same it will suffice if we consider only one of them. For this purpose, the egocentric argument seems the most striking and the most suitable.

Broadly speaking, it may be said to have three forms, and to rely, respectively, upon the supposed implications (a) of the egocentric relation, (β) of the egocentric perspective, (γ) of mnemic assimilation on the part of the ego.

(a) F. H. Bradley's *Appearance and Reality* compelled British philosophers to take the metaphysics of relation very seriously indeed. It would be absurd to pretend that agreement upon the point has now been reached, but it is permissible to express a strong conviction concerning the issue of the dispute. Briefly, then, it is possible to assert with some confidence that if A has some relation r to B, it is not only logically conceivable that A and B retain their characters unmodified in the relation, but it is logically inconceivable that they should not do so. Relations hold *between* terms, and form or express a tie *between those very terms*. Thus, in the propositions "3 is greater than 2" and "3 is greater than 1," one and the same 3 occurs in both propositions, not a 3 modified by its relation to 2 in the first instance and a different 3 modified by its relation to 1 in the second instance. Either the whole relational way of regarding things is mythopoeic, or this identity of terms must be preserved.

It follows that, in so far as some known object O stands in the relation of being known to an ego E, it can not be logically inferred that O is therefore different from what it would be if it were quite alone, or from what it would be if related to something that is not an ego at all.

(β) The argument from perspective is manifestly spatial in its mode of expression, and is usually spatial in its actual meaning. It is commonly the argument that each of us perceives from his own point of view, and that this singularity of standpoint affects the whole of any man's cogitation. In our discussion, we may keep to this form of the argument while conceding that some philosophers (like the great Leibniz) have maintained that the phrase "point of view" in ultimate metaphysics is only in appearance spatial, being, in the last analysis, a pictorial way of describing the different degrees of confusion and error that, metaphysically speaking, distinguish one self from another.

In sense-cognition, where our visual, auditory, and other sense-apparitions manifestly do vary according to the observer's point of view, it has to be said, in the first place, that this variation is in no way exclusively mental. The same difference relative to point of view affects a camera as it affects the human eye—the same foreshortening, the same variation of size with distance, and so forth. It is rather the cerebrocentral than the egocentric predicament that is in question.

Secondly, these facts are fully compatible, in principle, with a "selective" view of perception. It is quite possible, in other words, that from any given point of view a different selection must be made, but that each selection is fact and nothing but fact. It is not necessary to assume, in other words still, that egoity is projected into perceptible facts. All that need happen is that some particular station restricts the ego (or perhaps, rather, the cerebrum) to a particular objective selection.

Even if the case regarding sense-perception, however, remained highly dubious, it would be quite illegitimate to infer that all our cogitation is determined (or vitiated) by the same sort of egocentricity. The main business of intellectual thought is to correct the illusions of private perspective, and there is no good *a priori* reason why the intellect should not succeed in this part of its business and achieve, not only anthropocentric agreement, but genuine knowledge of things as they are. So far as I can see, the common *cliché* that "being human, we can only interpret things humanly" means, as nearly as possible, nothing at all. We have to use our human faculties, but may very well discover by their means, and yet with accuracy, what is not human at all. Taking our former instance, for example, viz. that "3 is greater than 2," is there any genuine meaning in saying that Jones can only judge that *his* 3 is greater than *his* 2; and similarly with Smith and his Smithian 3's and 2's? And is there any way of saying that *only* human 3's are greater than human 2's, without also confessing that there is *no real meaning* in the statement that 3 itself is greater than 2?

(γ) The adjective "mnemic" describes the fact of retentiveness, either in the way of memory and explicit association or in the unremembered, implicit way in which we retain the vestiges of former experience and learn from it. While retentiveness, in some degree, is shown, say, in the hysteresis of certain types of aneroids and other instruments, it is in every way probable that the elaborately mnemic character of our minds is one of the profoundest parts of them.

In the same way as before, however, we may argue, and indeed must argue, that one of the principal offices of thought is to correct what is merely biographical and in that sense personal, and in the end to discover what any man ought to think, precisely because the facts *are* such and such. The circumstance that we are mnemic beings has in itself no tendency towards showing the futility of thought's enterprise in this affair.

In so far, again, as explicit memory or explicit association are in question, what appears to happen is that there is a mnemic expansion of the field of attention. In noticing X, which is before us, we also recall Y. This is no proof, in itself, that there is anything wrong with our apprehension of X; and our previous argument concerning relations forbids us to conclude that X must become different when noticed in relation with Y. If, on the other hand, the stress of the argument concerns what is implicit and unremembered, it would appear that what is implicit in this way is really a *tendency* to associate or to remember. It is incipient recall, which, psychologically, is little more than a dawning impression of familiarity. And it is scarcely to be inferred that mnemic *expansibility* is logically upon a different footing from actual mnemic *expansion*.

None of these arguments from mental atmosphere, therefore, is at all a convincing proof that our minds are better known than other things. The last of them is probably the strongest, and would be difficult to dispute if knowledge were simply a species of assimilation. The assimilative view, however, begs the question. If the truth were that knowledge is based upon inspective apprehension—and this is what I have argued by implication—there is no mnemic reality sufficient to ruin this interpretation.

(ii) The argument from similarity depends upon the ancient, but still active, superstition that like must be known by like. Historically speaking, this argument, like so many of the others previously mentioned, was elaborated in connection with sense-cognition; and it fell into the common error of confusing between sense-cognition and the physical causes of sensation. Even with regard to causation, however, it is magic, not science, to hold that causes and effects must be *like* one another; and we should try to avoid the state of mind that seeks to injure an enemy by sticking pins into his effigy. In general, we may say that there is no more logic in maintaining that the eye *must* be sun-like in order to behold the sun, than in maintaining that the eye must be potato-like in order to behold a potato.

According to Shelley, in his magnificently Platonizing *Defence of Poetry*, there must be a certain affinity or propinquity between the higher capacities of the mind and the True, the Beautiful, and the Good. This may well be the truth; but it can not be inferred from the pseudo-axiom *Similia similibus*.

(iii) The argument from proximity is also based upon a confusion between the causes of perception, on the one hand, and the reality of sense-cognition, on the other hand. When our senses are stimulated, it is argued, the mind must be "in its own place," that is to say, in contact with the cortex of the brain. It can not take a walk among the stars. It is under our hats. In other words, the contention is that sense-cognition is an instance of causation by contact; and hence, with some confusion, that although the mind, properly speaking, is aware only of its own modifications, it yet can also be held to be aware of the adjacent causes of such modifications, although not of any remote cause.

This underhat philosophy is a tissue of confusion. It would be consistent, although quite unreasonable, to maintain that our minds are acquainted with themselves only, but it is wholly inconsistent to combine this view with any knowledge of adjacent but extra-mental regions in the brain. The principal fallacy, however, is to infer that because there must be cerebral excitation whenever we perceive, therefore we perceive nothing but this cerebral excitation. Any one who perpetrated this fallacy ought, in consistency, to conclude that the world we perceive is under our hats—a cerebral world. This cerebral world would have to contain our (physical) hats and our (physical) skulls. In other words, our heads, according to the theory, would be inside our heads. It is highly advisable, therefore, to excogitate something more sensible. If any one holds that the mind must be in its own place, he may be invited to consider where that place is; and if he holds, as well he may, that a thing *is* where it *acts* (action, in terms of this argument, being the "action" of sense-cognition), he might most logically conclude that the mind's place is wherever its cognition takes it. In other words, if it perceives the sun, its place, then, is in the sun.

The mind, however, is so much more than sensory, and the argument from proximity is so exclusively sensorial, that nothing further need be said about the palpable insufficiency of this doctrine.

(iv) The argument from appearances may be stated as follows:

(a) In all our cogitations we can not be concerned with anything except appearances. Such appearances may be shams, but they may also be authentic or veridical. The business of science and philosophy alike is to save the genuine appearances and to eschew the shams; and there can be no proper challenge to these statements, provided the term "appearances" is understood widely enough and defined in such a way as to include logical, inferential, and also introspective appearances as well as sensory apparitions. This being understood, we are told that the ancient adage holds universally: *De non apparentibus et de non existentibus eadem est ratio,* which is another way of saying that anything that does not appear to some given person is, in respect to that person, *nothing.*

(β) All appearances (we are informed) are mental. According to Hume, the mind consisted of sensory or passional appearances, together with their echoes in imagery, and was, indeed, a "heap" of such appearances. Suppose, however, that Hume was wrong both in his description of appearances and in his view that our appearances are loose and separate, constituting a mere heap. It still remains true (this argument states) that our appearances are *somehow* mental and also personal (although not necessarily merely private).

(γ) An appearance (it is further explained) must be what it appears to be. This is an identical proposition. Anything that seems so-and-so *must* seem so-and-so.

From (β) and (γ) taken together it follows that such part of our mental equipment as consists of appearances must be better known than anything else because it must be known quite infallibly, on pain of contravening an identical proposition. From (α), (β), and (γ) taken together it follows that everything thinkable consists of appearances and must be what it seems to be, i.e. is infallibly apprehended.

Clearly, there is something wrong somewhere—indeed, something *very* wrong; for sound arguments could not lead to so preposterous a conclusion. I have to suggest, indeed, that all the three steps in the above argument are mistaken.

The statement that something appears to us when we are aware of anything, and consequently that appearances and awareness are coextensive, seems innocuous so long as we are dealing with what is true. Even in this case, however, it is illegitimate to argue that because something seems such and such, therefore it presents a distinct entity, its seeming or appearance, to some knower. And in the case of falsehood it is surely clear that there are no such entities. Suppose, for example, that I believe that Marie Antoinette died in her bed. In that case, according to this theory, there would have to be a real, although false, entity—Marie Antoinette's death in her bed, appearing to me—whereas there was no such fact.

Another form of the same fallacy—which, as it happens, has been very common in European philosophy from Greek times onwards—is the view that every distinctive form of human cogitation specifies a distinctive form of "object." Thus let us suppose that Jones opines something, that Smith believes it, and that Robinson knows it. According to the fallacious view we are now considering, it has to be inferred that there are three distinct objects in the case, viz. Jones's *opinatus*, Smith's *creditum*, and Robinson's *cognitum*, or, still more fallaciously, that Jones's *opinatus* is a real piece of half-being, Smith's *creditum* a real piece of three-quarter being, and Robinson's *cognitum* a real piece of full being. Actually, all these inferences are false. There is only one thing that Jones opines, Smith believes, and Robinson knows. The only difference in fullness is the fullness with which each has severally grasped it. And although we often have to admit that our cogitative grasp of things may be very imperfect, we never (unless we are the dupes of a theory) attribute these limitations to things themselves.

In short, we are never entitled to conclude that because X seems such and such, there is therefore some intermediate epistemological entity, the seeming of X, which stands between us and X and is the mental apparition that we know.

For the same reason, it is illegitimate to infer that "appearances" are necessarily mental. If a stone wall appears to us, what appears may very well be part of the surface of the stone wall. And there need not be anything mental about this part of the wall.

The same objection, in principle, must be made to the very common argument that, at least in our consciousness, seeming and reality must be identical. It does not follow that, because we are conscious, we must therefore inevitably discern what our consciousness is. On the contrary, the greater part of introspective psychology was directed towards this very discernment. The introspective psychologist's entire orientation was towards the nuances in his own consciousness; and these nuances are not at all easy to discern. We *are* conscious, but it does not therefore follow that we fully and accurately apprehend what our consciousness is.

Our argument, at this stage, is largely directed against Hume's presentationism and against the type of argument employed by Mill in a quotation given in an earlier part of this chapter. It has, however, a much wider range. I do not pretend to know how Kant answered Hume—if Kant did answer him—but there is a prevalent opinion to the effect that Kant's answer took the following course: We have to distinguish within our mental appearances those that have a scientific significance from those that do not have it. Without the former, the latter would be a mere chaos, incapable of yielding the very foundations even of Hume's system, e.g. the certainty that I am seeing something now.

If so, it has to be said that the arguments we have stated apply with the same force to significant as to non-significant appearances. The object of knowledge can not be reduced to a significant kind of appearance. If our reference to an object were *only* a reference, there would, so far, be no object. There would only be an attitude of mind, whether or not this attitude were charged with, say, the necessary or the universal stamp. It is only when our significant experiences succeed in acquainting us with objects *themselves* that there is knowledge, properly speaking, at all. To distinguish within experience between experience of a necessary kind and experience of some other kind is no solution. On the contrary, it leaves us with a mass of balked cognitions, all awaiting the starter's pistol and none of them running the race.

(v). Many who follow or were strongly influenced by Kant (and perhaps some others) maintain that our knowledge of physical nature contains a passive or sensory constituent and an active or spontaneous constituent; and there is a prevalent opinion to the effect that our own activity must be known to us with a clarity and certainty that can not be reached elsewhere.

This point of view finds very complete expression in the *atto puro* of the New Idealism in contemporary Italy. I quote from Signor Gentile:

"When we speak of spiritual fact we speak of mind, and to speak of mind is always to speak of concrete historical individuality; of a subject which is not *thought* as such, but which is *actualized* as such. The spiritual reality, then, which is the object of our knowing, is not mind and spiritual fact, it is purely and simply mind as subject. As subject, it can, as we have said, be known on one condition only—it can be known only in so far as its objectivity is resolved in the real activity of the subject who knows it." [14]

And again:

"To find spiritual reality we must seek it. This means that it never confronts us as external; if we would find it we must work to find it. And if to find it we must needs seek it, we shall never have found it and we shall always have found it. If we would know what we are we must think and reflect on what we are; finding lasts just as long as the construction of the object which is found lasts. So long as it is sought it is found. When seeking is over and we say we have found, we have found nothing; for what we were seeking no longer is." [15]

The presuppositions of this argument are clearly (1) that knowing and existence are identical (nothing "external" or "foreign" to the knower being knowable), (2) that knowing is an active or constructive process, and (3) that this translucent constructive process, in which there is nothing foreign since knowledge and existence are identical in it, is known when and so long as it exists, but no longer.

Granting that knowing is an active process, whether or not in the sense understood by these new idealists, the first and third of these presuppositions ought to be categorically denied. It is not true that knowledge and existence are identical, e.g. that a stone, because it exists, knows the nature of its stoniness; and even if it were false to say that stones exist (on the ground, say, that nothing exists except minds), it would also be false to assert that minds know themselves simply because they exist.

The third presupposition is equally indefensible. There could be no time order if there is never any reality except the present moment. In other words, a "historical" process that has no *past* but contains the whole of a non-entitive "past" in a specious and conscious present is not a historical process at all.

---

[14] *The Theory of Mind as Pure Act,* English Translation, p. 12.
[15] *Ibid.,* p. 23.

This, I concede, is a very summary rejection of Signor Gentile's presuppositions. The excuse is that nothing except summary treatment is possible. Signor Gentile states his principles with the utmost dogmatism, because there is nothing to be said for them. They are either manifestly true or quite definitely false. Since, therefore, there is no middle way, it is best to take these presuppositions for what they are, viz. false.

On the other hand, the view that our mental activity is in fact known to us, in and through a special mode of knowing that is as good as infallible, has been maintained by so many philosophers, arguing from such widely different standpoints, that it can hardly be treated in the same summary fashion.

In general, what is contended is that the nature of our own voluntary activity is very plainly knowable and comprehensible by us. In the external world, it is said, the sequence of cause and effect is, so to say, mere brute sequence. Dip the blue paper in the acid and it becomes red. Here we have an invariable, but not an intelligible, sequence. It is otherwise, however, with our volitions. In their case we know what we mean to do, what our purposes are. And it is intelligible (is it not?) that we should accomplish what we mean to do. *Ex post facto,* at any rate, and in case of success, we can understand why certain results came about. The mere existence of serious willing shows that we have an intelligent and intelligible grasp of the situation.

These statements are plausible; but they will not bear the closer kind of scrutiny. We can not grasp a situation except on the basis of experience. If we know, or have reason to believe, that we can distinguish between what we can move and what we can not move in the external world, we may then proceed to make adjustments; but not otherwise. If we know what in our bodies (e.g. our limbs) we can move, and how far, or how fast, we can move them, we may then proceed to adjust our bodies. And similarly we may adjust our minds if we know the kind of control we have over our thoughts and imaginations. The whole of this distinction, however, between what we can do and what we can not do, has to be *learned;* and the distinction itself is just a "brute" fact, like any other brute fact of the causal sort.

There is no difference in principle between learning by experience how far a gun can shoot and similarly learning how far a man can jump.

Even if we had first-hand acquaintance with the efficacy of our volitions, however, in a sense much liker clear intelligibility and much less like brute fact than is actually the case, there would be a considerable deflection of the argument when our cogitative and speculative activity came into question. Speculative contemplation is clearly not identical with voluntary action; and if *pure* activity, activity without any admixture of passivity, is the crux and the core of the debate, there is a serious dubiety whether we are acquainted with pure activity either in ourselves, in our minds, or elsewhere. Our acquaintance with our bodily activities is obviously not non-sensory. It is, on the contrary, guided by postural and kinæsthetic sensa; and although these should be distinguished from "pure" mental activity, it is very questionable indeed whether such pure mental activity is not known rather by inference than by any direct and unequivocal revelation.

(vi). At an early stage in the argument of this chapter we distinguished between the epistemological presuppositions of Kant, the *Metaphysiker,* and those of experiential or empirical epistemologists like Hume or Mill. According to both, the mind was central in these affairs and the study of it in some sense prior to any other study. They differed widely, however, both in their interpretation of mind and in their accounts of its cogitative office. In the end, Kant belonged to a tradition which, following the Stoics and the Scholastics, regarded mind and reason as ultimately identical (at any rate as regards what is governing and distinctive in the mind) and regarded reason as nomothetic, supersensible, and a purely spontaneous agency. The "light" of reason was taken for granted, and what was discussed was its constructiveness and mode of operation.

As we have seen, however, this high priori way of arguing, while it is capable (on its own terms) of telling us a great deal about what reason *does,* may not be equally ready to give us any clear understanding of what reason *is.* According to the argument, reason is the order-producing principle, and logical necessity or logical universality is its sign manual. It is there-fore easy to tell (again according to the argument) when and where reason has been at work, as also to declare where it is indispensable.

These contentions, however, are quite consistent with the fur-ther view that the principle of order is in itself unknowable, or, at any rate, unknown. We infer the operation of an order-pro-ducing principle, because we are compelled to recognize orderli-ness in our experience, but the supersensible ground of orderli-ness may nevertheless be hidden from us. There is much in Kant's philosophy to suggest that this *was* his ultimate principle; and it is certain that he sharply distinguished between the for-mal or logical unity of self-consciousness, on the one hand, and any *knowledge*, either of the "empirical ego" through the internal sense, or of the noumenal, supersensible, or rational ego, on the other.[16]

In this case, the rational mind, or the logic-producing prin-ciple, so far from being better known than anything else, is, on the contrary, not known at all.

To be sure, it may well be contended that this attempt to dis-tinguish between orderly intelligibility and the principle of such orderliness is itself a dropping of the substance and an effort to pursue the shadow. What I am maintaining is only that the high priori way of demonstrating that epistemology comes first in these affairs is itself in great danger of being only a shadowy highway.

§8. Conclusion

I shall not attempt to summarize the long and complicated argument of this chapter, but should like to remind the reader of a few simple conclusions that emerge from it. These are, in the main:

(1). That epistemology has to be studied because there really are epistemic questions.

(2). That such a study is distinctive in its purpose and point of view.

---

[16] See especially his account of the "Paralogisms of Substantiality" in his *Critique of Pure Reason*.

(3). That a certain weight should be attached to the contention that the study of our faculties is more manageable than many ontological adventures; but

(4). That it is impossible to study our faculties *in vacuo*. They can only be studied in their use. And any arguments that purport to show the logical priority of epistemology are subject to this condition.

(5). That there is no good reason why our minds *must* be better known than anything else; moreover, that most of the "reasons" alleged in support of this contention, or tacitly presupposed when such support is given, are very bad reasons indeed.

(6). That the argument which asserts that, because we are human, therefore we can only know what is human (or can know nothing else *well*) is one of the worst of all the bad metaphysical arguments.

Book II

THE NATURE OF KNOWLEDGE,
BELIEF, AND OPINION

Chapter IV

THE NATURE OF KNOWLEDGE

§ 1. Preliminary

As we have seen, the great philosophers of the eighteenth century interpreted the term "knowledge" in a very stringent and, as some might say, in a very narrow sense. Knowledge consisted, in their view, either of *principia* or of *principiata e principiis*. In other words, they held that when we "know" we are conscious of what is evident, either immediately, by intuitive self-certification, or derivatively and demonstratively, by a chain of conscious intuitive steps.

It would not be correct to say, however, that the term "knowledge" is always employed in this sense; and the circumstance calls for inquiry.

It is not to be expected, of course, that words in common use are invariably (or even frequently) free from ambiguity. This happens only when nobody is likely to make a mistake. Everybody understands that a spade is a spade, because nobody has the least difficulty in distinguishing a spade. It is otherwise, however, when people begin to talk metaphorically about spades. For example, there is usually a good deal of ambiguity about the precise meaning of spade-work.

Since it is infrequent for the same sound to be employed *very* differently without at least some presumed connection, or partial analogy, between its various meanings and ambiguities, it is usually advisable to consider several different meanings—without prejudice to any final conclusion—with a view to discovering where the alliance or analogy between diverse meanings is supposed to reside.

Thus it is with the term "knowledge." Animals, we say, "know their way about," or may come to do so, like rats in a maze, after experience and habituation. The female of any species is sometimes said to "know" a great deal concerning maternity, whether or not she has ever become a mother. In short, what, in some sense, permeates any vital constitution is sometimes said to be "known" either by racial habit (or instinct) or by individual habituation without conscious memory.

In this sense it is hard to see why "knowledge" should be restricted even to animals. May not plants be said to *know* how to make use of air and of phosphates in the same sense as a vulture *knows* how to make use of air and carrion? And do not magnets *know* how to cajole iron filings? If we discriminate in these cases, we should be able to give a reason for our discrimination.

§ 2. On Samuel Butler's Views

It will be convenient, I think, to begin this discussion by considering some of the pregnant, if complicated, statements that Samuel Butler made in the early chapters of his *Life and Habit*.

"As long as we did not know perfectly [he says] we were conscious of our acts of perception, volition and reflection, but when our knowledge has become perfect we no longer notice our consciousness nor our volition." [1] "It would therefore appear as though perfect knowledge and perfect ignorance were extremes which meet and become indistinguishable from one another; so also perfect volition and perfect absence of volition, perfect memory and utter forgetfulness." [2] "In either case—the repose of perfect ignorance and of perfect knowledge—disturbance is troublesome." [3] "Certain it is that we know best what we are least conscious of knowing, or at any rate least able to prove, as for example, our own existence or that there is a country England." [4]

"Indeed, it is not too much to say that we have no really profound knowledge upon any subject—no knowledge on the strength of which we are ready to act at all moments unhesitatingly without either preparation or after-thought—till we have left off feeling conscious of the possession of such knowledge, and of the grounds on which it rests. A lesson thoroughly learned must be like the air which feels so light, though pressing so heavily against us, because every pore of our skin is saturated, so to speak, with it on all sides equally. This perfection of knowledge sometimes extends to positive disbelief in the thing known, so that the most thorough knower shall believe himself altogether ignorant. No thief, for example, is such an utter thief—so good a thief—as the kleptomaniac." [5]

"As the fish in the sea, or the bird in the air, so unreasoningly and

1 Pp. 10 *sq.*   3 P. 19.   5 Pp. 21 *sq.*
2 P. 18.   4 P. 20.

inarticulately safe must a man feel before he can be said to know. It is only those who are ignorant and uncultivated who can know anything at all in a proper sense of the word. Cultivation will breed in any man a certainty of the uncertainty even of his most assured convictions."⁶ "For the power to prove implies a sense of the need of proof, and things which the majority of mankind find practically important are, in ninety-nine cases out of a hundred, above proof. The need of proof becomes as obsolete in the case of assured knowledge as the practice of fortifying towns in the middle of an old and long-settled country. Who builds defences for that which is impregnable, or little likely to be assailed? . . . *Qui s'excuse, s'accuse;* and unless a matter can hold its own without the brag or self-assertion of continual demonstration, it is still more or less of a parvenu, which we should not lose much by neglecting till it has less occasion to blow its own trumpet."⁷

There is much more, in Butler's best manner, to the same effect. What, then, did Butler mean by "knowledge" in these passages?

Superficially, at least, the answer seems tolerably plain. According to him the marks of "knowledge" were, firstly, repose and security: secondly, unhesitating adjustment, without foresight or after-thought, to an alterable situation.

It seems clear that these characteristics may be interpreted in a way that has nothing to do with mind and consciousness, to say nothing of proof or reason. If we were asked, offhand, to give an example of utter repose and security, we might point to the everlasting hills. If unhesitating response to a stimulus were what we thought of we might refer to a hair-trigger.

Nevertheless, these statements are in reality metaphorical. They apply, in strictness, only to beings that are capable of being consciously secure or in repose. And if the poise and security of self-maintenance, on the one hand, and fearlessness in active response, on the other hand, are expressly conditioned by the qualification that these statements are metaphorical except in the case of beings capable of experiencing fear or confidence, it can not be supposed that conscious experience is irrelevant in this matter, even if, in certain given instances, this fear or this confidence need not be actually felt.

Let us, however, proceed in detail to what appear to be the distinctive counts in Butler's exposition.

⁶ P. 28.   ⁷ P. 30.

The main point is that unquestioning assurance is what Butler meant by knowledge. He therefore drew the natural conclusion that the most unquestioning sort of assurance is that which
is always unquestioned, never doubted, never so much as considered; and he suggested that serene self-maintenance or unhesitating action is the only possible evidence of this unquestioning assurance.

We have seen that there is no meaning in "assurance" unless
we are dealing with beings that are capable of thought and consciousness, unless in the palpable metaphor according to which
a Virginia creeper, say, may be held to "know how to creep."
This being granted, we have also seen that firm assurance may
exist in certain cases without our attention being drawn to the
nature or manner of the assurance. There may be instinctive, unlearned, congenital, or constitutional assurance, such assurance
being for the most part cognitive, but not necessarily, and perhaps not usually, self-cognitive. There may be hearsay assurance that persuades us without the smallest suspicion of doubt
or question. There may also be assurance due to familiarity,
habit, inseparable or indissoluble association, and the like. It
may also happen that what we were acutely conscious of during
the process of learning becomes almost, if not quite, unconscious
and "secondarily" automatic.

But is assurance of this kind necessarily or usually *knowledge*?

That is the question with which the present chapter is concerned; and it is best to approach it warily. Let us therefore consider two of Butler's arguments with some care.

Butler's statement that consciousness interferes with knowledge, and that sheer, blank ignorance does not interfere with
knowledge, is manifestly an intentional paradox. Is there, however, anything solid in the paradox?

It is clear that consciousness may impede action. Naturally it
does not always do so, else we could never guide our actions by
conscious attention; and we frequently guide them attentively.
On the other hand, when we have learned to dispense with attention, the entrance of attention may seem unnatural and therefore bewildering and a hindrance. In that case we may trip or

stumble or be afraid, whereas, if we had "gone right ahead," none of these mishaps need have occurred.

In actions which are learned, express attention has generally to be given to the early stages, and it is seldom true that actions thus learned can proceed wholly without attention. When they do, we are, for the most part, confronted with abnormal cases, like that of the parson who wrote sermons in his sleep; and even then it is not certain that the parson did not attend to what he was doing. All that is clear is that he did not remember having done so when he woke up. What happens, in fact (at any rate in the great majority of cases), is that there is a redirection of attention. The cricketer learns to "see the ball" as soon as it leaves the bowler's hand. He does not have to wait for it to pitch. This finer adjustment gives the cricketer an extra moment's grace, with immense advantage to his batting average.

In such cases, the consciousness of particular movements may be used, to a limited extent, *where it is needed*, without any impeding of action. Thus a golfer, on one of his more miserable and less successful days, may consciously correct certain faults (such as lifting his head), whereas, on happier occasions, he has only to stand up and hit the ball without thinking at all of his head, or of his grip, or of any other special movement. On the other hand, it is generally true that if he pays considerable attention to rapid movements that ought to be almost, if not quite, automatic, distraction and disaster will ensue. The rhythm of his swing is broken because he is dismembering his movements by lingering over some of the details in them.

Nevertheless, the proper contrast in such instances is not between consciousness and unconsciousness, but holds within consciousness regarding the direction of attention. The golfer who hits the ball without thinking of his stance or of his grip is not an unconscious golfer at all. For he does mean to hit the ball. And, although we say he "knows how to hit it" when he consistently hits it well, it may be doubted whether we really mean what we say. Obviously, he need not have the kind of (assumed) analytical knowledge that floods the market with books about golf.

Similar arguments hold of deliberation and of absent-mindedness. Deliberation is one thing, and action is another thing. We should not therefore be surprised if enterprises of pith and moment sometimes go astray owing to the intrusion or recurrence of an attitude appropriate to the planning of such enterprises before they were begun in earnest. Absent-mindedness, again, is not unconsciousness, but temporary lack of concentration upon the matter in hand. If and so far as it causes ludicrous mistakes in action, the cure is more or different consciousness, not less consciousness.

Even if we grant that there may (sometimes) be too much thinking, it does not follow that there is any evil in thinking as such, or in the appropriate amount of thinking. In general, there is no proof that consciousness is normally or usually a hindrance to efficient action, and that we should be the better if we dispensed with this impertinent meddler. All that is proved is that one direction of consciousness may easily hamper some other direction of it.

A second count in Butler's argument concerns the relation between proof and hesitation or doubt. "It must be so, Plato, thou reasonest well." When Addison penned these lines, he implied (did he not?) that his hero, Plato, was doubtful about the immortality of the soul?

We must concede that when any one is asked for a proof of something familiar that he always takes for granted, such as his own existence or the existence of his country, the request is apt to induce something very like a shock to his simple system. It is easy to be more certain of a conclusion than of the grounds we could give for it; and it may be disturbing to learn that something we do not doubt *is* a conclusion that must have grounds. Such shocks, however, need not last; and, as can not be too often repeated, if anything *abides* our questioning, we surely know it the better, and not the worse, if we see it proved.

Again, it must be conceded that there is a difference between undiscriminating attention, on the one hand, and critical attention, upon the other. This difference is so manifest that persons unaccustomed to critical reflection may readily become bewildered when the skeleton of reflection peeps out of the cupboard. At the best the thing appears an unnecessary subtlety. "Fiddle, we know, is diddle; and diddle, we take it, is dee." All that follows from this circumstance, however, is that certain people are unfamiliar with certain kinds of proof; and do not like to be forced to admit that other people ponder what they themselves would never dream of thinking about. And this is rather a trivial conclusion.

Nevertheless (we may be told), proof implies some sort of testing. Whatever is proved is *put* to the proof. Is it not legitimate, therefore, to argue that there are some things that (1) can not, (2) should not, or (3) need not be put to the proof at all? And is it not precisely these things that we know best of all?

I submit that if proof, in this case, means deductive proof, it is obviously true that not everything can be deductively proved. The chain of logical deductions must hang upon a peg that, in the last resort, is not itself suspended from a deductive chain. In any other sense of proof, however, it seems clear that some test is applicable. The mere fact that we are dealing with something conceivable, thinkable, capable of receiving attention, is evidence in itself that we can attend to the thing more carefully, give it closer scrutiny, raise questions about it. And to do so is to test it.

The great mistake that is apt to be made in these affairs is to insist that some *special* test must be applied. Conceivably, indeed, there is some universal test, e.g. clearness or, perhaps, consistency. Very frequently, however, we find quite special tests applied to everything, whether the tests are suitable or not. And if these special tests are inapplicable we are glibly informed that there is no meaning whatsoever in anything that can not be verified in this quite special way.

For example, I do not wish to maintain that we should or can believe in the Real Presence at the Eucharist. Suppose, however, it were argued, as we all know it has been argued recently, that there is no meaning in the doctrine of transubstantiation unless the consecrated bread and wine can be shown to be different from secular bread and wine either by a chemical or by a spiritual test. In that case, I suggest, the criticism is itself uncritical.

No one maintains that chemical analysis reveals any difference whatsoever. The gravamen of the statement must therefore be that a spiritual test is impossible. A devout person, we are given to understand, ought to know, without other evidence than his spiritual discernment, whether he is in the presence of consecrated elements or no. If he does not know (and it does not seem to be the fact that he does know), there is said to be no meaning in the doctrine of transubstantiation at all.

Surely it is obvious that if the effect of the consecration were to quicken the souls of believers, the history of the church might be said to verify the doctrine. Something of the greatest moment would occur on account of the consecration that (on this hypothesis) would not have occurred without it. It would be irrelevant whether a test that smacks of a psychological laboratory did or did not apply.

Omitting this point, however, it is clear that if substance is distinct from its accidents, and if any given accident, or set of accidents, might belong, in principle, to several substances, a change in substance without any change in the accidents is *not* meaningless. These critics of the doctrine, in short, have confused transaccidentalism with transubstantiation. It may be true, very probably it is true, that there is something wrong with these ideas concerning substance and accident. Perhaps, even, they are indefensible. But they are not meaningless, unless all errors are meaningless, which would be an abuse of language. Verification of the type in question does not constitute the meaning of the original theory. The theory, consequently, is not destroyed by the inapplicability of this particular test.

The same, I submit, is true of the refusal to admit any but pragmatic tests. This, however, is substantially a new question. And although the quotations I have cited from Butler are more than semipragmatist, it may be better to select some other expositor of that theory for discussion.

It seems to me that the contrast, as well as the similarity, between Mr. Dewey's opinions and Butler's on this matter repays a close examination.

§ 3. Mr. Dewey's Account of Knowledge

The salient features in Mr. Dewey's theory may be stated briefly by saying (1) that knowledge is the result of thought and can not occur without thought, and (2) that thought, in its essence, is instrumental or pragmatic.

(1). The first point is made abundantly clear. Thus we find it said:

"It may well be admitted that there is a real sense in which knowledge (as distinct from thinking or inquiring with a guess attached) does not come into existence till thinking has terminated in the experimental act which fulfils the specifications set forth in thinking. But what is also true is that the object thus determined is an object of *knowledge* only because of the thinking which has preceded it and to which it sets a happy term. . . . Seen from this point of view, so-called immediate knowledge or simple apprehension or acquaintance-knowledge represents a critical skill, a certainty of response which has accrued in consequence of reflection." [8]

Or again:

"The man in the street, when asked what he thinks about a certain matter, often replies that he does not think at all, he knows. The suggestion is that thinking is a case of active uncertainty set over against conviction or unquestioning assurance. When he adds that he does not have to think, he knows, the further implication is that thinking, when needed, leads to knowledge; that its purpose or object is to secure stable equilibrium." [9]

Hence Aristotle and others "were obliged to assume primary intuitions, metaphysical, physical, moral and mathematical axioms, in order to get the pegs of certainty to which to tie the bundles of otherwise contingent propositions." [10]

Mr. Dewey's account of knowledge therefore differs from Butler's in at least one critical respect. According to Butler, all security of response *is* knowledge; and consciousness, which indicates some degree of questioning or wonder, is therefore opposed to knowledge. Although Mr. Dewey also takes the "brief dogmatic" view that "where, and in so far as, there are unquestioned objects, there is no 'consciousness.' There are just things," [11] he asserts that what is known *has been* questioned but is now no

---

[8] *Essays in Experimental Logic*, pp. 15 *sq.*   [10] *Ibid.*, p. 204.
[9] *Ibid.*, p. 183.   [11] *Ibid.*, p. 225.

longer questioned. The security of knowledge is the result of a
reflective and conscious process, although there is always a tendency for knowledge to "pass naturally into a more direct and
vital type of experience, whether technological or appreciative,
or social." [12]

(2). An equally important matter, however (according to Mr.
Dewey), is to admit the instrumental character of knowledge
itself.

Thinking, or reflection, he tells us, always occurs in connection with a specific situation, and is to be regarded as a natural
occurrence prolonging or improving a response. "Reflection appears as the dominant trait of a situation when there is something seriously the matter . . . when . . . a situation becomes
tensional." [13] The different stages of reflection "denote various
degrees in the evolution of the doubt-inquiry function." [14] "Due
progress is reasonably probable in just the degree in which the
meaning, categorical in its existing imperativeness, and the fact,
equally categorical in its brute coerciveness, are assigned only a
provisional and tentative nature with reference to control of the
situation." [15] "The given is undoubtedly just what it is; it is
determinate throughout. But it is the given *of* something to be
done. The survey and inventory of present conditions . . . exist
for the sake of intelligent determination of what is to be done, of
what is required to complete the given." [16]

All thinking is to be regarded naturalistically. "The reorgani-
zation, the modification effected by thinking is, by this hypothesis, a physical one. Thinking ends in experiment, and experiment is an *actual* alteration of a physically antecedent situation
in these details or respects which called for thought in order to
do away with some evil." [17]

The most serious error in this affair is to suppose that we
have to deal with "the relation of thought, as such, or at large,
to reality as such, or at large." [18] "The instrumental type [of
logic], the type which deals with thinking as a specific procedure
relative to a specific antecedent occasion and to a subsequent

[12] *Essays in Experimental Logic*, p. 20. [15] *Ibid.*, p. 243. [17] *Ibid.*, p. 31.
[13] *Ibid.*, p. 11. [16] *Ibid.*, p. 341. [18] *Studies in Logical Theory*, p. 5.
[14] *Ibid.*, p. 206.

specific fulfilment" is the type of theory that corrects, not all abstraction, but the *undue* abstraction of most theories of knowledge. "Thinking is a kind of activity which we perform at specific need, just as at other need we engage in other sorts of activity: as converse with a friend." [19] This view is quite compatible with the further doctrine that we may think about thinking, because there may be a specific need to consider the nature of logical evidence more widely than in the way that immediately concerns some particular occasion.[20]

Taking these two contentions of Mr. Dewey's together, viz. that knowledge is the sequel to doubt and inquiry, and that doubt, inquiry, and knowledge, these three, are themselves a special and natural sort of purposive adaptation, we may remark:

Firstly, that it may be doubted whether a process of doubt-inquiry or of tentative explanation *necessarily* precedes the certainty we call knowledge. Perfectly convincing evidence might turn up, so to say, *ambulando,* when we are engaged in something irrelevant, or even when we are listless or languid. Landor, by his own account, once wrote a poem when he was brushing his teeth. He might, with equal casualness, have made some great discovery. It does not seem to be true that each specific piece of good evidence is an answer to some specific doubt.

Secondly, the doctrine that the business of the doubt-inquiry function, and of the reflective process generally, is to escape from some *evil* seems to require very close consideration. For:

(a). Suffering and the experience of calamity do not necessarily evoke reflection or doubt-inquiry. On the contrary, the primitive animal attitude seems to be rather to accept the suffering passively, or to respond to it unreflectingly by cries and spasmodic movements. Indeed, we might almost assert that reflection must *show* us the evil before we attempt to remove the evil by reflecting upon means of escape. It is when we notice that some painful event really is an evil, when we appreciate, by reflection, that our affliction, because of its character or on account of its menace, belongs to the class of evil things, that we begin to reflect upon ways of avoiding it. And even in that case our attitude may be one of reflective complaint and of rueful

[19] *Ibid.,* p. 2.   [20] *Ibid.,* p. 3.

acceptance of our misery, although in fact we might be able to excogitate a remedy if we gave our minds to the work.

(b). The evil from which we are said to escape by inquiry (with or without the hope of eventually stilling our doubts and attaining certainty) would seem, in the most general case, to be only a certain dissatisfaction (vague or explicit) with the adequacy of our ideas. In other words, it is a very special sort of evil. The "tension" in the situation, to use Mr. Dewey's language, may indeed be acute, as when a man has to think furiously in the chase or during a combat. It may, however, be a much less strenuous kind of tension, at any rate when judged from any practical standpoint. Indeed, the "evil" may be only the piquant and pleasurable excitement of a lively curiosity that is obstructed just sufficiently to be tempted to bestir itself. There is no sufficient reason for believing that a curiosity of this stimulating and pleasant kind is other than primitive. Children and savages, very frequently, "want to know" and are delighted to guess. The "problem of evil," on the whole, weighs much less heavily upon them than upon warier and more sophisticated members of the human species.

(c). In short, the "natural" event called reflection seems to be evoked by a special sort of stimulus and to be "satisfied" (or to fulfil its function) in its own peculiar way. What is more, if curiosity is admitted to be a proper or "adequate" stimulus to reflection (as well as a "baffled heart," or some grave and disturbing tension in what we usually call "practical affairs"), there would seem to be no constraining reason why such curiosity should not be, as we say, speculative, theoretical, and disinterested. If so, the line between pragmatists and their opponents becomes very hard to draw. "I have never identified any satisfaction with the truth of an idea," Mr. Dewey says, "save *that* satisfaction which arises when the idea as working hypothesis or tentative method is applied to prior existences in such a way as to fulfil what it intends." [21] Ideas, in a word, must do the work of ideas. But did any "intellectualist" ever maintain the contrary?

Thirdly, however, it has to be remarked that the reference to

[21] *Op. cit.*, p. 320.

prior existences in the passage quoted above is most peculiar in terms of Mr. Dewey's theory. For Mr. Dewey, time and again, lays emphasis upon the *future* as reflection's solitary goal and solitary test. Thus he tells us that thought is wholly concerned with "signs or indications of something else. . . . This something else is a somewhat not physically present at the time; it is a series of events still to happen." Again he tells us that thought yields "a sign or clue of a *future* reality to be realized through action." [22]

Even granting that the recognition of prior existences for what they *were* is the *terminus a quo* rather than the *terminus ad quem* of exploring thought, it is surely absurd to deny that such recognition, whatever it may lead to, may itself be a case of knowledge. Yet Mr. Dewey appears to deny any knowledge of what is prior, and to confine the certainty of knowledge to what is always *uncertain*, to wit the future. According to him, the future, and it only, shows what anything *is* or has been.

Take, for example, Mr. Dewey's marked preference for *inventio* as opposed to *judicium*, or for "discovery" as opposed to "proof." Surely, if we examine this contrast we find, in general, a complementary, not an antagonistic, relation. Indeed, Mr. Dewey himself says so. "So far as it is already certain that this *is* ice," he says, "and also certain, that ice, under all circumstance cools water . . . the entire work of knowing as logical is done." [23] In other words, some certainties apply to "prior existences" and not to future consequences.

Even where mistakes are possible, the same comment has to be made. Water, in general, may signify a means to health and the quenching of thirst; but *this* water may contain typhoid germs and probable death. Therefore, Mr. Dewey says, it may be uncertain whether "the right exclusions and selections have been made." [24] In other words, there *are* right exclusions and selections, not selected by the future but contained in the prior existences. And similarly of Mr. Dewey's favorite example of the doctor's diagnosis of symptoms. Since the doctor is by profession a leech or a healer it is true enough to say, as Mr. Dewey does, that a particular analysis of a particular swab from a particular

[22] *Ibid.*, p. 218.   [23] *Ibid.*, p. 236.   [24] *Ibid.*, p. 242.

throat *means* to him the prescribed treatment for diphtheria. Such is the practical significance to the doctor, unless we say that this practical significance is the collection of a fee. But if anything in the doctor's mind is to be accounted knowledge, surely the identification of the bacteria in the swab is to be accounted such. Mr. Dewey might as well argue that if the patient is dead, the doctor does not know of the death, but only knows that he is about to sign a death certificate.

Obviously, no prudent general would deny that consolidation is as important a part of a commander's business as advancing can ever be. He advances on the strength of the security of his lines of communication. And "proof," by Mr. Dewey's own argument, has the same relation to "discovery." Mr. Dewey would have been much more consistent if he had simply asserted that many things that we know are also, and subsequently, the basis for acting in a certain way. In that case, however, it would be illogical to infer either that knowledge always is a mode of action, or that there could not be knowledge that had nothing to do with action.

§ 4. The Gnostic Character of Knowledge

At this stage in our investigation it would seem prudent, on our own part, to attempt to consolidate our position, or at least to review the discussion of the present chapter. For we have now to pass from a pragmatist account of the knowledge situation and of its occasions to the express consideration of knowledge itself in its gnostic character.

Up to the present, then, I have argued in this chapter, firstly, that repose and security, combined with unhesitancy in action can not be *identical* with knowledge. Butler, at the cost of some violence to ordinary language, maintained, as we saw, that it is possible to have unconscious *assurance,* and he described this assurance wholly in terms of security of action. For our part, however, we were compelled to argue, *e contrario,* that even if such action can legitimately be said to be "certain" and "assured," it can not legitimately be called knowledge. For knowledge, whatever else it may be, must at least be *gnostic.* In other words, no one can know without possessing a clear and conscious apprehension of what he knows.

This conclusion entails a further consequence. Many who could not accept Butler's entire contention might still be disposed to accept a part of it. Unconscious *knowledge*, they would admit, is a contradiction in terms, whatever may be true of unconscious assurance. On the other hand, they might maintain that complete *conscious* assurance is indistinguishable from knowledge.

To this contention, by implication at least, we have also demurred, and the purpose of our discussion of Mr. Dewey's views was, in part, to indicate the nature of the demurrer. Even on pragmatist or instrumentalist grounds, we argued in effect, knowledge must be something more than consciously felt (or psychological) assurance. For, again, it must be gnostic. It must see and apprehend the truth of what it knows. Here Mr. Dewey himself would seem in a measure to agree. According to him, knowledge is *reflective* psychological assurance preceded by doubt or inquiry.[25] That, he says, is the sort of natural and pragmatic transaction that knowledge is. The implication is that any other kind of psychological or of conscious assurance is distinct from knowledge.

This gnostic character of knowledge, accordingly, is the point on which I want to lay emphasis. It does not seem to me, I confess, that every gnostic process, or all the insight that may be endemic to the process of knowing, must necessarily be preceded by doubt and inquiry; and it also seems to me to be possible that certain forms of insight may have an immediacy and a penetrative potency which the word "reflection," in its ordinary employment, is clearly unsuited to express. Again, it seems to me quite evident that no "instrumentalism," that is to say, no account of the *functions* of knowledge (whether future-regarding or more general) could conceivably be an account of what a gnostic process essentially *is*. On the contrary, I should maintain

[25] *Cf.* J. Grote (*Exploratio Philosophica*, Vol. II, pp. 201 *sqq.*); "Knowledge begins when reflection begins, and no earlier, for in immediateness it is dormant. . . . Immediateness is confusion or chaos, which reflection begins to crystallize or organize."

that all such pragmatisms and intellectualisms are logically bound to accept the reality of gnostic process, just as they ought to accept the reality of pleasures, or of colors, or of beliefs. Pleasures and colors, to be sure, have actually an instrumental function in our lives. Yet each has itself a distinctive nature which can not be resolved without remainder into its instrumental office. And we are now concerned with the *nature* of knowledge or of gnostic process.

Nevertheless, this, if it be granted, is palpably not enough. We need more than simple-minded acceptance.

It is tempting, indeed, to maintain that the reality which is gnostic process is not only familiar to all, but that it is also in some way understandable and understood by all. What has to be done, it may be said, is quite simply and frankly to rid ourselves of wrong-headedness. For knowledge, we may be informed, is really the plainest thing in the world. It is *sui generis*, ultimate and unanalyzable. Indeed, the only considerable effort that is needed for the comprehending of it is the effort to repel the seductions of certain plausible but mystifying sophistications. As "the man" said in Mr. Priestley's *The Good Companions:* [26] "It's as easy to explain as anything you could wish for, considering, that is, it's a bit of a mix-up."

I wish this were true: but I see no feasible way of avoiding "a bit of a mix up"; and I shall now try to explain why I think so.

§ 5. Questions Concerning Gnostic Process

How could a man set about to examine his gnostic processes with any confidence in the success of his enterprise?

(1). He might attempt to proceed by simple inspection, the principle of his method being "Look and see." In this case, however, he would be in a precarious position, argumentatively, if others, who also claimed to have looked, saw something different from what he claimed to have seen. This method, in short, even if it is in some ways unavoidable, seems to need help and support from other modes of inquiry.

(2). He might attempt to test and examine the usual certainties in the hope that, when once he had discovered what he

[26] P. 168.

knows for certain and had rid himself of merely apparent certainties, the general character of gnostic process might be manifest at a glance, or after an intuitive and very straightforward induction. This, as we shall see in Book III, is a very long method, whatever its promise may be. It is far too long for the present chapter.

(3). He might attempt to institute an elaborate comparison between knowledge, of the one part, and, of the other part, that which, although it is not knowledge, seems similar to knowledge in such a way as to require some niceness in discernment for the purpose of laying hold of the difference. Thus, for example, a relatively minute comparison between knowledge, judgment, belief, and opinion might well be highly instructive in this regard.

(4). He might attempt to *define* knowledge, especially if it seemed possible to define it *secundum artem*, as a subgroup (or species) of some larger group (or genus) according to some *fundamentum divisionis* (i.e. according to some general and intelligible principle of division).

These two latter methods (i.e. 3 and 4) and the results to be expected from them have been examined with great closeness in the recently published *Statement and Inference* of the late Professor Cook Wilson, and I propose to consider Cook Wilson's views in §§ 7 and 8 of the present chapter.

(5). It might also seem possible to discover by analysis some particularly direct or fundamental kind of knowledge (for example, acquaintance-knowledge) and to use this discovery as the clue to all further investigation of the general character of gnostic process.

It seems expedient to discuss this last suggestion in the first instance; and so I shall examine it now, with special reference to an important doctrine formerly maintained (although subsequently abandoned) by Mr. Bertrand Russell. (Despite Mr. Russell's abandonment of his doctrine, several philosophers are still disposed to accept it.) [27]

[27] *Cf.* McTaggart, *The Nature of Existence*, Vol. II, p. 63.

§ 6. KNOWLEDGE BY ACQUAINTANCE

In his little book, *The Problems of Philosophy,* pages 72 sqq, Mr. Russell enunciated the following theory.

"There are [he said] two sorts of knowledge: knowledge of things and knowledge of truths. . . . Knowledge of things, when it is of the kind we call knowledge by *acquaintance,* is essentially simpler than any knowledge of truths, and logically independent of knowledge of truths, though it would be rash to assume that human beings ever, in fact, have acquaintance with things without at the same time knowing some truth about them. Knowledge of things by *description,* on the contrary always involves . . . some knowledge of truths as its source and ground. . . . We shall say that we have *acquaintance* with anything of which we are directly aware, without the intermediary of any process of inference or any knowledge of truths." "All our knowledge, both knowledge of things and knowledge of truths, rests upon acquaintance as its foundation. . . . The fundamental principle in the analysis of propositions containing descriptions is this: *Every proposition which we can understand must be composed wholly of constituents with which we are acquainted.* . . . The chief importance of knowledge by description is that it enables us to pass beyond the limits of our private experience. In view of the very narrow range of our immediate experience, this result is vital, and until it is understood, much of our knowledge must remain mysterious and therefore doubtful." [28]

When we have knowledge of things by description only, Mr. Russell explains, we do not know them immediately but only know of, or about, them, that they are the so-and-so or that they are members of a class that is so-and-so. On the other hand, we have, he says, immediate acquaintance with sense-data (e.g. a patch of color as a personal apparition), with memory-data and introspective data, probably with our Selves or Egos, and clearly with general ideas or universals such as "whiteness, diversity, brotherhood and so on." [29] In other passages dealing with the same topic, Mr. Russell's main intention was to discuss the relation between acquaintance and judgment, with special reference to a theory of the latter process he was then engaged in propounding. "There seem to me," he said, "to be two main cognitive relations with which a theory of knowledge has to deal, namely *presentation* (which is the same as what I call *acquaintance*) and *judgment.* These I regard as radically dis-

[28] *The Problems of Philosophy,* pp. 91 *sq.*   [29] *Ibid.,* p. 81.

tinguished by the fact that presentation (or acquaintance) is
a two term relation of a subject to a single (simple or complex)
object, while judgment is a multiple relation of a subject to several objects." [30]

It seems plain that Mr. Russell, in these passages, is interpreting "knowledge" in the widest sense possible (if, indeed, this
general sense *is* possible) and meaning by it awareness or cognition. If so, the historical contrast (in John Grote [31] or in William
James [32]) between "knowledge by acquaintance" and "knowl-
edge-about" is not really exclusive. For an awareness that is
not by acquaintance need not be awareness *about,* unless the
word "about" is interpreted in a sense inconveniently loose. In
any case "about" is not the same notion as "by description" in
Mr. Russell's rather precise logical sense of the latter phrase.
And similarly it clearly should not be inferred that all cognition
is either presentation (or acquaintance), on the one hand, or
judgment, on the other hand.

Again, the statement that acquaintance-awareness is "direct"
may not be nearly as clear as it seems. The adjective "direct"
in this connection has the appearance of being positive, although
its reality is negative. And it is always very hard to prove a negative. In Mr. Russell's rather casual explanation of the point, we
are informed only that what is "direct" (in this sense) is non-inferential and not dependent upon knowledge of truths. Assuming
that there is no such thing as implicit or "unconscious" inference—a point, however, that in the slang phrase "verges on the
moot"—it is possible, no doubt, to speak quite definitely and
quite accurately about the presence or about the absence of
inference; and the same may perhaps be said about the presence
or about the absence of "knowledge of truths." On the other
hand, if "direct" means, as it appears to mean, *unmediated*
in every conceivable sense (including causal mediation of every
type) it would seem very presumptuous to deny the existence of
all such mediation, even if we can not, on inspection, see that
there are any intermediaries, and even if we can not point to any

[30] *Mind,* N.S., Vol. XXII, p. 76.
[31] *Exploratio Philosophica,* Vol. II, pp. 201 *sqq.*
[32] *Principles of Psychology,* Vol. I, pp. 221 *sq.*

sufficient reason why there should be any. That is always the disadvantage of attempting to prove a negative.

Perhaps we might put the point most simply (although not, I am afraid, with perfect innocence) by distinguishing between inspective and non-inspective "knowledge," and would take Mr. Russell to have meant that the apprehension of sensa, of universals, and the like is inspective, that descriptions and judgments imply and are based upon the inspective apprehension of their constituents, but that there can be no inspection of the truths and propositions that we judge, because propositions are not unities that *can* be inspected but, on the contrary, are ways of combining (or of constructing with) these inspected constituents. In that case, Mr. Russell's subsequent abandonment of the view we are now discussing would be due, in the main, to the circumstance that he came to agree, broadly speaking, with the "neutral monists" in contending that there is no such thing as inspection at all. Ultimately, however, the essential questions are (1) whether "acquaintance" is, or could ever be, knowledge, and (2) whether there is any intelligible sense according to which "knowledge" can be said to be based upon "acquaintance."

(1). Regarding the first of these points, it seems plain that *presentation* (as described by Mr. Russell) must be different from knowledge (as understood in any ordinary sense). For anything known is known to be *true;* and presentation is neither true nor false, in the sense of truth according to which we may know a proposition to be true. The same conclusion follows when we consider our "acquaintance" with the *constituents* of any proposition that contains "descriptions." It seems difficult, indeed, to deny that we *must* be acquainted with the elements in any proposition of which we are aware as a whole. Indeed, this is difficult to deny even in the case of propositions that are, and are known to be, false. The elements of such propositions in themselves, however, are neither true nor false.

Accordingly, if knowledge must be *true*, the kind of apprehension, or acquaintance (supposing it to exist) that is here referred to, can not strictly be *knowledge*. Nevertheless, it is possible that knowledge *implies* something still more fundamental than itself, viz. apprehension. And if misapprehension as well as (correct) apprehension may occur, there might conceivably be a relation between apprehension, on the one hand, and misapprehension, on the other hand, that corresponds tolerably closely (or even very closely indeed) with the normal relation between knowledge and error.

(2). If the last suggestion is tenable, it is further possible that all knowledge is based upon (correct) apprehension, and indeed that true belief and true judgment are similarly based. Again, it it conceivable that there is a quality of immediacy and of finality in the knowledge *of* something (as distinguished from any knowledge that is merely *about* something); and, yet again, that this immediate and final quality in the gnostic character has marked similarities to "acquaintance." Indeed, as we shall see in the later sections of the present chapter, some such view is pretty widely entertained.

§ 7. COOK WILSON'S ACCOUNT OF KNOWLEDGE

As I explained in § 5 above, I shall now attempt to discuss some of Cook Wilson's characteristic accounts of our subject.

Cook Wilson's method, in part, was elaborately to distinguish between "knowledge," on the one hand, and judgment, opinion, and belief, on the other hand; and this distinction, in many ways, was the central part of his theme.

Let us first consider judgment. Cook Wilson was strongly opposed to what may be called the "orthodox" position of British logicians in his time, viz. that judgment is the common form of all mental activity, that opinion, belief, and knowledge are varieties of it (as well as questioning, supposition, or wondering), and that inference, although a prolongation of those "units of thought" that are judgments, is, *prima facie* at least, distinct from and more complicated than judgment.

This orthodox opinion, Cook Wilson says, involves a confusion of thought. "If we take judging in its most correct and natural sense, that is as decision on evidence after deliberation, then inferring is just one of those forms of apprehending to which the words judging and judgment most properly apply." [33] There is no common form including non-inferred knowledge,

[33] *Statement and Inference,* Vol. I, p. 86.

opinion, and belief, and excluding inferred knowledge. "A judgment is a decision. To judge is to decide. It implies previous indecision; a previous thinking process, in which we were doubting." [34] And knowing, or apprehending, does not connote previous indecision. Opinion is a form of judging. It is decision upon evidence. "But still there will be something else besides judgment to be recognized in the formation of opinion, that is to say knowledge, as manifested in such activities as occur in ordinary perception; activities, in other words, which are not properly speaking *decisions*." [35] Judgment is not "the general form of the mental activities called thinking"; but it may be made "the key to the understanding of them" [36] if we clearly recognize that all our judging, wondering, and opining presuppose and depend upon "knowledge" in the sense of "apprehension."

Cook Wilson's account of "opinion" is very similar to the ordinary account of "probability." "For it," he says, "taken in its strict and proper sense, we can use no term that belongs to knowing. For the opinion that *A* is *B* is founded on evidence we know to be insufficient, whereas it is of the very nature of knowledge not to make its statements at all on grounds recognized to be insufficient; nor to come to any decision except that the grounds are insufficient; for it is here that in the knowing activity we stop." [37] Opinion, therefore, is said to be based on knowledge, but to go beyond knowledge; and it is sharply to be distinguished from knowledge precisely in so far as it exceeds knowledge.

Similarly (we are told) of belief. "Belief is not knowledge and the man who knows does not believe at all what he knows; he knows it." [38] What is significant in belief is not its gnostic character, but a psychological feeling of confidence which is *sui generis*. "To a high degree of such confidence, where it naturally exists, is attached the word belief, and language here, as not infrequently, is true to distinctions which have value in our con-

---

[34] *Ibid.*, pp. 92 *sq.* Note the difference between this view and Mr. Dewey's. According to Cook Wilson, it is judgment, not knowledge, that presupposes the doubt-inquiry function.
[35] *Ibid.*, p. 96.   [36] *Ibid.*, p. 95.   [37] *Ibid.*, pp. 99 *sq.*   [38] *Ibid.*, p. 100.

sciousness. It is not opinion, it is not knowledge, it is not properly even judgment." [39] Cook Wilson does not deny that a man who only believes and does not *know* may be just as sure as a man who knows. The man who decides with conviction upon a mistaken view of the evidence may be, he says, "in exactly the same frame of mind as when he decides that the evidence proves and it really does prove." [40] It is in fact a fallacy, he says, "that there could be a general criterion of knowledge by which we should know what was knowing and what was not." [41] Nevertheless, "the consciousness that the knowing process is a knowing process must be contained within the knowing process itself." [42] We may be under the impression that *X* is *A*, perhaps through a certain passivity and helplessness; it may not have entered into our heads to doubt what in fact is a mistake; and in that case there will be "real error other than false opinion" which "does not lie in false judgment, taking judgment in its strict and proper sense." [43] The existence of such ultimate *mis*apprehension, however (which is *not* an erroneous opinion), is held not to annul or to impair the foregoing analysis.

In short, according to Cook Wilson, "apprehension in general," not "judgment" or "thinking" is our true starting point. "This includes knowledge and is the key to the activities called thinking." [44] Belief, judgment, and opinion rest on apprehension, not it on them. He further maintained that the "ordinary idea of definition" is not applicable to the relations thus arising.

Cook Wilson, while admitting that certain very general terms such as "consciousness" apply to knowledge, apprehension, opinion, belief, and wondering, emphatically denies that these departments of consciousness (if I may stretch a point in describing them so) are in any strict sense *species* thereof. In their case, he holds, there is no proper *fundamentum divisionis*, no general principle according to which the subdivision can be conducted according to an intelligible logical specification. On the contrary, he says that belief is *sui generis* (in respect of its high degree of confidence), [45] that opinion and judgment are *sui generis* (in re-

[39] *Ibid.*, p. 102.   [41] *Ibid.*, p. 107.   [43] *Ibid.*, p. 108.   [45] *Ibid.*, p. 102.
[40] *Ibid.*, p. 106.   [42] *Ibid.*, p. 113.   [44] *Ibid.*, p. 79.

spect of the way in which they decide upon evidence), that wondering is *sui generis* ("Further in explanation we cannot go, for
the inquiring attitude is unique, cannot be expressed in terms of
anything else, is its own explanation"),[46] and, finally, and principally, that knowledge is *sui generis*. "For there are some
things," he says, "which cannot be made matter of question.
Indeed we cannot demand an answer to any question without
presupposing that we can form an estimate of the value of the
answer, that is, that we are capable of knowing and that we
understand what knowing means; otherwise our demand would
be ridiculous. Our experience of knowing then being the presupposition of any inquiry we can undertake, we cannot make knowing itself a subject of inquiry in the sense of asking what knowing is. We can make knowing a subject of inquiry, but not of
that kind of inquiry." [47]

We have to deal, it is true, with activities of consciousness
(and also with passive apprehension, in so far as apprehension
is wider than active knowing).

"This, then, is what is common to them: but it is a universal which
is not confined to them; for willing and desiring, which are not thinking, are also activities of consciousness. But beyond the common universal of activity of consciousness, these forms of thinking have no
further differentiation of it to unify them. What does unify them is
the fact that the one, thinking which is not knowing, entirely depends on the other, knowing, and is only intelligible through it. This
brings us to the general answer. The unity of the activities of consciousness, called forms of thinking, is not a universal which, as a
specific form of the genus activity of consciousness, would cover the
whole nature of each of them, a species of which thinking would be
the name and of which they would be sub-species, but lies in the relation of the forms of thinking which are not knowing to the form which
is knowing. Those which are not knowing arise from the desire to
know or from some other relation to knowing and are unified with
knowing by some special relation, depending in each case upon its
peculiar nature and *sui generis*, intelligible and only intelligible by a
consideration of the particular case. This therefore is a case where the
ordinary idea of definition is not applicable." [48]

§ 8. COMMENTS ON THE ABOVE

If a crabbed and scholastic-sounding paradox could ever be
pardoned, we might say that, according to Cook Wilson, the in-

[46] *Statement and Influence,* Vol. I, p. 37.
[47] *Ibid.,* pp. 39 *sq.*   [48] *Ibid.,* Vol. I, p. 38.

definability of knowledge is the key to any articulate understanding of what knowledge is—or, more boldly, that knowledge is comprehensible because it is inexplicable. Paradox-mongers, however, usually drop their guard to fate, and, when they fall, have only themselves to thank. Since, personally, I should like to avoid this calamity, I hasten to explain what, in my judgment, these paradoxes properly convey.

The marrow of them is that if we understand precisely *why* knowledge is indefinable, or the exact manner in which knowledge can not be explained by means of a certain (and the "ordinary") kind of definition, we can scarcely avoid obtaining a clear perception of what knowledge is and of its difference from everything that, not being knowledge, is liable, through misapprehension, to be confused with knowledge.

In my view, there is life in this contention, although not, perhaps, perfect health, and so I intend to dwell upon it for a little space. For this purpose, it seems expedient to consider some of the more outstanding among the many possible meanings of the word "indefinable," and the relation of Cook Wilson's argument to these outstanding meanings. I shall begin, then, by examining two meanings of "indefinable" with which Cook Wilson was not specially concerned, although each of them has a relevant bearing upon the chief of his arguments, and thereafter I shall discuss a third meaning with which he was very particularly concerned.

Firstly, then, when anything is said to be indefinable, what may be meant is only that the distinctive features of the thing in question can not be made characteristically manifest in terms of anything *else*. For this reason it is argued in some quarters that religion, let us say, is indefinable, the thesis being that no one could understand, even dimly, what religion meant unless he himself had had authentic religious experience. On similar grounds, J. S. Mill and other British logicians were accustomed to maintain that the "distinguishable sensations or other feelings of our nature" were themselves indefinable.[49] Persons blind from birth can not, properly speaking, have the essence of color explained to them. Fine gustatory distinctions must remain funda-

[49] E.g. *System of Logic*, Book III, Ch. xiv, § 1.

mentally unintelligible to those whose taste buds are dull or defective. And so forth.

In this sense of "indefinable" we should certainly hold that no one who had had no experience of knowing could conceivably be expected to understand the meaning of knowing, that no one who was without experience of believing would be able to appreciate the meaning of belief; and other similar propositions. Unfortunately, however, there are so many things of which the same could be said—scores of tastes or smells, for example, and hundreds of shades of color—that it may be doubted whether these admissions give us appreciable assistance in our present perplexities. More in detail, it would be legitimate to accept the indefinability of knowledge, in this particular sense of indefinability, and yet to argue that, having accepted it, we are left with all the really important questions unanswered. Granting that no one who had never had experience of knowing could know what knowing is, it does not immediately follow that those who have had such experience do know what knowing is; and no conclusion follows concerning the important question whether knowledge is or is not "ultimate" and is or is not "analyzable." All that follows is that there is *something* unique and quite distinctive in the specific experience called knowing.

Hence, secondly, we run upon another and perhaps upon a more considerable meaning of "indefinable," viz. that what is indefinable is, quite precisely, what is unanalyzable, definition being understood to mean the resolution of a complex notion into its simple notional elements.

In this second sense of "indefinable," it would appear that Cook Wilson held that knowledge, and even apprehension, were not *completely* unanalyzable. For up to a point he did analyze them. They are instances, he said, of consciousness, or (perhaps we might say) of awareness. Again, he apparently admitted that much knowing was an instance of mental activity, although he also maintained that apprehensions exist, particularly in sense-perception, which do not involve any originating activity on our part, and that such (passive?) apprehending is also knowing.

This analysis, it is true, goes a very short way, and it would be consistent to hold (as Cook Wilson, incidentally, seems to have held) that what is distinctive and important in knowledge (as also in belief) *is* ultimate and not further analyzable. The possibility of a certain degree of analysis, however, seems quite beyond dispute.

Supposing, however, that the analysis which is undeniably possible is also undeniably superficial and little more than a broad and sweeping classification, a certain interest would still attach to the unanalyzable residue, if this residue were indeed unanalyzable. In other words, it seems reasonable enough to ask what we could learn about knowledge if we knew simply that it was a piece of conscious activity having a distinctive and peculiar essence of its own, not further analyzable so far as we can see.

The answer to this question seems plainly to be that, directly, we could learn very little. Obviously, what seems to be unanalyzable need not really be so. On the other hand, if we knew for certain that, when we had to do with knowledge, we had to do with something that we knew to be altogether and ultimately incapable of analysis, our plight would be entirely different. For we could not know this for certain, unless we also knew for certain what knowledge, in itself, completely and essentially is. The very notion of it, *ex hypothesi*, would necessarily be completely uncomplicated, that is to say, a true logical simple. And it would not seem possible to *know* that an ultimate logical simple really is ultimate and simple without fully comprehending its ultimate simplicity. In other words, it would seem to be impossible to have such knowledge in any strict sense unless we possessed genuine noëtic or notional insight into the simplicity of this unanalyzable entity.

In that case, the negative "unanalyzable" could only be known and recognized to be what it is if we already possessed positive insight into the nature of what, verbally, is described by negation.

Thirdly, however, it is necessary to turn from what Cook Wilson may have meant but did not say (or did not usually say) to what, in fact, he meant and also said; in other words, to a third possible meaning of the indefinability of knowledge. What Cook Wilson explicitly maintained, then, was that what are frequently called the various "modes of cognition" were improperly so called, because this way of speaking implied that cognition is a unity specified in various "modes" according to a single intelligible principle, just as closed rectilinear figures may be subdivided into three-sided, four-sided, and so forth, or again into regular and irregular. The general property of being a rectilinear figure logically demands specification of this sort. *Per contra*, according to Cook Wilson, a merely general term like "cognition" makes no such demand, and, if it did, would demand what could not conceivably be fulfilled. These various "modes of cognition," he declared in effect, are only empirical groups, each requiring, and each based upon, specific factual apprehension. Each of them, indeed, was characterized by a unique flavor, not further analyzable. This flavor, however, is empirical in the sense that there is nothing to be said about it except that it is just what it is. And the list of *de facto* "modes of cognition" is empirical in the further sense that no conceivable reason could be given why there are just so many and no more.

If so (and I think Cook Wilson has given strong reasons in favour of his doctrine), the plight of knowledge, belief, and the rest, would not be at all singular, although many rationalists (who might otherwise be in sympathy with Cook Wilson's strongly noëtic and gnostic turn of mind) would doubtless be distressed to find that "thought" itself, the very palladium of their theme, was itself, in a sense, empirical because it developed by a kind of brute fission into a collection of singular, unanalyzable, empirical groups. For, after all, the thing is possible.

Nevertheless, it seems, in the end, to be most doubtful whether this reasoned argument concerning the indefinability of knowledge does actually enable every candid observer to discover what knowledge essentially is. Moreover, it seems clear that the term "knowledge" in Cook Wilson's pages is employed in two senses which appear to be and (I think) really *are* essentially distinct. For he seems to speak of "knowledge" *both* as something different from "thinking" or wondering or believing, *and* as something presupposed in the very foundations of all "thinking," judging, wondering, and believing.

In the first of these senses of "knowledge" we have to do with the discernment of final and completely evidenced truth. Indeed, when we speak (in this sense) of our knowledge of principles or even of our "knowledge" of matter of fact, we are speaking of something that is known to be capable of withstanding critical assault; and it would surely be preposterous to maintain that all, or even very many, of our beliefs, questions, and opinions are based upon "knowledge" of this type, even according to the extreme hypothesis that some or all of these beliefs, questions, and opinions are tinged or affected by such "knowledge."

In Cook Wilson's *other* sense of "knowledge," however, we have to do with a fundamental "apprehension" or "acquaintance" not dissimilar from that which was discussed in § 6 of the present chapter. We there concluded that any such "apprehension" was not, in any ordinary sense, "knowledge," although it might be a necessary part of the foundation of much that is "knowledge" and also of much that is not "knowledge."

Unfortunately, it is impossible to expect much assistance from Cook Wilson's pages on this cardinal matter. Indeed, Cook Wilson's editor himself complains that the important term "apprehension" "is nowhere defined by Wilson, who appears to use it as equivalent to Aristotle's νόησις. For long he used "recognition" to express the immediate cognizance of the object and conviction of its being." [50] In view of this absence of definition (and more importantly of explanation) it will be prudent to relinquish any further attempt to conjecture Wilson's meaning.

§ 9. On Certain Opinions of Mr. A. E. Taylor's

Another discussion of the foregoing general question, and a discussion not dissimilar from Cook Wilson's (although, oddly enough, Cook Wilson's name is never mentioned), is to be found in Mr. A. E. Taylor's presidential address to the Aristotelian Society in 1928. The title of this address is "Knowing and Believing."

After arguing, as Cook Wilson did, that knowing is *not* believing (even when the belief, in fact, is true) and that the difference between believing and knowing "is not to be detected by any mere examination of the act or process of knowing or be-

[50] *Statement and Inference,* Vol. I, p. 78 n.

lieving"[51] (one wonders what is meant by the little word "mere"), Mr. Taylor proceeds to argue that the difference can not consist in "giving an account" of the matter by demonstration (in knowing) and in being unable to do so (in belief). This, he says, is because demonstration both uses, and relies upon, indemonstrable principles. If, then, there is any demonstrative *knowledge* at all, there must be real knowledge of such undemonstrable principles. "The point which is important for my purposes," Mr. Taylor says, "is that νοῦς or *intellectus*, like knowledge, is sharply discriminated from opinion and belief (δόξα and ὑπόληψις), and held to have a still higher 'epistemological' status than demonstration, knowledge of proved conclusions as guaranteed by their premises. It is this recognition of an immediate knowledge as genuine knowledge, and indeed as the type of complete and perfect knowledge, which I am concerned to defend."[52]

"Neither inference nor judgment," he goes on, "can be the type of the most profound and thorough knowledge."[53] That type is *vision;* and it is in vision that extremes meet. In sense-perception we have immediate apprehension of something which, being but semi-intelligible, is "opaque" and also incommunicable. At the highest intellectual extreme, the opaqueness is done away, but the incommunicability remains. (Apparently Mr. Taylor, for no very obvious reason, connects or identifies communication with demonstration.) "In the case of what we see with the mind's eye," he says, ". . . there is nothing intermediate in the order of apprehension between the knowing mind and the principle it knows. And it is this kind of direct and immediate apprehension of truth which we should regard as the type of true knowing. . . . It is just because judgment is the characteristic form of *thinking* that, to the mind of St. Thomas, it is unjustifiable anthropomorphism to say that God thinks. God does not *think;* he knows with a knowledge which is vision."[54] And Mr. Taylor says in conclusion: "Since knowledge, so far as it really is knowledge, is immediate, there can be no 'theory of knowledge' in the sense of a theory of the way in which knowing

[51] *Proceedings of the Aristotelian Society*, 1928-1929, p. 12.
[52] *Ibid.*, p. 17.   [53] *Ibid.*, p. 19.   [54] *Ibid.*, pp. 20 *sq.*

is done. The whole of what can properly be called 'theory of knowledge' is contained in an answer to the question 'how does knowing differ from opining and believing?' And the true answer to this question can be given in three words, 'by being vision'." [55] It is unfortunate that limitations of space and proprieties of time prevented Mr. Taylor from further explaining and elaborating this very interesting view. As Mr. Taylor's argument stands, he stops short of maintaining with Aristotle (whom otherwise he follows so closely) that "actual knowledge is identical with its object," that such knowledge is "separable" and "immortal" and "eternal," and that "without it nothing thinks." [56] Mr. Taylor also does not employ Aristotle's very curious arguments in the same passage, viz. that the separate and unmixed activity of reason owes its eminence to the fact that "the active is always of higher worth than the passive, and the originative source than the matter." Mr. Taylor, indeed, seems to leap to his conclusion without explaining the reasons for his saltations. It does not seem clear, for example, why demonstration is *not* vision just because it is based upon, or has to employ, undemonstrable principles. Have we not to see our way, step by step, in our demonstrations? Is it not even possible that the attempt to apprehend the principles of demonstration, so far from being inevitably an instance of vision, is liker the attempt to see our seeing—which is rather difficult?

It is not to be pretended, of course, that these matters are easy, and it may very well be true that some genial *aperçu* is the most that we can expect in the end. Despite the menace of ultimate failure, however, something has to be said concerning what Mr. Taylor calls intellectual vision, or, as we might say, concerning noëtic insight.

§ 10. Noëtic Insight in Relation to Knowledge

In general, the term noësis and its derivatives were taken to describe godlike reason, that divine principle in man. It was supposed, from Greek times onwards, that the main business of investigators was to exhibit this noble thing in its exalted purity

---

[55] *Ibid.*, p. 30.
[56] *De Anima*, 430a (as translated by W. D. Ross).

and to distinguish it from anything crass or vulgar that, in some men's estimation, might be confused with it. For the most part, the nature of this argument, as we have seen, was a distinction between noësis on the one hand and passion (including sensation and emotion) on the other. This task was intricate both because passion might, on occasion, simulate noësis, and because it might attain an end not readily distinguishable from conclusions due to noësis.

According to many authors, indeed, nothing purely anoëtic occurs in our minds. Neither passion nor sense, it may be said, can be wholly blind, wholly unamenable to logic, wholly destitute of principle. And conversely, many have argued, despite Aristotle, that separate noësis is never to be found even in the most logical of men. A crude way of putting this argument is to hold, as a matter of "mere" psychology, that imageless apprehension does not occur, but that echoes of sense always reverberate in the most intellectual ear. This, if it could be established, would prove only that the two are always in company. It would not even prove that these echoes in imagery are relevant to thought's dialogue with itself. Even so, however, noësis, as a separate ingredient, may be very hard to discover; and the reason might conceivably be that it is *not* a separate ingredient.

Nevertheless, it is hard to deny that we do have insight, of a thoroughly intellectual kind, whether or not we are able to isolate, to discern, and to define any ingredient of pure noësis; and it is not unreasonable to hold (as has been incidentally suggested so frequently in this chapter) that every one, even the plainest of plain men, knows what such insight is, whether or not he can explain and intelligibly communicate the nature of his insight.

Accordingly, the path of tradition seems inviting. Has not all knowledge, properly to be called such, its roots in noëtic insight? Is not noësis, in a recent writer's phrase, the "chrysalis and incunabulum" of any authentic knowledge? And in that case is not our course, in general, plain? Should we not identify noësis with the exercise of certain intellectual faculties, and then argue down to the presumptive presence of noësis in semiopaque sensation and in other similar departments of twilight cogitation?

The noëtic, according to these philosophies, is usually said to be either (1) the rational or (2) the logical; and some discussion of the meaning of these terms seems advisable.

(1) In the narrowest sense, and having regard to the history of philosophy, the principal meanings of "rational" may be said to have been (a) complete and self-contained evidential clarity, (b) what follows deductively by self-evident steps from what is self-evident, and (c) whatever is universal, necessary, or *a priori*. Since the certainties of sense are also maintained, in a host of quarters, to be *evident* of themselves, it became incumbent on rationalists to show how intellectual or noëtic insight differed from the clearest sensible vision, and their answer almost invariably was conveyed in the metaphor that intellectual evidence was "transparent" or "translucent," so that, to continue the metaphor, sensible things (in an extended sense of vision) can only be *seen* while intellectual things are *seen through* with a vision that penetrates and also encompasses them.

It is difficult to deny that intellectual insight has a species of clarity all its own; but this does not seem to be enough for the theory before us, and the additional requirements of the theory seem to imply a very special and (if our arguments in Chapter III, § 7 were not fallacious) a quite indefensible view to the effect that the relation between intellect and the objects transparent to intellect is a community, propinquity, proximity, or identity of things invisible, a meeting place of pure noumenal essences.

Regarding universality and necessity, again, it should be conceded that the recognition that some law or connection *must* hold in every instance, observed or unobserved, carries us far beyond the brute and circumscribed particularity of sense-experience. On the other hand, any general name (e.g. in Aristotle's example, the snubness of snub noses) is a universal, and many such names do not seem to be transparent or translucent. Thus rationalists have to distinguish between universals *and* universals, and they usually claim in the end that some universals are elicited from their native source in pure intellect and in its spontaneous activity while others are elicited from sensible fact. This view again implies that the mind is at home only in its own invisible house, and that the mind's own activities are alone completely intelligible. It has, therefore, to be rejected if there is any substance in our former arguments in Chapters II and III.

(2) If logic is indeed the organon or instrument of all science and of all certain knowing its connection with noëtic insight must be quite exceptionally close—as close, indeed, as it was for Kant, who found the clue to the principles of natural knowledge in the forms of the logical judgment described in the current textbooks of his day. Nevertheless, there may be a good deal of touching credulity and of indefensible simple-mindedness in this appeal to logic, supposing, that is, that something more is meant by an appeal to logic than simply a general indication of some particular line of argument.

Personally, I am not one of those who believe that logic (or even "formal logic") is effete and a mere superstition, but there can be no doubt whatever that the ordinary school logic is a historical collection rather than a unified science. The appeal to logic, therefore, unless the nature of the appeal is specified much more closely, is but an appeal to a historical collection of topics, not all of which can conceivably be regarded as instances of pure noëtic insight.

Therefore, the advocates of noëtic insight have very frequently contended that they are not at all content with the traditional logic, and that they desiderate a new logic, or even a superlogic. They desire a purer insight than, as they think, logic ever affords.

To illustrate this view, it will be sufficient, I think, if I quote without comment from a recent writer. Mr. J. A. Smith asserts that his philosophical position "acknowledges the vanity of any hope adequately to express in words the self-certain grounds upon which Mind throughout all its busy activity reposes, yet for all that it does not decline to enter upon and pursue some formulation of their nature, some exhibition of their systematic structure, some estimate of their worth and strength. *Alea jacta est . . .*" What is here offered is in plain terms a doctrine concerning what is in itself unknown and unknowable, the inward and secret essence of mind, and of whatsoever in the universe surrounds it, constituting its whole and sole environment. The account here formulated is neither inventory of contents nor theory nor body of truth, does not claim or aspire to be any of these, but is, as I have said, a disclosure and exposure of what, if any of these be established, underlies them as their indispensable substructure, and if, so disclosed and exposed, it is criticized as paradoxical, the criticism is repelled as at once justified and *nihil ad rem.* Its soundness may be questioned, and indeed, ought to be and must be, but the cause cannot be determined before the tribunal or by the jurisprudence of ordinary logic.[57]

In general, of course, there is nothing amazing, or even surprising, in the contention that all things, pursued beyond a certain point, pass into mystery, but there is something more than amazing in the doctrine that insight should pass into mystery, or that knowledge in its purest forms should become ignorance, even of the special kind that is called *docta ignorantia.* In doctrines of this species the penalty paid is very severe.

Indeed, I do not think it would be too much to say that the penalty is unconscionably severe. Those who, like Mr. Taylor, maintain that a greater degree of intelligibility than logical deduction is required of the highest kind of knowledge, together with those who, like Mr. Smith, long for and have faith in, an inward and secret essence of pellucid rationality not to be obtained by any human knower, seem to go beyond reason as well as to go beyond the stabler and more reputable departments of traditional logic. On the other hand, those who ask less than this of knowledge, may, as we have seen so frequently, find themselves in a difficulty when they come to consider the various ways in which knowledge, as they say, becomes diluted or clouded. A few of them even maintain that the rational or logical is simply the deducible, according to the due forms of mood and figure, and so have to hold that any ultimate premises, not themselves capable of deduction, are in the end non-rational and alogical. This is an easy method of extending the province of the alogical; and may bring comfort to a few of the many who are anxious to assert that all our knowledge, as well as everything else in the human mind, rests ultimately on faith. The kind of faith, apparently, does not matter.

The "dilution" of "knowledge" in matters of belief and in infer-

[57] *Contemporary British Philosophy,* Second Series, pp. 234 *sq.*

ences based upon sensory observation is, again, a tantalizing story. It is *not* alogical and irrational, although it is not an invincible apprehension of what is certain. This aspect of the question, however, should be reserved to later chapters.

§ 11. Conclusion

I shall not attempt to make a formal summary of the argument of this chapter. I have tried to consider the respects in which knowledge is conscious, cogitative, and evidential; what its relations are to doubt, inquiry, and judgment; whether it includes, or is based upon, apprehension or acquaintance; whether it is definable; and whether it, or the higher kinds of it, are in reality a special and peculiar sort of noëtic insight. In dealing with these important problems, I have illustrated the various points that seemed to arise by rather copious quotations from modern and, for the most part, from contemporary authors, by way of counterpart to the more historical narrative of earlier chapters; and I hope that I have done something towards indicating the complexity, as well as the austere fascination, of the whole subject.

CHAPTER V

THE NATURE OF BELIEF

§ 1. Further Concerning Knowledge and Belief

Belief is not a univocal term either in common language or in philosophy; indeed it is not infrequent to find different and conflicting meanings of the word on adjacent pages. Thus J. S. Mill states on pages 77 and 78 of his *Examination of Hamilton* that "in common language, when Belief and Knowledge are distinguished, knowledge is understood to mean complete conviction, Belief a conviction somewhat short of complete; or else we are said to believe when the evidence is probable (as that of testimony), but to know, when it is intuitive or demonstrative from intuitive premises; we believe, for example, that there is a Continent of America, but know that we are alive, that two and two make four, and that the sum of any two sides of a triangle is greater than the third side. This is a distinction of practical value."

On page 80 (footnote) of the same work, however, Mill says:

"We do not know a truth and believe it besides; the belief *is* the knowledge. Belief altogether, is a genus which includes knowledge; according to the usage of language, we believe whatever we assent to; but some of our beliefs are knowledge, others only belief. The first requisite which, by universal admission, a belief must possess, to constitute it knowledge, is that it be true. The second is that it be well-grounded; for what we believe by accident, or on evidence not sufficient, we are not said to know. The grounds must, moreover, be sufficient for the very highest degree of assurance; for we do not consider ourselves to know, as long as we think there is any possibility (I mean any appreciable possibility) of our being mistaken. But when a belief is true, and held on grounds sufficient to justify the strongest conviction, most people would think it worthy of the name of knowledge, whether it be grounded on our own personal investigations, or on the appropriate testimony, and whether we know only the fact itself, or the manner of the fact. And I am inclined to think that the purposes of philosophy, as well as those of common life, are best answered by making this the line of demarcation."

129

I have quoted both these passages at some length, because, being an honest endeavor to explain a perplexing matter, they indicate a considerable stretch of the territory we are about to explore. Admitting their candor, however, we can not deny that the account of belief given in the first passage contradicts the account given in the second passage. For in the first passage belief is *opposed* to knowledge, the latter implying complete conviction, the former implying at least a residual doubt; yet in the second passage knowledge is said to be a *species* of belief, i.e., to be that sort of belief that is true and also well-grounded.

Concerning the usual meaning of belief, we may say:

(1) That if the criterion be conviction, it seems plain that belief does not *exclude* conviction although we sometimes say that we believe things concerning which we do not have full conviction. William James even says that he includes under Belief "every degree of assurance, including the highest possible certainty and conviction." [1] He might, however, have found some difficulty in explaining what he did *not* include at the other end of this scale.

(2) That if the criterion be assent, it seems plain that we may assent without experiencing any very active conviction. It seems doubtful, even, whether we necessarily believe all that we assent to. And Cook Wilson, as we saw, held that we assent to what we know as well as to what we believe although belief and knowledge are quite different.

(3) That if the criterion be the nature of the evidence, it is universally admitted that men may believe much for which they have no genuine evidence, as when their belief is due to mere hearsay, to mere authority, or to mere superstition; and (although questions might be raised about this matter) that "fully evidenced conviction" is a common and not untenable working definition of "knowledge."

(4) That it is universally admitted that we may believe what is false but can not know what is false.

In what follows, I shall not assume that conviction or assurance *has* degrees, but shall assume, unless the contrary is expressly stated, that a man who is *convinced* is *quite sure*. I shall

[1] *Principles of Psychology,* Vol. II, p. 283.

speak of *mere* belief when I wish to imply that a man's belief is not sufficiently evidenced, and, in general, I shall not try to distinguish between "knowledge" and beliefs that are completely evidenced.

§ 2. FURTHER CONCERNING HUME

As we have seen, Hume, following Locke, identified belief or judgment with probability, and sharply distinguished this type of conjecture from knowledge. He also maintained, however, that there is a wider and a narrower sense of "probability," and so that a distinction between "proofs" and "probabilities" arises within the general sphere of "probability." Hume did not deny, of course, that there were, in a few instances at any rate, rigidly demonstrative "proofs"; but he also believed that there were experimental proofs which belonged to the domain of judgment·or belief. Developing his position he says, "By knowledge, I mean the assurance arising from the comparison of ideas. By proofs, those arguments, which are deriv'd from the relation of cause and effect, and which are entirely free from doubt and uncertainty. By probability, that evidence, which is still attended with uncertainty." [2]

In other words, after employing Locke's term "probability" to denote the domain of assurance (perhaps in varying degrees) which is not genuine knowledge or science, Hume found himself confronted with the sense of "probability" which implies guesswork, whether of the mathematical sort called probability of chances, or the "probability of causes" which, as he acutely observed, was in fact, the application of the mathematical theory of chances in experimental induction.[3] Hume therefore had to distinguish between causal induction in general and problematical causal induction. Hence his distinction between proofs and probabilities within the region which, as a whole, he also called probability.

On the whole (we may say) there is no good reason why Hume should not have drawn this distinction, as may be seen if we select an illustration in which, by universal admission, rigid demonstration is not to be had. Suppose, for instance, that we are

<hr />

[2] *Treatise,* p. 124.   [3] *Ibid.,* Part III, Sec. xii.

dealing with so-called circumstantial evidence. Such evidence never yields mathematical certainty, yet we often regard it as wholly sufficient for its purpose, and therefore we are accustomed to distinguish between "proofs" and mere "suspicions" of a circumstantial kind. We do not hold that circumstantial proofs are worthless because they are not demonstrative proofs. On the contrary, if a certain consilience of such suspicions be held to be "proof," it seems plain that the separate suspicious items, none of which is itself a proof, must each have some weight.

On the other hand, as we argued in some detail in Chapter II, § 6, Hume's argument is open to at least one fatal objection. Insisting, as he did, that *all* belief is ultimately of the "vulgar" kind and identical with strength and firmness of conviction, he nevertheless affirmed that convictions due to repeated experience, although alogical, are nevertheless a more sensible and respectable kind of belief than what we call prejudice. According to him, the world that is "peopled" by the judgments or beliefs of scientists and of sensible men of the world has, somehow, a better warrant than a world that is peopled with phantoms and devils and miracles. Hume pilloried the latter type of belief, although constrained to admit that it *is* a type of belief, and that no type of belief is truly logical.

For example, he pilloried prejudice. "An Irishman," he says, using an illustration that strikes us to-day as very odd, "cannot have wit, and a Frenchman cannot have solidity; for which reason, tho' the conversation of the former in any instance be visibly very agreeable, and of the latter very judicious, we have entertain'd such a prejudice against them, that they must be dunces or fops in spite of sense and reason." [4] Where, we may ask, do "sense and reason" come in concerning an affair that is merely customary and destitute of logic? And in what other way could Hume's theory of "belief" be described with any approach to accuracy?

In general, as we saw, Hume held that belief belonged to the sensitive rather than to the cogitative part of our nature. It was an affair, as William James [5] later said, of "sensible pungency," although (*teste* what he said concerning prejudice) Hume did

---

[4] *Treatise*, pp. 146 *sq.*   [5] *Principles of Psychology*, Vol. II, p. 301.

not hold, with James and Bagehot,[6] that it is also an affair of emotional pungency, unless in the general and probably irrelevant sense according to which all Hume's "impressions of reflexion" may be said to be emotions. The general tenor of Hume's argument may be said to be that the sensible pungency of sensory experience and of sensory memory necessarily includes the "vivacity" or, to use another of James's terms, the "liveness"[7] of assurance, but that certain customary expectations, although in reality they are but customary imaginings, come, by a specific kind of indissoluble association, to acquire a sensible pungency almost, if not quite, indistinguishable from the sensible pungency of present perception. In such cases we also have assurance and belief which may very well be irresistible.

Before examining this theory more closely, something should be said concerning this sensible pungency, liveness, or, in Hume's language, "vivacity."

Much in Hume's account of "vivacity" is, *prima facie* at any rate, accurately described by critics like Reid when such critics refer to "that modern discovery of the ideal philosophy, that sensation, memory, belief, and imagination, when they have the same object, are only different degrees of strength and vivacity in the idea."[8] In so far as such descriptions are accurate, Hume clearly laid himself open to the very effective censure of these critics. "Suppose," Reid continues, "the idea to be that of a future state after death: one man believes it firmly—this means no more than that he hath a strong and lively idea of it; another neither believes nor disbelieves—that is, he has a weak and faint idea. Suppose now, a third person believes firmly that there is no such thing, I am at a loss to know whether his idea be faint or lively: if it is faint, then there may be a firm belief where the idea is faint; if the idea is lively, then the belief of a future state and the belief of no future state must be one and the same." In short, this doctrine, without serious modification, is clearly inadequate.

Even in those passages, however, in which Hume did speak as if an "idea" in sense-perception had a great deal of vivacity, in

[6] Quoted by James, *ibid.*, p. 308.   [8] *Inquiry*, Hamilton's Edition, p. 107.
[7] *The Will to Believe*, p. 2.

memory a lesser degree of vivacity, while in imagination the same idea became "a perfect idea" and was very "languid" indeed,[9] it should be noted that what Hume meant by "vivacity" was "the forcible *manner*" in which impressions "strike upon the mind"; and there can be little doubt that he meant all the time (as he later explicitly said) that this forcible manner of our believing was something quite characteristic and also something quite indefinable. He might therefore have agreed verbally with J. S. Mill, who held, as James later did, that belief was "ultimate and primordial," and even with Reid, who held that the nature of belief was indefinable although perfectly well understood. We shall see, indeed, that this verbal agreement is not a real agreement, because Reid, and also Mill, whatever may be true of James, did not understand this "indefinable" precisely as Hume understood it. Nevertheless, it is both necessary and important to quote Hume's amendments to his earlier and very defective statements.

In Section viii, Part III of the *Treatise*, Hume explained that he spoke of the "quality, called it *firmness, or solidity, or force, or vivacity*, with which the mind reflects upon (an idea) and is assur'd of its present existence" and further explained that he meant "that certain *je-ne-sçai-quoi* of which 'tis impossible to give any definition or description, but which every one sufficiently understands."[10] In the Appendix to the *Treatise*, and later in the *Enquiry*,[11] these explanations are given more elaborately and in quite unmistakable terms.

"We may therefore conclude [Hume says in the Appendix] that belief consists merely in a certain feeling or sentiment; in something that depends not on the will, but must arise from certain determinate causes or principles, of which we are not masters. When we are convinc'd of any matter of fact, we do nothing but conceive it, along with a certain feeling, different from what attends the mere *reveries* of the imagination. . . . Now that there is a greater firmness or solidity in the conceptions, which are the objects of conviction and assurance, than in the loose and indolent reveries of a castle-builder, every one will readily own. They strike upon us with more force: they are more present to us: the mind has a firmer hold of them, and is more actuated and mov'd by them. It acquiesces in them; and, in a manner, fixes and

---

[9] E.g. *Treatise*, p. 9.   [11] Sec. v, Part II, §§ 39 and 40.
[10] *Ibid.*, p. 106.

reposes itself on them. In short, they approach nearer to the impressions, which are immediately present to us; and are therefore analogous to many other operations of the mind." [12]

And finally he says:

"I conclude, by an induction which seems to me very evident, that an opinion or belief is nothing but an idea, that is different from a fiction, not in the nature or the order of its parts, but in the *manner* of its being conceiv'd. But when I wou'd explain this *manner*, I scarce find any word that fully answers the case, but am oblig'd to have recourse to every one's feeling, in order to give him a perfect notion of this operation of the mind. An idea assented to *feels* different from a fictitious idea, that the fancy alone presents to us: And this different feeling I endeavor to explain by calling it a superior *force*, or *vivacity*, or *solidity*, or *firmness*, or *steadiness*. This variety of terms, which may seem so unphilosophical, is intended only to express that act of the mind, which renders realities more present to us than fictions, causes them to weigh more in the thought and gives them a superior influence on the passions and imagination. Provided we agree about the thing, 'tis needless to dispute about the terms. . . . I confess that 'tis impossible to explain perfectly this feeling or manner of conception. We may make use of words that express something near it. But its true and proper name is *belief*, which is a term that every one sufficiently understands in common life." [13]

§ 3. WHETHER SEEING IS BELIEVING

Hume's theory of belief was, in brief, that what we believe in the way of confident expectation simulates the sensible pungency of present sensation. It seems advisable, therefore, to consider, in the first instance, whether "seeing is believing," or in other words, to examine the nature of the assurance we are said to repose in the "present testimony" of our senses.

To be sure, any one who asserts that we believe propositions, and these only, must in consistency assert that seeing is *not* believing. For we do not see (or sense) propositions.

This, however, seems too summary an expedient for dealing with an important question, and far too similar to Gordian knot-cutting by mere definition. I propose, therefore, to essay a longer route.

A crucial, and at the same time a puzzling, instance is the case of our dreams. Do we not believe what we dream, while we are dreaming it, and yet is it not the fact that these dreamy re-

[12] *Treatise*, pp. 624 *sq.*   [13] *Ibid.*, pp. 628 *sq.*

gions and somnolent territories are, in Hume's language, mere "ideas" and not "impressions"?

At any rate, Hume himself seems to have thought that the objects of our dreams are mere ideas. Speaking of the distinction between images (i.e. "ideas") and sense-apparitions (i.e. "impressions") he said that "in sleep, in a fever, in madness, or in any very violent emotions of soul, our ideas may approach to our impressions," but that "notwithstanding this near resemblance in a few instances, they are in general so very different that no-one can make a scruple to rank them under distinct heads." [14]

I interpret this statement as meaning that dream-apparitions really belong to the fancy and are not accredited sensible realities, although we may sometimes be deluded into taking them for such. Hence it should follow that we do not really believe when we are dreaming, although we may occasionally be deluded into a condition not dissimilar from belief. And yet it seems quite evident that we do believe in our dreams—until we wake up. The cloud-capped towers of our dreams, our levitations and journeys to Athens or to Timbuctoo, the voices that we hear and the murmuring of bees, all this fantastic "matter-of-fact" is, in general, something that we believe with utter conviction so long as we continue to dream. Very occasionally, perhaps, while not awake, we may convince ourselves that there is something unbelievable in the dream-experience, or, in other words, admit to ourselves while dreaming that we *are* dreaming; and, more frequently, we awake in a nightmare just at the point where the horror of the nightmare becomes too great even for a dreamer's sanity. Such instances, however (speaking in the large), are exceptional. For the most part, in dreaming, we do believe in our dreams.

This matter ought to have caused Hume no little difficulty. It is possible for *other* philosophers to explain dreaming, perhaps to their own satisfaction, by cerebral causes. Although our eyes are closed and our ears are shut (they say), something in the brain excites the dream-experiences, and these brain stimulations have some slight connection with such external causes as pressure

[14] *Treatise*, p. 2.

of bedclothes, flapping of a window-blind, and the like. That is as it may be. Most of the modern theories of dreaming are, as it happens, much more psychological, much less confidently physiological. It is suggested that the greater part of our dream-material consists of memories of the doings of the previous day variously dramatised into the "manifest content" of the dream, or, in other words, into the visible pattern and picture of the dream. We need not trouble ourselves, however, with this dispute. The point for us to notice at the moment is that Hume, being a thoroughgoing presentationist, denied any knowledge of the "external" causes of any impressions or of any ideas, and refused to speculate on the question.[15] For him, the experience alone was the thing. And yet, although dream-experiences are obviously perfectly good experiences, he committed himself to a theory of "impressions" and of the belief in "impressions" that manifestly has to do with *waking* impressions, and not, properly speaking, with any others.

Are we to say, then, that Hume was wrong in maintaining that dream-apparitions are images, not impressions, and that he should have maintained, instead, that dream-apparitions really are impressions which, just because they are impressions, automatically carry conviction with them?

This expedient is undeniably tempting. According to any psychology (not Hume's in particular) dream-apparitions seem to flit across the usual boundaries. They are not imagination, reverie, day-dreaming, or the like, for part of the meaning of such fancies is that we distinguish the fancy from what we call actual fact sensibly avouched to the open eye. We only *entertain* such images, suspending the question of their "reality," just as we read fiction, however vivid, without at all confounding it with an attempt at literally historical narrative. Yet, if dream-apparitions are not fancy (because we accept and trust them while we are dreaming), they are also not to be accounted fact (because we accept them *only* while we are dreaming and reject them completely when we wake up and remember them). In a word, they seem to be neither fact nor fancy.

Accordingly, the difficulties in Hume's theory would not have
[15] *Ibid.*, p. 84.

been appreciably lessened had he declared roundly that dream-apparitions are impressions and are not ideas. The plain truth appears to be that in dreams we accept *everything* just as it comes. We are (with rare exceptions) wholly uncritical in our dreams and avid of assurance from every quarter. Even what is faint and languid is accepted and believed *pro tempore*, not simply what is forcible and vivacious. Hume's entire distinction between impressions and ideas vanishes in dreamland, where everything, however faint, is accepted with all its pretensions and pretentiousness.

Such, then, being our plight when we dream, let us see what is to be said about it.

The dream mind, we have said, is in a state of complete visionary credulity. It is voracious, not veracious. It is not (as according to Hume's theory it ought to be) selective and discriminating in the special way of attaching conviction to "impressions" (together with strong habitual expectations) and of denying conviction to all other apparitions. On the contrary, it is omni-credulous. And when, remembering our dreams, we decide that they were fantasies, that we talked in our dreams to children we never had and were in terror of tyrants who never could have hurt us, the reason seems to be, not that our dreams had less vivacity than certain waking apparitions, but that, taken together, they are chaotic. It is not even true that "the" dream framework will not fit into "the" waking framework. If there were a single dream framework, as in the recurrent dreams mentioned by Mrs. Arnold Forster [16] or in the nightly progressive dream-world of one of Mr. Wells's heroes, the problem would be more acute than it is. As things are, there is, properly speaking, *no* dream framework for any of us. The system of our waking memories and of our waking "impressions" shows a tolerable degree of consilience. The different vanishing structures of dream experience have no logical consecution at all.

A plausible interpretation, both of dreams and of waking, therefore leaps to the eye; and it is not Hume's interpretation. This interpretation is that what is primitive in belief is not belief in impressions as opposed to the mere entertainment of "perfect

[16] *Studies in Dreams.*

ideas," but, on the contrary, primitive omnicredulity. We are credulous before we are wary, even with regard to the limited degree of caution implied in trusting our senses and in distrusting other apparitions. Our belief in impressions is not the sole fact of primitive conviction. On the contrary, the importance of this distinction between what Hume calls "impressions" and "ideas" is acquired and has to be learned.

If we consider the psychology of very young children, this alternative interpretation, surely, becomes very probable indeed. After reaching a certain age, it is true, children may be correctly said to be "imaginative" and even to give their fancies rein in what is at least half make-believe. Even then, however, their "imagination" is seldom complete make-believe or a "fantasy" in the sense in which adults understand "fantasy." It is but semi-critical regarding any final or utter separation between hard or workaday fact and a frankly imaginative realm. Santa Claus is first believed, then half-believed, then disbelieved. The younger the child, the smaller the probability of make-believe, and the stronger the likelihood of omnicredulity. The newly-hatched chick may discriminate between what is edible and what is not edible, but the human baby snatches at the moon.

Psychologically, therefore, the theory of primitive omnicredulity is very much more plausible than Hume's, and it may be remarked that our development from this primitive basis is by no means confined to a growing reliance upon first-hand sensory experience, on the one hand, and a growing mistrust of everything not visibly connected with such first-hand experience upon the other hand.

There are, I daresay, sound social, and even sound biological, reasons why we should accept almost as much as we do accept upon hearsay and upon uncriticized authority. For children have to depend for a very long period upon their parents, schoolmasters and elder companions; and adults, for the most part, have to rely to a very great extent upon their "superiors" as well as upon journalists and publicists. But, whatever the reason, the fact remains. We do not rely exclusively upon first-hand observation; and it may be doubted whether we always consider such evidence markedly superior, even for us, to other evidence.

The result may cause the judicious to grieve, just as it may induce authoritarians to rejoice. Welcome or unwelcome, however, it can not be gainsaid.

Admitting the fact of primitive omnicredulity, however, may it not still be maintained, with great show of reason, that a relative and qualified acceptance of Hume's position in this matter may still be justifiable? Our argument, a Humian objector might say, proves altogether too much. Whatever may be true of the beginning of our lives, we do *eventually* learn to distinguish between impressions and ideas in waking life, and, if we are sane, we continually distinguish between what we perceive and what we merely fancy. We may accept opinions upon hearsay, but we do not let fancies interfere with sensible facts.

Are there not, indeed, inescapable biological reasons for discriminating in these affairs? A man has to learn to rely on his own senses (has he not?) in order to live. Dreamers do not have to act upon their dreams. They lie immobilized in their beds; and consequently they are not in any real peril if they dream that they are swimming the Atlantic. The man who acts upon his waking impressions, however, is subject to quite a different sort of control. He *may* be drowned if he swims out to sea. He is very likely to perish if he attempts a leap over a twenty-foot gorge. To be sure, he may also perish if he acts upon hearsay; but opinions, in general, are less immediately helpful, or less immediately noxious, than sensation. In short, as Hume said we are not our own masters in this matter; and we have all to learn how to repose a quite special reliance upon our senses.

Again, it may certainly be argued, and with complete propriety, that the genetic way of approaching these questions is not the only legitimate way of approaching them. Suppose that we do begin with an undiscriminating, omnivorous credulity, and gradually learn to distrust much, but to trust our senses in a way in which we trust nothing else. What then? Is it not a fair inference that we come to recognize a cardinal distinction that was always present, although, in the beginning, we did not recognize it for what it is? Impressions, it may be said, always do, and always did, "strike upon the mind" in a different way from ideas. In the beginning, or in our dreams, we, confused creatures that we were or are, did not or do not appreciate the distinction. Nevertheless, it is a genuine distinction.

These contentions, in their several ways, seem to be very just. There is a biological reason for placing quite peculiar reliance upon our senses, however feeble these senses may be. In adult life, the impact of sense-experience is frequently beyond voluntary control. And there may be an ultimate distinction between sense and other categories. Nevertheless, the conclusion is not what Hume said it was. The biological argument, for example, does not prove that our senses and habitual expectations are alone to be trusted. On the contrary, we should often be the wiser if we distrusted our senses and corrected them. And in any case, the argument relies, not upon the vivacity of the *je-ne-sçai-quoi* of the senses, but upon their consequences. These consequences can not be deduced from the sensory pungency of the impressions or from the "manner" in which we conceive these impressions. They must be known, if they are known, in some other way, preferably in a logical way. If they are not known, the argument collapses.

More generally, if, as Hume often suggests, it is the "system" and "coherence" of waking impressions (and of habitual waking expectations) that are the criterion of their ultimate importance, the effect of any such argument is to bring the entire subject before the bar of logic (primarily of inductive logic) and to deny the sufficiency of mere psychological feelings, however vivid, in this connection. And when logic is admitted as the judge, several consequences follow. In the first place, Hume's argument must be transformed beyond recognition. What Hume held was that the natural or psychological fact of belief was prior (both temporally and in every other sense) to any species of logical evidence. Any logic that entered was but the servant of something fundamentally alogical. The conclusion now is that alogical sensory pungency does not have this sort of priority at all. In the second place, once logic is made the judge, it may very well decree that sensitive belief is not the only kind of conviction entitled to the name of belief.

There are sufficient reasons for pursuing this matter further.

§ 4. James Mill and His Critics

In the chapter on Belief in that once (and justly) celebrated book, *The Analysis of the Human Mind,* James Mill developed what was essentially Hume's theory on an extensive scale, and included what is often regarded as the central problem of belief, viz. our assurance of existence and particularly of the existence of "external" things. This development of Hume's theory deserves close consideration, not on account of its merits only (although these are considerable), but also on account of what it led to historically. For Bain, who was one of the editors of the later editions of the *Analysis,* made what we should now call a pragmatist protest long before the days of American pragmatism; and J. S. Mill, his father's other editor, made comments that have to be reckoned with in any serious discussion of this topic.

According to James Mill we believe (1) in the present testimony of the senses, (2) in the testimony of personal memory to past events, and (3) also in future events. The belief in physical objects, Mill further maintained, could be shown, on analysis, to be a union of these three. Even present sensation, he said, is accompanied, in developed minds, by a cluster of associations that provides the basis for the belief in so-called "external" things. And all sensation is inseparably accompanied by the idea of ourselves.

Memory beliefs, he declared, are not at all mysterious. "Memory is, in fact, a case of belief. Belief is a general word. Memory is one of the species included in it." [17] Or, again: "When the idea of a sensation which I formerly had, is revived in me by association, if it calls up in close association the idea of myself, there is memory: if it does not call up that idea there is not memory." [18]

In general, present sensation carries with it some testimony beyond the present, and this testimony is believed. This extension of the testimony, however, he declared to be entirely due to indissoluble association. For the physical objects we believe ourselves to perceive are (he said) associated clusters of ideas, and there is no material *substratum* that can not be resolved into a relation between or union within such clusters.

[17] *Analysis,* Vol. II, p. 359.   [18] *Ibid.,* p. 360.

James Mill considered, however, that his doctrine had to undergo a sterner test in the case of our expectations and of the beliefs that accompany *them*. (Expectation, perhaps, is hardly the right word, since all inductive inference to an unremembered past is included in his argument, as well as inductive inference to the future. The same kind of logic is required to establish our belief that William the Conqueror was not a tobacco-smoker as to justify our confidence that the sun will rise to-morrow.)

Regarding expectation, James Mill had to account for our belief in it. "I believe," he says, "that to-morrow the light of day will be spread over England: that the tide will ebb and flow at London Bridge," [19] and the like. And yet, in his view, the future was a nonentity. He also held that there could be no idea of a nonentity, much less belief in such an idea.

The answer to this perplexity, he says, is supplied by association. When an association is indissoluble or inseparable (Mill preferred the former phrase but did not distinguish the two phrases peremptorily) the occurrence of any idea implies the revival of its associate in such a way that the association is nonvoluntary. Therefore, because the associate is apprehended willynilly, we are constrained to believe in its reality. And James Mill inundated his readers with examples of the point. Among these, the mention of two may here suffice. "In passing, on board of ship, another ship at sea, we believe that she has all the motion, we none." [20] And similarly of ghosts. "In the dark, when this strong association is produced, there is the belief; not in-the-dark, when the association is not produced, there is no belief." [21]

Invariably, therefore, according to this author, belief, so far as it extends beyond present sensation or definite personal memory, is an affair of indissoluble association. James Mill admitted, indeed, that we also believe in propositions, but he held that such beliefs could be explained by verbal association, propositions being, in the end, but words.

This general doctrine, attractive in its simplicity, roused both of James Mill's sympathetic editors to vigorous protest.

Bain's protest, as has been mentioned, was pragmatistic. Accepting "primitive credulity" in place of the associationist hypo-

[19] *Ibid.*, p. 361.   [20] *Ibid.*, p. 371.   [21] *Ibid.*, pp. 372 *sq.*

thesis, Bain proceeded to limit this credulity by a species of pragmatic restraint. Conviction, he held, means in the end, readiness to act. In the beginning, we are ready to act on *any* suggestion, but experience restrains our action in some ways and accentuates our readiness to act in some other ways. Our beliefs, in any important sense, come *after* experience, not before it, and are, in reality, those among our active tendencies that are *confirmed* by experience. "To have gone a certain way with safety and with fruition," Bain said, "is an ample inducement to continue in that particular path. The situation contains all that is meant by full and unbounded confidence that the future and the distant will be exactly what the present is. The primary impulse of every creature is at the furthest remove from a procedure according to Logic. In the beginning, confidence is at its maximum; the course of education is towards abating and narrowing it, so as to adapt it to the fact of things. Every check is a lesson, destroying to a certain extent the over-vaulting assurance of the natural mind, and planting a belief in evil,[22] at points where originally flourished only the illimitable belief in good." [23]

In a tepid way, J. S. Mill accepted Bain's Aberdonian verdict. "We believe a thing," he conceded, "when we are ready to act on the faith of it; to face the practical consequences of taking it for granted; and therein lies the distinction between believing the facts to be conjoined, and merely thinking of them together." [24] Yet this very concession, in J. S. Mill's judgment, itself required explanation. *Why*, he asked, are we ready to act in the one case and not in the other? James Mill had said that the reason was indissoluble association. We sail up the river on a flowing tide because of a confidence in the ways of tides begotten by associative experience. J. S. Mill, while admitting that such association may beget this confidence denied that the association is the invariable or the sufficient cause of the confidence.

<hr />

[22] Bain might have noted the important point recently mentioned by Mr. R. Hughes (*A High Wind in Jamaica*), viz. "It is a fact that it takes experience before we can realise what is a catastrophe and what is not." It is not infrequent to encounter and experience horror and evil without appreciating them for what they are.

[23] *Op. cit.*, p. 397.   [24] *Op. cit.*, p. 403.

Part of the son's criticism of his father is verbal, and not altogether convincing from the standpoint of verbalism. J. S. Mill preferred the term "inseparable association" (which his father occasionally used) to the term "indissoluble association" (which his father habitually used).

This verbalism, however, gave place to something not verbal. As J. S. Mill clearly perceived, the plain truth is that "indissoluble association" does not yield the basis required in James Mill's theory. For what James Mill spoke of is not necessarily indissoluble (or inseparable) at all. An indissoluble association would be one that could not be dissolved, and there are very few associations (if there are *any*) that utterly resist disintegration in this way. In the ordinary way, we do not experience the least difficulty in contemplating connections and relations of ideas that are wholly contrary to all the associations we have acquired in experience.

There is no insuperable difficulty, for example, in *imagining* a purple cow or a grass-green swan, and the mere fact that we can imagine in this way is completely sufficient evidence that we are capable, temporarily and experimentally, of dissolving in thought the most stubborn of customary associations. In short, we do believe in the existence of dun cows and do not believe in the existence of purple cows, *although* the association is *not* indissoluble.

The same point, more fully expounded, entails the ruin of James Mill's theory. As we have seen, James Mill maintained that most of us believe in ghosts in the dark, because we have *then* an indissoluble association of ghostly import, but that we do not believe in ghosts in the daytime, because the friendly sun dispels the (so-called) indissoluble association. In any strictness of language, this opinion is manifestly absurd. An association can not be indissoluble, if, in fact, it is dissolved for twelve hours out of the twenty-four, or in the town (with its lighted streets) and not in the country. The most that could be meant by "indissoluble" in such cases is something that, at some given moment, is not, in fact, dissolved.

In that case, J. S. Mill admitted, belief may normally be expected to occur. If any association of ideas, at any given moment, is so strong as effectively and completely to exclude all other ideas for the time being, then, by the hypothesis of primitive credulity, there will, for the moment, be unquestioned belief. On the other hand, J. S. Mill correctly argued, it is not at all *inevitable* for a very stubborn cluster of ideas to induce genuine belief.

Distant objects, he pointed out, appear to be nearer, when observed through a telescope, than they otherwise would, and this appearance is "indissoluble" in the sense that such objects continue to look nearer after we have come to recognize that the telescope does not, and can not, affect their distance from the eye. In this case, does any one, "except perhaps an inexperienced child," [25] *believe* that the objects in question really *are* nearer? On the contrary, we decline to believe this, although we cannot rid ourselves of the sensory illusion of greater proximity.

Similarly, in a display of ventriloquism, the origin of certain spoken words is assigned to some other place than the actual speaker's larynx; and when we are apprised of the trick, we still, for the most part, continue to have the illusion. But we do not, in general *believe* that the sounds emanate from anywhere except from the actual speaker.

And so with a host of other examples. James Mill's instances prove the reverse of what he intended to prove by their means. Even in the case of the ghosts, we may say that, although in the dark certain associations frighten us, they do not, in general, force us to *believe* in ghosts, granting that, in our terrified condition, we may behave as if we really did believe in them. The Cornish Litany speaks of "ghoulies and ghosties, and long-leggetty beasties and things that go bump in the night." There are very few moderns who, even in the dark, do not distinguish between the "ghoulies" and the "things that (really) go bump."

J. S. Mill accordingly concluded that belief is "ultimate and primordial," not the product of imagination. He further explained that it is governed by logic and not by some mechanical clustering of ideas, and proceeded to give a summary of his own views concerning logical evidence. But that is another story.

[25] *Op. cit.,* p. 406.

§ 5. Belief and Volition

The connection between conviction and what we can not help believing has obtruded itself at various stages in the narrative of the present chapter, and should now be expressly considered. This is the more necessary because the connection between pragmatism and the *will* to believe is commonly supposed to be very close indeed, and because William James, in his *Principles of Psychology*, professed to found his doctrine of belief very largely upon Hume's theory, although it may well be doubted whether the agreement between them was, in reality, at all substantial.

As we have seen, Hume held that "the mind is more actuated and mov'd" [26] by its convictions than by mere ideas; and also that our convictions "must arise from certain determinate causes and principles, of which we are not masters." [27] The latter was his main reason for distinguishing between belief and imagination; for, according to him, "The imagination has the command over all its ideas, and can join, and mix, and vary them in all the ways possible"; [28] and therefore can never reach belief.

It seems clear that Hume, in making these statements, greatly exaggerated the extent to which even creative imagination is amenable to voluntary control, and wholly neglected what is sometimes called "passive" imagination. It is also probable that he exaggerated the degree in which sensation and expectation are involuntary.

In the main, however, the contrast on which he relied in these passages is very generally admitted to be an essential contrast. Whatever else may be true in these matters, according to the usual opinion, it is at least certain that we can not believe what we like, unless by the slow and very indirect means that are occasionally employed to silence a troublesome intellectual conscience.

If so, it should be noted that belief is not by any means confined to the sensitive part of our nature. It might equally well be logical; for inferences are not under our control in the sense that we can make them do just what we like. We may shut our eyes to the evidence of logic, just as we may shut our physical eyes and,

[26] *Treatise*, p. 624.   [27] *Ibid.*   [28] *Ibid.*, p. 629.

as in the fabulous habit of the ostrich, refuse to look. We may also be negligent in our inferences, just as we may be negligent in the employment of our senses. But inferences that we clearly understand do compel our assent, and as J. S. Mill's example of the telescope showed, if the senses conflict with logic, it is the latter, not the former, that compels our assent, once the nature of the circumstance is recognized and appreciated.

Again, in terms of this criterion, belief might very well be emotional, as James (sometimes) would have it, and as Hume, in the main part of his theory, was anxious to deny. For it is usually held that our emotions, particularly our loves and our hates, are as little subject to direct voluntary control as any sensory fact or as any logical inference. Love, we say, can *not* be commanded. One of Hume's major difficulties, therefore, was to distinguish our alogical belief in the senses from our illogical beliefs due to emotional prejudice.

Let us turn, next, to the pragmatic side of belief, the way in which we are "actuated and mov'd" by (or in) a state of assurance. And first let us consider sensory conviction in this connection.

It may be doubted, in the first place, whether the connection between sensation and action is by any means so close as it is sometimes taken to be. Suppose, for example, that I notice in the springtime that the leaves at the top of my lime-trees come out before the leaves on the lower branches. What direct connection has such an observation with any of my actions? I do not propose to climb the trees, or even to paint them; and my sensory interest in them seems purely contemplative. For, although I am accustomed to mow my lawn and otherwise to bestir myself practically in portions of my grounds rather near these trees, I can see no logical connection between the leaves at the top of my trees (at any rate in springtime) and the lawn beneath them. What the pragmatists have to argue, therefore (if they follow Hume), is something highly indirect, viz. that the function of sensation is to guide our actions, and that contemplative sensing is an irrelevant by-product. An emotional pragmatist, on the other hand, would refer, in the above instances, to my esthetic and other emotions concerning the tops of these trees, although it is very doubtful whether any "action" of mine, other than my enjoyment of the trees, is at all relevant. The same must be said of convictions due to memory. While it may be true, in a general way, that we tend to remember what is likely to be serviceable, much more readily, and much more accurately, than anything else, it remains an incontestable fact that we all have many "useless" memories, wholly irrelevant to any probable action.

And similarly of many logical and scientific convictions. It is possible, no doubt, to argue that *ultimately* the function of intellect is practical, and that we would not be logical at all (even to the extent in which we *are* logical) if logic were altogether a biological luxury. But it is quite absurd to deny that many of our speculative notions and beliefs are directly contemplative, and have no obvious relevance to any probable piece of practice.

Passing the point, however (although it is not without importance), let us turn to the cases in which belief and practice do obviously go together.

What is argued, or taken for granted, in such cases, is that we act according to our beliefs, and do not act when we are doubtful. In this statement, however, the positive assertion should be modified and the negative assertion should be denied.

Regarding the positive assertion, it is quite obvious that each of us does not in fact perform a great many actions that we believe to be practicable, and practicable for us individually. It is quite practicable for me to go to church every Sunday, or to take a voyage round the world. In fact, however, I do not do either of these things. Such beliefs, in other words, do not determine action even if they are prerequisites for many actions.

The negative part of the assertion, on the other hand, must be emphatically denied. Any one who consciously takes the bigger kind of risks, or embarks upon what he clearly perceives to be a genuine adventure, does not, unless he is hopelessly muddle-headed, *believe* that the success or even the practicability of his course of action is other than doubtful. The most he can be said to believe, unless he becomes quite ridiculously confident in his excitement, is that it is not impossible he should succeed. A cricketer hopes, let us say, that he may make a "century" for his country, but knows that he may make a "duck." This is too obvious to need further comment.

Something further, however, should be said concerning the time-relations between belief and action.

In many discussions of this topic, it seems to be assumed that we believe first and act afterwards. This may be true of deliberate action, where the planning of the action comes first, and where, in general, we plan according to the best of our beliefs, although, as must be added in fairness, according also to the best of our mere conjectures. Very often, however, especially in impulsive and in very rapid action, the truth would seem to be that we act first and believe afterwards, if, in reality, we believe at all. And very often concomitance and not priority seems to be the correct description of the situation.

Consider, again, another circumstance. In Bain's view, as we have seen, primitive credulity preceded belief, but was sufficient to induce action. Belief, or *settled* conviction, supervened in the cases in which our actions were repeatedly successful, that is to say, in the cases in which our actions turned out to be safe and not to hurt us. Bain might just as well have said, however (as he did say in other parts of his theory), that primitive impulsive tendencies came first, and that the successful ones become established principles of action which, at the conscious level, are described as practical convictions or beliefs.

This leads to a further criticism. According to Bain, primitive credulity through a process of limitation due to trial and error, becomes canalized (to use a modern phrase) into settled practical conviction, and it is *success* that turns the spreading waters into a deep and unflurried canal. It should be noted, however, that absence of striking failure rather than positive success seems to describe the facts that occur. Take, for example, the beliefs of savages in dreams, in omens, in ordeal, or the great mass of "credence" to which most civilized people give a negligent, but firm and tranquil, assent. Such beliefs survive, not because they are true and not because they are beneficent, but because their falsity may not be readily and strikingly apparent, or the evils to which they lead sharp, crushing, and indisputable. For the most part, it takes a very poignant lesson to overcome the inertia of our credulity.

These considerations regarding belief and action are essential to any accurate description of the facts at issue. They are only preliminary, however, to the central theme of this section of our discussion, viz. the connection between belief and volition.

According to Hume, and also according to Bain, we believe because we can not help believing, and, for the same reason, are constrained to act according to our beliefs.

This position is readily intelligible, although it would be more precise if it explained further that we are constrained to act according to our beliefs in the cases, and in these only, in which our beliefs are obviously and immediately relevant to some given action. Yet William James, from very similar premises, reached, in appearance, a very different conclusion. "The whole psychology of belief, disbelief, and doubt," he said, "is grounded on two mental facts—first, that we are liable to think differently of the same: and second, that when we have done so, we can choose which way of thinking to adhere to and which to disregard." [29] In other words, James asserted that belief was a phenomenon of voluntary choice.

As they stand, I do not think these two positions can possibly be rendered consistent. It can not be true that we believe where, and only where, we have *no* voluntary choice, and *also* that believing *is* an instance of voluntary choice. Nevertheless, if we examine the main tenor of James's argument we may be able to diminish the degree of the difference.

In the first place, the word "will" is ambiguous, and among the many things that may be meant by it two that are readily distinguishable are closely connected with our present theme. Sometimes when we speak of "will" we mean voluntary choice between alternatives, either of which may be chosen. Sometimes, on the other hand, we mean settled principles of action.

Accordingly, there is no substantial difficulty in holding that belief is an affair of the will in one of these senses, although

Principles of Psychology, Vol. II, p. 290.

quite involuntary in the other sense. In other words, belief might be essentially allied with settled principles of action, and these principles might be so thoroughly settled that we had no choice in our beliefs but *had* to believe.

On the whole, although James sometimes *says* that belief is volitional choice (as in the passage I have quoted), he is referring, for the most part, to "voluntary" in the other sense.

Essentially, James's contention is that belief, or assurance of reality, is a *live* thing, something intermingled with a man's *life*, and that what we turn to *with a will* is precisely what our life takes hold on. Affirming, as he did in the *Principles of Psychology*, that the "emotional and active" part of us was the really living part, he consequently maintained that the living part of us determined our beliefs.

Incidentally, this view involves him in another inconsistency. On page 284 of his *Principles* (Volume II) he says that "the true opposites of belief, psychologically considered, are doubt and inquiry, not disbelief." It is readily apparent, however, that doubt and inquiry may be very live things indeed, and may strongly affect action even when they paralyze it. They may also be emotionally most disturbing. In short, the opposite of belief, regarded as the "live" part of us, is indifference, and not doubt. Belief, in this sense, is a category of *value* in the wide sense of "value" according to which anything is said to be a value or a disvalue to a man in proportion as it *matters* to him. Value, in this sense, is just the non-indifferent; and its opposite, in the French phrase, is *le n'importisme*.

Quite clearly, the effects of this second ambiguity are rather extensive. In any ordinary sense, we do not either doubt or disbelieve many things to which we are indifferent. I do not doubt that light from Jupiter takes about twelve minutes to reach the earth, but personally I am quite indifferent to the circumstance. If the light took half a century to arrive I should not care. But I do not on that account doubt that it takes about twelve minutes. On the other hand, it must be confessed that this doctrine of James's (which seems so thoroughly opposed to any ordinary interpretation of *belief*) has rather close affinities to what is usually meant by strong *conviction* or assurance. We do not usually squander our deep convictions upon anything that does not burn within us.

The logic, however, of James's celebrated essay on "The Will to Believe" is very peculiar indeed. Having distinguished, firstly, between living and dead options (which may be taken to include a further distinction between momentous and trivial ones) and secondly between forced and avoidable options,[30] James states his thesis (in italics) as follows: "Our passional nature not only lawfully may, but must, decide an option between propositions whenever it is a genuine option that cannot by its nature be decided on intellectual grounds; for to say, under such circumstances 'Do not decide, but leave the question open,' is itself a passional decision—just like deciding yes or no—and is attended with the same risk of losing the truth." [31]

This thesis is remarkable in several respects. In the first place, it is concerned ostensibly, not with all assurance, but with assurance in the truth of propositions. Secondly, it not only admits but affirms that passional conviction has no legitimate place where anything can be decided "by its nature on intellectual grounds," thus affirming something very different indeed from what was affirmed in the *Principles of Psychology.* Thirdly, it states (quite falsely) that the (intellectual) decision that there is a conflict of evidence, apparently pretty evenly balanced, is itself "a passional decision—just like (an intellectual) yes or no." Fourthly, there is nothing in the argument to forbid the interpretation that in the lives of most of us these passional decisions, in the limited sphere in which James holds that they legitimately occur, are in reality forced acceptances rather than forced "options." The "precursive faith" [32] in life and in society of which he speaks may well be the necessary condition under which men live and participate in communal relations. "Where faith in a fact can help create the fact" [33] in another of his phrases (and that is not everywhere) there may be little choice about the faith. If doubts remain they need not be of the kind that ought to perturb. Faith in our fellow-men, and social credit generally, may not indeed be something we know for certain, but can hardly

[30] *The Will to Believe,* p. 3.   [32] *Ibid.,* p. 24.
[31] *Ibid.,* p. 11.   [33] *Ibid.,* p. 25.

be other than a settled principle upon which (unless there are strong contrary reasons in particular instances) we all habitually act.

§ 6. BELIEF AND EMOTION

As we have seen, a part of James's contention in "The Will to Believe" was that, in certain cases rather carefully limited and defined, a passional decision *ought* to go beyond an intellectual decision. We have also seen that, although pretty firm, James was also somewhat apologetic about the matter. He did not maintain that passional decision should ever go against intellectual, but argued instead that, where intellect fails, passion, in certain cases, may rightfully enter. This qualified defense of passional decision is, in itself, a frank admission that passion may be, and frequently is, irrelevant in these affairs.

Here there is general, although not universal, agreement. Passion, we are commonly told, packs the jury and prevents a fair trial. Certainly it may *persuade*, and in that sense may induce the strongest of strong convictions; but the fact (we are usually told) is to be deplored both in science and in ordinary life. The great fault of the social sciences, we are further informed, is that we are constitutionally incapable of studying them disinterestedly and without prepossessions. Such studies, therefore, are not at all similar to the study of lines and of angles, and they are much less likely to be successful. For sentiment combined with good intentions plays havoc with the truth.

The contrast here may easily be overstated, and may readily be misstated. In the first place, it is very common, and very perverse, to omit to distinguish between what is *dis*interested and what is *un*interested. In reality, there is no incongruity in a "passion" for abstract justice, or for intellectual candor; and there are very few eminent scientists and very few eminent jurisconsults who do not possess this passion in a marked degree. No one, indeed, ever set about in seriousness to discover truth without having a passion for truth; and no one has ever tried to solve a puzzle without having some interest in the puzzle and in its solution.

Secondly, it should be remarked that passion and emotion are not irrelevant to all beliefs. If the question be: "Do you love me?" or "Do I love God?" or "Do we hate time-servers?" the answer obviously should be settled by the presence or absence of a certain emotion; for that is what the question is about. Again, it is not necessarily illogical to hold that emotion may be a prior condition for certain kinds of insight or penetrative beliefs. It is at least quite conceivable that we can never understand our fellow-men unless we love them and sympathize with them and, as in Peter's injunction, "honour all and love the brotherhood." [34] Active benevolence, as Hutcheson [35] and other moralists have maintained, may in this way precede any insight into virtue. And there is no need to deny that doing the will of God may be the only sure means of coming to understand or to divine His mind. The just who live by faith may thereby also come to believe and to see.

Granting, however, that emotion *may* exercise an irrelevant suasion and cheat us into believing, a certain interest attaches to the way in which the thing is done.

In the main, the phenomenon is a phenomenon of *pre*possession, although it is also a phenomenon of psychological integration.

Prepossessions have an inhibitory influence. They are, or have the effect of being *choses jugées*, and therefore, by a natural inertia, we are reluctant to admit, and even to examine, fresh evidence. In other words, sentimental appeals (where sentiment should not enter) act both directly and indirectly. They act directly in so far as they stimulate interest in one side of the case, and lead us to attend to it (often with considerable logical acuteness) whether the interest be pity or hope or fear. (For we are the dupes of fear as well as of self-confidence.) And negatively they inhibit attention to what is distasteful and troublesome, that is to say, to matters which, for the time being, run counter to the general trend of our thoughts, feelings, and actions.

Particularly on the negative side, this phenomenon, seen from another angle, is a phenomenon of integration. We are, so to say, wound up in such a way as to pursue a certain course, and therefore arrest any obstacles that, in a sense, might be of our own making and not forced upon us. And if we can be soothed, or flattered, or cajoled, or frightened into such an attitude, our

---

[34] I Peter, ii, 17.   [35] *Inquiry,* 4th edition, 1738, p. 132.

primitive credulity is not, for the time being, disturbed, and conviction (partly from inertia) is apt to follow: Psychical integration, in brief, may come about in various ways, and only one of these ways is logical. Even where logic appears to rule, a certain massive and cumulative effect of one-sided argument frequently does duty for it. We are stunned rather than instructed; and we are too weary and too dull to attack the edifice that stuns us.

An interesting point in this connection is still more indirect. It is tempting to hold that emotion is a very good test of belief, conviction, and even of knowledge. No one, it is said, can really believe very strongly unless he is liable to be roused when he is flatly contradicted. Take, for example, our reliance on memory. In general, as we have seen, we have many useless memories and many trivial ones; yet, for most of us (as we have also seen), nothing is more aggravating (and, indeed, more exasperating) than to have a *clear* memory contradicted, whether or not the affair remembered was important. Consider any ordinary family. Tom and James have gone on an expedition, and Tom, at a later date, recalls, in conversation, some incident in the expedition that he remembers clearly and that James (he is sure) ought also to remember. If James denies recollection a family squabble is almost certain to ensue, and James is lucky if he is not accused of grave moral delinquency. Small wonder, too. For Tom, if he is in any way normal, is almost certain to lose his temper.

In general, I think, the extent to which we are liable to be roused to anger when contradicted by people whose counter-assertions have some weight is a very good test of the strength with which we hold any given conviction. On the other hand, it is not, of course, an infallible test. Some persons are roused by *any* contradiction, even of their slightest opinions. Other persons, like some of the mystics, have, they say, so deep a conviction that surface gusts of anger are, to their minds, unthinkable.

It must be confessed, however, that certain mystics have very sharp tongues.

§ 7. Retrospective

A *coup d'œil* over the argument of the present chapter may conduce to clarity.

We began with the general conception that belief implies psychological conviction or assurance, and that it involves unqualified assent. (It is no great matter, in substance, if the term "belief" should also be applied to instances in which this assurance is psychologically not quite solid but includes, in a minor degree, a certain potential reserve or residual provisional character.) We also assumed that "belief" is either a mistaken or a misleadingly weakened term when the assurance of genuine *knowledge* is in question. On the other hand, we did not attempt to separate belief from knowledge further than by holding that knowledge occurs whenever a conviction is fully evidenced (or certified in a logical sense) and that mere belief occurs when a conviction is not fully evidenced.

This being premised, we proceeded to examine Hume's opinion (which, directly or indirectly, has continued to have great subsequent influence even to the present day) that belief, as opposed to knowledge, is fundamentally alogical because it is based upon the sensitive, not upon the cogitative, part of our nature, and because the extension of sensory pungency found in practical "judgment" and in workaday "probability" (which are the principal species of the plain man's beliefs) is also alogical, being, in the end, an instance of invincible association or inveterate expectation.

Our conclusion, here, was directly negative. Hume's "impressions" are not the only experiences that convince us at any time, and they do not have a monopoly of primitive impressiveness. On the contrary, this impressiveness, with its bearing upon conviction, is, very largely, acquired. We have to *learn* the distinction between what, in Hume's language, we "are pleas'd to call a reality" and the "unrealities" that also win our childlike and inexperienced assent.

What is more, there is no good reason to assume, and there are very good reasons against assuming, that the (common sense, practical, or scientific) "system" that (again according to Hume) we erect on the foundation of these first-hand sense-impressions is altogether, or even predominantly, alogical. The associations of *homo sapiens* are not mere brute clusterings of impressions and ideas. For that matter, there seems to be a stout thread of inarticulate logic even in the associations of the brutes. The burnt dog dreads the fire as well as the burnt child. Hume, by admitting the existence of (logical) rules whereby to judge of causes and effects, and by distinguishing horse-sense from prejudice, unintentionally gave testimony in favor of the potentially logical character of expectation, and the point became quite clear in the later discussions of his successors (e.g. the Mills). The clearness of the result, to be sure, is partly in spite of what these later authors said. For the most part, their associationism was not logical enough. But J. S. Mill's proof of the "ultimate and primordial" character of belief, with its explicit recognition of the essential logic in belief, is as frank as it is cogent. The younger Mill pointed out, as we saw, that we all refuse to believe that what we see through a telescope *is* nearer than the same thing seen by the naked eye. In other words, he proved that, given a sufficient reason, we all deny the "evidence" of our senses and prefer the evidence of our reason. Similarly, he proved that no association is completely indissoluble (since we can always conceive the opposite) and that we need not *believe* in the most stubborn associations, even if, as in our terror of ghosts in the dark, we sometimes act as if we did believe.

Hume's unwitting testimony to the presence of at least a certain degree of logic in the "system of realities" with which, as he explained, the plain man's world is "peopled" is shown, once again, in his anxiety to distinguish the beliefs that are due to custom (that is to say, to repeated experience) from those that are due to prejudice (or logically irrelevant emotion). If belief were wholly alogical, or wholly illogical, why should this distinction matter at all? As Hume's argument stands, he appears to evince an alogical prejudice against prejudice. For there can be no doubt that prejudiced people really are convinced. All that we can say against them is that they should not be. Emotion, as we have seen, is not invariably irrelevant to all our beliefs; but, where it is irrelevant, we conclude that logic applies *de jure,* although it is frequently overborne *de facto.* In such cases there are genuine convictions, but ill-grounded ones.

The connection between the sensitive part of our nature and our actions is obviously very close, although, as we have argued, the two are not the same, since sensitive acquaintance, in certain instances, seems to be contemplative only. There is great danger here, however, of confusing between actions (and "will" in the sense of a settled disposition to action), on the one hand, and voluntary choice (or "will" in this narrower sense), upon the other hand. Hume, Bain, James Mill, and others expressly repudiated the view that we can believe what we choose to believe. Like the great majority of us, they held that we believe what we can not help believing, indeed, that a conviction is firm and assured precisely in proportion as it is involuntary. Our beliefs are things over which we are not the masters; and our sensitive nature, together with its more stubborn associations, is just the part of us over which we have least control. Belief, therefore, is active and *also* involuntary.

On the whole, there is no good reason for disputing the substantial accuracy of this part of their contention; and the truth of it does not at all conflict with the main conclusion that has emerged from our discussion, viz. that belief is not fundamentally alogical, need not be predominantly alogical, and should never be flatly illogical.

It may be true, as Newman said, that "obstinate men give their own will as their very reason for assenting, *if they can think of nothing better.*" [36] It may be doubted, however, whether persons who reach this pitch of obstinacy truly *believe* that the "reason" they allege is a reason at all.

§ 8. "Notional" and "Real" Assent

As I have said, any one who puts his trust in "logic" (and indeed any one else who deals with logic) should be careful to explain what precisely he means by "logic." For the "logic" of the schools is an amalgam rather than a system, and e.g. Mr. Bosanquet's "philosophical logic" (which he called the "morphology of thought") is very different indeed from the "logic" of other authors (who have difficulty in distinguishing their science from pure mathematics).

Let it be said, then, that the logic of belief (when belief is distinguished from intuitive or from demonstrative and deductive

[36] *Grammar of Assent,* p. 164 (Italics mine).

certainty) must be concerned, in the main, with inductive logic (particularly problematic induction) and with the theory of probability. These topics will be considered later in the present work; and the present chapter may be regarded as an introduction to them. Accordingly, since the discussion of these central matters is postponed, it is unnecessary to offer any further explanations concerning them now. On the other hand, there is a point of great philosophical importance that should not be postponed.

A cardinal doctrine in Hume's philosophy is that there is no such thing as a separate or distinct idea of "reality." There is no difference in the world, he says in effect, although not quite in this language, between saying that such and such a thing *is* so-and-so, and saying that it *really* is so-and-so.[37]

I have chosen to put this statement in a form very slightly different from Hume's because I hold it to be true in the form in which I have stated it. Regarding *assertions,* it is true, I conceive, that "is really" simply means "is," and that the logical copula "is" expresses, on the epistemic side, simply the fact that I affirm such and such a connection to hold, and on the side of fact, the circumstance that the facts support my assertion.

Hume, however, had, properly speaking, *no* theory of assertions or of propositions.[38] He was wholly concerned with the fact of presentation. Therefore (taking "existence" and "reality" to be synonyms), he said that "to reflect on anything simply and to reflect on it as existent, are nothing different from each other." [39]

On the other hand, Hume could not deny, and did not attempt to deny, that there is a very considerable difference between imagining a thing as existent and believing it to be existent. Accordingly, when faced with what he called "the inevitable dilemma" that "either the belief is some new idea, such as that of *reality* or *existence,* which we join to the simple conception of an object, or it is merely a peculiar *feeling* or *sentiment,*" [40] he was forced to accept the latter, not the former, alternative.

In various ways (although frequently with modifications not

[37] *Treatise,* pp. 66 *sq.*
[38] See especially *Treatise,* pp. 96-97 note.
[39] *Ibid.,* pp. 66 *sq.*
[40] *Ibid.,* p. 623.

altogether easy to defend) this type of opinion is very frequently held. The touch of sense, it is said, is necessary for any acquaintance with existence. Without it, all our thoughts and all our imaginations bombinate in the void. As Kant declared, a hundred possible dollars have the same *meaning* as a hundred actual dollars, and yet we have the right to deal with conviction with the actual dollars whereas the possible dollars could serve, at the best, for an imaginary subscription to an imaginary bazaar. Even our notions must, in the last resort, be blended with sensory tidings (although perhaps in a fashion that is involved, tortuous, and obscure) if they are not to vanish into a shadowy limbo of bloodless nonentities.

Much of the argument, in contentions of this species, is concerned, not with the principle at issue, but with a certain interpretation of what "notions" are. The allegation is that notions are nothing but "abstract" ideas derived from sense by the *omission* of certain sensory characteristics and by the retention of others. If this account of our notions were true, the procedure, as Hegel said when he parodied it, would be very similar indeed to peeling the coats off an onion. Abstraction would give us rather less onion without any other essential difference, and in the end would leave us either with a coatless shred of onion or with no onion at all.

There would be no great difference in principle if notions were regarded as formed by an "abstraction" less crudely similar to physical division—if, for example, thought were regarded as only a pale and circumambient reflection of things, attaining at the best a partial grasp of their surfaces, atmosphere, and aroma, and achieving a flat and savorless synthetic compound of these; or, again, if the notion, say of whiteness, were but a shorthand device for expressing a troop of associations by similarity, such as snow, milk, Roman togas, bread, surf, a hoary head, and an albino mole.

On the other hand, if notions are essences discovered, not by physical separation or by superficial cogitative circumambience, but by penetrative insight into structural, although general, facts, there would be no occasion for any such criticism, and it would be mere assumption that sensory pungency is better evidence of acquaintance with fact than this notional insight. In showing, or in attempting to show, that Hume's doctrine in this particular should be amended so as to refer to belief in propositions (which have always a notional structure) and should not be confined to sensory presentation, I have endeavored, from the outset, to guard against the superstition that "notional" assent is not "real."

I must still, however, offer certain further observations concerning the distinction between belief and imagination.

§ 9. BELIEF AND IMAGINATION

The term "imagination" being ambiguous, it is necessary to say something of the principal senses in which it is contrasted with belief.

In so far as imagination is merely passive, or merely reproductive, its contrast with belief need not be at all acute; and in general it does not seem advisable to pay any special attention to the type of "imagination" that is almost, if not quite, synonymous with the absence of critical capacity. The essential contrast is between belief and *creative* imagination; indeed, for the most part, between belief and what Coleridge called "fancy," [41] that is to say, not between belief and the "primary esemplastic power" that according to Coleridge "dissolves, diffuses, dissipates, in order to recreate," but between belief, on the one hand, and romance or day-dreaming, upon the other hand. The imaginative sweep of some great scientific theory, to be sure, may be said to be a higher exercise of the "creative" imagination than the shyer, more elf-like constructions of romance; and scientific "imagination" is quite certainly "imagination" in so far as it outstrips its data, and leads, without following, the evidence. Nevertheless, this species of imagination, in its finest examples, is so intent upon distilling the subtler essence of the facts, and so suffused with analogies and the control of some world-pattern, that its contrast with belief may become very difficult to explore.

In a romance, on the other hand, we are dealing with some-

---

[41] *Biographia Literaria*, Ch. XV. I have somewhat extended Coleridge's account of "fancy."

thing that, *on the face of it,* is made up or concocted. This ostensible meaning, it is true, may convey another, and perhaps a most truthful message in an indirect way. There may be more truth in *Hamlet* than in a hundred histories of Denmark; more human nature in Tartuffe or in Pecksniff than in a shelf's weight of treatises on psychology; more historical life in the fictitious than in the real D'Artagnan; and Mrs. Crupp may be the quintessence of all landladies. But that is by the way.

Again, we must take for granted the usual qualifications that are presumed in discussions of this matter. For example, a narrative that is romantic in form may be substantially autobiographical or may otherwise record fact very faithfully.[42] And the converse may happen equally well. Rousseau's *Confessions* may be more of a romance than his *Emile*. Similarly, a narrative scrupulously careful of its factual statements (e.g. *Gulliver's Travels*) may incorporate much that is true in the literal sense, or true with some adjustment to scale. And, no doubt, *The Supper of Trimalchio* may be better historical evidence than much that was intended to pass for history.

These obvious points being presumed, we have to examine the contrast between our non-acceptance of romance, despite its romantic pungency and its close relation to our lives, on the one hand, and our acceptance of "literal" narrative, on the other hand. Let us consider, then, what might be said in some of the better-known schools.

An epistemological realist would say that, in the last analysis, we inspect fact or select from it; and that the truth of our thinking depends upon the accuracy of this inspection and selection. Other epistemologists have other theories. For the most part, they say that our thinking constructs something that corresponds to facts, if it is true. And a few would say that "truth" consists in the coherence of what we construct, or, at any rate, that there is no other conceivable test of it.

[42] As in the extreme literalism of *Gulliver's Travels* or in the romances of Defoe. Of Defoe, Mr. D. McCarthy has recently said that "he was so unimaginative that he could not conceive that a story could be interesting to others, unless they believed it." Mr. McCarthy further explains that Defoe was inventive, not imaginative. In particular, he had no emotional imagination, with the result that his characters, whether pimps or saints, "are all exactly the same inside."

How then do these theories apply to works of imagination?

Realists may argue with complete propriety that the elements, connections, and plausibilities of any romance are drawn directly from observed facts. (Indeed, it is a canon of romance that a plausible impossibility is better than an improbable possibility.) Similarly, they may point out that Maupassant's plan was a very good one, that is to say, that many romantic artists select real people, put them into imaginary proximity, and deduce the result. And finally, realists may argue that an artistic selection may be quite as accurate, and also quite as inaccurate, in its artistic way, as any other selection. As Stevenson wrote to Barrie, "*The Little Minister* ought to have ended badly. We all know that it *did*, and we are infinitely grateful to you for the grace and good feeling with which you have lied about it. If you had told the truth, I, for one, could never have forgiven you."

The fact remains, however, that we do not believe a romance, as it stands, and as the incidents and characters are assembled; and that, rightly or wrongly, we do believe a literal narrative, unless we have some special reason for disbelieving it.

Mutatis mutandis, the adherents of the correspondence view may also maintain that there are several kinds of correspondence, and that a romance, a poem, and the others correspond to fact in a romantic and poetic way, which is not the way of scientific description, biographical narrative, or the like. Nevertheless, the same sort of belief does not arise.

The coherence view is also in a difficulty. For skilful works of fancy are more coherent than most other human constructions, and yet are *prima facie* less "real." It may be permissible to hold with Mr. Yeats that "whatever of philosophy has been made poetry is alone permanent"; but the same could hardly be said of history or of science.

Is there, then, nothing "real," in a direct and literal sense, about a work of imagination or about its ostensible "content"?

Several answers may here be given, most of which are quite consistent with one another.

Firstly, any work of art really is a work of art. The painting, the poem, and the rest "really" are, that is to say, *are*, manipulations of pigments, of words, and so forth. This is not in dispute, for the dispute is about what the words or the pigments signify. If they signify nothing, as on purely formal esthetic theories, no such question arises. A good painting, according to the formal view, is a beautiful color-pattern and nothing more. It is degraded if any other significance creeps in. And—what is still harder to believe—a good poem is a beautiful sound-pattern and nothing more.

If, on the other hand, significance or representation (not the literal copying of nature, one must admit) be allowed to pertain to art, there need be no objection to the view that fine art may signify the life or the soul of nature, provided that it signifies in its own way, and not by photographic reproduction or by literal verbal description.

Again, if we hold an "expressive" view of art, of imagination, and of their functions (or combine this "expressive" view with the former), it may, of course, be literally true that all valuable art expresses a state of the artist's soul and incites a somewhat similar state of soul in the beholder or in the reader. It has, therefore, the same reality as these souls possess.

More generally, if a romance be regarded as the record of a fancy, there really has been such an event as this fancy—in the author's mind.

It is sometimes held that an "object of the fancy" exhausts itself in being fancied, and that *therefore* it is less real than anything else. "It is of the very essence of fiction, "Mr. Bertrand Russell writes, "that only the thoughts, feelings, etc., in Shakespeare and his readers are real, and that there is not in addition to them an objective Hamlet. When you have taken account of all the feelings roused by Napoleon in writers and readers of history, you have not touched the actual man; but in the case of Hamlet you have come to the end of him. If no one thought about Hamlet, there would be nothing left of him; if no one had thought about Napoleon, he would have seen to it that someone did." [43]

This is excellently said, and may readily be combined with Croce's view—rather disturbing to the vanity of most authors— that what any one expresses in a work of art is the whole, at

[43] *Introduction to Mathematical Philosophy*, pp. 169 *sq.*

the time, that he has in him to express. We certainly hold this of our dreams, although psychoanalysts would tell us we are wrong. Our dream-objects, we say, exhaust their reality in the mere circumstance of their appearing. This is very different from the "reality" of buildings or of tax-collectors.

If, on the other hand, art and dream-objects are symbolic of something beyond themselves, their truth and their meaning is not exhausted in their naked or non-symbolic selves. For part of their being is to symbolize.

In the end, however, it is impossible seriously to overlook the circumstance that if our fancies are real (and plainly there really are fancies) and if they really have, or may have, significance beyond themselves, they are not the same kind of facts (although they *are* facts) as perceptions or as logical discoveries, and they do not signify in the same way as what is perceived or as what is thought. The stuff they are made of may not be altogether different from perceived stuff, but it is not literally identical in all important respects. Fancied stuff may be at least as different from perceived stuff as the workaday stuff of the moon is different from the workaday stuff of green cheese.

This commonplace observation may be too simple-minded to be dignified by the name of a theory, but I am inclined to suspect that it is "really" the last word on the matter. It is not true that we do not believe in the existence of fancies, for plainly we do. What is true is only that we do not believe that fancies are anything except fancies.

CHAPTER VI

CONCERNING OPINION

§ 1. GENERAL

ACCORDING to Cardinal Newman, Catholics speak of theological opinion, not as of something necessarily doubtful, but in contrast, firstly, to anything known for certain; and, secondly, to the vital and essential assurance that is implied in the faith a Christian must live by.[1] Opinion, in this sense, is something not necessary to believe, although perhaps overwhelmingly probable, according to Catholic premises; and, at the same time, something which, being but probable, can not be fully evidenced knowledge. On the other hand, many opinions do not even approach cogitative conviction and assurance. They are qualified and provisional decisions upon evidence known to be insufficient, where there should be no question of a categorical Yes or No. And logically-minded persons recognize the fact perfectly well.

Semilogical and illogical persons, it is true, are frequently inclined to forget that their opinions are *only* opinions. It is the easiest thing in the world to jump to an unqualified assent, where there is no logical title to do more than incline towards provisional assent upon a favorable balance of probability, relative to decidedly insufficient evidence. In this respect, all of us, unless we are on our guard for special reasons, are frequently only semilogical. And obstinate men very often are quite illogical in this matter. "I am of opinion that the works of Burns is of an immoral tendency," Sir J. M. Barrie's Bowie Haggart said; "I have not read them myself, but such is my opinion."

The upper limit of opinion, in this sense, is belief (or something very near it), although it is never knowledge. The lower limit, on the other hand, would seem to be simply what is not beyond all conjecture or supposal. True, an opinion is an opinion

[1] *Grammar of Assent*, p. 57.

based, even at the lowest level, upon a survey of conjectures, but some opinions are such that only one conjecture is before the opiner's mind, so that the survey is of this one conjecture only. The limiting case of the opinable, therefore, seems to be just the limiting case of potential surmise that is conceivably plausible.

It is possible, of course, to attempt to restrict "opinion" to a narrower connotation. Thus Cardinal Newman also held that opinion came midway between what he called profession and credence (which came below it), on the one hand, and what he called presumption and speculation (which came above it), on the other hand.[2]

Newman's criterion in this instance was logical. Profession he defined as a "notional" assent that had no personal intellectual effort behind it. To follow the fashions of the day in wine, or dress, or literature; to call oneself a Whig or a Tory because of the family tradition—in a word, to give lip-service to catchwords and allegiance to the unexamined—is what "profession" means. It is unworthy of the name of opinion. Credence, again (he maintained) is the same thing a little improved when judged by the standards of logic, but not, according to Newman, sufficiently improved to be, properly speaking, an opinion. What we pick up from newspapers in the way of information of an incapsulated, journalistic sort, or what reverberates as an echo from our travels is to be accounted mere credence. It is a gentleman's information, as opposed to a professional man's, the "ungrudging prompt assent" of a mind that may be polished and tolerably acute, but that has no particular reason for *thinking* about the matter. It is the kind of belief, according to Newman, that has never been subjected to any shock or strain, although it might very well be capable of surviving such an ordeal if the ordeal came.

By "opinion," in contrast to "profession" or "credence," Newman meant neither more nor less than strict logical probability. "I shall here use the word," he said, "to denote an assent, but an assent to a proposition, not as true, but as probably true, that is, to the probability of that which the proposition enunciates;

[2] *Grammar of Assent*, pp. 40 *sqq.*

and as that probability may vary in strength without limits, so may the cogency and moment of the opinion." [3]

Above opinion, Newman placed presumption and speculation on the ground that these latter came nearer to (or might actually reach) cogitative certainty, although not deductive knowledge. By presumption he meant the assent to first principles (i.e. to fundamental principles regarded as inevitable and as true although not necessarily as self-evident). And by speculation he meant cogitative insight, quoting in corroboration of his terms the Shakespearean statement, "Thou hast no speculation in these eyes."

On the whole, since "probability" precisely defines what Newman here called "opinion," it seems unnecessary and inexpedient to have a second technical term for the same thing, unless usage plainly constrains us to have one. And commonly we do not thus restrict the term "opinion." When we speak of a "climate of opinion" (the phrase, I think, was Buckle's), we certainly include profession and credence in the "climate," and mean only to indicate that there is logical uncertainty in the air, whether or not the majority of the people who breathe it are, for the time being, convinced. When we speak of our own opinions, we may normally refer to those surmises concerning which we have tried to do a little original thinking, but may also refer to personal credence that we admit we have not attempted to examine. When we speak of political opinions, we think of views that are not shared by all members of the community, although many who hold such opinions do so with strong conviction. We use the word because we know that persons legally sound in mind, and in many instances not less capable than we ourselves are of coming to a decision upon evidence, nevertheless decide differently from the way in which we ourselves decide, or, it may be, decline to decide.

From the logical standpoint, we do mean to imply, in all such cases, that we are dealing, not with certainties, but with plausibilities. On the other hand, we do not deny individual psychological assurance or conviction, and we do not mean to say anything at all about the extent to which those who opine

[3] *Ibid.*, p. 51.

have even an inkling of the logical status of their opinions. Our point is that such conclusions *are* matter of opinion whether those who hold the opinion are, or are not, aware of this logical circumstance.

Again, we *want* the word opinion to be as broad as is reasonably possible, but we tend to restrict the range of "probability" to something that is measurable according to an intelligible scale of equiprobability. This tendency to restrict probability to measurable probability is perhaps a mistake, but there are advantages in possessing a term that indicates only what inclines us to assent (but does not logically necessitate assent) whether or not this inclination is too indeterminate to be measured. And this, I think, is precisely the sense in which we commonly, and correctly, speak of "opinion."

§ 2. WHAT IS MEANT BY A "COMPETENT" OPINION

In general, we distinguish between a "competent" or a "sensible" opinion and an opinion that is not to be described in any such terms; and as we all know, a competent opinion is often very hard to come by. Is it possible, then, to indicate with some precision what is meant by a competent opinion? The attempt is worth the making, because no other opinions are worth the having.

Negatively, we may affirm with some confidence that a mere opinion can not be competent where knowledge or definitive proof is available. There might be relatively skilful guessing in such instances, but knowledge decrees a better way. A bridge player, for example, who guesses that the seven of trumps in his hand is higher than the last remaining trump in his adversary's hand, is not, properly speaking, a competent player, although he need not be frankly incompetent. He ought to have counted all the trumps and to have noted all their denominations. If he had done so, he would *know*.

At the other end of the scale, we should say, with somewhat diminished confidence, that, where the evidence is *very* insufficient, a competent person would decline to give, and a very competent person would decline to form, any opinion whatsoever. This view appears to contradict much that is frequently stated *ex cathedra* by writers on the theory of mathematical probability, but the contradiction need not be more than apparent. Mathematicians measure a "probability" relative to the least scrap of evidence, and hesitate (if, like Mr. Keynes [4] and Mr. von Kries, they hesitate at all) only if they have strong grounds for suspecting that some few of these scraps of evidence are too indeterminate to yield a basis for any measurement. In general, however, the obstacle that prevents a "competent" person from expressing any opinion at all is his knowledge of the extreme inadequacy of the relevant information he possesses. Relative to his evidence he might give an opinion, but he is too prudent to do so. He does not expect to have exhaustive evidence, but he prefers to have an appreciable, perhaps a very appreciable, *weight* [5] of evidence before he ventures to pronounce an opinion.

In addition to the above, the chief point that arises concerns the relations between a competent expert opinion and the competence of a layman's opinion in matters partly of expertise. This problem bristles with difficulties. In professional circles, a competent opinion, especially if challenged in the law courts, means little more than an opinion that a duly qualified person might give, without revealing gross negligence, and without making the sort of mistake that no one except an ignoramus could possibly perpetrate. In this sense, the standard of "competence" is very low indeed; and for the purposes of this discussion it seems preferable to indicate a higher standard of "competence" in opinion. We might say, perhaps, that an "expert" opinion is one that a proficient, or even an eminent, member of some given profession might give without making an obvious slip, and which, although it might be mistaken, showed the influence of a master hand to some appreciable extent even in the mode of its error.

Are we, then, to say that no one except an expert is entitled to form an opinion at all in matters that require technical experience, and that common sense opinions are to be accepted, either with or without a pinch of salt, only in the instances in which any one man's views, given reasonable care and attention, are just as good as another's? Are the experts, in all other instances, the sole depositaries of such logic as is to be had?

[4] *A Treatise on Probability*, pp. 42 *sqq.* [5] *Cf.* Keynes, *op. cit.*, e.g. p. 312.

Such a view would seem unreasonable. In the first place, it is easier to criticize with effect than to construct with effect, and therefore, in subjects not excessively technical (and in some parts even of highly technical subjects) a layman may be entirely competent to form an adverse or a favorable opinion about expert evidence, although he might be quite incapable of taking the lead in such matters. He might similarly (sometimes at least) be capable of acting as an umpire between divergent experts, as judges in the courts frequently are, although not, of course, always. Again, experts may have the defects of their expert qualities. They may be over-subtle. They may be too eager to obtain a "system," and insufficiently aware that what is sketchy or lath-and-plaster in the system ought to be more solid. They may also have an axe to grind.

Laymen do not have all these defects in quite the same way. They are under- rather than over-subtle. They have reverence only for well-established "systems," and the axes they have to grind are, in general, different axes. It does not follow, of course, that these opposite defects cancel one another. To pit under-subtlety against over-subtlety is a dangerous and a stupid way of attempting to reach the truth; and the standing problems of trial by jury, or of the practice of appointing Royal Commissions that contain only a few "experts," must remain standing problems. There is no doubt that an ordinary jury is not competent to form a sound opinion (in many cases) without proper direction from the judge, and also no doubt that the judge may misdirect or the jury grievously misapprehend their directions. On the other hand, there are grave dangers in officialdom and in professionalism, and there are certain reasonable objections to be taken to the extent to which matters of literary criticism, philosophy, economics, and political or natural science are in the hands of "academic" people. Hence the theory of Royal Commissions, according to which (on the whole and in most instances) experts have to explain and to defend their opinions in such a way as to persuade a majority of persons well versed in public affairs but not specially trained on the severely technical issues. (The experts, however, have a good deal to say, in private, about the other members.)

In various ways, therefore, although not in all particulars, a layman's opinion, or a general practitioner's, may be worth considering by a specialist, and a specialist's (perhaps) by a super-specialist. If it were not so, where is the principle to stop? No one can be a super-specialist in everything pertaining to his job, to say nothing of everything else, and we pity the patient who has to be examined by a dozen super-specialists. His ailments, however, may be numerous and complicated.

Opinions of some weight, therefore, may be pretty widely diffused. But how widely?

§ 3. THE LIMITS OF CONJECTURE

A celebrated passage in the concluding chapter of Sir Thomas Browne's *Hydriotaphia* runs as follows:

"What Song the *Syrens* sang, or what name *Achilles* assumed when he hid himself among women, though puzzling questions are not beyond all conjecture. What time the persons of these Ossuaries entred the famous Nations of the dead, and slept with Princes and Counsellors, might admit a wide solution. But who were the proprietaries of these bones, or what bodies these ashes made up, were a question above Antiquarism. . . . There is no antidote against the *Opium* of time, which temporally considereth all things. . . But the antiquity of oblivion blindly scattereth her poppy, and deals with the memory of men without distinction to merit of perpetuity."

This, in sum, is our question. What is beyond all conjecture, and does not admit even of the widest solution, can not be matter of serious opinion. Where there are no data, or data so slender as to be completely worthless, there can not be an opinion that earns its name.

I think we may say, firstly, that whatever is meaningless can not be either supposed or conjectured. Here, however, explanations are clearly required. For, as recent philosophical literature has shown, the meaning of "meaning" is not at all self-evident.

In the first place, "meaning" may be simple indication, as pointing with the finger, or some other such gesture. "I mean *that*" or "Keep off the grass. This means *you*" are illustrations. Private individuals are aware that they are pointing out something in particular and not something else; and in various ways we believe ourselves capable of inducing other people to refer to what we refer to. The first meaning of "meaning," therefore, is simple indication; and anything may be meant in this sense that may be pointed to.

In the second place, "meaning" may refer to the way in which, as we say, one thing indicates another, or suggests it. In a certain sense, this interpretation of meaning includes gestures. For these are events that signify other events. The same is true of the abbreviated gestures in conventionalized gesture language, in spoken language, in hieroglyphics, in mathematical symbols.

Most of these are arbitrary signs in which the symbol suggests what is symbolized through a conventional association. There might, however, be "natural" signs, as Reid suggested when he set about to improve Berkeley's theory whereby a divine (but essentially arbitrary) language made the evidence of sight suggest the evidence of touch to all men at all times. Again, most of the above signs are *substitute* signs, where the sign *stands for*, or does duty for, the thing signified, a point that does not hold of the first sense of "meaning," viz. simple indication.

The clearest and most important instance of this second kind is the connotative indication of logic, where one term means-what-is-meant-by, or indicates-what-is-indicated-by, some other term. This also is a phenomenon of suggestion. Anything that indicates or suggests anything else must do so *to a mind*. Without a mind, things might be connected but could never be suggestive. On the other hand, the suggestion may be due to a logical or to a factual connection, and need not be arbitrary or the product of mere (or alogical) association.

When we say that an opinion must at least have some meaning, we refer, in general, to this second sense of "meaning," and this second sense of "meaning" may be so very wide, or, again, so very conventional and so very personal and subjective, that it may be doubted whether this restriction of opinion to what has "meaning" is actually an effective restriction. To say that an opinion must be somehow suggestible to some one is not to say very much. Even dreams would be included in this category.

Attempting, therefore, to amend a statement that is far too wide, we might say that an opinion must seem to have logical or evidential meaning. It must be a possible interpretation of the kind of suggestion that is, or seems to be, relevant logical evidence. To that extent opinion can not be wholly uncritical.

This amended description carries us a certain way, but not very far. What may *seem* to be relevant or logical to a savage, to a child, or to a peasant is a wide and curious collection, much of which would be summarily dismissed as "meaningless" by warier and more sophisticated persons. And the more sophisticated part of the world's population lives itself in a brittle shelter. For there are few who would have the effrontery to affirm that many, at least, of their best attested opinions might not prove, in the end, to be logically indefensible, or to have mistaken a spurious for a genuine analogy. What is consistent with itself and with the evidence, and what does not seem to be inconsistent with itself and with the evidence, are obviously very different indeed. Yet actual opinions are of the latter, not merely of the former, class.

Even where inconsistency is admitted and recognized in any opinion, the reality of the opinion is not always questioned. "I see that the thing can't be quite what I say it is, but you know what I mean" is a common form of statement and is not necessarily indefensible.

Again, where inconsistency arises, the state of affairs may be highly complicated. We have to consider (1) the parts and (2) the specific manner of their alleged conjunction. Even in the case of some plain absurdity like a round square, the parts, viz. "round" and "square," have meaning in the sense both that they can be indicated and that they can be defined. What is absurd is their conjunction in such a way that whatever has all the properties of the first has also all the properties of the second. Where the manner of the specific conjunction is less brutally obvious, impossible inconsistencies may easily escape notice, and in that case there may be genuine, although not defensible, opinion. It is always possible, moreover, that some analogous but slightly different conjunction may avoid inconsistency. If we suspect that this is possible, we adhere to our opinions, while admitting that they may need some revision in what we airily call matters of detail.

A point historically momentous in this connection concerns the logical status of the mysteries of the Christian religion. I may illustrate, once again, by referring to a contention of Cardinal Newman's concerning the Holy Trinity.

What Newman argued in substance was that the "Tres et unus" of Augustine, which gives the substance of the Athanasian Creed, is only an intellectual or theological mystery. Regarded as a "lex orandi et credendi" or, in other words, as a part of the believer's faith and vital participation or communion with deity, it is not a mystery at all. The various parts of this doctrine of the godhead (Newman enumerated nine of them in all)[6] are all laid hold on by every genuine believer. Each is a part of his Christian life, and as a simple believer he is neither asked nor expected to combine every feature in his life intellectually into a coherent pattern. There is, therefore, no mystery at all at the level of faith, and of good works, and of prayer, just as there is no mystery in a man's living his own existence. If a man creates a mystery about his life when he tries to form a philosophical theory about living, so much the worse for his intellectual capacities. Similarly, if he can not understand how deity can be three and also one (Newman did not try to say, as some have said, that God was numerically one and non-numerically three), the fault should be assumed to lie in the man's intellectual or theological capacity. "We know one truth about Him and another truth,—but we cannot image both of them together; we cannot bring them before us by one act of the mind; we drop the one while we turn to take up the other. None of them is fully dwelt on and enjoyed, when they are viewed in combination."[7]

In this argument several different strands should be disentangled.

(1) If the mystery be simply that no theologian has hitherto succeeded in stating all the vital truths that describe man's communion with God in a fully comprehensible fashion, it is not even an intellectual *mystery*, although it remains an intellectual, or theological, *problem*.

(2) If what is meant is that certain theologians (and particu-

larly the framers of the great creeds) have succeeded in describing the principal attributes of deity in a consistent, although in a very abstract, fashion, but that most humble folk can not understand the theological solution, and can not even keep nine propositions in their minds at once, there might be mystery for the laity, but there would not be mystery for the better theologians. But

(3) If what is meant is that certain of these theological propositions clearly contradict one another, and that each several proposition indisputably describes, without the possibility of mistake, a necessary aspect of religious experience, then there is something more than mystery. There is utter impossibility; and it should be doubted whether any one either believed or opined what he clearly perceived to involve such a contradiction.

It seems unnecessary to proceed further with the consideration of this particular boundary of the territory of the opinable —the boundary, namely, that results from the requisite that what is opined must not be meaningless. What sometimes purports to be an alternative expression of the same view, however (although it may be substantially different), requires separate consideration. I mean the view that every opinion must at least be "conceivable."

The difficulty in this view is that the word "conceivable" suffers from a very mischievous ambiguity. It may mean "logically thinkable," and in that sense there is no difference whatever between "being conceivable" and "having an authentic meaning." The word, however, may also mean "imaginable in a pictorial way" (whether fanciful or otherwise), and this alternative and different meaning of "conceivable" should not be held to be a necessary prerequisite of a serious, or indeed of any, opinion.

In the first place, it need not be true that whatever is thinkable is imaginable in a pictorial way. Consider, for example, the statements, "A point has position but no magnitude" or "*Mere* position in time or space is causally irrelevant in Nature." These statements, whether or not they are true, are at least thinkable, but they are not pictorially imaginable. The first is intelligible, say, if, following Eudoxus, we think of the logical meaning of the intersection of the boundaries of two surfaces in the same plane; and it is separately intelligible although not separately imaginable. The second, similarly, is an affair of conception, not an affair of possible imagery. *Mere* position is unimaginable, but is thinkable if anything in these subjects is thinkable. (I am speaking, be it noted, not of mere position in "absolute space" or in "absolute time," but of the intelligible, yet unimaginable, meaning of position as such.)

A second, and more difficult, question is whether that which is pictorially imaginable is *therefore* thinkable, and consequently something that might be accepted, at least in the provisional way of opinion.

If our conclusions in Chapter V, § 8, were not mistaken, much that is imaginable is not a possible decision on evidence. For fancies are imaginable; and, in so far as the conceivable includes the fancied, it is not true that everything fancied is either believed or opined to be possible. It is possible *as a fancy* but need not be considered possible as an object of perception or as a thinkable member of the executive order of the world. The mere fact that in a day-dream we might fancy ourselves Kings of Afghanistan, renouncing European ways, is not a proof that we could ever be definitely and seriously of this opinion, and yet retain our sanity.

Opinion, in short, is a narrower conception than imagination in one way, although in another way there is more logic in it (that is to say, more in the way of evidence) than in pictorial imagination. We might say, indeed, that opinions can not be utterly incredible, at any rate to the opiner, although many fancies may be utterly incredible, even to the fancier. This is not to say that opinion and belief are ultimately the same. It is only to say that an opinion must be a possible candidate for belief. And the mere absence of incredibility is not a sufficient ground for believing, or a usual cause of belief.

§ 4. The Limits of Credulity

Are there, then, any limits to human credulity, or to possible human opinion, other than the proviso that anything believed or opined must have some apparent meaning in the opiner's mind, and that it is not confessed to be frankly fanciful?

There is at least the appearance of prudence in answering this question in the negative. How can we set limits to what *somebody* has opined?

Consider, for example, witchcraft, demonology, and the other superstitions which human beings have not only opined but have believed in the mass for many centuries. Consider "magic, astrology, sorcery, divination, omens, the raising of spirits, auguries, auspices, necromancy, cabalism, oracles, the interpretation of dreams, pythonesses, sibyls, manes, lares, talismans, the presence of demons in flesh and blood, incubi, succubi, familiar lemures, vampirism, possession, lycanthropy, spirits, ghosts, spectres, phantoms, lutins, sylphides, fairies, goblins, the evil eye, enchantments, etc." [8] Consider old wives' tales concerning, in the language of the poet Burns, "devils, ghosts, fairies, brownies, witches, warlocks, spunkies, kelpies, elf-candles, dead-lights, wraiths, apparitions, cantraips, giants, enchanted towers, dragons and other trumpery." Consider the alleged miracles of the early Christian saints and fathers, how St. Hilarion sprinkled the horses of the Christian Italicus with holy water, thereby enabling Italicus to win a chariot race against the pagan duumvir of Gaza, and all the "other trumpery" of this grotesque legend. Consider what St. Augustine regarded as evidence of fact, how he declared that the salamander lives in fire, that the hardest diamonds may be cut by the help of goats' blood, that the flesh of peacocks is incorruptible, how he related that seventy miracles had been wrought by the body of St. Stephen within two years in his own diocese of Hippo, and how he had knowledge of five authentic cases of the restoration of the dead to life. [9]

In the face of these considerations is it possible to allege that there is any limit to human credulity, even among the greatest of mankind?

In the main, these catalogues of signs and wonders refer to an order of belief and of opinion that has ceased to be held by most persons educated in the European tradition at the present day, although not by the majority of the world's inhabitants even now. To pile illustration upon illustration, there-

[8] *Boismont on Hallucinations*, Translation by Hulme, pp. 280 *sq.*
[9] *Cf.* Lecky, *The Rise and Influence of Rationalism in Europe*, p. 163.

fore, should not be more impressive than to proffer a necessarily abbreviated catalogue of the wonders of modern science. In the days before the reign of experimental science, men's beliefs and opinions were not so much pre-logical as pre-experimental, and they had time in which to elaborate their pre-experimental views. We are critical to the extent, and in the way, in which we have been taught to be critical; and so were they. What they accepted on the authority of a saint, a herbalist, or a medicine-man is not in itself more incredible than what we accept on the evidence of a doctor, a psychologist, a physicist, or an astronomer, and it may not be less conformable to the accepted standards of the day. We shall be fortunate indeed if future ages do not have a good deal to say about *our* credulousness; and although future ages, let us hope, will be unable to deny that our prepossession in favor of natural science is much better grounded than the prepossessions of medicine-men, it is not unlikely that our tendency to shut our minds to everything that does not profess to have received experimental proof will call for, and receive, the severest animadversions.

Writing in the middle of last century, Mill pointed out that "the facts of travelling seventy miles an hour, painless surgical operations, and conversing by instantaneous signals between London and New York, held a high place, not many years ago, among reputed impossibilities." [10] The list to-day might be greatly extended; indeed the reputed impossibilities seem to be dwindling every day. This, indeed, is no evidence that the older magics will return. Old women will not learn the more easily to ride upon broomsticks, because the wealthier among them can now be transported by aëroplane at a moderate fee. If the dreams of the alchemists come true, these dreams will not be fulfilled according to the ancient prescriptions of alchemy. Certain ancient superstitions may be revived—and withdrawn from the category of superstition. But more is to be hoped from the enlargement of our outlook than from any reversion to ancient and discarded methods.

To say that anything is utterly incredible is to say that it is met, and that it ought to be met, by a shut mind; and it is rash,

[10] *System of Logic*, Book III, Ch. 25, note.

to say the least, to boast that there are limits to open-mindedness other than the limits of demonstrable impossibility. To insist upon proper caution is quite another thing. An open mind need not be a careless mind, and it is possible to be hospitable without accepting all one's acquaintances as lifelong companions. The range of what is not beyond all conjecture and admits of a wide solution should be as extensive as the canons of proof permit.

BOOK III

THE USUAL CERTAINTIES

CHAPTER VII

CONCERNING CERTAINTY

§ 1. GENERAL

IN this third part of our inquiry, I mean to examine the question: What is it that (as we commonly assert) we know for certain? or, in other words: What is it of which our assurance is asserted by us to be not only complete, but also completely evidenced? The ambitious character of this enterprise is only to be excused by the inexorable demands of the subject. We *have* to examine the usual certainties.

As we have seen, the term "certainty" is not univocal, any more than the term "knowledge" is. "Knowledge" may be a generic or blanket term for cogitation in general, or even for awareness in general (assuming, that is, that cogitation and awareness *are* generic terms), but may also be restricted to "knowing for certain with completely evidenced certainty." And "certainty," similarly, may be a generic term for assurance in general, as when we say, "I am certain," and refer, ostensibly at least, to a state of mind which may, in the main, be even emotional.

Indeed, when we say "This is certain," our statement, although ostensibly factual, is actually in great part epistemic. It is a statement like "This is undoubtedly true," not a statement like "This is red." On the other hand, evidenced certainty is not simply identical with personal assurance, any more than "truth" must mean, quite simply, just what a man "troweth." And it seems better (as we have argued) to speak of "conviction" or of "assurance" when we refer only to psychological trust and confidence without raising the question of the evidence upon which the confidence either is, or is taken to be, based, and to use the term "certainty" only when we mean to imply that the evidence is completely sufficient to justify the assurance.

We might, of course, use other terms not improperly. For example, we might follow Newman in taking "certitude" as the generic term, and in employing "certainty" only for justified gnostic assurance. On the other hand, it would be not less improper to use "certainty" for the first of these senses, and some term like "certified" for the second. Within rather wide limits, in short, it is quite permissible for any author to use these terms in his own way, provided always that he explains his choice and abides by it.

We are asking, then, with Locke, where certainty, *real certainty,* is to be found, and are not to be put off with what *passes* for certain, or with what, for practical purposes, is *accounted* certain, in the law courts, say, or in daily life. Similarly, we are not to be put off with what, for scientific purposes, is accounted certain, e.g. with what is, *de facto,* accepted or unchallenged "proof" in physiology or geology or history, according to the prevailing and modish standards of those sciences. What passes for certainty in this way is just what is not disputed so long as the discussion retains a certain argumentative level. On the contrary, the circumstance with which we are now concerned is that there is always a tendency for any discussion to become metaphysical under stress, that is to say, to become uneasy unless it examines its own foundations in a more thoroughgoing fashion than the accepted traditions or conventions of the type of discussion are accustomed to contemplate.

Pilate's "What is truth?" for example, need not have been spoken in jest or in any spirit of levity. Pilate was satisfied (we may infer from the record) that his prisoner did not claim to be the King of the Jews in a way that was literally seditious, and that the "truth" which Christ had come into the world to proclaim was not an entity that the law-courts had legitimately to deal with. Pilate need not, on the other hand, be supposed to have denied that there was such an entity to think about. And similarly, if notions such as Cause or Substance seem, within any science, to demand examination on their proper merits, the stage of metaphysics has been reached, whether or not it is a "science" that has thus become metaphysical.

In any ultimate analysis, nothing can be *certain* in the metaphysical sense unless it is able, with complete success, to defend itself from attacks from every quarter; and there are so many quarters from which objection may be raised that it may seem impossibly dogmatic, *ab initio*, to assert that anything whatsoever is so utterly certain that it always must prevail in every conceivable conflict. Even if a "certainty" has prevailed in the past in all its serious encounters—and truly enormous erudition might seem to be required in order to establish such a point—what of the future? May not some new revolution or hyper-Einsteinism upset all our present certainties?

On the other hand, it seems at least equally extravagant to suggest or to suspect that nobody knows, and that nobody ever has known, anything whatsoever for certain. If we made this suggestion because of evidence, would we not be relying upon the *negative* evidence? What seemed the plainest truths, we say when we argue in this vein, frequently have been seen to have a flaw in them, or at least have gone out of favor because a flaw seemed likely. In the first of these cases, we allege ourselves to know for certain that there was a flaw, and therefore we do assert that we know *something* for certain. Even in the second case we do the same thing; for we affirm that we know for certain that this or the other specific tenet was at one time accepted as unshakable by a great many people, whereas, at a later date, it appeared to many to be very shaky. The change in the fashion is *something;* and, contrary to the hypothesis, is declared to be known for certain.

In short, there is still vitality in the age-long refutation of scepticism, that to assert that you know that you don't know anything at all *is* a contradiction, and that to suspect that you don't know anything at all can not be justified by logical evidence. The statement "I tell you I'm a liar," it is true, may be one of a series of "paradoxes" not all of which can be false. It may be similar, for example, in its logical type, to the true statement "All propositions are either true or false," which is itself a proposition. The statement, however, "I know that I know nothing," is not on a par with the conceivable statement of an omniscient being that such a being knows that he knows everything (including this statement of omniscience). The former is a contradiction, and the latter, although the explaining of it may need some logical ingenuity, is not a contradiction. That is the difference between them.

Apart from this venerable elench, however, it is surely plain that past failure, in directions not formerly suspect, is not a sufficient proof of necessary failure everywhere, that the necessity for modification due to imprecision of statement does not deny that *something* is known. And so forth. It is at least as hard to deny that nothing is known for certain, as to prove that the more stubborn of the usual certainties are not known for certain. Hence our problem.

§ 2. Certainty and Infallibility

It is sometimes said that any one who claims that he knows anything for certain thereby claims, *pro hac vice*, to be infallible; and that no mortal beneath the moon has any right to make any such claim.

This is an excellent example of the way in which we may cheat ourselves with abstract terms. To say that no man is infallible is just to say that every man sometimes makes mistakes, or is liable to do so; and this statement is far too general to be informative upon the specific point in question. We admit that Simpkins is not infallible, but deny that his general fallibility is a sufficient proof that he never knows anything at all. Simpkins, for instance, may not have an infallible memory for cards, and may even be a nuisance in the card-room for that very reason. It does not follow, however, that he is liable to be mistaken if he believes that the bed in which he is lying does not contain a baby hippopotamus. Similarly, he may be liable to illusions. Like the rest of us, he may exaggerate the size of a lamp-post in a fog. But this is no evidence that he has made a mistake about the absence of the baby hippopotamus.

To be infallible is to be incapable of error; and to be infallible in some special way is to be incapable of error in that special way. This is not our problem. We are not asking whether the man is never wrong, but are asking whether he is ever right. To speak of "infallibility" is a mere confusion of the issue.

§ 3. Concerning "Human" Knowledge

We have to remark, once again, that it is easy to misstate the problems now confronting us. Thus it is usual to ask, "What do *we* know for certain?"—the thinker, as it were, trying to sweep all humanity along with him, or, at the least, proclaiming himself a perfect representative of the human race in this particular. We seem to be asking, in other words, what it is (if anything) that every human being at all times has known for certain.

Plainly, any such view is wholly impossible. There are no materials for an exhaustive survey, by enumeration, of the common knowledge of the human race at all times; and since it is plain, in every field, that men come to know what formerly they did not know, it also appears to be manifest that we should not dogmatize concerning the flashes of illumination that "must" come in every one's way. Again, if we speak of universal human knowledge, we perplex ourselves, from the outset, with problems concerning boundaries—when men became men and ceased to be apes, when a child's intelligence passes into maturity, whether morons and defectives are to be counted as "men." It is foolish to incur these perplexities gratuitously.

To take a slightly different point, if we say that a man *knows* such and such, we imply that he can not now doubt it, even tentatively, whatever may have been true of his past history. Therefore, in asking whether this or that is *known*, we may embarrass ourselves unnecessarily if we permit the interpretation that we are asking about something that no one, or at any rate no sane person, has ever doubted. The truth, on the contrary, is that if we hold that anything is certain, all we have to hold is that, if any one doubts it, he is wrong and can be shown to be so. Even if it were maintained that any one who knows therefore knows that he knows, it would also have to be explained that many knowers have an amazing capacity for persuading themselves, temporarily at least, into the unknowing of much that they habitually know, and can contrive to raise and entertain doubts where they feel none. This is generally due to extraneous questions masquerading as relevant difficulties. But whatever the explanation, the fact is quite apparent.

§ 4. "Philosophic" Doubt

For the most part, when people are asked to distinguish between what they really know, on the one hand, and what, on the other hand, they are merely disposed to pass without question, they commonly become pretty cautious; but it is possible that a slight acquaintance with Descartes's "philosophic doubt" may make them over-cautious.

As Dr. Carr has recently reminded us,[1] Molière's Don Juan gives a faithful picture of the effect of Descartes's philosophy upon certain minds. When Sganarelle pressed Don Juan to declare what, in the end, he took to be completely certain, Don Juan replied that he believed that two and two made four, and that four and four made eight. Beyond the plainest kind of plain arithmetic Don Juan was not prepared to go.

To be sure, Descartes himself would not have said what Don Juan said in the play, although it may be doubted whether Descartes would have impressed Sganarelle much more than Sganarelle's master did. Descartes himself built up an elaborate system, much of which he professed to demonstrate in the strictest sense of demonstration. He began with the *Cogito*—"I think, hence I am"—and, although it may not seem very much to profess to demonstrate that at least I must exist in order to doubt my own existence (or anything else), it is at any rate a good deal more than simple arithmetic.

"There is but one perfectly indefectible truth," William James once wrote, "and that is the truth that pyrrhonistic scepticism itself leaves standing—the truth that the present phenomenon of consciousness exists."[2] If a skeptic admitted even this—and it is considerably less than Descartes's *Cogito*—he might be constrained, supposing that he also accepted the rules of logical inference, to admit very much more, although, in all probability, not enough. He would not be compelled to fall back, in good order, upon the multiplication table.

[1] *The New Idealist Movement in Philosophy,* pp. 4 *sq.*
[2] *The Will to Believe,* pp. 14 *sq.*

Let us try, however, to consider these matters in a more comprehensive way.

§ 5. CONCERNING MR. G. E. MOORE'S VIEWS

Mr. G. E. Moore's essay entitled "A Defence of Common Sense" contains an important series of observations upon the nature of certainty, and also upon the usual certainties. These observations form an admirably pertinent introduction to the present part of our theme.

Premising that "in his own opinion" he *knows* a number of propositions "with certainty, to be true," [3] Mr. Moore proceeds to explain that he and nearly all other philosophers, notwithstanding what some of the others may say, must really be in agreement concerning such propositions.

As a sample of what (in his opinion) Mr. Moore knows for certain to be true, we are given the following:

"There exists at present a living human body, which is *my* body. This body was born at a certain time in the past, and has existed continuously ever since, though not without undergoing changes; it was, for instance, much smaller when it was born, and for some time afterwards, than it is now. Ever since it was born, it has been either in contact with or not far from the surface of the earth; and, at every moment since it was born, there have also existed many other things, having shape and size in three dimensions (in the same familiar sense in which it has), from which it has been *at various distances* (in the familiar sense in which it is now at a distance both from that mantelpiece and from that book-case, and at a greater distance from the book-case than it is from the mantel-piece); also there have (very often at all events) existed some other things of this kind with which it was *in contact* (in the familiar sense in which it is now in contact with the pen I am holding in my right hand and with some of the clothes I am wearing). . . ." [4]

In short, each human being knows several familiar propositions *for certain* concerning his body, its spatial, temporal, and material environment, as well as concerning his own mind and experience.

These statements explaining what we know for certain, we are further informed, must be taken to be absolutely, not partially, true, and must be understood in the "ordinary" or in the "familiar" sense, not in any recondite, esoteric, philosophical

[3] *Contemporary British Philosophy*, Second Series.   [4] *Ibid.*, p. 194.

sense. Moreover, each of *us* knows these things with regard to himself, and accordingly knows himself to be a member of a class of human beings all of whom have such knowledge.

What, then (Mr. Moore asks), are we to make of the facts (1) that many philosophers have denied the reality of time, bodies, space, and much else that Mr. Moore (in his own opinion) knows with certainty to be true, or (2) that other philosophers, apparently more modestly and more cautiously, have denied that they *know* these things, while admitting that they *believe* most of them, perhaps with well-grounded assurance.

Regarding (1), Mr. Moore (as I understand him) says that a philosopher *is* a person who has a living human body born upon the earth, etc. Therefore, if there were no bodies on the earth there would be no philosophers. Therefore, if a philosopher denies these truisms he is denying his own existence, which is absurd. The case is still worse if any philosopher denies that "we" know these things. For "we" are human beings who were born, etc.

Mr. Moore further explains (a) that because these propositions are true, it can not also be true that they lead to contradictory conclusions, and (b) that Time, Space, and the rest *might* not have been real, but in fact are real. In favor of their being real Mr. Moore has, he thinks, "no better argument than simply this" [5]—that the propositions he enunciates are true.

(2) The view that we may *believe*, but do not *know*, that Space, Time, and the like exist is, we are told, self-contradictory, because any such belief implies the *knowledge* that there are believers "in the familiar sense." The proposition, "Each of us believes but can not know that other human beings exist," is self-contradictory, because it implies that there are many human beings, and that the human being who has the belief knows that there are other believers.

Superficially, this type of argument bears an undeniable resemblance to what is commonly called dogmatism. When Mr. J. G. Vance, for instance, quotes the "Filosophia fundamental" of the Spaniard, Jaime Balmes, as "the code of an unflinching dogmatist," he is quoting something that, verbally at least, is

[5] *Contemporary British Philosophy, Second Series*, p. 204.

very hard to distinguish from much that Mr. Moore says. Thus we read the following in Mr. Vance's excerpts from Balmes: "That bodies exist is a fact that no man of sane mind can doubt. . . . Explain it, perhaps, we cannot: but we certainly cannot deny it: we submit to it as to an inevitable necessity. . . . Philosophy should begin by explaining, not by disputing, the fact of certainty. . . . A thoroughgoing sceptic would be insane, and that too with insanity of the highest grade. . . . Certainty is to us a happy necessity: nature imposes it, and philosophers do not cast off nature. . . . There never was, in all the rigour of the word, a true sceptic." [6]

Perhaps it is a good thing to be dogmatic. In the alternative, very likely, Mr. Moore (as we shall see) is much less dogmatic than he seems to be. On the other hand, Mr. Moore's qualification that "in his own opinion" he knows these propositions is at the best a very slight qualification and at the worst (as Cook Wilson maintained) a flat contradiction. Again, any one who says, "Of course there are Space and Time and Material Bodies," seems to be affirming impenitently what Leibniz, Berkeley, Hegel, and McTaggart stoutly denied for reasons that can not be ignored even if they may be overcome. And to say, "I define a human being as one who possesses an animate body born upon the earth at a particular date," is surely an odd answer to those who assert, "What you call being born, being in contact with cradles and rattles and swaddling clothes, etc., can not be what you say it is, because there can not really be Space, or Time, or Material."

This, however, is not Mr. Moore's point of view. We have to distinguish, he says, between two utterly different questions, viz. (a) whether we understand the meaning of the statement that we have bodies, etc. (this, he says, we all certainly do understand) and (b) whether we are able to give a correct analysis of this meaning [7] (a task, he thinks, almost always of the utmost difficulty). In other words, Mr. Moore combines an apparent dogmatism concerning the first type of question with extreme hesitation concerning the second type. "I hold," he says, "that the proposition 'There are and have been material things'

---

[6] *Reality and Truth*, pp. 51 sq.   [7] *Op. cit.*, p. 198.

is quite certainly true, but that the question how this proposition is to be analysed is one to which no answer that has been hitherto given is anywhere near certainly true." [8] And he even says, "We are all, I think, in this strange position that we do *know* many things, with regard to which we *know* further that we must have had evidence for them, and yet we do not know *how* we know them, i.e. we do not know what the evidence was." [9]

Is it possible, seriously, to accept this position?

Concerning the minor question whether those who attempt to avoid dogmatism by asserting that they only believe, but do not profess to know, the usual certainties, are in reality contradicting themselves by asserting probabilities which *imply* definite knowledge, we may comment somewhat as follows. If we know that a belief is widely entertained, we know, *ex hypothesi*, that there are many believers; and similarly, if we know that all believers have living human bodies, it follows that we must know that many living human bodies exist. Again, if we know that living human bodies are spatio-temporal continuants in a spatio-temporal world, we know, *ex hypothesi*, that there is space, and time, and a world.

If, on the other hand, I only believe that such beliefs are widely entertained, I need only maintain (as I might maintain without contradiction) that, to the best of my belief, although not to my certain knowledge, there are other believers whom I believe to hold certain views concerning what I believe they call space and time and matter. If I assert these things about Mr. Moore and his beliefs I may, no doubt, contradict myself by asserting the existence of Mr. Moore's beliefs as well as the existence of my own. But if I am careful I need not make this slip.

The major and more intricate question, however, is whether it is possible to accept Mr. Moore's contention that we may know, with complete certainty, that propositions like "Mr. Moore was born" or "Mr. Moore's hat is on his head" are true in their ordinary and familiar sense, although we can not expect to be able to make more than a tentative approach towards explaining with precision what the correct analysis of such state-

[8] *Reality and Truth*, pp. 222 *sq.*   [9] *Ibid.*, p. 206.

ments is. If Mr. Moore had held only that we have excellent reasons for believing that *some* intelligible and ultimately defensible meaning is to be found in such statements and that the principal occupation of sound philosophy is to search for such a defensible meaning, his contention would have been much less startling. As it is, he makes the bolder assertion that we know, and know that we know, without knowing (and perhaps without being able to conjecture) the analytical implications of what we know.

If we say that there is an ordinary and familiar meaning of Time, Space, or Material, we imply that many conscious beings do mean one and the same thing by Time, or by Space, or by Material. There is surely a question, however, whether this is true in fact; and Mr. Moore, in explaining the matter, seems content to affirm that he means the sort of thing that is meant by saying that a mantelpiece is above a fender in most rooms, or that apples ripen after the apple-blossom is shed. It may be doubted, however, whether any such alleged explanation is really an explanation at all.

It seems to be the very type of "definition" against which Socrates protested. For example, Socrates explained to Euthyphro in the celebrated dialogue that piety could not be defined as the sort of thing Euthyphro was then about to do, i.e. to prosecute his father for incurring the pollution of homicide.

This matter deserves inquiry. The word "piety" presumably meant *something* to Euthyphro, and this *something* probably corresponded pretty closely to what Socrates meant by it, because both, in the main, would agree to call certain actions decidedly impious and certain other actions decidedly pious. Suppose, however, that a doubtful case arose, as in the accusation of impiety that Meletus was about to bring against Socrates in the law-courts. Socrates could not believe that he himself was guilty of impiety, but many of the jury might believe that very thing. According to Socrates, it was necessary to *know* what piety was, not merely to be able to describe it without obvious absurdity as "the sort of thing that. . . ." And the matter, according to Socrates, was of some little importance, since Socrates's life depended upon the verdict at the trial.

According to Socrates, if he and his judges knew what impiety essentially was, they could then determine with precision whether or not Socrates had been guilty of impiety, but if they only "knew" the sort of thing impiety sometimes was they would grope helplessly in a maze of confusing examples. And Socrates was forced to conclude that Euthyphro could not tell him (because he did not know) what impiety was, and that he, Socrates, did not know either, although he had a better understanding of the point than Euthyphro had, with much less pretence and arrogance.

This parable seems very apposite. Is it really credible that everybody knows what space is, according to an "ordinary" meaning, if all that such "knowers" can say about their "knowledge" is that they mean the sort of thing that is meant by saying that one's hat is on one's head, or that the eaves of a house are above its foundations?

I can not think the point at all obvious. It is possible to hold, no doubt, that Socrates and Euthyphro both knew *the* meaning of piety, although neither of them could explain quite accurately (and Euthyphro very inaccurately) what they both meant. Even on this supposition, I think, it would be contrary to sound sense, and even to common sense, to affirm that such knowledge was accurately described by such a name. If they knew for certain, why should they boggle at doubtful cases? Why should there be any doubtful cases at all? Could they really know in some cases and not in others, if there was no logical reason for restricting the knowledge to such particular cases? Would that not be like saying that some one may know that this 2 and this 2 make this 4, without knowing what the sum of 2 and 2 is?

The alternative analysis would be that each of them held vaguish opinions on the point (yielding approximate agreement in their use of the word "piety"), and that each of them could, by reflection, greatly improve the exactitude of such opinions. This would include the possibility that there *was* a single meaning of piety, and perhaps a common or ordinary meaning that each of them could ascertain if each reflected upon the point with an assiduity not wholly beyond the capacity of human nature. It would deny, however, that either of them, at the time just before the trial of Socrates, actually did know "the" meaning of piety.

Is it quite certain that this alternative analysis is false?

Speaking of time, St. Augustine said, "Si non rogas, intelligo." This statement of the Bishop of Hippo is so similar to the Cambridge professor's that we may be excused for dwelling upon it in this connection.

Several interpretations may be put upon Augustine's assertion. Let us consider some of them.

(1) What might be meant is that time is unique, as well as fundamental, and so that it is impossible to explain time in terms of anything else. As well attempt to explain color to a blind man or beauty to Peter Bell.

This type of consideration must always be kept in mind. It is easy to be too clever and to demand the impossible in our explanations. There may be much that is plain of itself; and there is much that, if it is not plain of itself, is not plain at all. We may have to train ourselves to accept the unique for what it is. But what is unique or quite singular *need not* be plain to see; and we need not know what it is just because it somehow confronts us.

(2) Augustine may have meant that he knew what time was, but could not tell his hearers all about it. He apprehended time and its nature, but was ignorant of, or did not care to argue with precision about, its context, conditions, and remoter implications. It is quite permissible to distinguish in this way between our knowledge *of* time and our knowledge *about* time. It is also permissible to maintain that we may know the former, but be very ignorant indeed concerning the latter.

(3) Augustine may have meant, and probably did mean to assert, a part of what Mr. Moore means, viz. that he knew what time is although he was unable to express his meaning with precision when asked to give an analysis of time.

Here, I think, we must distinguish. Precise, unambiguous expression is an art that needs practice. Accordingly, in any ordinary sense, it is possible for a man to know something or other perfectly well and yet to be unable to describe what he knows with technical art. If, as seems likely, the logician's or the philosopher's art has to be learned by practice in the schools, it should be usual for the laity to understand much that they can not express either according to the etiquette or according to the more serious requirements of the schools.

We have all, of course, acquired a certain art of self-expression because we can all speak, but if we have learned only the art of common speech, we need not be expected to have learned the art of philosophical speech, and so may be tripped, *secundum artem*, when we are not really confused at all.

Apart from this question of technique, however, I think it should be assumed that a man who knows can also *say* what he knows; and that if he says anything badly or inaccurately, at any rate after due consideration, he does *not* know what is meant by that thing. We should distrust these fountains of verity who can never express anything even tolerably veracious. Therefore,

(4) We have the possible interpretation (which is the main part of Mr. Moore's) that we know Time although we can not think Time out with sufficient clearness, especially in our analytical thinking.

Let us return to Socrates and Euthyphro. It may be argued (a) that both of them knew there was such a thing as piety although neither of them knew what piety was or (b) that, although they both knew what piety was, neither of them knew its essence (if it had one) in the way in which they both knew the three-sidedness and the rectilinear character of a triangle.

(a) The former point, that we know *that* x is, although we do not know *what* x is, is a familar distinction in philosophy that is not without its difficulties. Frequently, it does not seem distinguishable from saying that we know there is something that has the character x, although we do not know the character of the thing that has this character x. The trouble in this case is that x *is* the disputed character. So far, therefore, there is nothing, as Hegel said, more easily known.[10] Our statement, therefore, is intelligible only if we mean that we do not know any of the thing's characters *besides* x. And that is a very different statement indeed.

[10] *Smaller Logic* (Wallace's translation), p. 92.

For the most part, those who argue in this vein mean yet a third thing. They mean, e.g. that we know that there is freedom, although we do not know how freedom can come about, or be a characteristic of the world, or be consistent with the many necessitated things we know to occur in the world. In this case, the distinction is between knowing "that" and understanding "how," rather than between knowing "that" and knowing "what."

(b) As we have seen, if we know that there is piety, we must also, in one sense, know what piety is. For it is piety. It might be contended, however, that what happens in most instances thus described is only that we use the word piety to signify, not some meaning clearly known, but a number of things resembling one another more or less closely.

The view we are now considering offers precisely the opposite interpretation. Piety, we are informed, has one and only one meaning. Socrates, by self-communing or by a dialogue with Euthyphro, might *elicit* this single essence of piety. And what he elicits must be already present, although disguised. *The* meaning of piety acts, as modern psychologists would say, as a "control" or as a "censor," whether through the Platonic reminiscence of eternal verities or otherwise. And Mr. Moore says the same thing, although without any Platonic myth to help him. "It is obvious," he says, "that we cannot even raise the question how what we do understand by (some given expression) is to be analysed, unless we do understand it." [11]

Of this I can only say that I am not satisfied. Let us put the matter thus. Socrates and Euthyphro, let us say, do not really know the meaning of piety for certain, but agree in the conviction that there is something that the word piety ought to indicate and, for the most part, does indicate pretty clearly. They attempt, therefore, to make these indications quite precise, and in doing so come to a clearer and fuller understanding of piety. It surely does not follow that they have actually possessed this fuller understanding all along; and it does not seem quite certain that they knew the meaning of piety before they had this fuller understanding. To clear contradictory rubbish away, to notice

[11] *Op. cit.*, p. 199.

what is irrelevant to piety although frequently not considered irrelevant, may enable the vision to flash upon them; but that is no evidence that they always possessed this clear vision although it was also obscured, for a time, by mists and clouds.

In any case, it seems difficult to hold that Mr. Moore is entirely consistent in all that he says and still more difficult to deny that some restrictions must be put upon his argument, although he himself does not mention any such restriction.

Mr. Moore insists that the obvious implications of a plain statement must be admitted to be known along with our knowledge of what is directly asserted in the statement. He maintains, for example, that any one who says, "We all believe," must be admitted to know that others have bodies as well as he. Psychologically, this statement is very dubious. It is possible to miss such implications, and Mr. Moore says that many philosophers *have* missed the point. If so, they did not know it. But if these obvious implications are to be admitted into such knowledge, why should we stop short, and deny the knowledge of so many other analytical implications?

Mr. Moore says that we know that there was good evidence, e.g. of our birth, although we may not know what the good evidence was. We have lost our birth certificates, so to say, and can not recover them; and there are now no living witnesses of our birth. If so, the evidence seems to be inductive, and it is generally held that inductive evidence is not quite certain. Does Mr. Moore seriously mean to assert that it is? And if being born (among philosophers) means being born of human parents, is it not worth while pointing out that some human beings were once born of prehuman parents? We can not *define* a man as one who was born of human parents.

In such cases, we can give a *better* reason for our "knowledge" than simply the fact that we do "know" them. We are also aware, however, that inductive evidence of this kind is frequently not conclusive, and that it is difficult to assert that it can ever be completely conclusive. Hence, in such cases, we do not know for certain.

CHAPTER VIII

THE LAWS OF THOUGHT

§ 1. INTRODUCTORY

ACCORDING to a rough but serviceable division, the objects of human knowledge may be classified into those which are highly general, abstract, formal, or *a priori*, on the one hand, and those which are particular, concrete, "material," or *a posteriori*, on the other hand. This division, question-begging though it be, should suffice for the purposes of preliminary demarcation; and so we may turn, in the first instance, to the commonly accepted certainties that are highly formal and very general.

The chief of these, in the general estimate, are logic, arithmetic, and geometry, the latter pair being sufficiently representative of what is called "pure" mathematics. This trio, therefore, may be regarded as affording adequate examples of the usual claims to formal certainty. Since rational certainty of a formal type has also, however, been claimed very persistently in connection with the formal or intuitional part of ethics, it seems expedient to append a discussion of ethical intuitionism.

§ 2. "FORMAL" LOGIC

We begin, then, with logic, and have to ask whether there is such a thing as complete and final logical certainty.

Writing at the close of the eighteenth century, Kant declared that the science of logic had been complete since the time of Aristotle and that it could not permit of addition.[1] Even in Kant's day, however, and before it, this statement might have been questioned. For example, the Cartesian authors of the *Port Royal Logic* would not have assented to it; and the post-Aristotelian accretions to logic (such as the additions due to Porphyry or to Proclus) did not clarify what Aristotle said.

[1] *Critique of Pure Reason.* Preface to the Second Edition.

Traditional logic, indeed (as we have remarked on an earlier page), contains a somewhat amorphous collection of debates partly grammatical (e.g. much in the doctrine of terms), partly practical (e.g. a series of "tips" to avoid fallacies), partly metaphysical (e.g. the doctrine of the categories and of the predicables), and only partly "formal."

We are now concerned with the formal part of the subject, and shall deal in the present chapter with the Laws of Thought. In the next chapter we shall deal with the nature of inference.

The Laws of Thought are commonly said to be three in number, viz.

The Law of Identity: If anything is A, it is A.

The Law of Contradiction: If anything is A, it can not also be non-A.

The Law of Excluded Middle: Everything must either have the property A, or not have it. *Tertium non datur.*

§ 3. The Law of Identity: General Considerations

The Law of Identity obviously seems indisputable. Nevertheless, a skeptical *advocatus diaboli* would have something to say about it.

He might, in the first place, invite us to explain its meaning. In what sense, he might ask, is it a law of *thought?* Is it a psychological law describing our mental processes, and in that case do we know for certain what our mental processes are? If we are supposed to know our mental processes by introspection, has not introspection become suspect in these days?

Since the law is not a piece of psychological description—for we infringe it whenever we contradict ourselves, as we do "at least once a day"—it has to be said that the law is normative, not positive, that is to say, that it is a law according to which we ought to think, not a law according to which we invariably do think.

But what does "ought" mean? Is it a moral duty, or what sort of duty? And is it absolutely certain that there is such a thing as duty at all? If, again, we say that the Law of Identity is a law of "true" or of "right" thinking, have we not to show what "truth" is or to explain what "right" in these matters can possibly be or mean? And does not the law hold even in cases in which the question of "truth" may be left by the wayside? A politician M, let us say, objects to the proposal of a politician G, asserting that G's plan implies a loan that, like all loans, will simply fatten the Shylocks of industry; and straightway proposes the raising of another loan himself. It is unnecessary, in such cases, to consider the truth of M's objection to G. True or false, M ought to stick to it in his own case if he applies it to G.

A simple way, perhaps the simplest way, of putting this point is to say with Mr. Johnson that "the function of formal logic . . . is not permissive but rather prohibitive"; [2] and this enables us to state the Law of Identity in a form to which it is at least very hard to take exception. So formulated, the Law states that whenever we attempt to hink about anything, we know in advance that the thing must be precisely what it is and can not be other than it is. We need not know, completely and fully, what "truth" is, or what psychology is, or what "right" means, in order to see, with complete confidence, that at least *this* preliminary requirement must be fulfilled. Our thoughts must *somewhere* deal with nonentities, if the "objects" to which they refer turn out sometimes to be and sometimes not to be what, according to us, they are.

§4. TIME AND CONTEXT

Assuming that the devil's advocate has now to alter his tactics, he may be expected to raise difficulties concerning time and context.

In the statement "Everything is what it is," the word "is" need not, of course, be confined to the present tense. The Law does not affirm that everything is what it was, or that everything is what it will be. On the contrary, if tense is introduced, it states that everything was what it was (at some given time) and that everything will be what it will be (at some particular date in the future). Again, the Law is fully competent to deal with timeless relationships. For example, the number 3 "is" (timelessly or tenselessly) greater than the number 2.

According to certain philosophers, an alternative statement of
[2] *Logic,* Part I, p. 222.

the Law of Identity is "Once true, always true." In other words, the time of assertion is stated to be irrelevant to the character of that about which the assertion is made.

This principle, of course, does not imply that what is true of anything at *any* given moment is true of it at *every* moment. If I say, "It is raining," meaning to say that rain is falling at the time I am making the assertion, I am not saying that rain is always falling—even in Scotland. What is meant is simply that the characteristics of any event are always completely determinate, so that, when any occurrence is sufficiently and unambiguously designated, then, whatever is determinately true of it, *is* true, irrespective of the time at which we think of the determinately true characteristics of the occurrence.

While I can not personally doubt the Law as thus stated, many people aver that they do; and therefore there is a certain risk in claiming utter certainty for this statement of the Law. For many people assert that what is past (i.e. earlier than the moment of assertion) is nothing, and also that what is future (i.e. later than that moment) is also nothing. According to this philosophy of time, therefore, we are entitled, at any moment, to make assertions only about what occurs at that moment, but otherwise are condemned to make assertions about *nothing*. Therefore, if we speak at 10 P. M. about a sunset that occurred at 7 P. M., we are saying of *nothing* that it had the properties of a sunset.

As I say, I cannot accept this view of time, which seems to me to neglect time's elementary properties and to leave the word "moment" without meaning. Since the view is commonly held, however, and is even held to be *certain* in some quarters, it is necessary to point out the possibility of a conflict of (alleged) certainties in this matter.

Another interpretation of the Law is "True for me, true for all," or, in other words, that truth is not concerned with the private affairs of any one who knows the truth. This also appears to me to be certain, but it is hotly disputed by many philosophers for reasons they assert to be good reasons. Moreover, it is very frequently qualified by persons who do not deny it utterly. Granting that truth can not depend upon Smith or

Robinson, these philosophers say, it implies at least *some* knower, or perhaps a universal knower; and therefore they infer that Smith and Robinson belong to a collection, at least one member of which is indispensable, or, in the alternative, are consubstantial with the indispensable universal knower.

Both of the above enunciations of the Law may be said to assert the irrelevance, in certain determinate ways, of our psychological context in any assertion. The first states that truth is independent of the temporal context of the person who asserts it, the second that truth is wholly independent of the person who makes the assertion. Can we, then, go further and maintain that truth is *always* independent of its context, and that things are what they are *in spite of* the rest of the universe?

It is a presupposition of ordinary logic that any true proposition is absolutely and finally true, and also that any such proposition is, in a certain sense, a self-contained unit. If, for example, a proposition is proved to be true because it follows from grounds that are true, the proposition is true, not relatively to its grounds, but absolutely. This is the logical Principle of Assertion, and it implies a certain atomicity or pluralism of truths.

This principle is therefore disputed by all logical monists, who hold that there is no truth short of the whole truth, or, in other words, that every so-called truth is relative to its context, unless that context be The Whole. The major difficulty here is that "*x*-relatively-to-*y*" is an entire entity and therefore, that the-truth-of-something-particular-relative-to-its-partial-context is, according to the theory, true (i.e. absolutely true) and yet something that falls short of The Whole. Again, and more simply, the doctrine itself is partial and very abstract. Consequently, by hypothesis, it is not "true."

These are very serious objections to logical monism; but it can not be denied that any one who asserts that logical monism is quite certainly false has eminent authority against him, although he has authority not less eminent on his side. Another conflict of alleged certainties seems, therefore, impending.

§ 5. The Identity of Propositions

The Law of Identity may refer primarily to terms or to things. As Bishop Butler said, "Everything is what it is," or, as F. Jammes said, "Une chose est cela qui n'est pas autre chose." The Law, however, is stated in the form of a proposition, and it is a law of propositions in such formulations as "once true, always true."

Accordingly, those who are in quest of certainty have to consider whether there may not be something dubious about the whole propositional way of looking at things.

A proposition is sometimes regarded as the verbal expression of a judgment. If so, it is subject to all the unavoidable difficulties that attach to the use of words, and also to the criticism (if this be sustained) that knowledge and judgment may be quite different.[3] It is unnecessary, however, to define a proposition in such a way as to be forced to meet these criticisms. We may regard it simply as something propounded, perhaps quite wordlessly, to which we may assent as being true, or which we may reject as being false.

According to the traditional logic, the main types of assent are those in which (1) a character is assigned to a logical subject, or (2) a logical subject is included in a certain class. The latter type, however, is less important than the former. We speak of the "class" of horses as if we were referring to an actual collection of them in a paddock. That is not the nature of a logical paddock, or class, because the class "horse," in logic, is defined, not as a collection, but as anything which has, or may have, a distinctive and complete equine nature.

The important case, therefore, is the possession of a certain property, say, the equine property. *A* is *B*, that is to say *A* has the character, or more generally, the property *B*. (In this language, a "character" is always an attribute, but a "property" may be a relational property.)

Is there, then, anything seriously dubious about this logical way of looking at things?

The main ground of objection, variously formulated, is that

[3] *Cf.* Chapter IV, §6, on Cook Wilson's views.

propositions are always distinct from reality, and are therefore a little aloof from what we expect to discover in the real. In the proposition, it is said, our mental capacities work upon fact, dissect it, and reconstitute (with additions) something that expresses fact but is not identical with fact. In the process, Mr. Johnson suggests,[4] something may be lost. Somewhat more generally it may be held that a proposition is thought's reconstruction, and that thought, often a bungler, may never be wholly successful. In a *fact* there is no room for error. There is just the fact. But propositions may be false; and the artifice in them may destroy any proper claim to our complete allegiance.

In assenting to a proposition we always assent to something more than a proposition, viz. to the state of fact (whether general or particular) that the proposition signifies. (By "fact" I mean "reality," for example, sausages or marmalade, not "the fact that" there are sausages or marmalade for breakfast, where "the fact that" is propositional.) A proposition that does not signify some fact (in this sense of fact) is only a fainéant proposition which does not perform propositional functions. Hence, if the Law of Identity is *only* a law of propositions and not also a law of what propositions signify, it is scarcely a law even of propositions. Yet, if we do not know precisely what we signify when we use the Law, what business have we to proclaim its invincible certainty?

These doubts, if they may be called such, are so vague in their complaint that it is difficult to take them very seriously. On the other hand, if it could be shown that there are elements of weakness or of vagueness in the structure of every proposition, it would be prudent to hesitate in this matter.

Here specific doubts may be raised concerning the status of universals and the status of relational properties in propositions. Every proposition of the traditional type, it may be said, asserts either a universal or a relational property, and there are solid obstacles in the way of accepting either of these assertions.

[4] *Op. cit.,* Part I, p. 16.

§ 6. Universals

To the ordinary, unsophisticated view, nourished upon the firm traditions of European speech, nothing seems plainer than the apparent fact that different things may have precisely the same quality. Take, for instance, the stock illustration of whiteness. In a celebrated chapter in *Moby Dick* [5] we are conducted through a world of white things, all of them having the same general quality as Captain Ahab's albino whale: the whiteness of marbles, japonicas, and pearls, the white elephants on the banners of the grand old kings of Pegu or of the modern kings of Siam, the white stone with which the Romans marked a joyful day, the snow-white bull in which Jove was incarnated, the whiteness of albs and tunics, the white bear of the poles and the white shark of the tropics, the White Steed of the prairies, white friars and white nuns, the snow-howdahed Andes, and the White Hoods of Ghent. All these things are said to be characterized by the same livid pallor, and, although certain distinctions might be drawn between milk-white, snow-white, creamy-white, and the like, there is no doubt in the ordinary mind that one and the same character of whiteness belongs to several different things.

Obviously, the same *word* is used of them all. We say that Congreve was witty, that Goldsmith was witty, that S. L. Clemens was witty. But is there not an individual flavor in the wit of each that no one is likely to confuse? And if this is the truth concerning *some* so-called universals, why should we be forbidden to hold that, in the last analysis, it is true of all? If an inch of linen is equal to an inch of silk, and a yard of twine equal to a yard of pitch-pine, may not each of these equalities be an individual entity?

Let us look at this matter in another way. In the main, there are two sets of instances to consider, viz. (1) the relation (to use Mr. Johnson's language) [6] between a determinable and its determinates, and (2) the relation between a completely determinate quality (if there is one) and the things that have the quality. Thus, color is an instance of (1); for to be colored is to be red, or

* Ch. xlii.   * *Op. cit.*, Part I, Ch. xi.

green, or orange, or mauve, etc.; but, as an instance of (2), we have or seem to have precisely the same shade of red, let us say, in British penny stamps, British pillar-boxes, certain British uniforms, and the like.

Regarding (1) it may fairly be argued (may it not?) that there is no such thing as being colored in general, but that every actual color is a color fully individuated. Determinables are only determin*ables*, mere potencies of colors, not anything real in the way of color. Has a penny stamp *three* different characters, viz. (a) this shade of red, (b) red generally, and (c) color in general? Is not the truth that the stamp has only one character in the way of color, viz. (a)?

Turn now to (2). Is it really *quite* certain that *this* penny stamp and *that* penny stamp have precisely and numerically the same color? They have a quality indistinguishable to our senses, we may agree, but that is a very different statement. Is it not possible, at least, that each such stamp has its own individuated redness, and that there are no general determinables in the sense supposed? And although a "character," however clearly individuated, must be distinguished from a "thing" (since a penny stamp, for example, is not exhausted in its coloredness), is it not simplest to suppose that the stamp is the individuated union of its individual characters?

As the result of a prolonged historical controversy, it seems pretty clear that the "nominalist" and the "conceptualist" theories of universals are untenable, and that some form of "realism" concerning universals must be held, unless there are no universals at all. If a universal were *only* a *flatus vocis*, a *mere* name or a *mere* noise, there would be no more sense in saying that two separate penny stamps were red than in saying that smells and the multiplication table were red. The use of the name "red" would be a mere convention with nothing to justify the convention. And that is absurd. The convention, again, could not be justified by a merely conceptualist theory, in the historical sense of conceptualism. For suppose that the mind did form a "general" concept or image. We should then at once have to ask whether this general concept did or did not correspond to any general character of the facts, and without even raising the notorious difficulties concerning Correspondence Theories of Truth, we should have to say that if the concept represented anything general in the facts, then there *are* general facts, and that if it did not, there are no such facts. Conceptualism, in short, is a reputed half-way house that turns out, on inquiry, not to be a habitation at all.

Yet the realistic theory, as we have seen, is not without its difficulties; and if it is not quite certain, it follows that all propositions of the traditional form that ascribe a universal property to a logical subject *may* have an element of weakness in their very structure.

For the purposes of this discussion it is sufficient to indicate the nature of the difficulty, together with the grounds (or some of them) that compel us to recognize the difficulty. Many philosophers, it is true, will not admit any serious objection. The penny stamp, they say, "has" obviously a certain shade of red, completely determinate and literally identical in vast numbers of penny stamps, and also the more general property "red," and also the still more general property "color." All are distinct universals, although connected in a logical hierarchy. If it is difficult to suppose a literally common property of wittiness in a number of individual jests, this is no proof that there is any difficulty about ultimately determinate characters like some given shade of red or of green. Perhaps wittiness is the common property of making people laugh; and what makes many people laugh, surely, is mirth-provoking in them all. The circumstance that each of them may laugh in his own individual way seems irrelevant to such philosophers.

Other philosophers, however, are less easily satisfied. In their view, there is something wrong about universals, although it may be very doubtful indeed what precisely *is* wrong about them. They seem indispensable, yet altogether too peculiar, and so are the sort of entities we should like to get rid of if we could, although all the historical attempts to get rid of them have been much less plausible than the frank acceptance of them.

That is as it may be. It seems important, however, to distinguish reasons of this order from certain spurious objections that have assumed a quite disproportionate place in many historical discussions on this question and, even now, are far too common.

Berkeley, we may say, admitted the use of universals in predication. "It must be acknowledged," he said, "that a man may consider a figure merely as triangular; without attending to the particular qualities of the angles or relations of the sides." [7] (Therefore there must *be* three-sidedness to attend to, and the three-sidedness can not be what is *not* attended to). Again, Berkeley admitted that an image, particular in itself, may represent a great number of other particulars. This must mean "particulars of the same kind"; and the *kind* of the particulars is just a universal. Even Hume's modification of Berkeley's theory can not escape the same comment. Hume's theory, in brief, was that a "universal" is a word or other image that tends to arouse a stream of associations by similarity. [8] Yet if the things associated in this way really are similar, they must be things of the same kind or possessing the same properties. Otherwise we should have to suppose that what is associated "by similarity" is not similars, but dissimilar things that are invested with an induced and spurious similarity by the association. And this is absurd.

The preconception of both these authors, and of many both before and after them, was that universals, if there are any, must be mental images or pictures, and that all such images are completely determinate. This opinion is mistaken in both parts of it. The whiteness of white things is not an image or illustrative picture that we may form, but a character of the white things, and also, if we do form the image, a character of the image. If the image "represents" by similarity, it does so because it possesses this character, i.e. because it also is white. Secondly, the supposed complete determinateness of "representative" images is mythical. Every mental fact (if the Law of Identity be accepted) is what it is, but a mental image which is a sign is not necessarily more determinate than any other sign. It may signify *vaguely,* and in any ordinary sense it may *be* quite vague.

[7] *Principles,* Introduction, § 16 (Second and later editions).
[8] *Treatise,* pp. 21 *sqq.*

§ 7. Relational Properties

As we have seen, traditional logic expressed all propositions in the subject-predicate form. Here the fundamental case is that in which S (a substantive) is characterized by the predicate P. This form of proposition clearly implies the subject-predicate relation. Therefore, if all relations are suspect, this relation must be. The discursiveness, aloofness, etc. alleged to destroy the fundamental unity of truth whenever relations enter must, according to the argument before us, impair the complete truth of every proposition whatsoever, including the proposition that expresses the Law of Identity.

The specific nature of this difficulty (as we noted very briefly in Chapter III, § 7) is that it is characteristic of a relation to hold *between* two terms. Strictly speaking, this is true of the subject-predicate relation as well as of all others. Certain philosophers, however, having digested the subject-predicate relation so thoroughly as to forget that it does, or ever did, hold *between* different terms, decline to swallow any other sort of betweenness. Hence Leibniz held that a relation must be a purely mental thing [9] because it does not properly belong to one subject (as an attribute does) but straddles in an ultimately unthinkable fashion, having one leg in one subject (or substance) and another leg in another subject (or substance). Other philosophers have similarly maintained that such relationships must be "external" to the terms they profess to unite, and proceed to argue as if things that were "external" to one another in this sense must in the last analysis be disconnected.

One way of attempting to avoid this conclusion is to hold that relations, other than the subject-predicate relation, express *secondary* adjectives. A character or primary adjective qualifies a substantive *sans phrase*. A secondary adjective also qualifies a subject S, but not without reference to another subject. Thus, in the statement A is equal to B, the property "equal to B" does hold of, or characterize A, but only with reference to something that is not A but B.

This view does not seem satisfactory. In the statement given

[9] *Cf.* B. Russell, *The Philosophy of Leibniz*, p. 13.

above the so-called "secondary" adjective "equal to B" contains the very "external" relation of equality that is in dispute. If all such externality is unthinkable, the alleged secondary adjective is unthinkable. There is something quite peculiar about these secondary adjectives, and this peculiar thing is just the "externality" and the "betweenness." Alternatively, we may say that there is no way of getting rid of this ultimate betweenness in any proposition expressing relation. Take, for example, the argument: A is precisely six feet high and B is precisely six feet high; therefore A and B are precisely equal in stature. The first of these statements qualifies A and the second qualifies B; but neither statement (nor the two conjointly), expresses any relation between A and B. The equality *between* A and B has to be inferred from the two statements, and is a fresh discovery.

Instead, therefore, of speaking of primary and secondary adjectives, we ought to employ terms of greater precision, and speak, say, of immanent and communicating or transitive [10] adjectives. This course has a double advantage. In the first place, it does not attempt to disguise the circumstance that the communication or relation between different substantives is a matter of salient importance, and quite distinctive. In the second place, however, it asserts that substantives that stand in relation to one another *are* characterized by their relational properties in the same fundamental sense as each substantive may be characterized by an immanent adjective.

I would suggest that the greater part of the difficulty so many philosophers give voice to concerning "external" relations is due to misleading associations of the *word* "external." The *word* is taken to imply mere juxtaposition in space, without any communicating relation through the nature of the things juxtaposed, or it may even be taken to imply the juxtaposition of discrete things in space. To speak in this way is to assert that whatever is thus external *is* disconnected and non-communicating according to the nature of things. Hence the word "external" is question-begging; and, in a subtler way, the word "internal" is also question-begging. For it is taken to imply that whatever is not "external" is not separate and therefore *must* be united, although

[10] Mr. Johnson's term. *Logic*, Part I, Ch. xiii.

in fact the coexistence of properties within the same boundary may be just as "unintelligible" (that is to say, just as hard to explain) as any relation between "external" things. The celebrated truth (mentioned by Darwin) that all white tom-cats with blue eyes are deaf is a sufficiently striking illustration, and Locke's pages (as we have seen) are full of other illustrations.

Ultimately, therefore, the question is whether a relation between things can describe a genuine connection or unity between the things. If it can, there is no mystery; for the fact, *ex hypothesi*, is intelligible. If it can not, such relations do not relate and are unintelligible if they pretend to do what they can not do. An immanent relation, however, is neither more nor less intelligible than a communicating one.

According to the logical pluralists, relations do relate, and when they relate are part of an intelligible unity. According to Bradley and others, this view is "incomprehensible." "If there are such unities, and, still more, if such unities are fundamental, then pluralism surely is in principle abandoned as false." [11]

For those who, like myself, are unable to see what relations could conceivably do if they did not relate, it seems sufficient to say that, if relations can not relate, there is no hope for any proposition or for the "laws of thought" referring to propositions. This Bradley admits. His "unities," he holds, are of the type of immediate experience,[12] not of the type of judgment; and he supposes that ultimate truth overcomes the externality and disunion that judgment and reflective or logical thinking vainly endeavor to suppress, although it retains the kind of unity that we feel, but may not understand, in our immediate experience.

§ 8. The Law of Contradiction

Given in full Bishop Butler's statement was, "Everything is what it is, and not another thing." In other words, the Laws of Identity and of Contradiction go constantly together, and are like concave and convex in an arc. Therefore, it seems useless to separate them, and I have not attempted to do so in the fore-

---

[11] *Essays on Truth and Reality*, p. 281.   [12] *Ibid.*

going discussion. On the other hand, certain logicians, and particularly Bradley, have held that negation is "subjective" and at a further remove from reality than affirmation. Accordingly, a distinct point emerges in this regard.

Grammatically, of course, and for the purposes of ordinary logic, affirmation and negation are on the same level, since any affirmative proposition has an equivalent negative form, and conversely. Thus to deny the absence of X and to affirm its presence are precisely equivalent.

It is argued, however, that this is only a formal device, and that, although there are positive facts, there are no negative facts.

Here it may be suggested there is a confusion between "positive" and "affirmative." It is, for example, a positive fact that a baby's cradle is too small to contain a living elephant, but it is a negative statement that no cradles contain elephants. Indeed, every negative statement may be said to express the positive fact that X is of such a nature, or so circumstanced, that it excludes Y.

In short, it is not true that negative statements are statements about nothingness or about non-facts. Even absence, in this sense, is a fact and not a non-fact. It is a fact, not a non-fact, that my study is characterized by the absence of a swimming bath or a crimson ceiling.

Again, every affirmative statement has a negative implication, and the implication seems to be as determinate, descriptive, and factual as the original affirmative. If a thing is red it is not blue or any other color. This implication seems completely factual, and in no way subjective. More generally, the fact of *otherness* is factual and positively descriptive. Red is other than green, and also other than sour. All such statements are completely factual. Red things, again, may be sour (as many berries are); but, in so far as they are red they can never also be green. This distinction between possibly coexistent otherness and otherness incapable of coexistence is again an important characteristic of fact.

I think we should conclude, therefore, that the "problem of negation" does not add to our perplexities in this matter.

§ 9. The Law of Excluded Middle

I have argued that negation is not merely a symbolic device, but fundamentally an expression for that *otherness* which is characteristic of reality. There may, however, be "laws" that are only symbolic devices, and the Law of Excluded Middle might conceivably be one of them. It would therefore be imprudent to lay any great stress upon the formal equivalence between "Not both *A* and Non-*A*" (the Law of Contradiction) and "Either Non-*A* or *A*" (the Law of Excluded Middle). The essential question is whether the Law of Excluded Middle expresses an invincible and distinctive certainty concerning fact. Is it, or is it not, in terms of the beautiful and justly celebrated printer's error, a Law of Excluded Muddle concerning the nature of things?

A serious objection to it appears to be that if we say, "*A* is either *B* or is not *B*," we appear to characterize *A* by an *alternative* mode of being, although one of the usual certainties is that everything that *is* must be completely determinate. How can a thing be "either-or"? Must it not be completely and invincibly its definite self? Must not "either-or" express our ignorance as much as our knowledge, and is it not an insult to truth and to reality to affirm that anything is characterized, in itself, by *our* frame of mind, and, what is worse, by our ignorance? As a Scottish judge recently said, "What has a frame of mind to do with the matter?" [13]

Similarly, it may be argued that we use the Law only when we are dealing with what to us is vague, but that vagueness can

---

[13] In a recent debate on Negation (at Nottingham in July 1929) Mr. G. Ryle drew a useful distinction between what a proposition *asserts* and what it *evinces*. In terms of this distinction, we have to say that a proposition asserts what is claimed to be a true state of affairs, but may also indicate or evince a condition of the speaker's mind, although not asserting this or claiming truth regarding it. (An ejaculation, for instance, *merely* evinces and asserts nothing at all.)

Applying this distinction to the Law of Excluded Middle we should say, I think, that statements in the "either-or" form properly assert that *A* is included in the class subdivided into the two divisions *B* and non-*B*, and so that its absence from the one subdivision implies its presence in the other; but that such statements also evince ignorance or doubt on the part of the speaker concerning which of these subdivisions *A* belongs to.

not be a characteristic of any fact, except a mental fact that is vague or obscure in its reference. The Law in short, does not *exclude* but, on the contrary, *expresses* muddle, or at least cogitative insufficiency. At the best, therefore, it expresses a certainty about our own uncertainty. And this an odd kind of certainty.

The Law, moreover, may be attacked from precisely the opposite quarter. If it is taken as a statement to the effect that realities must consist of "fixities and definites," whether we are or are not in a position to ascertain these fixities, it may be argued that many *continuous* pieces of existence are *not* composed of fixities and definites in this sense. You may select any number of "parts" in a continuous series, but the series is not made up of such parts. And there may be series which are neither completely continuous nor completely discrete.

Mr. Brouwer's account of the theory of assemblages (*Mengenlehre*) is expressly formulated "in independence of the logical law of excluded middle." [14] His "intuitive" mathematics is profoundly disturbing to a great many mathematicians. But it is not negligible.

Without necessarily committing ourselves to any of these theories, we have to confess, I submit, that the Law of Excluded Middle may be much more vulnerable than the Laws of Identity and Contradiction.

§ 10. GENERAL CONCERNING THE LAWS OF THOUGHT

It is generally conceded that the three traditional Laws of Thought are not the only laws of similar status. The list is manifestly capable of extension, and should include separate formulation of the Reiterative, Commutative,[15] and Associative Laws, as well as of others. This extension of the traditional formal logic along traditional lines has recently been attempted by Mr. W. E. Johnson with marked success.[16] Other extensions,

---

[14] See, e.g. *Mathematische Annalen*, No. 93, pp. 244 *sqq.*

[15] It may be remarked that D. Hilbert (*The Foundations of Geometry,* English translation, pp. 103 *sqq.*) gives a proof that "for a non-archimedean number system . . . there exists a system of numbers for which the commutative law of multiplication (ab = ba) is not valid."

[16] *Cf. Logic,* Part I, Ch. xiv.

along lines that do not pretend to be traditional, are a common-place of modern mathematical logic.

Mr. Johnson, however, has to admit that he can not attempt either to prove the complete independence of the logical first principles he enumerates or to show conclusively what is the smallest set of such principles from which the system of logic can be generated.[17] These problems, he suggests, may be principally of technical interest, but he comes very near to annulling the slight implied in this suggestion by noting the fundamental difficulty of all such attempts, viz. the extreme circumspection required in seeing that "in explicitly deriving formulae from an enumerated set of first principles, we are not surreptitiously using the very same formulae that we profess to derive."[18]

That is the principal difficulty, as we have sufficiently seen in our discussion, say, of the Law of Identity. For we saw that certain interpretations of this Law regarded it as asserting, *inter alia*, the irrelevance of asserting the same thing twice, or, in other words, the truth of the Reiterative Principle.

On the whole, while laws other than the three traditional ones are manifestly lacking in the traditional list, it may be doubted how far any of the others are comparable in point of apparently self-evident certainty to the three we have examined, especially if the traditional trio is interpreted with some breadth. It seems unnecessary, therefore (for our present purpose of examining the usual certainties), to cite other instances of obvious laws of thought. Most of the others are too simple to be obvious.

In general, therefore, we have to conclude that while the traditional laws and others like them seem pretty clearly to indicate the whereabouts of certainty, it is seldom easy or rational to be fully convinced of the utter certainty of any particular formulation of such laws. On the contrary, there are definite (although often, very likely, inconclusive) reasons for dubiety in this affair.

Indeed, there is a growing tendency on the part of mathematical logicians to renounce every claim to the certainty or self-evidence of the "primitive" propositions from which (as they maintain) their science may be generated by a series of logical

[17] *Op. cit.*, p. 223.   [18] *Ibid.*

inferences. According to this latter view, the choice of logically primitive propositions is principally a matter of technical convenience. What is logically primitive in one system may be derivative in another, or, in other words, the *certainty* of any primitive proposition is largely irrelevant.

It is even said that primitive propositions borrow their certainty from their success in the orderly development of the system. For the most part, certainty resides in the middle regions of the science, or in what Bacon called *axiomata media*. It is a mistake to search for it among the *axiomata prima*.

If certainty meant mere psychological assurance, and if the "evident" and the obvious were always the same, it would be difficult to avoid the conclusion of these formalists. If, on the other hand, we follow the older-fashioned but (I think) the correct opinion that much that *is* certain may be very hard to discover, and the very reverse of an easy or obvious plausibility, we can scarcely escape from the traditional conclusions that what is logically prior to an inference must itself be certain if what is inferred from it is certain, and that the certainty of this entire procedure must remain under suspicion until the principles necessarily employed in the procedure are capable of exhibiting and vindicating their certainty.

That is why the traditional Laws of Thought supply a crucial intellectual experiment in this important matter. They are said to be not only certain but *apparently* certain or obvious, and their implications are not too technical to be grasped with relative ease. Other laws of the same logical order need not be so fortunately circumstanced.

Chapter IX

OF INFERENTIAL CERTAINTY

§ 1. Inference and Truth

We are frequently informed that inference should never be included among the primary verities since, even if it is correct, it is no guarantee of truth. Correct inferences may be drawn from false or from merely supposed premises as well as from true and certain ones.

The mistake in this opinion concerning inference is not hard to discern. The laws of inference do not claim to guarantee the truth of any conclusion that is correctly inferred, but they do claim to guarantee the truth of a conclusion correctly inferred from premises that are true.

Again, there is a serious oversight in maintaining that inference is concerned, not with truth, but only with consistency; for it *is* concerned with certain truths, the truths, namely, of certain types of connection between premises and conclusion. The laws of inference assert the truth of an inevitable interconnection between premises and conclusion. They assert the truth of logical dependence, and this logical dependence is necessary even when it holds between whimsies and falsities. Indeed, the necessity of the dependence or interconnection may reveal the sham and the caprice in the premises. Your idea, we say, looks good to you, but it logically implies such and such a consequence which you must admit to be preposterous. Therefore, you must relinquish your idea. There would be no occasion to relinquish the idea on these grounds except for the *truth* of its necessary interconnection with what is admittedly absurd. In other words, if the interconnections expounded in inference were not *true* interconnections, we could never explore the extent and force of our ideas and conjectures by means of inference, and could never be stopped short by means of a *reductio ad absurdum.*

In the present chapter, then, I propose to consider our certainties regarding inference, or, in the alternative, to consider any doubts that may be raised concerning the validity of the inferential process other than the dubieties already considered concerning the nature of propositions.

§ 2. IMMEDIATE INFERENCE

It is commonly held that there are two principal species of inference, viz. mediate and immediate. Of these, the latter variety occurs when a conclusion may be inferred from a given premiss without the aid of an intermediate proposition. In ordinary formal logic the two fundamental types of immediate inference that are currently recognized are the processes of obversion and of conversion. In the former process, we infer S is not non-P (or S is not other than P) from S is P. In the latter, we infer a proposition having P for its subject from a proposition having S for its subject, e.g. from "All predatory nations are strong" we infer that "Some strong nations are predatory."

In the traditional formulation of logical problems, the proposition to be converted or obverted (in technical terms, the convertend or the obvertend) must be in subject-predicate form, and so must the proposition inferred by immediate inference (i.e. the converse or the obverse). Propositions so formulated, it is further maintained, must belong to one or other of the four traditional groups A, E, I, and O; i.e. they must be of the form All S is P, or of the form No S is P, or of the form Some S is P, or of the form Some S is not P.

Various criticisms have been brought against this traditional formulation of propositions, especially with regard to the ambiguity of the little word "all." For example, the "all" in Lady Macbeth's "All the perfumes of Arabia will not sweeten this little hand" plainly refers to the totality of Arabian perfumes and so has a different meaning from the "all" in "All philosophers are human beings," where (in addition to the implication that there are philosophers and that there are human beings) the gist of the assertion is that if anything is a philosopher that thing is a human being. Omitting such points, however, we have now to ask (1) whether the traditional processes of conversion

222 KNOWLEDGE, BELIEF, AND OPINION

and of obversion may be valid, (2) whether they are genuine inferences, and (3) whether there are other valid types of immediate inference.

(1) Regarding conversion, doubts may be raised concerning the transition from substantival to adjectival expression. This stone is white, i.e. it has whiteness. Can we legitimately pass from "whiteness" to white substances and say (by conversion), "Some white substance is this stone"?

The answer, pretty clearly, is that we may. In the given proposition the use of the adjective "white" is concrete, that is to say, the adjective asserts the factual character of a factual thing. The proposition asserts the existence of something white which is a stone, and there is nothing in the converse illegitimately extracted or inferred from the convertend.

Regarding obversion, vigorous aspersions have frequently been cast upon the so-called "infinite" term non-P. Non-turtles, it may be said, are just as absurd as mock-turtles. Is it not therefore equally absurd to argue that from the true proposition "All pelomedusidae are turtles" we may infer the absurd proposition "No pelomedusa is a non-turtle"?

In this argument there appears to be a confusion between what is absurd and what is linguistically uncouth. If by a "non-turtle" we mean, quite simply, "anything that is not a turtle" or "anything other than a turtle," we may not be able to plume ourselves upon the elegance of our language, but surely we are not committing ourselves to anything frankly absurd. And manifestly no pelomedusa is other than a turtle.

Accordingly, we have to maintain that these objections fall; and in general, I think, we may reasonably conclude that (ambiguities of formulation apart) no serious objection can be taken to the accuracy of the traditional processes of obversion and of conversion.

(2) The general accuracy of these processes being admitted, however, the question may at once be raised whether such "eductions" (as Miss Jones called "immediate inferences") are inferences at all. May not the truth be that eduction is not an inference but a dodge? When we infer, it may be said, we must pass from one proposition to another proposition necessarily

interconnected with the first. It is a very general logical opinion, however, that in so-called "immediate inference" there is no passage from one proposition to another (and distinct) proposition, but that "eduction" is only a technical device for restating some given proposition in such a way as to facilitate the manipulation of the logical machine. The whole problem, we are told, concerns the alternative formulation of one and the same thing.

In this argument, there appears to be an *ignoratio elenchi.* Even if conversion and obversion *were* technical manipulations, it would not follow that they were not *inferences.* Indeed, if we are dealing with an equivalent that is not identical, an inference, somewhere, is plainly required.

Thus, in obversion we have to pass from "*S* is *P*" to "*S* is not other than *P*." To be sure, any one who understands that *S* is *P* should be presumed to understand that *S* is not other than *P*. But he asserts something of *S*, viz. that it is *P*; and, since non-*P* is obviously different from *P*, there must be a difference between obverse and obvertend. The inference may indeed be obvious; or, again, with practice, such logical manipulations may become "mechanical"—that is to say, having learned what they mean, we may proceed to perform them without the necessity of interpreting their meaning step by step. The more obvious inferences need not startle us at all with any flashes of novelty.

Similarly, in the process of conversion, the question is whether the proposition "*S* is colored" is a different proposition (although equivalent) from the proposition "Some colored thing is *S*," not whether there is a connection so very obvious that no one who grasps the first could conceivably fail to grasp the second. And here there does seem to be a transition in thought. The steps are "*S* is colored. Therefore, *S* belongs to a set of colored things. Therefore, one or more of this set of colored things is identical with *S*." It is possible that the third of these propositions does not express anything more than the second proposition does, and is *only* a restatement of the second without any need for inference. This can not be said, however, of the relation between the first and the second. *Ergo,* in the usual case, at least, the process of conversion *somewhere* involves an inference.

In view of the notorious fact that most university students

of formal logic find considerable difficulty in immediate inferences—indeed, in my experience, I have been forced to anticipate
a greater degree of initial mulish obstinacy concerning immediate
than concerning mediate inference—it is very unplausible to
maintain even the irrelevant proposition that immediate inferences are so very simple and obvious that novelty can never be
expected of them or intellectual effort required in their case.
Take, for example, the process known as contraposition, in which
the rule is first to obvert the contraponend and then to convert
the obverted contraponend. Let us suppose that we are told, for
instance, that all politicians are deficient in complete candor, and
that we want to know the contrapositive (which should tell us
how candid people stand in relation to the class of politicians).
Therefore, we proceed to infer (a) by obversion that No politicians are candid, and (b) by conversion of this proposition
that No candid people are politicians (or (c), by subsequent
obversion, that All candid persons are other than politicians).

If this conclusion is obvious to any one who understands the
first proposition even negligently, 'tis well. It is a pleasant
thought that so much logical acumen is distributed universally
among the human race. Those who entertain this pleasant
thought, however, may be reminded of a rather unkind little
footnote in Mr. J. N. Keynes's *Formal Logic.* "It will be found,"
Mr. Keynes says, "that, taking Euclid's first book, proposition
6 is obtainable by contraposition from proposition 18, and 19
from 5 and 18 combined; or that 5 can be obtained by contraposition from 19, and 18 from 6 and 19. Similar relations subsist
between propositions 4, 8, 24, and 25; and, against, between axiom
12 and propositions 16, 28, and 29. Other examples might be
taken from Euclid's later books. In some of the cases the logical
relations in which the propositions stand to one another are obvious; in other cases some supplementary steps are necessary."[1]

If contraposition is so very obvious, it seems odd that Euclid
should have neglected the circumstance in so signal a fashion as
to have given independent proof of matters that needed no proof,
and (might we add?) that so many teachers and students of
Euclid's *Elements* should have neglected to notice the fact.

[1] *Studies and Exercises in Formal Logic,* Fourth edition, p. 136 note.

(3) When we assert relational propositions instead of retaining the simple subject-predicate form, we run upon a new set of immediate inferences and at the same time include the ordinary immediate inferences of daily life. To most people, indeed, there appears to be something almost incredibly jejune about the immediate inferences in traditional formal logic. "X is greater than Y. Therefore, something greater than Y is X." This traditional inference is not, in general, what we want to know. For the most part our attitude is: A certain relation holds between X and Y. What is the converse relationship between Y and X? It is this extended relational conversion with which mankind, despite traditional formal logic, is principally concerned.

Thus, from "X is greater than Y," we infer that "Y is less than X." From "Edinburgh is north of London," we infer that "London is south of Edinburgh." From "James struck John," we infer that "John was struck by James." And so in a host of other instances.

The main distinction here is between symmetrical, asymmetrical, and merely non-symmetrical relations. A symmetrical relation is one in which the "sense" or direction of the relation is necessarily reversible. There is the same relation between X and Y as between Y and X, for example in $X = Y \therefore Y = X$. An asymmetrical relation is one in which the sense of the relation is necessarily opposite. Thus "X is greater than Y," $\therefore$ "Y is less than X." A non-symmetrical relation is one in which the sense of the relation and the sense of the converse relation may be the same and also may not. Thus, if X is Y's lover it may or may not be the case that X's affection is reciprocated.

Such inferences are clearly immediate, and seem clearly inferences. Indeed, for the most part, they are inferences that may require something very like hard thinking. It is only by a series of intellectual experiments in the process of conversion that we are usually able to decide whether some given relation is symmetrical, asymmetrical, or non-symmetrical.

§ 3. Mediate Inference

In traditional school logic the syllogism is the supreme example of mediate inference, and there is even a tendency to argue that although most of the mediate arguments employed in common life are not, on the face of them, perfect syllogisms, they really are abbreviated syllogisms (or, in technical language, enthymemes) and are always (if they are valid) capable of being exhibited in the full-dress uniform of mood and figure, that is to say as a syllogism in Barbara, in Celarent, or in some other of the nineteen valid moods.

It seems advisable, therefore, in the first instance, to consider the traditional syllogism and the certainty it is reputed to yield.

The traditional syllogism, although now so much of a commonplace, is also one of the major achievements of the human intellect. It was not without its critics, however—Bacon [2] and Locke,[3] for instance, as well as Mill—although it was very generally accepted at its own valuation.

For the most part, these critics did not impugn the validity of the traditional syllogism. They impugned its usefulness, and held that the traditional syllogism could only attest and consolidate what had been already gained. According to most of the critics, the syllogism was not a process of discovery but the etiquette of expressing a discovery already made. On the other hand, J. S. Mill's theory is a notable exception to the general tendency of these criticisms. Mill maintained that the syllogism is *not* valid but that it *is* useful. It is invalid, Mill said, because it always begs the question; but the process of begging the question in the "high priori" way of the syllogism may incidentally yield a useful precaution which, on occasion, may even be indispensable.

Since an attack upon the syllogism's validity is much more serious than any attack upon its utility, we must consider the question of validity first. Let us, then, begin by examining Mill's attack upon the syllogism in Barbara,[4] that traditionally "perfect" syllogism that was the head and front of the *art d'infaillibilité*, as Leibniz called the syllogism.[5]

Take: "All men are mortal. Socrates is a man. Therefore,

---

[2] *Novum Organum*, I, 11-14.
[3] *Essay*, Book IV, Ch. xvii.
[4] *System of Logic*, Book II, Ch. iii.
[5] *Nouveaux Essais*, commenting upon Locke, *loc. cit.*

Socrates is mortal." Traditionally, this conclusion concerning Socrates in relation to mortality is said to be deduced from the major premise "All men are mortal" through the mediation of the middle term "man"; and it is clear that this procedure is tainted by the fallacy of *petitio principii* if the conclusion is already contained in the major premise from which it is said to be deduced. Otherwise, it is not so tainted, and the conclusion remains unbegged.

The crucial question, accordingly, is whether the premise "All men are mortal" already contains the proposition "Socrates is mortal"; and the answer commonly and (I think) correctly given to this question is that if the distributed term "all men" were an enumeration of Socrates, Plato, the Duke of Wellington, and every other particular man, it would include Socrates as one of the enumerated particulars, and otherwise would not include him. Since, however, it is absurd to maintain that the distributed term "all men" enumerates each individual man who has lived, is living, or will be alive, it is clear that the major premise is not enumerative, and therefore that, to speak with intentional meiosis, there is no *blatant* begging of the question.

The way in which Mill formulates his charge of *petitio principii* is slightly different from the criticism examined above, but is not essentially different. According to Mill, we pass, in the psychology of such reasoning, to the conclusion, Socrates is mortal, from the minor premise. Socrates is a man. We connect Socrates with mortality by a particular inference, Plato with mortality by another particular inference, and so forth. The traditional major premise of the traditional syllogism is, therefore, Mill says, only the record of a number of particular inferences, and this record is mistranslated, by tradition, into an alleged principle from which the connection between humanity and mortality may be deduced in this or in the other particular case.

Our criticism obviously applies to this way of arguing also. Does the premise "All men are mortal" *enumerate* the particular inferences "Socrates is mortal," "Plato is mortal," and the rest? Clearly it does not; and therefore the *petitio* does not stand forth. Indeed, Mill himself admitted the point, although he did not see the force of his own admission. For he said that major premises of the traditional type are records of particular past inferences *"and short formulæ for making more."* [6] The addition I have italicized destroys Mill's previous argument. Mill's formula might have been reached without any knowledge of the case of Socrates. Moses might have inferred it from the deaths of Jacob, of Esau, and of Pharaoh's host.

According to Mill, syllogistic procedure is really a process of hermeneutics, or of interpreting notes. On the basis of past experience we make a note of the inescapable liability of former human beings to an eventual demise. On the strength of this note we proceed, by inferential extension, to affirm that any one who had not died at the time Mill wrote (e.g. Sir William Hamilton) would nevertheless die.

These statements are not inexact concerning such major premises are as reached by induction. The major premise in Mill's syllogism about mortality is such a note, and the minor premise states that Socrates conforms to the note. On the other hand, the interpretation that Mill puts upon his note-taking implies the use of the formula in the very way that Mill decries.

In a major premise derived from induction the note is to the effect that because in a certain number of observations (deemed sufficient and in the absence of any verifiable counter-observations concerning Enoch, say) all *observed* men had the property of mortality, we are entitled to accept the general principle that *all* men, observed or unobserved, noted or unnoted, have this property, and therefore we are logically entitled to apply the formula forthwith to any new case not recorded in our notes. This is the syllogistic, or the applicative, principle, and it yields a result totally different from the proper logical conclusion of Mill's strictures. If Mill had been consistent, he should have argued: "You ask about the mortality of Socrates. Let me examine my files. If the name of Socrates is not on the files, I can naturally tell you nothing about his mortality. No doubt I have the name under the heading 'man'; but if I have no record under the heading 'mortal' I am afraid you will have to consult

* *Loc. cit.,* §4.

some other set of records. Perhaps there are records about executed persons in some Athenian archives."

The same considerations hold of principles not reached by induction. Take, for example, legal enactments. If the law enacts that any person attempting to purchase tobacco after 9 P.M. is to suffer certain legal pains and penalties upon conviction, it is clear that (unless the enactment is retrospective) none of the *future* infringements of the enactment can in fact be enumerated in the enactment. On Mill's principles, all accused persons should plead: "There is no logic in the court unless my name is mentioned in the statute as one who has purchased tobacco after 9 P.M. Since the framers of the law were not prophets, my name can not be mentioned. Therefore, you must let me go."

We must conclude, accordingly, that the syllogism is not invalid on the score of *petitio*, and so we need not trouble ourselves with Mill's further (and curious) contention that although invalid it is a useful precaution because it tends to restrain the exuberance of our generalizing propensity.[7] We have to consider, however, whether there are any other reasons for nonsuiting the syllogism.

Here we may remark with some confidence that any denial of the validity of the syllogism, within its selected formal province, has undertaken a very formidable task. It is easy to point out, of course, that there are nineteen formally valid syllogisms (leaving weakened moods out of account) and to suggest that nineteen is a lot. The theory and enumeration of valid syllogisms is, however, unusually defensible because it is quite complete. Indeed, if the validity of conversion and of obversion be admitted (and we have seen that there is no good reason to deny the validity of either) *any* syllogism can be, in technical language, "reduced" to any other, that is to say, the conclusion that follows from any pair of syllogistic premises may, by the employment of obversion and of conversion, be shown to follow from these premises according to any other valid syllogistic mood (or determinate syllogism).

Again, if conversion only be employed, it can be shown that

[7] *Ibid.,* § 5.

any valid syllogism in the second, third, or fourth figures can be reduced to some valid syllogism in the first figure, the process in two instances requiring a *reductio ad absurdum*. Hence, if syllogisms in the first figure are valid, all other syllogisms are valid, and instead of attempting to defend nineteen distinct syllogisms we have only to defend four, for that is the number of valid unweakened moods in the first figure.

This logical exercise in the reduction of syllogisms is certainly, in a historical sense, germane to our present theme. For reasons principally technical (or perhaps rather as an exercise in skepticism) it was held, or suggested, that the principles of the reasoning in the second, third, or fourth figures might not be quite self-evident, and so that a scholastic disputant might deny them during the formal disputations that, in medieval times, served the purpose we now assign to examinations in our horrible, semi-Chinese educational system. It was therefore important to reduce the fifteen syllogisms not in the first figure to some one of the four in the first figure, provided, of course, that the principle of the first figure *was* self-evident.

This principle, or *dictum*, of the first figure was called the *dictum de omni et nullo*. It may be stated in the form Mr. Joseph [8] quotes from Zabarella, viz. "Quod de aliquo omni praedicatur (dicitur *s*. negatur) praedicatur (dicitur *s*. negatur) etiam de qualibet eius parte," or *Anglice*, "What is predicated (stated *or* denied) about any whole is predicated (stated *or* denied) about any part of the whole." In this form, the nerve of the argument refers to the "wholes" that are "classes," any member of the class being regarded as a part of that whole; and there are reasons for denying that classes are wholes. If we said bluntly, however, that any property that belongs to *everything* of a certain nature must belong to *each individual instance* of that nature, we should avoid this difficulty and at the same time should have enunciated a principle that seems quite self-evident, provided that the propositional form according to which characters and properties may be predicated of logical subjects is not disputed.

It is not surprising, therefore, that (as we saw) the validity

[8] *An Introduction to Logic*, p. 274.

of the syllogism is seldom disputed (apart from Mill's charge of *petitio*), the usual complaint being that, although valid, the syllogism is trivial. This is not so. The examples given in the logic books may frequently be trivial, but the syllogism itself is not. Our present question, however, is the certainty, not the utility, of this mode of argument.

Another complaint is that the traditional syllogism is not the form of all valid mediate inference, but that there are certain valid mediate inferences (even of propositions in subject-predicate form) that are not syllogisms, and that there is a host of relational mediate inferences, particularly in mathematics, which can neither be stretched nor chopped into the precise boundaries of the syllogistic bed. An example of the former is the ancient illustration given in *The Port Royal Logic*, i.e. The Persians worship the sun. The sun is a thing insensible. Therefore, the Persians worship a thing insensible—which looks like a syllogism but is not. Examples of the latter, as we shall see, abound.

This complaint is correct in what it asserts, but it can not deny the certainty of traditional syllogistic inference. It is no true inference to say that, because the "infallible instrument" of the traditional syllogism is restricted to its own sphere, and does not include all mediate inference, therefore there is any valid objection to it *within* its own sphere. It is not the sole instrument of mediate inference; but it operates with certainty when it is the instrument.

§ 4. Extension of the Traditional Syllogism

The categorical syllogism of traditional formal logic, in the "perfect" form of the first figure, is an instance of argument by subsumption.

Following Mr. Johnson,[9] we may state its principle thus:

Everything is *p* if *m*   or *m* implies *p*.
This is *m*   or Here is an instance of *m*.
∴ This is *p*.   ∴ This is *p*

Here the major premise states an implication, the minor premiss assures us of the existence of an instance in which the

* *Logic*, Part II, Ch. v.

implication holds. We have, in short, an *instantial* argument concerning a given implication.

As Mr. Johnson demonstrates in full,[10] this principle may be extended functionally in a way not included in the traditional categorical syllogism. Thus, in his example, let $a =$ acceleration and $s =$ distance. Then the Newtonian gravitation formula concerning the inverse variation of acceleration with the square of the distance becomes $a = 1/s^2$. We can then draw inferences, not merely by the subsumption of any given instance, but, without any new principle of reasoning, for all the determinate values to which the governing formula may apply. Thus,

> a implies $1/s^2$
> If a is 7, it implies $1/49$
> In this instance a is 7
> In this instance it is $1/49$.
> And similarly for all values of a.

In addition to the categorical or subsumptive syllogism we have the hypothetical, which deals exclusively with transitive relations of implication. The hypothetical syllogism may be written: If a then b; and if b then c ∴ If a then c. And similarly *da capo*. We have, in fact, an implicational progression wherever a series of transitive relations are united by appropriate implicational middle terms.

Here what is essential is that the terms of the implicational series should be transitive, that is to say, that if a transitive relation r holds between a and b, and also between b and c, it always and necessarily holds (being transitive) between a and c. Thus (to illustrate transitiveness), "ancestor of" is transitive because if X is the ancestor of Y and Y the ancestor of Z, X must necessarily be the ancestor of Z. This would not hold of the relation of fatherhood, say. For if X is Y's father and Y is Z's father, X would not be Z's father but, on the contrary, Z's grandfather.

On the whole, therefore, we may conclude that the validity of inference is very hard to impugn, and that its claims to certainty in its own kind are very firmly established. This conclusion applies both to inferences of the traditional form (mediate

[10] *Logic*, Part II, Ch. v.

or immediate) and to the many extensions of these that modern logicians have discovered and examined. Even here, however, some modern Cromwell might reasonably beseech us to think it *possible* we might be mistaken.

CHAPTER X

THE CERTAINTIES OF ARITHMETIC AND GEOMETRY

§ 1. PRELIMINARY

As we saw in a reference to Molière's Don Juan, and also in our discussions of Hume's account of *knowledge*, even those who pose as skeptics in most of their cogitations, or those who would gladly be accounted skeptics, are inclined to make an exception in favor of arithmetic and to admit, without question, that 2 and 2 make 4. The rationalists, similarly, regarded mathematics as completely certain and evident. In the skeptical exordium to his *Discourse on Method*, Descartes, for example, complained, not of the rigor of mathematics, but of the scurvy use to which this magnificent discipline was currently put; and Spinoza said that truth would have been hidden from mankind forever, if mathematics had not shown the way to deal with the essences and properties of figures, and so had destroyed the misleading and improper ideals of popular theology on the one hand, and of impressionistic, empirical humanism, on the other.[1]

The same, no doubt, might be said to-day. "It seems to me," a recent author has assured us, "that no philosophy can possibly be sympathetic to a mathematician which does not admit, in one manner or another, the immutable and unconditional validity of mathematical truth." [2] As an instance, this author cites Lagrange's discovery that "any number is the sum of 4 squares." On the other hand, many mathematicians would make no such ultimate claim; and neither mathematicians nor their philosophical camp-followers would speak with Spinoza's confidence concerning the demonstrable certainty that the sum of the interior angles of a plane triangle is equal to two right angles; for the necessity of this equality is denied in Riemann's non-Euclidean geometry, and also in non-Archimedean geometry.

[1] *Ethics*, Part I, Appendix.   [2] G. H. Hardy in *Mind*, N.S., No. 149, p. 4.

More generally, it would be freely admitted in the present century that a great part of the important mathematical work upon the logical foundations of arithmetic and geometry has been very recent work. Even now, however, it is not agreed that mathematics can be completely "logicized," that it ought to be capable of being logicized, or that, if it were completely logicized, the result would be immutable and unconditional truth, and not, in the main, symbolic elegance. There is not, again, anything like universal agreement concerning what numbers, say, essentially are. According to Hilbert, they are marks upon paper. According to Frege and Russell, they are classes of classes. According to others, they are ultimately spatial or even material; for they are derived, it is said, logically as well as genetically, from constant and readily identifiable bits of matter that can be moved about without alteration in size or shape. Similarly, there is still an unresolved dispute whether transfinite numbers really are numbers or not, whether ordinal number is essentially prior to cardinal, and the like. It is also not agreed whether the axioms of mathematics are simply accepted without demonstration, or are self-certifying, immutable verities.

§ 2. The Nature of Number

According to Peano, the meaning and proper application of number is adequately and completely determined by the following primitive propositions:

(1) *0* is a number.

(2) The successor of any number is a number.

(3) No two numbers have the same successor.

(4) *0* is not the successor of any number.

(5) Any property which belongs to *0* and also to the successor of any number which has the property, belongs to all numbers.

The criticism commonly passed upon this scheme, by those who are sympathetic towards it, is that it is imperfectly logicized, since "*0*," "number," and "successor" must be independently understood before the scheme can be said to be intelligible. According to Mr. Bertrand Russell and others, this defect was overcome by Frege in his *Grundlagen der Arithmetik* (Mr. Russell modestly omitting his own independent discovery). Let us then consider Mr. Russell's corroborative formulation of the point.[3]

Number, it is held, is a property of a set of things. Thus, two is the number of all couples, three the number of all trios, etc.

Accordingly, we have to ask, "When does this, that, or the other set of things have the same number?" And the answer, according to Russell, is that two sets of things have the same number when there is a one-one correspondence, between the things comprised in the sets. Here "one-one" means "item for item," or "logical individual for logical individual," i.e. the "one" in question is not the number 1 but something more fundamental.

If we denote one-one correspondence by the term "similarity," we have to say that all classes or collections that are "similar" have the same number; and in general, according to Russell, we may define number as "the class of all classes similar to a given class."

If class means "collection," as Russell sometimes says it does, this definition is surely most questionable. The collection of all couples (say of 'Arries and 'Arriets on a Bank Holiday) does not have the number 2, although each separate couple has. Mr. Russell further explains, however, that it is possible to state the properties of classes without introducing the notion of "class" in the sense of "collection."

What are held to be strong points in favor of this definition are (1) that, in terms of the definition, it is possible to have knowledge of the number without enumeration of the separate individuals in any class, and (2) that the definition of number applies equally to finite and to infinite numbers. This is important because we can not attain the infinite by an infinite enumeration, and therefore (like the finitists in mathematics, e.g. Brouwer), would have to reject infinite number if number could be attained by enumeration only.

In any finite collection, say a dozen, it is plain that

1, 2, 3, 4 . . . 12 contains 12 members; that

1, 3 . . . 11, i.e. the odd numbers in the collection, consist of

[3] *Introduction to Mathematical Philosophy*, pp. 11 *sqq.*

12/2 members; and that 2, 4, 6 . . . 12, i.e. the even numbers in the collection, consist of 12/2 members.

But according to Mr. Russell, in an infinite set of numbers a "proper" part of the series must have the same number as the number of the series, for there is always a one-one correspondence between the numbers of the infinite series 1, 2, 3, etc., and, say, 1, 3, 5, etc., (i.e. the odd numbers in it).

It is claimed, therefore, that one and the same conception of number applies both to infinite and to finite numbers, and is workable without the necessity (which might be the impossibility) of separate enumeration. This may fairly be called an advantage, since it seems quite arbitrary to hold that any non-enumerable number is also inevitably unintelligible. When the claim to certainty is made, however, it may well be asked whether we are not asked to pay too high a price in accepting these definitions. For it would seem quite legitimate to argue that, *because* infinite numbers have such very different properties from finite numbers (e.g. regarding their "proper" parts, or regarding the fact that infinite numbers are not increased by the addition of 1), they *can not* be numbers in the same sense as finite numbers, and hence that one-one correspondence can not exhaust the meaning of finite number, or, in the alternative, affords a proof that infinite numbers are not numbers at all.

§ 3. The Application of Number to Fact

According to Mr. Russell, "we want our numbers not merely to verify mathematical formulae, but to apply in the right way to common objects. We want to have ten fingers, and two eyes, and one nose." [4] This seems reasonable. But can we satisfy these wants with certainty?

If we say that we have two eyes and one nose, we depend, presumably, upon perception for our information, and must therefore hold that two eyes and one nose are distinguishable units to our percipience. If we were dealing with the microscopically perceptible cells in the nose or with the imperceptible electrons in it, the number of such entities would be quite different from 1

[4] Ibid., p. 9.

Such perceptual discrimination, however, is not always easy. When two drops of a fluid coalesce, does not 2 seem to become 1? When mercury rises continuously in a tube, is the arithmetic of this *continuous* alteration at all simple in terms of discrete numbers? Mill suggested,[5] we remember, that 2 and 2 might not be 4 in some remote part of the stellar universe. This, we say, is nonsense; but it would not be at all nonsensical to suppose that what we perceptually identify as 1 in our present environment might not be so identifiable in some other environment. In our present environment, indeed, alcohol may have precisely this effect. It is not necessary to make a long and impossible journey to illustrate this supposition.

Perceptual discrimination of units, therefore, is neither wholly certain nor necessarily invariant, and arithmetic, as such, has nothing to say about the certainty of its application to perceptual data. It may be argued, however, that once the units are admitted, the work of arithmetic proceeds apace and untrammeled. "It is certain," Mill also said, "that 1 is always equal in *number* to 1; and where the mere number of objects, or of the parts of an object, without supposing them to be equivalent in any other respect, is all that is material, the conclusions of arithmetic, so far as they go to that alone, are true without mixture of hypothesis."[6] On the other hand, it may be doubted whether the application of the merest of mere arithmetic is ever properly significant without implied assumptions, often very difficult to translate into certainties, concerning the comparability of the units to which the reckoning applies. It is obvious, for instance, that lengths multiplied together do not really yield an area. To multiply a numbered set of things is to take the set once, twice, etc. It is as impossible to multiply an inch by an inch (obtaining a square inch) as to multiply an egg by a prayer. Apart, however, from such obvious misapplications of arithmetic, it may be doubted whether we can say that the Apostle Peter, $\sqrt{2}$, and my typewriter really comprise a set of entities whose sum is 3. It is generally held that numbers themselves are non-

[5] *System of Logic,* Book III, Ch. xxi, § 4. *Cf.* Book II, Ch. vi, §§ 2 and 3.
[6] *Ibid.,* Book II, Ch. vi, § 3.

addible. The number 2 is just one entity, and so is the number 3. Therefore, if 2 and 3 were added the sum would be 2 (i.e. 2 entities), not 5. But if only things and not numbers can be added, is it truly certain that any "set of things" forms a significant arithmetical sum? And if it does, what is the ultimate justification? According to certain authors, 2 and 2 would make 4 even if there were nothing to which the numbers applied. According to others, the twoness of any couple is a property of fact in the same sense as astuteness is a property of Mr. Lloyd George. If so, there could be no numbers if there were no couples, trios, etc., any more than there would be astuteness in a mindless universe. In that case, however, some special comparability in things may very well be prerequisite to the arithmetical treatment of them, whereas, in the former case, the application of numbers thus *independent* of existence *to* existence may well seem a problem in itself, quite additional to any particular problem of the particular application of particular numbers.

§ 4. COUNTING

The attempt made by logicians such as Sigwart to base arithmetic upon the unity of each mental act seems to impede rather than to aid our comprehension of this matter. It is quite true, as Sigwart says, that anything that *is* one need not be *recognized* as one, and hence that it must be singled out in thought whenever it is treated as a unit; and it is also true that this elementary consideration was neglected by thinkers like Locke, Hume, and Mill. On the other hand, it is not true that the unity of our acts determines the unity of the objects we count. On the contrary, we may wittingly include several objects in the scope of a single act, and indeed must always do so when we recognize that several units make a single sum. Again, when Sigwart says that "counting appears as a general form which brings into consciousness its own laws as a process from one unity to another, accompanied at each step by the combination of previous acts into a new unity,"[7] he appears to be proving far too much; for counting in this sense would be a formal property

[7] *Logic,* English translation, Vol. II, p. 34.

of all connected thought, and Sigwart would therefore be compelled to admit the monstrous piece of nonsense that we count whenever we think.

In general, counting presupposes the correlation between the ordinal number of successive acts of selecting or singling out and the entities thus singled out. While the process and the sum must, in one sense, be held together in a single connected thought-process, it seems pretty clear that we rely when we count not on unaided memory but upon permanent units set out before us, or upon correlation with such units (e.g. our ten fingers or the notches we make upon a stick). What Sigwart describes, therefore, can not be the whole of the relevant process; and it would seem undesirable to attempt to decide upon psychological or philosophical grounds whether ordinal number is prior to cardinal. If Weyl is right in his criticism, say, of Dedekind, ordinal number must be prior, in the sense that certain ordinal notions are involved in cardinal number. But cardinal numbers seem to be logically simpler than ordinal, and, despite Weyl,[8] do not seem to require the temporal process of counting.

§ 5. A Conspectus of Modern Mathematical Ideals of Proof

In the article in *Mind* already referred to at the beginning of this chapter, Mr. G. H. Hardy gives so clear a *vue d'ensemble* of the present situation in mathematics, and at the same time appends observations so pertinent to our theme, that it seems highly politic to follow his lead very closely. First, then, his *vue d'ensemble*.

Mr. Hardy distinguishes three contemporary views of the nature of number, viz. (1) the views of the logisticians Russell, Ramsey, and others, (2) the views of the finitists or intuitionists Brouwer and, in the main, Weyl, and (3) the views of the formalists, among whom Hilbert is the chief.

(1). The aim of the logisticians is completely to logicize number, and consequently to claim for it the pellucid evidence that ought to pertain to logic, together with freedom from any elements that have an empirical or other non-logical source. (Since, on this view, much in logic may be rather a matter of formal

[8] *Philosophie der Mathematik und Naturwissenschaft*, p. 28.

elegance than of certainty in any ordinary sense, a greater degree
of certainty need not be claimed for pure arithmetic than for
logic itself.)

Russell definitely claims that pure logic and pure mathematics
are "continuous," and hence that it is "quite arbitrary" to attempt to distinguish between them.[9] Mr. Hardy points out, however, as others have done, that Russell's scheme involves certain
extra-logical axioms, such as the Axiom of Infinity, Zermelo's
Axiom, and the Axiom of Reducibility, and that it does not
seem possible to avoid all such extra-logical axioms on any
scheme of this general sort.

(2). Mr. Hardy's criticism of the finitists is in effect that they
are dogmatic where they should be cautious. While they may be
right in dealing with the more secure parts of the subject, they
are wrong, positively, in regarding either perceptual intuition
or the signless integers as something sacrosanct—as when Weyl
appears to quote with approval Kronecker's curious dictum that
"the good God made the whole numbers; everything else is the
work of man"[10]—and they are wrong, negatively, "in rejecting
all attempts to push the analysis of mathematics beyond a certain point."

This criticism seems in part unnecessarily lacking in sympathy. There is surely a certain show of reason at least in
Brouwer's criticism of Cantor to the effect that Cantor's *Mengenlehre* failed to distinguish, as it should have distinguished,
between a field of free constructive possibility, on the one hand,
and fixed determinate concepts, on the other. As Weyl says, "The
continuum should not be treated as an aggregate of fixed elements, but as a matrix of free becoming,"[11] or again, "the continuum is not made up of parts."[12] This is at least a defensible,
not an arbitrary, view; and if it involves the consequence that
"mathematicians have to observe with sorrow their supposedly
solid towers leaving their foundations and disappearing in the
clouds,"[13] this consequence, after all, may have to be faced. On
the other hand, it may be much more doubtful whether the

[9] *Introduction to Mathematics*, pp. 194 *sq.*
[10] *Op. cit.*, p. 27.   [12] *Ibid.*, p. 43.
[11] *Ibid.*, pp. 42 *sq.*   [13] *Ibid.*, p. 44.

merely general is logically incomplete, whether non-logical intuition yields any great degree of precision, and whether step-
by-step procedure through free acts of choice ensures the presence of definite and intelligible entities as opposed to the mere
possibility of making such choices. The laws of possibility, it
may be said, must themselves be actual, and a whole (whether or
not continuous) that contains parts really must contain them
(even if they are discrete), although it may not be entirely constituted of such parts.

(3). In certain respects Hilbert is not out of sympathy with
Brouwer and Weyl, as is sufficiently proved by two passages
Mr. Hardy quotes from him. These quotations run: "Mathematics is occupied with a content given independently of all
logic and cannot be founded on logic alone," and "in order that
we should be able to apply logical forms of reasoning, it is
necessary that there should first be something given in presentation, some concrete extra-logical object, immediately present
to intuition, and perceived independently of all thought." In
Hilbert's view, however, problems of this order belong to what
he calls metamathematics, not to mathematics proper, and Hilbert's primary interest is in the latter.

Let us, then, consider Hilbert's personal views more closely.

"My researches towards establishing mathematics on a new
foundation," Hilbert says, "aim at nothing less than the total
removal of the general doubt concerning the certainty of mathematical proof." [14] The instrument for accomplishing this ambitious task, Hilbert is convinced, is the "axiomatic method,"
meaning thereby not the self-evident axioms of an older mathematical theory, but a still more rigorous formalizing of mathematics than heretofore. i.e. the establishment of a complete *Fach-
werk von Begriffen,* or apparatus of rules and terms. The cardinal principle of such ultra-formal treatment is absence of contradiction, and Hilbert's view appears to be that the formalist's
task, when accomplished, carries with it a certain non-formal
metamathematics or well-grounded application to reality and
fact. "The formal rules," he says, "are the images of the thoughts
that traditional mathematics is concerned with, but are not them-

[14] *Mathematische Annalen,* No. 88 (1923), p. 151.

selves absolute truth. On the contrary, absolute truth is the insight to be achieved through my formal proofs on account of the conclusiveness and absence of contradiction in the formal system." [15]

In expounding the character of the formalism in mathematics proper, Hilbert commits himself to the untenable view that "in mathematics the objects of our study are the concrete signs themselves," i.e. the marks upon paper. This view is untenable because, for example, the mark 2 made by my typewriter is a different physical mark from the number 2 drawn with chalk upon a blackboard, yet these different physical marks signify the same mathematical entity. Formal mathematics, in other words, can not be *simply* a game played with utterly meaningless counters, because no counters, even in a game, *are* utterly meaningless.

In the same way, it can easily be shown that many mathematical signs, e.g. the 2 in "2 miles from Pitlochry," do have a concrete meaning and plain application. Nevertheless, in the main, this type of criticism seems only partially justified. Hilbert's essential point is that for formal purposes (i.e., in his view, for mathematical purposes) it is not at all necessary to show that there is a concrete intelligible application of any particular sign employed. It is sufficient if the sign is necessary for the purposes of formal construction. The question of truth comes in when the whole construction is applied to fact, not necessarily when the items in it are so applied. And that is why Hilbert is entitled to maintain, as he does maintain, that although mathematics itself may be regarded formally as a game proceeding, like chess, according to certain rules, the game, when played out, differs from other games precisely because it provides metamathematical insight of the highest order and importance. As he says at the conclusion of his paper upon Axiomatic Thinking: "I believe that everything that can properly be the object of scientific thinking is the result of the axiomatic method, and therefore indirectly of mathematics, as soon as it is ripe for the construction of a complete theory. By pressing on to ever deeper strata of axioms in the sense explained we also gain ever

[15] *Ibid.*, p. 153.

deeper insight into the nature of scientific thought itself, and become ever the more convinced of the unity of our knowledge. Through the symbols of the axiomatic method mathematics seems to appoint us to the rôle of discovery in science in general." [16]

Nevertheless, although it may be a mistake to pass carelessly or at random from formal or mathematical requirements to a further metamathematical meaning, it can hardly be a mere accident that the formal game should have so much metamathematical importance. In particular, the central position of the absence of contradiction in the game has itself a metamathematical basis. Formally regarded, it is the supreme rule of the game; but the game would not be worth playing except for the metamathematical importance of this principle.

Hilbert's distinction between mathematics and metamathematics, being the apotheosis of formalism, is manifestly of the first importance for our general theme. If we accepted it, we should be forbidden to look for certainty or immutable truth in any part or step of the formal structure. Any such inquiry would be a piece of metamathematics, and we should not be ready for metamathematical inference until the formal structure was complete. And even then, the argument would be: "This is the whole. Take it or leave it." It would also appear to be dubious whether there might not be *several* mathematical wholes, each formally consistent. In that case, how could we rationally select our certainties?

Commenting upon Hilbert's view, Mr. Hardy is moved to distinguish between demonstration and proof. The former is Hilbert's "mathematics" or *formal, mathematical, official* demonstration inside the mathematical system and concerned only with that formal system. The second (which is Hilbert's metamathematics) Mr. Hardy calls "informal, unofficial significant proof" —not very happily, because, as he admits, such proof need not be "in any sense slacker or less 'rigorous' than the formal mathematical demonstration."

According to this distinction, "demonstration" is concerned with the formal patterns of mathematics. Regarded metamathe-

[16] *Ibid.*, No. 78 (1918), p. 415.

matically, these patterns are the subject of discussion. The object of "proof," on the other hand, is to produce conviction, a point on which formal demonstration has no direct bearing. It is therefore an open question how far mathematics is concerned with conviction at all. Mr. Hardy himself says he can not really doubt that there is a class which is the logical sum of any given set of classes; and Hilbert does doubt this—metamathematically. Ultimately, the question is how far mathematics can afford to be purely formal, and therefore to put aside for its own purposes the kind of proof that is directed towards achieving conviction or certainty.

§ 6. Geometry

It is related of Thomas Hobbes, the philosopher, that, being unacquainted with Euclid's *Elements* before the age of forty, he exclaimed, on first seeing the proof of Euclid I, 47, "By God, this is impossible," thereby evincing his astonishment (as we may suppose) that spatial matters could be treated with such rigor and generality. If this was indeed the cause of Hobbes's astonishment, we may conjecture that he was not very different from the common man in this particular, supposing, that is, that the common man had not learned Euclid at school. Most of us, like Hume, find it difficult to believe that simple arithmetic is other than purely rational. We have to be convinced by argument that it may be otherwise. Geometry, on the other hand, seems to be concerned with something empirical, perceptible, and closely allied with what (if we are not restrained) we call matter; and we all know that doubts may arise concerning the certainty and generality of demonstrations upon such topics.

To be sure, the "logisticians" did not regard geometry in this empirical way. So far from holding that geometry dealt with empirical space, they averred that pure geometry could be completely "arithmetized," and therefore ultimately "logicized" (since arithmetic, in their view, could be logicized). Thus, as late as 1919, we find Mr. Russell writing: "All traditional pure mathematics, including analytical geometry, may be regarded as consisting wholly of propositions about the natural numbers. That is to say, the terms which occur can be defined by means of the natural numbers, and the propositions can be deduced from the properties of the natural numbers—with the addition, in each case, of the ideas and propositions of pure logic." [17]

The criticism that many might have been disposed to make upon this statement would be that a geometry so very "pure" would not be geometry in any ordinary sense; and Mr. Russell himself seems to have gone very far towards accepting the censure, for in 1927 we find him saying:

"Any geometry, Euclidean or non-Euclidean, in which every point has co-ordinates which are real numbers, can be interpreted as applying to a system of sets of real numbers—i.e. a point can be taken to *be* the series of its co-ordinates. This interpretation is legitimate, and is convenient when we are studying geometry as a branch of pure mathematics. But it is not the *important* interpretation. Geometry is important, unlike arithmetic and analysis, because it can be interpreted so as to be part of applied mathematics—in fact, so as to be part of physics. It is this interpretation which is the really interesting one, and we cannot therefore rest content with the interpretation which makes geometry part of the study of real numbers, and so, ultimately, part of the study of finite integers. Geometry as we shall consider it . . . will be always treated as part of physics, and will be regarded as dealing with objects which are not either mere variables or definable in purely logical terms. We shall not regard a geometry as satisfactorily interpreted until its initial objects have been defined in terms of entities forming part of the empirical world, as opposed to the world of logical necessity." [18]

Helmholtz, as is generally known, maintained that geometry is dependent on mechanics, since it requires us to assume that rigid bodies actually exist and are freely mobile in space.

The criticism usually passed upon this view is that in geometry we abstract the pure spatiality of bodies, and thus arrive at the theater in which the movements take place. If so, it is not at all evident either that the abstraction is legitimate or that its result is certain. Do we abstract (or extract) pure Newtonian "absolute" space? All the world knows to-day that the existence of this "absolute" space is highly questionable. Do we abstract by a species of idealization, constructing in thought ideally straight lines that lie "evenly" on the same plane, and so forth? It seems clear that such idealization may very well be of the

[17] *Op. cit.*, p. 4.
[18] *The Analysis of Matter*, p. 5.

kind that mathematicians call improper. And if we perform some other kind of abstraction, what in the world is it?

In any case, if geometry (or geometry of the "important" kind) is logically derived from our experience of bodies in space, it must be subject to any uncertainties that are necessarily attendant upon such derivation. These, in the main, will confront us later; but some of the problems so arising may conveniently be considered now.

It seems plain that Euclid himself, and the great majority of the ancient geometers, did not, in fact, purge geometry of all reference to spatial bodies and probably did not consider it advisable to attempt to do so. This is evident, for example, in many of the traditional and inaccurate definitions of a "point" as the limit of the process involved in supposing a grain of sand or a mote in a sunbeam gradually to become smaller and smaller. It is evident, similarly, in Proclus's definition of a line as the "flux" of a point, or its path when moved, or in Heron's definition of a straight line as a line (i.e. a material string) stretched to the utmost. The clearest instance, however, is probably the axiom of congruence which is one of Euclid's κοιναὶ ἔννοιαι. Commenting on this axiom Sir T. L. Heath says, "The phraseology of the propositions . . . in which Euclid employs the method indicated [i.e. superposition], leaves no room for doubt that he regarded one figure as actually *moved* and *placed upon* the other." [19] If so, there is the obvious difficulty (according to the traditional account of "absolute" space) that *space* can not be moved about at all, together with the additional difficulties that what is required for any such geometry is the superposition of *non-deformable* bodies, that we can not be certain empirically that any bodies *are* non-deformable, and that we presuppose the notion of space as soon as we begin to compare bodies according to the degree in which they are deformable. Consequently, it would seem that such geometries rest upon an assumption that can not be adequately verified by experience, and that is in part opposed to experience, viz. the assumption of bodies that do not alter shape or size when they are pushed about. If, on the other hand, we omit this assumption, and say, for instance, that with-

[19] *Euclid's Elements* (Second Edition, 1926), Vol. I, p. 225.

out physical superposition we may direct our attention from one figure (or from the geometrical properties of one figure) to another, it is not at all clear that the reply is satisfactory. For if perceptual attention is meant, the look of figures varies with their distance, and triangles identical in shape and size appear very different when, as we say, one of them is tilted or partly turned round and the other is not.[20]

As we have seen, the Axiom of Congruence is one of Euclid's κοιναὶ ἔννοιαι , or "common notions." These common notions were "axioms" in the Aristotelian sense, which is most precisely opposed, say, to Hilbert's. Axioms, for Aristotle, were very thoroughly metamathematical, for Aristotle held them to be rationally self-evident as well as indemonstrable. Such common notions were also held by Euclid to be common both to geometry and to arithmetic, although the fourth axiom (of congruence) may seem to us to be geometrical and not arithmetical.

In addition to his "common notions" and "definitions," however, Euclid also required certain "postulates," and the history of his fifth postulate concerning parallels is admitted on all hands to afford a very instructive commentary upon the nature of geometrical certainty.

Euclid's statement of his fifth postulate runs as follows: "That if a straight line falling on two straight lines make the interior angles on the same side less than two right angles, the two straight lines, if produced indefinitely, meet on that side on which are the angles less than the two right angles."

Sir T. L. Heath finds this statement of the postulate "epoch making," and remarks, "When we consider the countless successive attempts made through more than twenty centuries to prove the postulate, many of them by geometers of ability, we cannot but admire the genius of the man who concluded that such a hypothesis, which he found necessary to the validity of his whole system of geometry, was really indemonstrable." [21]

The postulate, however, is also not self-evident, either in Euclid's form or in such alternative forms as "Playfair's Axiom"

("Through a given point only one parallel can be drawn to a given straight line") or Gauss's ("If I could prove that a rectilineal triangle is possible the content of which is greater than any given area, I am in a position to prove perfectly rigorously the whole of [Euclidean] geometry"); and those who are accustomed to believe that traditional geometry exhibits the very paradigm of rational certainty can not withhold their sympathy from the long succession of geometers, Ptolemy, Proclus, Wallis, Saccheri, Lambert, Legendre, and others, who believed that the postulate could be proved and should not simply be assumed.

The history of this celebrated controversy is briefly that all attempts to demonstrate the postulate failed, but that Saccheri and others discovered important truths in the course of their attempted demonstrations, although they were unable to make full use of these discoveries owing to their rooted conviction that the postulate could not seriously be challenged; that Gauss seems to have been the first to perceive (after much hesitation) that the postulate might be "false" in the sense that a consistent geometry might be developed independently of it; that, following Gauss, Lobatschewsky and Bolyai developed the species of "non-Euclidean" or "astral" geometry now called hyperbolic; and that Riemann's work, based upon a more general standpoint concerning the measure of curvature in a continuous manifold, laid the foundations of the present system of the axioms of geometry. In these, Euclid's postulate is proved to be indemonstrable, and is not assumed to hold necessarily and universally.

According to Riemann, the straight line is not infinite (as is required in the Axiom of Archimedes). He says:

"In the extension of space construction to the infinitely great, we must distinguish between *unboundedness* and *infinite extent;* the former belongs to the extent relations; the latter to the measure relations. That space is an unbounded threefold manifoldness is an assumption which is developed by every conception of the outer world; according to which every instant the region of real perception is completed and the possible positions of a sought object are constructed, and which by these applications is for ever confirming itself. The unboundedness of space possesses in this way a greater empirical certainty than any external experience, but its infinite extent by no means follows from this; on the other hand, if we assume independence of bodies from position, and therefore ascribe to space constant curvature, it must necessarily be finite, provided this curvature has ever so small a positive value." [22]

The empirical unboundedness here referred to applies to the *measured* objects of physics in the neighborhood of the earth. It does not apply strictly to visual or to tactual apparitions (i.e. to immediate sense-experience), for such apparitions are *not* unbounded. Indeed, it is to physics, or to some supposed theater of physics, that all these controversies apply. The parallel lines in question are those, for example, of railway tracks, which the train seems to prove parallel however far it journeys. To the eye, such "parallel" lines converge. And there is a marked curvature, not a Euclidean flatness or approximate zero curvature, within our visual horizon. The sense, again, in which our visual apparitions are strictly three-dimensional is highly dubious. Having regard to eye-movements, such space may well be six-dimensional.

We need not, however, proceed with these reflections in this chapter. Instead, it will suffice if we recall the very neat paragraph with which the authors of the *Britannica* article on non-Euclidean geometry complete their argument.

"Finally [these authors say] it is of interest to note that, though it is theoretically possible to prove, by scientific methods, that our geometry is non-Euclidean, it is wholly impossible to prove by such methods that it is accurately Euclidean. For the unavoidable errors of observation must always leave a slight margin in our measurements. A triangle might be found whose angles were certainly greater, or certainly less, than two right angles; but to prove them *exactly* equal to two right angles must always be beyond our powers. If, therefore, any man cherishes a hope of proving the exact truth of Euclid, such a hope must be based, not upon scientific, but upon philosophical considerations." [23]

[22] Quoted by Bonola, *Non-Euclidean Geometry*, English translation, p. 142.
[23] *Encyclopædia Britannica* (Eleventh Edition), Vol. XI.

Chapter XI

OF CERTAINTY IN ETHICS

§ 1. General

At the first look, it may seem downright absurd to discuss ethical certainty as if it might conceivably be *in pari materia* with arithmetical. Are not "moral" and "mathematical" certainty flatly opposed? Is ethics not the study of *mores* or customs—as Ulpian said, "Tacitus consensus populi, longa consuetudine inveteratus"? And is it not plain that customs are highly variable, as well as largely irrational? What, on the face of it, could be more ridiculous than a solemn inquiry into *certainty, pro* or *con*, in such matters as the suicide of defeated generals, the duty of hospitality in countries where there are few, if any, inns, the limits of generosity, and the like? The Bedouins do not accept the code that our bank clerks accept; and that should be an end of the matter.

Such objections, however, depend upon a certain definition of ethics which need not be accepted, and it has frequently been maintained that ethics is based upon rational intuitions, and not on habits or on a variable *Sittlichkeit*. These intuitions, it is also claimed, can be known for certain. Indeed, we are sometimes told that they furnish the *best* examples of what is generally known by rational intuition. While it may be held that the ultimate simplicities in mathematics, say, are of a type in which laymen and experts are on a footing of equality, it is hard to believe this contention. It is much more plausible, however, to urge that the simpler moral duties, at least, are not only incumbent upon all but are also known by all who are mature in any appreciable degree.

Such contentions, therefore, may fitly be considered in this place. We have consequently to deal with ethical intuitionism of a rational, not of a merely impressionistic, type. Such intuitions are usually held to apply to a part, at least, of our duty, i.e. to something right and wrong, although it may also be maintained that there is such a thing as rational insight into "good" or "value."

Let us, then, begin with the former, and more usual, type of intuitionism. What is claimed in this matter is usually (1) that "right" is an elementary notion, incapable of further definition; (2) that every one knows for certain what this elementary notion is, although such knowledge may be temporarily occluded in the vertigo incident to intellectual gymnastics; and (3) that, for the most part, at all events, everyone is capable of applying this notion to his practice in such a way as to distinguish clearly (at any rate in a host of simple instances) between what is right and what is wrong.

§ 2. Varieties of Intuitionism in Ethics

It is usual to distinguish three varieties of intuitionism in ethics which (following Sidgwick, although without adopting his terminology) we may call particular, general, and formal.[1] According to the first of these doctrines, we are said to know intuitively that *this* action is right, and *that other* action wrong. According to the second alternative, we are said to know intuitively that any action of a certain class is right or wrong. According to the third view, we are said to know that any action that is right must be conformable to some structural or supremely general principle of a self-evident, formal type, although such a structural formal principle, while necessary to any right action, may not be sufficient to determine completely what is right in any particular case or in many rather special classes of actions.

These three types of ethical intuitionism are not, of course, necessarily exclusive.

§ 3. Particular Intuitionism

This species of intuitionism may be defended in various ways. In the Aristotelian way,[2] for example, it may be said to be due

---

[1] Sidgwick's terms are Perceptual, Dogmatic, and Philosophical. See *The Methods of Ethics*, Book III.
[2] *Ethics*, 1098b.

ἐθισμῷ τινι, that is to say, to a species of habituation among persons who have been trained in commendable ways. Again, these particularistic intuitions may be said to be the inevitable fruit of some type of emotion, say of a loving heart, or a public spirit.

Neither of these, however, necessarily implies rational vision or insight. The good habits of which Aristotle spoke are the habits that the statesman (or the director of public education) desires to induce among the young. The statesman may possess insight regarding the fitness, propriety, or "good form" of such habits, but the essential point is that the young should be trained in these habits whether or not they appreciate the reasons for them. In Platonic phrase, they should be indelibly dyed with the right opinion.[3] It is, of course, entirely possible that such habituation should be a necessary psychological precondition of genuine ethical insight; but the question before us concerns this insight itself, and can not be answered by matters relating to the usual, predisposing, or desirable causes of any such insight.

Similarly, while it may be true that love and affection (or, in the old and stilted phrase, "benevolence"), may, although they are reputed blind, clarify and induce our insight into the right way in which to act towards our fellow-men, it can not be argued with any plausibility that love (even the love of women) is invariably exempt from imbecility, or that affection and its promptings can not occur without yielding clear insight into duty. If there are *raisons de cœur* these must really be *raisons*. Otherwise, the argument falls. Mere promptings and inclinations are not enough for intelligible insight; and it seems tolerably clear that public spirit and mere good-heartedness do not necessarily lead to right conduct in ethics any more than in politics.

Omitting these species of "intuitionism," then (and also omitting others like them), it seems difficult to deny that rational intuition into any particular case is at least implicitly general, and so that the first variety of such intuitionism can not consistently be sundered from the second.

The conclusion seems inevitable that if any particular action is right for A to perform, any other action similar to this particu-

[3] *Republic*, 429.

lar one in relevant ethical respects must also be right for B or C
or D to perform, provided that B, C or D do not themselves
differ relevantly from A. Unless some given action is wholly
unique, and not in any way fitted to be a precedent or a parallel,
this implicit generality seems to be part of the meaning of what
is morally right. The question is always one of principle, and
ethical principles, if they are rational, can not vary on account
of trivial irrelevancies.

It is quite likely, to be sure, that a man who clearly discerns
that *this* is right may not be able to generalize his intuition in a
way that would satisfy a trained moralist. The reason here is
partly (as in so many other cases) that accurate generalization
is a highly technical art, and partly that most ethical principles
apply *differently* to cases that come within their scope, and that
unusual niceness of discernment may be necessary in order to
apprehend the relevant ethical difference. Even apart from such
niceness of discernment, if it is the duty of a wealthy husband to
support his wife, and also a poor husband's duty to support his
wife, there will be a relevant difference in the amount of the
allowance to be given, and subsidiary principles (which need not
be equally evident or known to both parties) may therefore
require to be introduced. Too much, however, should not be
made of this circumstance; and it is difficult to see how any one
could be said to know that he ought to support his wife, simply
because she is his wife, and yet could conceivably be ignorant
that this duty (so understood) could be other than general, that
is to say, could have a lesser application than to any husband
of any wife. If it be replied that it is *not* the duty of certain
husbands to support certain wives (e.g. faithless wives or very
rich ones) and that it may even be the duty of certain wives to
support certain husbands (e.g. invalid husbands or husbands
under a different economic régime to that to which we are accustomed), the answer is manifestly that, in that case, no one
can really know that it is *his* duty to support his wife *simply
because she is his wife*. He must know that it is his duty to support her (supposing that he does know it) because she is not
rich and not faithless and because he is not an invalid and has

promised to support her. These reasons have the same implicit generality as the former.

In other words, any rational intuition concerning the rightness of a particular action must, if it is *knowledge*, be capable of discerning the precise respect in which any such action is right. Otherwise, particular intuitionism can scarcely be distinguished from impressionism; and it is hard to see how a mere impression can be said to yield clear ethical knowledge or defensible ethical insight. In one sense, no doubt, it is correct to argue that no reason can be given for any self-evident intuition—that is to say, no reason other than the reason which is given by the intuition itself. But to hold this is very different indeed from holding that any impression of certainty in ethical matters is to be accounted rational knowledge simply because it is inarticulately convincing.

§ 4. GENERAL INTUITIONISM

According to general intuitionism, it is possible to know for certain that every instance of actions of a given class is right, and that every instance of actions of some other given class is wrong.

This doctrine, if at all plausible, must be freed from some prevalent misconceptions.

Firstly, it is not necessary for a general intuitionist to hold that any man (or woman or child) has an infallible "conscience." All he need maintain is that some men do authentically know that certain specific classes of actions are right and others wrong. The general intuitionist has no greater reason to be afraid of the bogy of infallibility in this kind of alleged knowledge than in any other alleged kind.

Secondly, he need not maintain that such knowledge is easily attained or very usual, although, in fact, he probably will make this claim. (There are not many general intuitionists who are advocates of esoteric knowledge of the fundamental duties.)

Thirdly, he need not maintain that these self-evident moral rules are uncomplicated. When faced with the problem of the "conflict of duties" (e.g. the telling of a truth that may kill or necessitate lifelong misery), he may consistently maintain that the general rule that he knows to be true is not of the simple type "never tell a lie," "never destroy a human being's happiness," but may be much more complicated.

These explanations being premised, it seems reasonable to consider some instance of such a general intuition in ethics, and I shall select one of the most important of them, viz. promise-keeping.

We may define a promise, for the purposes of the present discussion, as an express assurance given by A to B, that A will do everything in his power to perform a certain future action, and that B may count upon his doing so. Such promises may be relatively indeterminate (e.g. "Count on me if ever you are up against it") or quite specific (e.g. "I promise to pay your son's fees at Winchester next term as soon as they fall due"); and on trivial matters B need not understand that A will do *everything* in his power to implement the promise. A and B may also be groups acting in a corporate capacity. But with these explanations the definition seems sufficiently accurate.

We have therefore to consider, firstly, the making of promises, and secondly, the keeping of them.

It is clear that some promises should not be *made*, e.g., in some instances at least, suicide pacts or a promise to run away with another man's wife. If this were not so, we could make any sinful action right by promising to do it, and therefore it also seems reasonable to conclude that *some* promises that are made should not be *kept*. On the other hand, while promises to commit a definite sin ought not to be kept, it is a nice point of honor whether many rash and foolish promises, which it would have been better not to have made, ought not, nevertheless, to be kept. An explanation and an apology to the promisee, at least, is required if such promises are not kept; and very often such apologies, in the general judgment, are not enough. If A's word has been given, it should not, in general, be affected by A's afterthoughts or by A's subsequent coldness of feet. Obviously, however, there is the greatest possible difficulty in knowing for certain where the boundary should be drawn in cases of this kind.

Another difficulty concerns promises made in relative ignorance. The kind of ignorance normally to be expected concerning the future, no doubt, is irrelevant. To choose a trivial instance, a man is not to be excused from attending a dinner party because he is *rather* more tired than he expected to be. Consider, however, the case of a husband deserting his wife on the ground that she had tricked him into marriage by representing herself to have become pregnant by him although in fact she was not pregnant,[4] or the case of a good Catholic promising to marry a lady without knowing that she was a *divorcée*. Any simple rule of promise-keeping seems to founder on rocks such as these, and the rule can hardly be less complicated than "All promises other than promises to sin or very foolhardy ones ought to be kept, provided that no change in the circumstances reasonably presumed to be understood by both parties is sufficiently considerable to destroy the plain or ordinary meaning of the promise."

A further difficulty concerns the question whether a man is morally bound to keep faith with those who do not keep faith with him. Suppose that *A* and *B* enter into a mutual covenant of secrecy, and that *B* "spills the beans," perhaps in a mischievously inaccurate fashion. Is *A* then bound to say nothing at all?

What, then, are we to say concerning the *certainty* of promise-keeping? Obviously, there are a great many promises not for a sinful, unlawful, or highly imprudent end, not made in ignorance, not annulled by bad faith on the part of the promisee, not completely trivial, and well within the promiser's power to perform. In such cases, it may be said, that every one *knows* that he ought to keep his promise. Yet surely such knowledge is very odd if it is not accompanied by some measure of recognition of the occasions in which perplexity may reasonably arise. In short, it seems plain that if we take our stand on intuitionism, we should interpret such intuitionism in a different way from what is usual. What is certain, we may say, is that the giving of a promise always makes a relevant and inescapable difference to the moral situation. A man who has passed his word has done something that he can not disown—something that necessarily affects the morality of his future action, particularly with respect to the

[4] Dawson, E. *vs.* Dawson, T., as reported in *The Times* (London), April 12, 1929.

promisee. This seems true even of promises to sin. And, in general, it may fairly be argued that, unless very strong evidence to the contrary is adduced, every one is morally bound to keep all his promises punctually and faithfully. This highly significant and inescapable alteration of the moral situation has a strong claim to be considered quite certain knowledge, but it is not an assertion that every promise should be kept, and it does not give any direct information concerning the instances in which the duty of promise-keeping ought morally to be overborne by a still weightier obligation. For it does not determine what these weightier occasions are.

In order to show how serious such questions may become, and how exceedingly difficult it often is to be anywhere near certainty that we have attained definitive rational guidance in such matters, it may be well to choose some concrete historical example, and I shall select the theses of Luther's work *On Monastic Vows*.

A few years after Luther's challenge to the Roman hierarchy at Worms, the question of the morality of monks and nuns repudiating their vows—particularly the vow of celibacy—and joining the Protestant movement became vitally acute. Indeed, there could hardly have been a more serious question for many thousands of perplexed souls, as a very slight exercise of historical imagination is sufficient to show.

Luther's contentions, in the main, were as follows: [5]

(1). He argued that the vow was made under a misapprehension. The novice supposed that he could obtain salvation by works, by calculated and formalized austerities. But this is contrary to Scripture, false, and even sinful. When the misapprehension is corrected and the truth of justification by faith alone shines forth, the supposed obligation vanishes.

(2). He argued that the vow was a vow to something sinful, because the whole monastic system was sinful. The monasteries were an unscriptural attempt to found a vast worldly corporation, ostensibly for inward spiritual benefit, but actually for wealth and political power as well.

(3). Regarding celibacy, he held that celibacy was contrary

[5] See Mackinnon, *Luther and the Reformation*, Vol. III, pp. 24 *sqq.*

to nature; that, in fact, the monastic life led to sexual impurities far more hideous than the marriage tie, even in the eyes of those who take the "flesh" to be an inevitable hindrance to the spiritual life; that some monastic vows were made by parents for their oblate children, and that the children were consequently not consenting parties in any adequate sense; and finally, that many monastic vows were taken so early (in particular before puberty) that those who took them could not possibly know what the vow meant.

It seems unreasonable to contend that these arguments have no force at all, or that no one (including Luther) who had taken such vows could conscientiously become a Protestant or even preach Protestantism. Yet the arguments are of varying and somewhat doubtful cogency, and it is difficult to see how an intuitionist could show precisely how far real certainty resided in them. Since Luther himself admitted that a man might, without sin, remain celibate for spiritual ends and might even, without sin, remain a monk if he reinterpreted the character of the monastic system in the light of his knowledge of the gospels, many of his arguments are proportionately weakened. Others of his arguments, again, clearly have to do with special cases only, e.g. those referring to oblate children, or to monks and nuns who take their vows before puberty. Such arguments have no bearing upon the case of persons who took the vows after puberty, knowing what they were about. And in such cases, it can scarcely be contended that the point of ethics was altogether plain. A soldier can hardly be absolved from the oath he took as a recruit, merely because he can not know in advance what his actual feelings upon the battle-field will be, and a monk, similarly, can hardly plead that, as a novice, he did not know how strong his repressed sexual impulses would become. Again, the argument that the monasteries in fact became very impure places may be a good enough argument for abolishing the system, but is hardly a justification for any individual monk's renouncing his vows, especially if most of the monks, when they took these vows, shared the common knowledge concerning the conditions of the monasteries, but vowed themselves to remain unspotted.

§ 5. Formal Intuitionism

The third type of intuitionism may be illustrated by Sidgwick's "axioms." These are:

(1). The principle of Justice: "It cannot be right for A to treat B in a manner in which it would be wrong for B to treat A, merely on the ground that they are two different individuals and without there being any difference between the nature and the circumstances of the two which can be stated as a reasonable ground for difference of treatment." This Sidgwick declared to be self-evident "as far as it goes," [6] and he further stated that a "somewhat different" application of the same principle was impartiality in the application of general rules, e.g. in a court of law.

(2). The principle: "Hereafter as such is neither less nor more to be regarded than now." No reference is here made to the past, but Sidgwick says that the important application of the principle is Prudence, viz. "a smaller present good is not to be preferred to a greater future good (allowing for difference of certainty)." [7]

(3). The principle of Benevolence, Sidgwick holds, is deducible with certainty from these two propositions, and is the principle "that each one is morally bound to regard the good of any other individual as much as his own except in so far as he judges it to be less, when impartially viewed, or less certainly knowable or attainable by him." [8]

This statement of the principle of Benevolence is not without difficulty; for some would argue that the important question is whether another's good *is* as great as his own, not whether he judges it to be so when (if he ever can) he is "impartial." Again, it might be maintained that the important point is "attainable" not "knowable or attainable."

Sidgwick's statements of the principles of Justice and of Prudence, again, seem suspiciously like tautologies. In an apparently accurate paraphrase, the Principle of Justice becomes "I know for certain that the differences between A and B are morally

---

[6] *The Methods of Ethics* (Seventh Edition), p. 380.
[7] *Ibid.*, p. 381.   [8] *Ibid.*, p. 382.

irrelevant unless they are morally relevant in respect of capacity, circumstances, etc." What, in effect, Sidgwick's axioms proclaim is that we may be capable of making certain sweeping, and also certain highly specific, judgments of moral irrelevance. We can not, however, know for certain that differences that we do not know to be morally relevant therefore *are* morally irrelevant, or again, unless we have quite certain knowledge of moral relevance, that what we believe to be (or to be possibly) relevant, really is so. The brunt of the certainty, therefore, according to Sidgwick's theory, must depend upon specific judgments of moral relevance, and the only respect in which his axioms appear to be *not* tautological is the important principle that *if* we knew for certain that there was no relevant moral difference in any two or more given cases we ought not to act differently (in a moral regard) in such cases. (It is hardly axiomatic that this principle holds if we only *think*, but do not *know*, that there is no relevant moral difference.)

It seems clear that this attenuated axiom has a good claim to self-evidence, and that many of our judgments of moral relevance seem very firm indeed. To claim complete certainty for the latter, however, is something different, and the claim can hardly be made without temerity. At any rate, the majority of moralists of the intuitional type include much that should be doubtful in what they declare to be certain.

For example, Thomas Reid, in his *Active Powers*,[9] enumerates six of these formal axioms in ethics, but states some of them in such a way as to involve the very doubtful conceptions of merit and desert, and even the meriting of punishment. Some of his axioms, however, are exempt from this type of criticism, and of these two may be noted here. These are Reid's fifth moral axiom "We ought to use the best means we can to be well informed of our duty," and his sixth "It ought to be our most serious concern to do our duty as far as we know it, and to fortify our minds against every temptation to deviate from it."

These injunctions may perhaps be axiomatic, broadly speaking, although some would question the formulation of them in detail. Another moral axiom that might be suggested is the

[9] Essay V, Ch. I.

following: "It is wholly certain that we ought always to do the best that we can."

The special interest attaching to this "axiom" is that it endeavors to state an evident and necessary relation between "right" and "good," the two cardinal conceptions in ethics. Before considering this central theme, however, it seems necessary to make some preliminary explanations concerning the "axiom."

It is commonly held—this is another of Reid's first principles of morals [10]—that "What is in no degree voluntary, can neither deserve moral approbation nor blame," or, in other words, that actions wholly involuntary are not ethical at all. The mere production of good consequences (e.g. the human happiness that sunlight or some other inanimate agent may produce) is altogether beyond the purview of ethics.

It is not unlikely that modern Western ethics pays too much attention to the legal or semi-legal conception of express volition, and that love, purity, and other conditions of soul not usually regarded as volitional (or even, more generally, as "voluntary") pertain to ethics and may suffice to make conduct or character ethical. On the other hand, some restriction of the type in question seems essential. An action can not be ethical unless it is either (1) capable of being chosen or controlled in some conscious or reflective decision, and in that sense "voluntary," or (2) the expression of a moral character or condition of soul which, indirectly at least, is potentially obedient to such control.

Another explanation (which is, in part, a consequence of the foregoing) is suggested by the qualification contained in Reid's sixth axiom.[11] Ought we not to say that we ought to do the best that we can, *in so far as we know what is best?*

This qualification raises serious special difficulties. It can hardly be maintained, with any pretense at plausibility, that a man's duty is completely at the mercy of what he happens to know or not to know at any moment. The man must at least, in the sense of Reid's fifth axiom, have done his utmost to learn what is best for him to do. And even in that case, since, after the most sedulous examination, the man may nevertheless, like

[10] *Active Powers* Essay V, Ch. I. Reid's second axiom.   [11] *Ibid.*

most of us, over- or underestimate his capacities, he may in fact be capable of performing better actions than he thinks he is capable of performing. If so, does the "axiom" refer to what he *can* do, or to what he *thinks* he can do? If we seek to evade this difficulty by saying that it is *knowledge* and not opinion that should here be considered, our troubles are even more considerable. Are we seriously to hold that there is *no* duty unless there is utterly certain knowledge; and that ethics, so far from being a wide and sane reflection on the ways in which the lives of men and women and (perhaps) other rational creatures may be lived to the best purpose, is restricted to the slender sheaf of moral commandments (if indeed there is such a sheaf) that men know for certain to be true?

A further, and very important point, concerns the interpretation of the phrase "the best that a man can do." This is often taken forthwith to mean "the action that will have the best possible consquences"; and it is objected that more than the future counts ethically, that a man should be mindful of his past obligations, and that it may be a man's duty to keep his word, because of the past obligation, although no advantage need be expected to accrue.

This particular difficulty would seem to be met by the explanation that a man's moral action must be directed towards the immediate or proximate future (since all action must be so directed), but is nevertheless an adjustment to the entire moral situation, including the man's past obligations.

On the other hand, it seems clear that if we say that a man ought to do what will, in fact, bring about the best possible consequences (respect being paid to his past obligations and to other features of his moral situation that are not future), we are setting up an impracticable moral ideal. For what human being can *know* what the consequences of his actions are going to be? We never have this complete certainty regarding the future. And although it may not always be an objection that a moral ideal is something "too high for mortal man beneath the sky" (in the sense that men must be expected to fall short of its exacting standards), there is manifestly a serious objection in the present instance. For it is usually held that "ought implies can"; that is to say, that it can never be a man's duty to do what he could not conceivably accomplish. And if we were to say that a man ought to act as if he could foresee all the consequences of his possible actions and choose the best among them *although* he can not conceivably have such foresight, we should be running counter to the maxim that "ought implies can" in most of the intelligible senses of this maxim.

In order to escape from this difficulty it is frequently suggested that our "axiom" ought to be "A man ought always to do what is probably best." In this case, the burden of these perplexities is thrown upon probable inference, and, as we shall see, there is a great deal to be said, *pro* and *con*, concerning the rationality of "probability." Even if probability could be accepted as something completely intelligible, however, dubieties might still assail us. Probability is relative to evidence, and it would seem, not only that some agents have much more adequate information concerning the probable effects of action than other agents have, but that it is quite unreasonable to expect that every agent could expect to have the same degree of adequate information concerning the data from which probable inferences could be drawn. A mother bringing up her children, for example, can not be expected to have the same knowledge of probabilities as a doctor has, or necessarily to be able to conjecture when she should consult the doctor about them. And since conjecture according to statistical or other logical forms of probability is a very difficult art, it is also unreasonable to expect that everyone *could* form a correct logical estimate of probability from the data in his possession, or that different persons, having the same data, could reasonably be expected always to form the same probable estimate.

Thus, even if we knew for certain what *would be* good or valuable or excellent, supposing that we could achieve it, or what *would be* the best among alternative goods, supposing that we could attain them, there would still be a thicket of perplexities in our way when we began to ask what it is *likely* we should do in order to "maximize" the good in the world according to the best of our lights and the best of our powers.

§ 6. RIGHT AND GOOD

If the "axiom" we have just been considering were acceptable, the effect would be that "right" could be based upon "good" in the sense that if we knew what was *best* to do we could thence infer what was right to do. This would not imply that "right," on the one hand, or "good," "value," or "excellence," on the other hand, had the same meaning. All that would follow would be that they had this kind of equivalence and that they had this deductive relation.

In view of the difficulties we have mentioned, as well as in view of difficulties we have not mentioned, it is not surprising that many moralists renounce any hope of discovering any such equivalence, and therefore (if they do not also renounce ethics altogether and substitute some variety of sociology, psychology, or anthropology for it) adhere to an intuitionism concerning right that is wholly independent of any intuitions into value or "axiology."

This intuitionism is usually combined with an entire rejection of the relevance of "consequences" to ethics. A man who is careful, candid, and sincere, it is argued, may "damn the consequences" in a moral regard, not because consequences do not matter, but because they do not matter *morally*. If the man is negligent, say, his defect is moral, and he should experience moral contrition. But if he is faithful and not negligent, the defects of his skill, intelligence, and acumen are not to be imputed to any deficiency in his moral character.

While it is plainly not unreasonable to argue along these lines, and while (on the surface at least) there is much to be said for the view that we may know our duty without knowing anything about probable consequences, it is surely very difficult to believe in this complete separation between right and good. *Fiat justitia, ruat cœlum* has an elevated ring, but is hard to dissever from our belief that justice has no tendency towards making the heavens fall and a very marked tendency towards making human relationships stable and even delightful. It may be true that most human beings would prefer to live under a just than under a pleasant régime; but this, in its turn, may be taken to mean

that they rate the worth of justice above the worth of content-
ment. To argue that no values, esthetic, hedonic, or whatever
they may be, have anything to do with what is right and wrong
in action, that the good life is not a thing that men ought to
aim at, and the like, is surely a most violent paradox. In short,
the principle that men ought to strive after the *best*, whatever
difficulties it may contain, plainly does seem relevant to all moral
conduct, and it is repugnant to the judgment, if not flatly immoral, to maintain that any one *ought* to do what is worse than
the best, even in following one of the firmer moral rules.

Many, indeed, are of opinion that the most plausible way of
defending general intuitions concerning right conduct is to hold
that the value of fidelity, say, is so considerable that it is very
improbable indeed that any misfortunes that might accrue from
breaking one's word outweigh the dignity and intrinsic worth of
being faithful to it; and hence that, in general, it is unnecessary
to attend to actual, probable, or possible results. This view, if
it could be sustained, would base these moral rules upon the
value of the qualities of character exhibited in the keeping of
the rules. Even, however, if the value of these qualities was so
great that it could *never* be overborne by any accumulation of
contrary and competing values, it would not follow that such
contrary and competing values were *irrelevant;* and the paradox
contained in this type of opinion would, to that extent, be miti-
gated. On the other hand, it would still be a very hard saying,
and one concerning which it would be extraordinarily bold to
claim utter certainty, if we were to maintain with Newman that
"it were better for sun and moon to drop from heaven, for the
earth to fail, or for all the many millions who are upon it to die
of starvation in extremest agony, than that one soul—I will not
say should be lost—but should commit one venial sin, should tell
one wilful untruth though it harmed no one, or steal one poor
farthing without excuse." [12]

§ 7. Intuitions into Value

If there is any respect in which what is right is based upon
what is best, and if it is possible to *know* this basis, it follows

[12] *Anglican Difficulties*, p. 190.

that we must not merely be able to know for certain that particular things (or kinds of things) are good or excellent, but that we must be able to compare these "values." Such judgments concerning "better" and "best" ultimately imply what is called the "commensurability" of values.

While particular judgments (as that happiness is better than misery, or courage a finer thing than mere politeness) may claim very well to be as nearly certain as any judgments we ever make, it is quite another thing to defend the *certainty* that all values are significantly comparable and form a single scale such that it is always possible in theory to say how "white" a lie must be if it is not incomparably worse than the evil of so much toothache. And without further argument it should scarcely be necessary to point out that a rational man may doubt whether all values are "commensurable" in this sense.

To be sure, it might be maintained with consistency that we have completely certain knowledge of certain (indeed of many) values, although we are necessarily uncertain concerning any single and far-flung scale of values; and I am far from attempting to deny that we do have rational insight into values, and are entitled to be confident concerning this insight. Indeed, I should try to enforce this contention, if this were the place for it.

The entire nature of value, however, is at present a subject so hotly disputed among philosophers (who seem, for the most part, to be capable of understanding one another very well) that it would be a piece of effrontery for any disputant upon this topic to claim more than strong conviction of a grounded kind for his views upon it. I believe, then, that we have rational insight into values. But Spinoza [13] or Mr. Dewey [14] would say that value, in principle, is simply what helps anything (particularly any living thing) in its temporary self-maintenance. If so, value is an expression for the *conatus perseverare in esse suo* (together with whatever favors any such *conatus*) in *everything*, whether good, bad, or indifferent; and in this sense value is strength, not excellence. Other philosophers, such as Meinong,[15] von Ehren-

---

[13] *Ethics, especially* Part III.
[14] *Essays in Experimental Logic,* pp. 349 *sqq.*
[15] E.g. in his *Zur Grundlegung der allgemeinen Werttheorie.*

fels,[16] or Mr. Perry,[17] would say that value must be interpreted psychologically as a function of pleasure and desire. If so, there is the bare possibility of rational insight into excellence, although psychologically, it is entirely possible, and not at all unusual, to take pleasure in pursuits and experiences that we call mean and ignoble. Up to the present time, however, all such theories have been very tentative and exasperatingly vague.

[16] *System der Werttheorie.*
[17] *General Theory of Value.*

CHAPTER XII

OF SENSITIVE CERTAINTY

§ 1. EXPLANATORY

UP to the present, our discussion in Part III of this book has been concerned with the usual "noëtic" certainties, logical, mathematical, or ethical. We have been engaged in debating the claim to pellucid intelligibility put forward on behalf of some fundamental intellectual principles and propositions. Many philosophers would hold, however, that, in the last analysis, intellectual "certainty" concerning *noëta* (or the things that are intellectually limpid and diaphanous) is something of a fetish, and that authentic, invincible certainty is to be sought and found, not in *noëta* but in *æstheta*, that is to say, in immediate sensuous experience or in the throbbing vital experience of feeling and passion. Rationalists have asserted, indeed, that such *æstheta*, being "unintelligible" (or refractory to intellectual treatment), are not to be regarded by those who endeavor to *think*, not furiously but seriously. Yet these rationalists, we are told, were quite plainly wrong. Our immediate momentary experience, the "present phenomenon of our consciousness," is a piece of "shining apparency" and is wholly indubitable. Nothing else is either apparent or indubitable in anything approaching the same degree. Rationalists, according to this argument, may say, if they choose, that such *æstheta* are muddy and feculent, because they cloud and perturb the pure vintage in which intellect takes delight. Yet these *æstheta* are *certain;* and instead of being negligible lees and dregs, receiving a passing and rather shamefaced mention after the main work of philosophy has been done, are the source and the spring of whatever is completely indubitable.

Among such *æstheta,* those of a sensory kind, variously described as "sensations," "sensa," "sense-data," or "sensibles," occupy a commanding place in most discussions of this question. We may therefore consider sensitive certainty, or "the testimony of our senses," in the first instance. Other supposed certainties of the same order but of different types, such as mnemic or memorial certainty (i.e. the "testimony of memory"), introspective certainty regarding our own minds, and the extrospective certainty (if there is any) involved in our acquaintance with our fellow-men, will be considered in subsequent chapters.

§ 2. THE CERTAINTY OF SENSA

Before the introduction of a slightly altered terminology, it would commonly have been said that sensitive certainty is an affair of sensation, with the further explanation that what strictly was meant was a man's private, momentary sensation, here and now. It would also have been usual to say that a "sensation," in this sense, is a "present phenomenon of consciousness," although Locke defined his "ideas of sensation" as the *objects* of the understanding when a man thinks" [1] (*sc.* in a perceptual or sensory fashion) and although Berkeley himself declared that "those qualities [i.e. of sense] are in the mind only as they are perceived by it;—that is, not by way of *mode* or *attribute*, but only by way of *idea.*" [2]

More recently, when the New Realism began (although Mr. G. E. Moore, who inaugurated the movement with his article on "The Refutation of Idealism," [3] and others who agreed with him, did not covet the title of "realism") the term "sensation" tended to pass out of currency, because it was declared to be ambiguous. A so-called "sensation," it was said, necessarily included two distinct parts, viz. the "act" of sensing and the entity (e.g. "a patch of color") that was sensed. There were always the -*ing* and the -*ed* (for example the hear*ing* and the hear*ed*) and these twain were never the same. On the contrary, the -*ing* must be "mental" and the -*ed* might very well be non-mental or even material.

In the light of this analysis, it was declared that we could always, by attending with sufficient care, notice the difference

---

[1] *Essay,* Introduction, § 8.   [2] *Principles of Human Knowledge,* § 49.
[3] *Mind,* N.S., Vol. xii, 1903. Reprinted in *Philosophical Studies.*

between our (mental) "acts," say, of seeing (not to be confounded with movements of ocular adjustment or other kinæsthetic sense-data), and the "sense-datum" that was seen, although these "acts" were, so to say, "diaphanous"[4] and although it might be wholly impossible to distinguish any qualitative difference between the "seeing" of blue (i.e. the "act" of seeing) and the seeing of red, or again between the "act" of seeing a color and the "act" of smelling an odor.

In the more recent developments of this analysis (including, as I apprehend, the development of Mr. Moore's own thought) a part of this contention is abandoned. It is conceded (I do not say correctly conceded) that "acts" (or at any rate acts of sensing) are not introspectively observable, and that the word "act" is, to say the least, unfortunate, because it connotes the dangerous and difficult notion of "activity" which, even if it were readily intelligible, might be misplaced in this connection, since apprehension, properly speaking, is perhaps neither active nor passive. (A recent suggestion from Oxford[5] is to the effect that the Latin term "actus" might be preferable to the English "act," since the Latin does not imply activity but only actualization.)

In terms of these developments and explanations, the -ings in sensation may be said to have become suspect; but it is still firmly asserted that the -eds remain. We do sense odors and patches of color, and these entities quite plainly *appear* to us (and therefore *are* entities since they can not be nothing). We might call them, perhaps, sense-apparitions.

It has also become usual to describe these apparitions by what is intended to be the neutral term "sensa" rather than by the more question-begging term "sense-data." This point may seem to be verbal, and, of course, very largely *is* verbal; but the verbal dispute indicates points of real importance and should therefore be pursued, although not at interminable length.

The term "sense-data" implies that sensa are *given*, and the nature of this *givenness* may include a jungle of thorny questions which it is eminently desirable to avoid in a definition

---

[4] *Philosophical Studies*, p. 25.
[5] The suggestion is due to Mr. H. H. Price.

of entities that are declared to be wholly certain and indubitable. Among these menacing if shadowy, thorns, the following spiky dangers may be noted.

(1) In the epistemological sense, an entity may be said to be *given* if it confronts us, so to speak, as something *there* to be non-voluntarily apprehended without any admixture of our own activity; and plainly we can not infer with certainty, from the mere circumstance that a red patch appears (or even from the statement that there is a visual apparition tolerably well described as a red patch), that such a patch confronts our senses willy-nilly, or that our activity may not suffuse, or be an ingredient in, the apparition. A neutral term that does not contain this implication should therefore be chosen in preference to any term that might be taken, not unreasonably, to contain the implication.

(2) In view of the inveterate tendency of so many philosophers to confound sense-apparition with the *causes* of sense-apparition (and particularly with its physical and physiological causes, if there are such), it is of the utmost importance, especially in views of the type we are now considering, that our descriptions of sensa should not be moored to any dogma concerning their causes. In speaking, then, of the certainty of the existence of sensa or of sense-apparitions, it is necessary to avoid the appearance of suggesting any theory about their causes, and in particular to explain that what is meant is not the stimuli of such apparitions, or the brain states that (with an uncomfortable number of omissions in detail) are usually held to induce sensation, but the apparitions themselves. In the minds of many, to say that a sensum is *given* is just to say that it is *caused*, or even that it is caused by what physiologists call an "adequate" stimulus (i.e. by an appropriate stimulus, as when our sensing of a stelliform apparition is caused by an actual star and not by a blow on the head); and no accounts of the causes of our sense-apparitions (however plausible these may be) can approach the certainty (in some sense) of the apparitions themselves. Again, the "stars" that are seen on account of the blow on the head are perfectly good apparitions, and so are the pink rats of delirium tremens, together with the *fata morgana*, the Brocken specters,

and the entire phantasmagoria of illusion and hallucination. It is essential, accordingly, to avoid any theory of causation in our definition of sensa, and therefore to omit any reference to a "givenness" that might be confused with causation.

(3) It is natural, and not unreasonable, to distinguish between what is *given* in (or to) sense, on the one hand, and, on the other hand, the suggestions and associations that are blended with, or overlaid upon, what is thus "given." Hence, many conclude that if the "given" is not something protoplasmic and embryonic, it is at the best a naked infant, and therefore must be distinguished from any actual sensation or perception which is wrapped round and round with layer after layer of clothes (in the way of association and suggestion) like the large bundles with which we are familiar that are so largely clothes and so little baby. Obviously, however, if *certainty* is to be claimed in these matters, we have to take our apparitions as we find them, and as we find them *now*. To attempt to distinguish between the "given" parts of them, and all associative accretions to their "given" simplicity, is an endeavor of high conjecture and of resolute imagination in which even the boldest could not expect to find certainty. "I am as true as truth's simplicity, and simpler than the infancy of truth" might conceivably be written of the "given" in this sense; but such simplicity can never be said to be separately apparent.

In short, if appearances are to be taken just as they show themselves, they can not, for that very reason, be stripped of anything that they appear to have. In other words, they would *not* be the same appearances if we tried to rid them of everything except the nudity of their givenness. Similarly, if our sensa really are "suggestive," this "suggestiveness," whether primitive, ancestral, and prior to individual experience, or acquired in individual association, must also be allowed to be part of the apparition. The "innocence of the eye" of which Ruskin spoke, or, in other words, the freeing of visual apparitions from any suggestions concerning workaday fact or practical enterprise, would *not*, on this view, characterize our customary visual appearances. On the contrary, this innocence, supposedly primitive, has to be recovered by painstaking and continued training. Our visual sensa appear with their associative visual auras.

If sensa, then, are given, these particular interpretations, viz. mental passivity, causal occurrence, or absence of association and suggestiveness should not be read into the "givenness." And the term "sensum" does not imply any nuance of such an interpretation.

The view before us, then, is that the existence of sensa, properly understood, is quite indisputable and completely certain.

§ 3. The Momentary Sensum

"Our whole certainty is momentary," Huxley said; and this is the usual opinion of those who put their trust in sensitive certainty. The point, indeed, may be said to be a matter of definition. For it is usual to define both sensation and perception as processes confined to the immediate present, and to distinguish them sharply from any species of memory. Since memory, in the opinion of many philosophers, can not be supposed to yield certainty, being notoriously liable to be mistaken and infected with theoretical perplexities, this restriction of sensitive certainty to the present moment is supposed to smooth the way for those who believe in utter sensitive certainty.

There are grounds for holding, however, that restriction to the present moment makes the way more rugged instead of smoothing it. For what is the "present" moment?

It is generally said, and it seems reasonable to say, that the "present" in sensitive certainty must be the "sensible" or "specious" present. This term, the "specious" (or apparent) present, is due to a Mr. E. R. Clay who is quoted by William James as saying: "The present to which the datum [6] refers is really a part of the past—a recent past—delusively given as being a time that intervenes between the past and the future. . . . Time, then, considered relatively to human apprehension, consists of four parts, viz. the obvious past, the specious present, the real present and the future. Omitting the specious present, it consists of three . . . nonentities—the past, which does not exist, the future, which does not exist, and their conterminous, the present;

[6] E.g. any sense datum.

the faculty from which it proceeds lies to us in the fiction of the specious present." [7]

This definition and explanation is not very encouraging to believers in momentary sensitive certainty. But let us proceed.

One of the things that may be meant by the "specious" or apparent present is that what appears to be *present* is always, in reality, *past*, although very recent. According to this view, whatever we apprehend in sensation and in perception is apprehended when it is waning and has just escaped our simultaneous apprehension of it. Accordingly, if sensitive certainty, as Huxley seems to have thought, attaches to what is *apparently* "momentary," the conclusion is that we are certain, in this matter, of what is *really* past, although it *seems* to be present. And many philosophers would pretend to discover a flat contradiction in any such statement. The past, they argue in effect, can not be immediately apprehended. For, by definition, it is remote, even if it is ever so slightly remote (as in the very recent past). And an *immediate* apprehension of what is *remote* is a plain absurdity.

This argument, I think, is mistaken. An immediate apprehension is simply an apprehension in which there is nothing mediate, an apprehension that is "direct" in the sense that what is apprehended is not apprehended *by means of any apprehended intermediaries*. There is no contradiction of any sort in believing that we may, in this sense, have "direct" unmediated apprehension of what is past.

Consequently, there is no contradiction contained in the view that, in sensitive certainty, we are acquainted with the very recent past, although we misstate the circumstance when we say we are certain of the "present" moment. On the other hand, any such view seems extremely unplausible and excessively arbitrary. For if we may thus be quite certain concerning the very recent past (which seems to be present), what is the reason for denying our certainty concerning the less recent past (which not only *is* past but is obviously so)? If that which is past may nevertheless be certain, what grounds can any one have for asserting that what is *obviously* past can not be certain?

[7] From *The Alternative*, p. 167. See James, *Principles of Psychology*, Vol. I, p. 609.

A second set of arguments concerning the "specious" present is to the following effect. The "mathematical" present, it is said, is a "point" without the magnitude of duration, and it is impossible for us to sense or perceptually to discern such a point, limit, or boundary *in isolation*. We can only discern (in sense-perception) a temporal magnitude, that is to say, a stretch of duration or slab of passage. The "mathematical" present, therefore, can not be the "specious" or apparent present, because, by itself, it can not appear at all. We perceive a saddle-back and not a knife-edge whenever we perceive what occurs *now*.

Hence it follows that the "momentary" sensum of which we are said to be certain must have duration, because it is sensibly "momentary" and not mathematically so. Furthermore, assuming that we can not apprehend the future directly, it follows that when we apprehend any saddle-back of temporal passage, the saddle-back is bounded, on one side, by the limit called the "mathematical" present. In this, however, nothing is said about the limit, if there is one, at the other side; and it seems evident that any apprehended stretch of duration, bounded on one side by the "mathematical" present, must contain parts that are *earlier*, in time, than this "mathematical" boundary.

Here a distinction may perhaps be drawn between "past and present," on the one hand, and "earlier and later," on the other hand. To many it seems a plain contradiction to say that the "specious" present, which by definition appears to be *present*, can contain any part or feature that appears to be *past*. Whatever appears to have duration, however, must also (again according to this definition) appear to contain a transition from what is earlier to what is later.

In terms of this distinction, therefore, it might be accounted legitimate to assert that whenever we apprehend a slab of duration as being *present*, we apprehend the earlier portions of this duration simply as *earlier*, and not at all as *past*. On the other hand, this may well be considered an unnecessary refinement, and a simpler solution may be welcome. Why in the world should we hold that what is called the "specious" present appears to be *exclusively* present and to contain nothing that (correctly) appears to be past? Why should we not hold that the phrase is simply a rough description of the circumstance that when we apprehend a short stretch of duration, bounded on one side by what is intellectually, not sensibly, discernible as the "mathematical" present, we call such a duration the "present," although we can perceive, as well as intellectually discern, the earlier portions of it to be already past?

This would seem, at any rate, to be the natural explanation of the examples commonly cited. To quote again from James's excerpt from Mr. Clay, "All the notes of a bar of a song seem to the listener to be contained in the present." What, precisely, does this statement mean? It can not be contended, surely, that the notes are struck all at once, or ever appear to be simultaneous. It can not be contended that the earlier notes do not appear to be earlier. And is it evident, in any genuine sense, that they do not appear to be *past*, although apprehended to be continuous with the "present" conclusion of the bar? In short, there is no serious objection to the view that the sensible or apparent present is simply that stretch of apprehended duration that is apprehended as being sensibly continuous, at any given mathematical moment, with the mathematical *now*, and bounded, at one side, by the mathematical *now*.

If this be so, what is the proper conclusion concerning our alleged "momentary" certainty in sensation? As the result of psychological experiments, it is commonly said that the stretch of duration that normally appears to be sensibly continuous with the mathematical limit called the "present" is in the neighborhood of $\frac{7}{8}$ths of a second, although it may sometimes be appreciably less, and sometimes considerably more. Without examining the nature or the conclusiveness of these psychological experiments, let us take them for granted, and consider what follows from them. Can it be said to be wholly certain that what appears to be sensibly continuous with the mathematical present for $\frac{7}{8}$ths of a second (or thereby) necessarily *is* thus continuous—that there might be gaps in an apparently continuous duration of a second, but that there could not conceivably be gaps in a duration of $\frac{7}{8}$ths of a second? I do not see how any sane person could have the effrontery to say such a thing if he clearly understood what it meant. In general, the conclusion surely is that the length of the "specious" present is simply the length of what appears to be sensibly continuous with the mathematical present, that there can be no certainty that what appears to be sensibly continuous really is thus continuous, that there may be any number of very short gaps in anything that does appear to be sensibly continuous, and that there is no general reason of principle why what appears to be sensibly continuous with the mathematical present might not be of any imaginable length, or, in God's case, might not literally be an eternal "now."

It does not, of course, follow from these arguments that there is no such thing as sensitive certainty, but it does follow that if such certainty attaches *only* to the present moment there are the gravest reasons for doubting whether we can ever know for certain what the *sensible* "present moment" is. And if the criterion of the "sensible" or "specious" present moment is quietly put away on account of these difficulties, it is not at all evident what the claim to sensitive certainty precisely is, or what temporal restrictions concerning it should be conceded. As Dr. McTaggart said, "When the object and the apparent perception are simultaneous, the certainty takes the form 'this that I perceive is as I perceive it while I now perceive it,' in which there is no absurdity. But if the object was earlier or later, we should get 'this that I perceive was as I perceive it while I now perceive it,' or else 'this that I perceive will be as I perceive it while I now perceive it.' And both of these are absurd. The period, for which the guaranteed correctness is asserted, is declared in each of them to be simultaneous with the perception, and also not to be simultaneous with it." [8]

§ 4. DOUBTS CONCERNING SENSA

Passing the point of time, the existence of sensa, as was indicated in § 2 of this Chapter, may seem very plain indeed. "I quite certainly am at this moment acquainted with many different sense-data," Mr. Moore once said, "and in saying this, I am merely using this language to express a fact of such a kind, that nobody has ever thought of disputing the existence of facts

[8] *The Nature of Existence,* Vol. II, p. 293.

of that kind. A solipsist, if there is one, may perhaps doubt whether *I* am acquainted with sense-data; but nobody has ever doubted that he himself is acquainted with them." [9]

Since Mr. Moore was here arguing against at least one philosopher (i.e. Mr. Dawes Hicks) who *had* expressed such doubts, and since quite a number of philosophers profess to share the doubts (although not necessarily for Mr. Hicks's reasons), Mr. Moore must be taken to mean that, although certain philosophical interpretations of the nature and status of sensa may be disputable and dubious, the fact of the existence of sensa, *in some sense*, must be admitted to be beyond dispute or question. As I myself am one of these doubters, I have to show, or attempt to show, that this is not the fact. To be sure, if any one doubts the existence of sensa, he doubts their existence according to *some* interpretation of their nature. The word "sensum" would be meaningless unless it had *some* definite significance. In doubting the existence of sensa, therefore, I am doubting the existence of distinctive entities called sensa, understood as I believe Mr. Moore and his followers understand them.

The point is very fundamental, and far too simple to require, or permit, many words in the explanation of it. It is the point, briefly stated in subsection iv, § 7 of Chapter III of the present book, viz. that, as was there maintained, "it is illegitimate to argue that because something seems such and such, therefore it presents a distinct entity, its seeming or appearance, to some knower."

What I am trying to dispute is what seems to me the illegitimate assumption that because anything, say *X*, *seems* such and such, therefore it must be conceded that a distinctive entity exists, viz. the "seeming" or "apparition" of *X*. This illegitimate assumption is very persistent indeed. Sensa, we are told, are just show and appearance. A visual sensum, for example, is just a way of naming the look of something or other; a tactual sensum is a way of naming the "feel" of something or other. Therefore, our grasp of sensa leaves no room for error so long as we do not raise any questions that go beyond sensa. Keeping to the instance of vision, the look of a thing, we are told, ex-

* *Aristotelian Society Proceedings,* Supplementary Vol. II, p. 180.

presses, quite simply, what the thing seems to be. The thing may not *be* what it seems to be, but the *seeming* must be what it seems to be. For what is it except a seeming?

Without disputing the statement that something seems red, or green, or square to our senses, we may, and should (I think) dispute the inference that there is therefore a number of distinctive entities, a red sensum, a green sensum, and/or a square sensum. And if I am not entirely mistaken, Mr. Moore himself, in one of his essays, has laid bare precisely this fallacy.

In this essay he disputes "an assumption, which, though it seems to me to have great force, does not seem to me quite certain."[10] "This assumption," he continues, "has, if I am not mistaken, seemed to many philosophers to be quite unquestionable; they have never even thought of questioning it; and I own that it used to be so with me. And I am still not sure that I may not be talking sheer nonsense in suggesting that it can be questioned. But, if I am, I am no longer able to see that I am. What now seems to me to be possible is that the sense-datum which corresponds to a tree, which I am seeing when I am a mile off, may not really be perceived to *be* smaller than the one which corresponds to the same tree, when I see it from a distance of only a hundred yards, but that it is only perceived to *seem* smaller";[11] and similarly in other instances 'in which, as we say, "things" appear to vary with the position and state of the observer.

What I am arguing, then, is that these statements of Mr. Moore's are not, as he fears, "nonsense," but very good sense, and that *because* they are not nonsensical they abolish the necessity for believing in the existence of distinctive entities called sensa.

The language here employed by Mr. Moore is expressed in terms of the view that there is a (probably imperceptible) physical object called a tree to which certain perceptible sensa "correspond"—a smallish sensum when, as we say, we are a mile away from the tree, and a largish sensum when we are only a hundred yards away from it. Mr. Moore's suggestion is that

[10] *Philosophical Studies,* p. 244.
[11] *Ibid.,* p. 245.

the *same* sensum may appear to be smallish in the first instance and largish in the second instance. What I am suggesting is the possibility that the *tree* seems smallish at a mile's distance and largish at a distance of a hundred yards. In that case there need be no distinctive sensa at all. There would simply be the fact that the tree looks small in the first case and the fact that it looks large in the second case. There is no need for supposing that a sensum *corresponding to* the tree looks small in the one instance and large in the other. If there were such a correspondent sensum we could not surely infer that when it looks small there is a small secondary sensum corresponding to the primary one, and that when it looks large there is a large secondary sensum corresponding to the same primary one. There would only be one sensum in the case, which sometimes, for sufficient reasons, looked small, and at other times, for similar reasons, looked large. And what holds for this hypothetical sensum holds also for the tree. If the fact were simply that the tree sometimes looked large and sometimes looked small there would not need to be *any* sensa, large or small, at all.

I am not saying, of course, that this counter-interpretation is itself certain. I am well aware of the formidable difficulties that attach to every interpretation of this subject. All I am saying is that it may be true, and that it is not nonsense. And if it were true there would not be any sensa *in rerum natura*, that is to say, there would be no distinctive entities variously called, sensa, sense-apparitions, or sense-presentations.

Without laboring the point further, I should like to mention two subsidiary considerations. The first is that, if from the fact that "*X* seems to be red" we are entitled to infer that "there is a red sensum" (or apparition), this argument is quite general and would also apply to judgment. Thus from the rumor "Lord Kitchener seems to have survived the wreck of the *Hampshire*" we could infer the real existence of a false *judicatum*, viz. Lord Kitchener's subsequent existence; and this conclusion seems as little necessary as historical.

The second consideration is that a sensum seems to have all the marks of what may be called a merely epistemological object, and that it is quite unnecessary to suppose that *merely* epistemological objects actually exist. As we saw,[12] if Jones only opines something that Smith believes, it is illegitimate to infer that Jones's *opinatus* is one thing and Smith's *creditum* another thing. The personal limitations implied in these epistemological terms need not be applied to reality itself. The difference is only between something in so far forth as Jones apprehends it, and the same thing in so far forth as Smith apprehends it. There need not be two different things, and neither Jones nor Smith need suppose so. The same argument, however, seems to apply to sensa. For a sensum may simply be some *thing* in so far forth as some one senses it.

§ 5. The Testimony of the Senses

We have now examined the view that the senses yield indubitable evidence or testimony of the existence of present sensa, and have concluded that the only genuine certainty is the certainty of the perceptual fact expressed in the judgment that "something seems so and so." If the word "something" is understood generally enough (perhaps one should say vaguely enough), this statement seems beyond cavil, or at any rate as nearly beyond cavil as any statement can be.

A more extended testimony, however, is frequently claimed for the senses, and it is plain that, somehow or other, we all do believe that we are acquainted, *through* our senses, with what we call "the" physical world. On the other hand, so many and such divergent accounts of the nature of this acquaintance are given by philosophers that neither certainty nor the absence of serious theoretical difficulty can be claimed for any one of them; and the same must be said of all specific doctrines concerning the nature of "the physical world."

Even if it be false that our senses acquaint us *only* with momentary, personal apparitions, they reveal, at the best, something very fragmentary and very partial in comparison with what we believe the physical world to be. In other words, their immediate testimony, or the fleeting glimpses they directly yield, must be distinguished pretty sharply from any wider or more remote testimony they may furnish; and this wider testimony

[12] Chapter III, § 7 above.

can not be simply a function of sense but is at least equally a function of thought, judgment, and intellect. If we were to employ the (partially misleading) language of those who traffic in epistemological objects, we should have to say that "physical objects," regarded simply as entities evidenced by our senses, are neither mere æstheta nor mere noëta, but a subtle and intricate blending of the two. We might call them, perhaps, *epidoxasta,* meaning thereby to describe a peculiarity of their epistemological status, viz. that they *require* æstheta as part of the evidence for their existence but are not themselves mere æstheta in any intelligible sense.

This being premised, it seems unnecessary for our present purposes to do more than indicate, in a general way, some of the principal philosophical theories concerning the precise character and scope of sensory testimony; but at the same time it seems advisable to attempt this general survey.

(1) Many of the most celebrated arguments upon this question have revolved round the theses of a species of idealism. "Idealism" itself is a very wide term, and there is perhaps no good purpose to be served in attempting to define the term with greater precision than common usage warrants. An "idealistic" analysis of sense-perception, however, is generally understood to be a "mentalistic" analysis. It may be stated thus. The objects we immediately perceive are sensa. But sensa are mental, each man's sensa being states of his own mind. A less explicit theory (which, as it happens, was also Berkeley's) states simply that sensa are "in" our minds.

This theory can not be said to become precise until a precise account is given of what the "mind" is, what its states are, and what can reasonably be maintained to be "in" it; and since the terms employed in this controversy tend, like old coins, to be worn out of recognition by frequent use, it may be expedient to invent some new ones. Let us, then, describe the theory by saying that, according to idealism, we directly perceive sensa, and that the sensa we directly perceive are either *idiopsychic* or are *mentefacts.* By idiopsychic in this connection, I mean the theory that sensa are part of the stuff of our individual minds (supposing that there are such minds and whatever this stuff may be) in the same sense as that in which our attention, our belief, or our pleasure may be said to be idiopsychic. By a mentefact, I mean that which is mind-constructed, whether or not the materials of the edifice so constructed are themselves idiopsychic.

Without inquiring more minutely into the nature of "mind," it may be affirmed with some confidence that many sensa have properties that we hesitate (or flatly refuse) to ascribe to mind in any ordinary sense, and for that reason (as Berkeley himself admitted)[13] appear *not* to be idiopsychic in the way in which our attention or our pleasure is idiopsychic. There are, for example, red sensa and square sensa, if there are sensa at all, and it is, to say the least, very far from certain that any mind can be red or square. There is no such doubt regarding pleasure or attention.

These difficulties do not attach to the view that sensa are mentefacts, for our minds might construct such mentefacts out of materials not themselves mental. *Per contra*, it may always be argued that what is said to be "constructed" may in reality be only *selected*, and that if sensa were mind-selected, and not mind-*made*, this form of "idealistic" theory would not necessarily have any quarrel with, say, a realistic theory.

Speaking generally, it has to be said that most of the traditional arguments that purport to prove that sensa are "mental" have little or no bearing upon the question whether sensa are idiopsychic. What is commonly shown is that sensa vary with the observer to an extent and in a fashion that would be remarkable, if not miraculous, in "neutral" or "public" physical objects. This concomitant variation between the observer and his sensa, however, is for the most part (according to the theory) a concomitant variation between the observer's *body* and his sensa. He "sees" yellow when he is jaundiced, or dosed with santonin, as well as when there "is" something yellow to see. Such concomitant variation might be expected to occur if the observer's body played an effective part in his perceptual processes, and has no necessary reference to the functions of the observer's *mind*. On the other hand, so far as these arguments refer to the fact, if it be a fact, that the characters of sensa vary with the

[13] *Principles*, § 49.

observer's memory, attention, and associations, they would prove, or go far towards proving, that sensa are frequently, in part at least, mentefactual, if not definitely idiopsychic. As we have seen, if we stopped short with sensa (whether or not sensa are idiopsychic) we should not even begin to have a world. We should only have a rather disorderly consecution of fleeting glimpses. Nearly every theory, therefore, that is based on sensa gives some account of the "reference," "meaning," or "significance" of sensa beyond their private selves. The exceptions, I suppose, are theories which either *are* solipsistic without knowing that they are, or are, so to say, blatantly and triumphantly solipsistic.

According to Berkeley, it is sheer, downright (and also mischievous and atheistical) nonsense to say that "ideas of sense" (i.e. sensa) could conceivably be *like* material objects,[14] and since Berkeley also maintained that there was no meaning in "matter" *unless* it had properties *like* those of certain sensa[15] (e.g. unless it had shape like the round "ideas" that are "in" our minds), it follows that Berkeley (given these premises) correctly inferred that the truth about the universe must be immaterialistic, and was entitled to urge (on certain further premises) that a spiritual interpretation of the universe was legitimate and even necessary. As we have seen, however, it is not at all evident that squareness, color, and other important groups of properties in what are called sensa *are* spiritual or idiopsychic at all, or that they are "in" the mind in any other sense than that they are perceived *by* it. And even if a square sensum were in some respects "mental," it does not (despite Berkeley) seem at all evident that a square sensum could not resemble a square non-mental physical object.

Accordingly, when we pass from sensa to epidoxasta, that is to say, from the immediate apparitions of sense (supposing that there is no considerable error in describing them so) to the "physical" objects these sensa may signify, there is no entirely constraining reason why sensa, even if they are "mental," should not signify a non-mental physical object, or why there should not be at least a certain correspondence and resemblance be-

[14] E.g. *Principles,* § 8.   [15] E.g. *Ibid.,* § 9.

tween their properties and some of the properties of such physical objects.

It is sometimes claimed by ultra-modern writers that because the "revolution" in the science of physics to-day has destroyed many of the ancient certainties concerning "matter," idealism, in some form, has ceased to be a sort of fairyland, and has, instead, become inevitable.

Idealism never was a fairyland, but there is no sufficient evidence that these changes in the scientific interpretation of the physical world, although they may be ruinous to old-fashioned materialism, have any appreciable tendency to prove the truth of mentalism. To grant that space and time are inter-relative, and that their measurement is relative to this or to the other frame of reference (which may be specified, in particular cases, as some particular observer's frame of reference) is no evidence that what is spatio-temporal (according to an orderly physical scheme) is in any sense engulfed in this or in any observer's mind. To grant, if it must be granted, that physical science no longer requires us to assume the existence of *indestructible* physical substances is no reason for believing that it has to do only with destructible (or is it with indestructible?) human minds. Even if the so-called laws of nature are, to an extent formerly inconceivable, a species of scientific bookkeeping by double or *n*-fold entry, the mental character of nature is not thereby attested. And even if scientific "schedules of pointer-readings" are properly to be regarded as "symbols," it does not follow that they are symbols of that which is mental. We need not pause to consider whether these schedules symbolize sensa, or whether sensa symbolize these schedules, or whether the truth be simply that schedules and sensa correspond, and therefore, in so far as they correspond, may be correctly described as inter-symbolic. For if the entire edifice of modern physics *were* but a symbol for all (or for a particular selection of) sensa, it would still have to be shown, if idealism were to prevail, that sensa themselves are mental.

Mr. Eddington, and others who argue in this vein, simply *assume* that sensa are "mental." They are "mere mind-spinning,"

Mr. Eddington says.[16] Yet he somehow concludes that the species of mind-spinning that he calls "schedules of pointer readings" is ultimately inferior, in point of truth and reality, to the species of mind-spinning that Berkeley called "ideas of sense."

(2). A brief reference may be made to a type of theory that may be called "cerebral realism."

According to this view, sensa are events within our heads. In sensing a sensum each percipient senses a state of his own brain, and does so in the realistic sense. That is to say, when he senses his brain states, he senses what is really present in his brain. These brain states are not mind-made or idiopsychic.

It is not at all evident why the notorious difficulties concerning the direct perception of physical objects should suddenly cease when the perception of the brain is in question. For the brain is a physical object, or at least an epidoxaston, and never merely a sensum or set of actual sensa. In so far, again, as the brain is an epidoxaston, it *requires* sensa as an essential part of the evidence for its existence. The theory consequently implies a *circulus in probando,* and this is a vicious circle. It has to say, as we saw, that the world is inside my head, and therefore that my head (which is part of the world) is also inside my head. More generally, we may say that the theory is based upon an elementary confusion between sensum and causal stimulus. Because I do not sense unless my brain is excited, it is inferred, quite falsely, that I sense this excitement and this excitement only.

(3). We saw that what came nearest certainty in these matters was the simple statement that something seems to have certain sense qualities, as red or fragrant or square. This simple statement does not, of course, make any express assertion concerning what the "something" is. If it did, it would not be nearly so certain. But having explored the answer of mentalism (i.e. that it is our minds or their states that have these qualities) and the answer of cerebral realism (i.e. that states of our brain have them), we may now approach the commonsense answer that physical "things" have, and seem to have, these

[16] *The Nature of the Physical World,* p. 94. See this work *passim.*

qualities. This doctrine in some one of its many forms is usually styled "realism."

In any ordinary sense, a physical thing is a continuant (not necessarily an indestructible "substance") and our sense-glimpses are highly intermittent. Therefore, we may not identify "things" with "sensa," but it is at least conceivable that "sensa" are selections from "things"—a visual sensum, for instance, being literally a portion of the surface of some "thing"—and even that physical things have no parts that could not possibly be sensed. According to this view, physical nature contains more than we ever sense, but need not be supposed to contain anything of a different order from what we sense. The science of physics may indeed employ imperceptible concepts, but these may be scientific fictions, legitimate for purposes of explanation, but not realities *in rerum natura* except in so far as the logical character of the sensible world is not itself an object of sense, but an intellectual selection from the world of sense.

This common sense theory has certain obvious advantages. It "explains," for example, why we see primroses to be yellow and delphiniums to be blue, by the simple straightforward doctrine that there *are* primroses (which are yellow) and that there *are* delphiniums (which are blue). In other words, it exploits a species of crude physics that is not absurd and that, despite its crudity, may be true.

On the other hand, it has to face obvious and serious difficulties. We say that a penny looks elliptical when seen from the side although it *is* round; that a vase looks double when, regarding it, we press an eyeball; and so forth. Whatever may be true of these "double images," however, it would seem, in the case of the elliptical-looking penny, that there is no conclusive philosophical reason for regarding any one position from which the penny is seen as peculiarly privileged, or, in other words, it would seem that the elliptical shape is just as good a selection as the round shape. The conclusion, therefore, would appear to be that pennies have a great many shapes all the time and that we select visually from this collection of shapes. What we call a "round" object would not, indeed, have the *same* collection of shapes as what we call an "oval" object, although some of the shapes might coincide. But we should have to specify (if we could) the point from which we are looking in order to make the difference clear.

In this general way it seems possible, with entire consistency, to retain the common sense view while altering the common sense language in which the view is expressed; but there are, perhaps, insurmountable difficulties when we attempt to explain all the sensible appearances of things in terms of the selective view.

The elliptical-looking penny looks elliptical to every normal percipient who looks at the penny sidewise. But who is completely "normal" in this way, and who is able, with reason, to claim a position of privilege on account of his "normality"? If what any man does when he senses or perceives is simply to select, from the *facies totius universi*, what nature reveals, it must follow that all who are abnormal *also* select in this fashion from what is already *there*, and consequently that what a man visually selects when he is standing on his head, or drunk, or in a fever, is "there" to be selected just like the round penny. And this seems very hard to believe.

Perhaps it must be held, on any theory, that mis-sensing is an ultimate form of error which can never be explained in terms of any other sort of error (e.g. an error of judgment), although it is a different type of falsity from the falsity of an erroneous proposition; and that no explanation of error, however far it may circumscribe the *locus* of error or help to make error intelligible, can avoid the ultimate brute fact that wherever there is error there is something wrong somewhere that can not itself be explained away. The "selective" theory we are now examining, however, would have to make a very wholesale use of this facile, if defensible, explanation, and so might have to stretch our credulity until genuine belief snapped. While I can not think this objection utterly conclusive (since personally I believe that by far the most plausible theory of these matters is the view that attempts to base our knowledge of the physical world upon the high probability that certain, at least, of our "sensa" may be authentic, unmodified selections from physical nature) I can not deny that the objection is very formidable indeed, and I should be the last to affirm that any such hypothesis could conceivably be regarded as *certain*.

I should also mention another point, which many philosophers find to be a point of difficulty. Suppose, for example, we look, as we say, at the planet Jupiter. Light from Jupiter, we are informed, takes twelve minutes (or a little more) to reach our eyes. Therefore, if Jupiter, after emitting these rays, exploded or disappeared, we should continue to perceive the planet, quite unaltered, for this space of twelve minutes or more, just as we hear the boom of distant guns some time after we see the puff of smoke.

Accordingly, if what we perceive when, as we say, we perceive the planet, is really part of the surface of Jupiter, it must be part of a *past* Jupiter. While this conclusion does not seem to me to contain any very serious difficulty, or even to be very paradoxical, many philosophers appear to regard it as absurd, and see in it a conclusive objection to perceptual realism.

Even the selective view, as we have seen, can hardly be rendered plausible unless it is accompanied by the explanation that physical nature contains *more* then we ever sense. The question therefore arises: What grounds do we have for this extension to something *more?*

The principal answers given seem to be that these additional parts and properties of nature are (a) inferred from, (b) "suggested" by, and (c) constructed from, our sensory glimpses; and it seems probable that there is both inference and suggestion in the affair. (The further alternative that "things" are "logical constructions" [17] is that we construct fictitious "things" for our convenience, and speak in terms of them, although, in reality, no such things can be made out of sensory glimpses).

If we were always, and from the outset, confronted with a physical world of the same order as those portions of it that we glimpse in sense, these inferences (according to the inferential theory) and these suggestions (according to the suggestion theory) would seem to be well warranted and to need no special explanation. It is otherwise, however, if the selective view (or some view akin to it) is abandoned, and the theory put forward,

[17] *Cf.* Mr. Russell's *The External World.*

in its place, that we perceive sensa distinct from physical nature, and infer nature from (or have nature suggested by) these sensa. According to such alternative theories, it is usually held that these inferences would be so precarious that it is impossible to believe that human beings really become acquainted with physical nature in this way. It is, however, equally hard to believe that our stubborn trust in the reality of "the external world" can be due to ordinary association (i.e. to "suggestion" in that sense). It is therefore maintained that a "natural" or "unacquired" suggestion (that is to say a primordial "significance" or "meaning" prior to individual experience) must ultimately be presupposed in these matters.

But all such doctrines are highly speculative and can not be said to be certain.

The status of sensa, moreover, on views of this description, would seem to be highly peculiar. If sensa were idiopsychic, or, again, if they were states of men's brains, something intelligible would transpire concerning what sensa *are*. And similarly, something intelligible is being said, if sensa are declared to be parts of the surfaces of physical objects. If, however, sensa are none of these things, they would seem to have a mysterious origin—perhaps to be struck off, as it were, from the contact between mind and brainpan. Difficulties of this type, to be sure, do not arise at all when sensa are regarded simply as epistemological objects. In that case, we start from "apparitions" (whatever these may be) and maintain, with resolute simplicity, that our ultimate evidence in these matters comes from the apparitions. If, on the other hand, we attempt to translate these merely "epistemological objects" into entities actually subsisting in their own right, we would appear to have several gratuitous problems to tackle, and to be perambulating a region very far indeed from being certain.

Chapter XIII

OF MNEMIC CERTAINTY, WITH SOME REMARKS CONCERNING HISTORY

§ 1. The Description of Mnemic Phenomena

The Greeks distinguished μνήμη from ἀνάμνησις. Plato, for example, defined the former as the safe-keeping or preservation (σωτηρία) of sense-impressions, and plainly regarded it as bodily, biological, or at least as psychophysiological. The latter (which is usually translated "recollection" or "reminiscence") was, Plato thought, an instance of something that the mind caught up without bodily admixture, although it had formerly been experienced in connection with the body.[1]

Some distinction of this general kind—not necessarily, of course, with any express acceptance of Plato's psychophysics— has seldom been absent from psychology, and the term *mneme* has recently been revived by the late R. Semon in a sense predominantly biological, as may be seen from the subtitle of Semon's principal book *Mneme, as the Sustaining Principle in the Process of Organic Becoming*. It is convenient to revive the term for psychological and epistemological purposes, also.

Since our present topic is the testimony or evidence of our mnemic processes, and particularly the claim of this evidence to *certainty*, it is clear that our principal concern is with these processes at what is called the conscious level. Much that is in some sense mnemic, therefore, may be irrelevant to our discussion. For anything completely unconscious is obviously incapable of evidential certainty. If the evidential phenomena, however, are themselves part of a wider division of nature, this circumstance, plainly, should never be overlooked. And if anamnesis, or recollection, is essentially distinct from mere mneme, although circumstantially conjoined with it, this matter is also very noteworthy, especially if the claims to evidential

[1] *Philebus,* 34.

certainty are made on behalf of anamnesis and not on behalf of simple mneme.

It is usual for psychologists to deliver themselves to the following effect concerning what is mnemic. We have, they say, to distinguish three (possibly continuous) stages in any complete or typical mnemic process, viz. registration, conservation, and reproduction. [2] At the bodily or biological level this means (1) that there is stimulation or some reaction on the part of the organism, (2) that the effects of this stimulation or reaction are somehow retained in "traces" or "engrams," and (3) that when such stimulation or reaction is repeated, the second action is modified by these traces or engrams, and so is different, in a growing way, from the original stimulation or reaction.

Such accounts may be dangerously metaphorical, and, at any rate, are suspiciously reminiscent of the familiar process of making a jotting in one's note-book, leaving the book on a shelf, and consulting it on a later occasion. The convenience of distinguishing these three stages, however, may readily be admitted to counterbalance any disadvantages arising out of the metaphorical names that are employed.

Semon's interest was largely directed to the second stage, that is to say, to the "traces" and "engrams," although, from the nature of the case, his account of relevant and effective "engrams" had to be speculative rather than experimental. At the conscious level of ordinary psychology, on the other hand, the second stage appears to be a visible gap and plain lacuna. For consider the conscious facts. We notice something, with or without the intent to remember it. That is a conscious phenomenon. We may also, at a later date, recall or recollect this something, which is again a conscious phenomenon. But what happens in the interim? There are no conscious traces or engrams persistently noticed by us even in the vaguest way when we are not actually remembering. The most that could be alleged is that we *could* recall the readier of our "memories" if we chose to do so. In short, from the psychological standpoint, these "traces," regarded as persistent agents of conservation or as a "storehouse" of memory, are wholly hypothetical, and their very existence is doubtful.

[2] *Cf.* Morton Prince, *The Unconscious,* pp. 3 *sqq.*

It is impossible to evade this psychological lacuna, however sedulously we endeavor to ease the situation by reducing the requirements of "recollection" to the barest minimum. The gap would persist, even if the vaguest sense of familiarity sufficed for the existence of "memory." When we are not remembering, these traces are not consciously present *at all*, either vaguely or explicitly. And if we are bent upon certainty, it is almost superfluous to point out that there is at present nothing approaching certainty regarding the physiological character of such engrams, or regarding the relations of body and mind. On the first point, we are still at the pictorial stage of speaking of paths being worn in the nervous system, or of (supposititious) patterns being formed. On the latter point, has not Mr. Broad recently formulated seventeen possible theories? [3]

§ 2. REPRODUCTION versus RE-INSPECTION

Taking mnemic phenomena generally, the broadest question concerning their certainty is whether we have invincible assurance that our experience grows and develops, retaining the impress of former experience and being, in M. Bergson's language, interpenetrated by its past. The answer to this question can scarcely be other than affirmative, but when we examine the evidence for this affirmative answer, we readily perceive that it is based upon memory in the sense of conscious recollection or anamnèsis. It is because we recollect our earlier condition that we are able to say that the growth or development has taken place. Even if we had written memoranda on the point, these memoranda would themselves be the record of what, when recorded, were recent recollections.

Such recollections, then, are commonly said to be reproductions of the past. We manufacture, it is said (or otherwise come in contact with) certain *present* images (called memory-images) and these transient and embarrassed phantoms reproduce the past (or rather *our* past) in a ghost-like but veridical fashion. Moreover, to save this view from palpable inadequacy, certain further explanations are appended. The mere repetitive reproduction of something that in fact was similar to something past,

[3] In *The Mind and its Place in Nature.*

would not, it is conceded, be memory at all. It would simply be a present event x' that was similar to a former event x'', and would have no greater claim to be considered a memory than to-day's flash of lightning has if it is similar to yesterday's flash of lightning. Again, it has to be conceded that the mere circumstance that these repetitions are personal, the x' and the x'' belonging, in some sense, to the same person (for Jones does not remember Smith's past, unless Jones himself has been a witness of Smith's doings), does not affect the logic of the situation. What does affect the logic of the situation, we are told, is that the reproduction in question is a *conscious* reproduction in which our memory-images *consciously* resemble the past.

It is to be feared that this explanation, although it has satisfied, and apparently still satisfies, a great many psychologists, owes its plausibility to an equivocation. If by "consciousness" we mean "awareness," it seems abundantly clear that a series of states of awareness in which the later states happened to resemble the earlier would not necessarily be a memory series at all. What is needed, if there is memory, is not merely a temporal series of similar states of awareness, *but the awareness of the similarity of the series.* In other words, the "conscious reproduction" here in question is a "reproduction" in which there is awareness of *re*production, and also of the nature of the former fact that is said to be reproduced. In short, this alleged explanation assumes the very fact that it professes to explain. It assumes acquaintance with our past, because it assumes that we are conscious, or aware, in memory, that we are reproducing our past.

Clearly, the point is of great importance. If it is urged (as, in fact, it is urged again and again) that since the past is dead and gone, it can not possibly be recalled literally and bodily, but can only be *represented* from the standpoint of the present, the question obviously arises: How do we know, or what right have we to believe, that our so-called reproductions of the past really do reproduce it, or that our "memory-images" actually resemble anything that is past? To satisfy ourselves regarding this important particular, it would be necessary (would it not?) to compare the present image with the past event it is said to copy (no doubt in its own peculiar fashion). And if we can not conceivably recall the past event itself, how in the world can we have satisfactory evidence of the accuracy of our memory images, or even of their very meaning?

According to certain philosophers, this strange, mysterious fact has simply to be accepted. "It is mainly the *habit* of memory that testifies to the truth of memory"; Mr. Santayana says, "I believe I remember, and do not merely imagine, what I have always said I remembered; just as we believe events to be historical and not invented, when historians have always repeated them." [4] That is to say, memory is *not* evidence. And Mr. Santayana says several other things about memory which, although many of them are penetrating, appear to be quite singularly difficult to hold consistently. He lays stress, for example, upon the directness of memory. "Memory," he says, "deploys all the items of its inventory at some distance, yet sees them directly, by a present glance. It makes no difference to the directness of this knowledge how great the distance of the object may be in the direction of the past." [5] Yet Mr. Santayana's account of memory is pertinaciously *indirect*, because he regards it as a projection from a present image,[6] and does not regard our acquaintance with our own past experience in memory as at all different from our prophetic projections of our future [7] (or, so far as I can see, from projections into anybody's else past or future). Again, he says that memory is not a literal or faithful reproduction of the past. It is ghostly elusive, and treacherous. "Healthy memory," he tells us, "excludes pictorial fulness and emotional reference to the past"; [8] and memory is the more thoughtful and the more spiritual in proportion as it is able to select those ghostly essences that are most relevant to its purposes. It achieves thereby, he says, a truer perspective.[9] (All this may be true, but the inexactitude of memory is an odd reason for trusting it.) And when Mr. Santayana says that "memory is genuine if the events it designates actually took place, and conformed to the description, however brief and abstract, which I give to them," [10] he is telling us something that would be very

[4] *Scepticism and Animal Faith*, p. 160.
[5] *Ibid.*, p. 151.   [7] *Ibid.*, p. 151.   [9] *Ibid.*, p. 156.
[6] *Ibid.*, p. 155.   [8] *Ibid.*, p. 152.   [10] *Ibid.*, p. 152.

heartening if we could know it, but also something that would be forever unknowable if memory were, as he says it is, "incipient dreaming." [11]

An important question, therefore, is whether we are compelled to reap this crop of mysteries according to any tenable account of memory; and I should like to suggest that there is no such compulsion. To be sure, there is a "present glance" in all memory, but there is no need to assume that this present glance is a present *reproduction*. On the contrary, it seems reasonable to hold (and conformable to common language and opinion, although opposed to much philosophical speculation) that any man's present memorial glances are what he says they are, that is to say, that they are present glances *at* his past. We can not, indeed, in one sense of the word, *recall* the past literally and bodily; i.e. we can not *make* it present. For, by hypothesis, it is past. It does not follow, however, that we have no alternative except to re-create or reproduce it. We may simply reinspect or re-examine it, that is to say, we may direct our present attention to former things and events. And this reinspection may very well be "direct" in the sense that it is not mediated by any apprehended intermediaries.

I suggest, then, not that it is certain, but that it is legitimate and very plausible to regard our *anamnesta*—to use the appropriate Platonic [12] term for the immediate (epistemological) objects of recollection—as literally past events inspected from the standpoint of the present.

§ 3. THE SPECIOUS PAST AND THE SPECIOUS PRESENT

If the considerations advanced in connection with the "specious present" in § 3 of Chapter XII of the present book have any weight, they would seem in part to compel, and in part strongly to suggest, this reinspective interpretation of *anamnesta*.

Our conclusion there was that the "mathematical" point called the present is imperceptible; that the perceptible events we are accustomed to call present are, in fact, any perceptible stretch of duration whose boundary, at one side, is the "mathematical"

[11] *Ibid.*, p. 158.
[12] ἀναμνηστός = "that which one can recollect." *Meno*, 87b.

present; that (as the illustration of the notes in the bar of a melody shows) portions of any such sensible stretch of duration are, and appear to be, earlier than other and later portions. If we insist upon saying that any such perceptible stretch of duration is speciously or apparently present, and if we also hold that what appears to be present can not also appear to be past, we obtain the conclusion that the earlier portions of such a "specious present," although perceptibly *earlier*, are not perceptibly *past*. As I explained, however, I can see no considerable advantage, and certainly no constraining necessity, in employing familiar language in this peculiar way. On the contrary, it seems to me simpler, and at least equally accurate, to say that the earlier notes of the bar are perceived to be past (although very recent) and to be apprehended as sensibly continuous with the concluding note that is apprehended.

If this be so, it follows that if direct sensitive acquaintance with the *present* is ever possible, this direct sensitive acquaintance includes such portions of the very recent *past* as are sensibly continuous with the present. For (to repeat what was said) the "present," strictly speaking, is a mathematical limit or boundary and is itself imperceptible. In short, the very recent past always confronts our "present glances," and the truth of this circumstance is demonstrable in terms of the interpretation now before us. Another way of putting our conclusion would be to say that, if anything is directly perceptible, the very recent past (which is sensibly continuous with the boundary of the present) *must* be directly perceptible.

What, then, of the "obvious" past that is not sensibly continuous with the present, but is obviously and speciously separated from the present by a temporal gap?

The considerations we have adduced do not, of course, *demonstrate* that the obvious past must have the same epistemological status as the earlier portions of a specious present. It is conceivable that these temporal gaps should make all the difference in the world. But they do not seem to do so, and there is no good reason why they should do so. If the very recent past, sensibly continuous with the present, is perceptible, the past, in principle, is *capable* of being perceived. Why, then, should we not perceive the "obvious" past, as most people think that they do?

It is to be noted that pastness is not a proper attribute of an event, as the event's defining attributes are. The event called the death of Queen Anne does not change, although we recede from it. There is always the same event to be apprehended, if only we are capable of discerning it. This statement, however, does not imply, in its turn, that such events continue to exist—that Queen Anne goes on dying now, or remains at present transfixed *in articulo mortis*. It is only her past condition, not anything subsequent to it, that is the past event in question.

On the other hand, we may not infer that an event now past looks just the same as it looked when it was a present event, and when it was apprehended as such. We of the twentieth century can not, of course, remember Queen Anne's death, for our anamnesta seem to be restricted to those past events of which we ourselves had personal former experience. There is, indeed, no contradiction in supposing that we may apprehend what is past, although this past thing is not a thing that we could remember. (As we saw, our perception of a twelve minutes' old planet Jupiter may be an instance.) But if we can trust our memories (although not otherwise) it is possible for us to compare our (past) anamnesta with our (present) æstheta and to find the former, as Mr. Santayana says, "ghostlike" in comparison with the latter, as well, it may be, as more spiritual and better evidence of a thoughtful and logical mental selection. A selective theory of apprehension, however, finds no peculiar difficulties in this circumstance. Reinspection is a *different* selection from perceptual selection, at any rate when we are dealing with the "obvious" past. But this reinspection may well be a selection from the same reality that we call an event, and that (if this interpretation be justified) we may inspect and also reinspect.

§ 4. The Place of Memory-Images

According to William James, "the first element which memory-knowledge involves would seem to be the revival in the mind of an image or copy of the original event." [13] In other words, memory is based upon some *present* memory-image.

This statement is definitely opposed to the account of anamnesta that we have called "legitimate and very plausible." We may therefore expect a hostile critic to ask: "What, then, do you make of memory-images? Do they not exist and are they not present phenomena? And if they exist, can you seriously maintain that they are mere superfluities in the memory-situation"?

Here several points call for remark.

Firstly, we should notice the very wide range of memory. We remember, we say, persons, things, and propositions as well as events. An image, in any ordinary sense, mimics that, and that only, which is sensory.

It would therefore appear that memory images, even on the hostile critic's theory, must be expected to play very different parts in different types of memory, and further, that such images might sometimes, on his own theory, be unnecessary. Since the memory of events, however, seems to be the most fundamental instance of memory, it would be imprudent to lay very considerable emphasis upon the other instances.

Keeping, then, to our memory of events, we have to note, secondly, that the status of images themselves may be made a matter of dispute.

As we saw in Chapter V, § 8, it is usual to distinguish between reproductive and creative imagination, these being different employments of what Coleridge called our "primary esemplastic power." In terms of this contrast, memory must be supposed to belong to the reproductive, not to the creative, group, for, despite Mr. Santayana, memory is *not* "incipient dreaming."

We have therefore to ask whether so-called reproductive imagery (apart from the special case of explicit "memory-images") is properly either reproductive or esemplastic. May we not, borrowing another of Coleridge's excellent phrases, regard such images, not as something reproduced in the present, but as something "emancipated from the *oraer* of time and space"? Our memories are either dated in our past histories, or at any rate

[13] *Principles of Psychology,* V. 1, p. 649.

datable, more or less accurately, if we give our minds to the question of their place in our past, although, to be sure, such dating is not primarily according to the calendar, but according to salient remembered events whose calendar date might be indirectly ascertained. But what of floating, dateless, intermittent images? Is it really necessary to assume that these are *revivals*, or that they are *present* existences? We see them *now*, but need they *occur* now? Is it not simpler to suppose that they are, as it were, *our past*, stretching out before the mind's eye, but not in any orderly perspective? We "carry our past about with us," not necessarily in the sense that we keep on reviving and resuscitating what by definition is incapable of resurrection, but in the sense that we discern it, afar off, as we recede from it. Is it not possible, at least, that all our images are nothing but this distant prospect, intermittently revealed, and such that the portions that are out of perspective, or devoid of distinctive individual marks, are, as we say, "free" and "floating" images, moving nebulously in a haze?

In the third place, even if this account of "reproductive" imagery could not be sustained, it might well be the fact, notwithstanding, that memory-images are misnamed, and that so-called "memory-images" are in reality past events that are mistaken for images proper because of that ghost-like quality to which reference has been made. If this were so (and it is hard to conceive of any cogent reason why it should not be so, unless the habitual language of traditional psychology has to be regarded as a cogent reason), it would be quite consistent to admit the presence of supplementary, illustrative, or imitative images in many instances of memory, and yet to deny that the primary fact of memory is the existence of a supplementary, illustrative, or imitative image which, with any propriety, could be called a present and not a past event.

In short, it is in every way probable that the function of "memory-images" in this affair has been either misinterpreted or seriously exaggerated.

§ 5. An Alternative Theory

Mr. Broad, in an interesting account of memory phenomena, agrees that memory apprehension is in one sense "direct" and 'immediate." [14] "Memory beliefs," he says, "like perceptual beliefs, not only *are* not reached by inference . . . but can not be supported by such inference without logical circularity." [15] He claims, however, that the immediacy and directness of memory is rather a character of memory-belief than of any inspection of the distant past at all comparable to perceptual inspection; and for the most part his arguments are directed towards showing that memory is *liker* belief than it is like perception.

His principal arguments seem to be the following:

(1) It is generally agreed, he says, and it is also true, that when we remember anything clearly, we apprehend not only a past event but also our former experience of this past event. In clear perception, however, we apprehend, say, a colored surface *simpliciter*, without any explicit apprehension of our own participation. [16]

This argument, we may agree, supplies an indication that memory is more complicated and also somewhat more reflective than perception. In the main, however, the argument is weak, because it is very doubtful indeed whether we do not invariably apprehend the personal character of our perceptions, although we may not always trouble to mention the fact, even to ourselves. Whatever I perceive is certainly perceived *cum corpore meo* (where *cum* means "along with") and, I should say, is also perceived *cum mente mea*, although not necessarily in a sense that makes mind and æstheton indistinguishable.

(2) Mr. Broad points out that the past we remember may be indicated with very varying degrees of determinateness, e.g. "I remember that man's face though I do not remember seeing it before." [17]

It is difficult to see what can be inferred from this. Our perceptual æstheta may also be vague and indeterminate in varying degrees. And if the point of the argument is vagueness regarding

<hr/>

[14] *The Mind and its Place in Nature*, p. 235.
[15] *Ibid.*, p. 233.   [16] *Ibid.*, p. 237.   [17] *Ibid.*, p. 239.

our former *acquaintance* with the event, Mr. Broad's example may easily be matched by a precisely contrary one, e.g. "I clearly remember hearing Basque spoken, although I can not remember what the sounds were like."

(3) He says that in so far as memory is aided by imitative imagery, the relation between a memory-image and any past event it may signify contains "glaring" difficulties.[18]

This point we have considered.

(4) He argues that "negative memory-situations exist." Suppose that some one says to me, "Was the tie that your friend wore yesterday, red?" I may answer at once, "I remember quite distinctly that it was not *red*, but I can not remember what its color was." And Mr. Broad denies that there are negative perceptual situations.

This argument would show, at the best, that we use the word "memory" both for memory-inspection and for memory-judgments. So far as the point of language goes, however, it would not seem to be difficult to find a parallel in matters of perception, e.g. "I can see that that painting isn't a genuine Raeburn though I can't see precisely what is un-Raeburn-like in it."

The meaning of this last statement would be that something vaguely discerned in the appearance of the picture (i.e. in the æstheton) can not be made to *fit* Raeburn's methods. These vague, unidentified perceptual characteristics are our evidence for the negation. Why, then, should we not say, in the other instance, that certain vague, unidentified characteristics of the *anamneston* conflict with the possibility of the tie's redness, and supply the evidence that leads us to reject the belief that we saw the gentleman wearing a red tie?

Mr. Broad's conclusion is as follows: "I suggest that the objective constitutents of memory-situations are not in fact past and that they do not even seem to be past. But they do seem to have (and there is no reason to doubt that they actually do have) a certain peculiar characteristic which is not manifested by most images or most sensa. Let us call this "familiarity."[19] Now we are so constituted that, when we are subjects of a cognitive situation whose objective constituent manifests the charac-

[18] *Ibid.*, p. 244.   [19] *Ibid.*, pp. 244 *sq.*

teristic of familiarity, we inevitably apply the concept of past-ness; and, if we make an explicit judgment, it takes the form: "There was an event which had such and such empirical charac-teristics." [20]

In other words, memory is an instinct which is part of our "constitution." We apprehend nothing empirical except the pres-ent, but we "inevitably" apply the *concept* of pastness when we have a certain kind of present feeling.

In that case, it is surely most doubtful, not only whether the "past" can be ascertained in any way, but also whether the con-cept of "pastness" has any meaning whatsoever.

More generally, it would surely be an amazing thing if we could know, or have good reason for believing, that our memory-beliefs *fitted* the past without being capable of verifying their adequacy in any way by inspection *of* the past.

§ 6. THE COGENCY OF MEMORY-EVIDENCE

It is always possible to argue that these disputes concerning the *way* in which we remember should never be supposed to affect the certainty of the *fact* that we do remember. As Thomas Reid said, the principle *"that those things did really happen which I distinctly remember* . . . has one of the surest marks of a first principle; for no man ever pretended to prove it, and yet no man in his wits calls it in question. . . . When I remem-ber a thing distinctly, I disdain equally to hear reasons for it or against it. And so I think does every man in his senses." [21]

As we saw, however, in Chapter VII, § 5, this truculent type of assertion is itself most questionable. Clearly, these epistemo-logical perplexities do not in the ordinary way shake our *assur-ance* in our memories. Possibly, indeed, they do not even disturb the assurance of the most sophisticated people in their most sophisticated moments. And there is force in the contention that we may know that we remember, although we do not know how the thing is done. On the other hand, there is a great gulf fixed between assurance, of the one part, and evidenced certainty, of the other part; and it is the latter with which we are concerned

---

[20] *The Mind and its Place in Nature*, p. 266.
[21] *Intellectual Powers*, Hamilton's edition, pp. 444 *sq.*

in the present inquiry. "The way in which the thing is done" is just the character of the evidence; and if the character of the evidence is obscure, it seems presumption to declare that we know, or are entitled to assert, that our evidence yields, or is capable of yielding, complete and authentic certainty.

Accordingly, while I am personally of the opinion that many of the classical perplexities concerning memory are manufactured without adequate warrant, I have endeavored duly to set them forth, and am the last to claim certainty for any particular solution hitherto propounded.

It remains to say something regarding our everyday assurance in affairs of the memory.

While in general, as Reid said, we "disdain" to argue with any one who impugns the clearer among our memories, we have nevertheless to admit, on occasion, that even our clearer and more recent memories are delusive. For the most part, however, these admissions that our memory has cheated us are themselves based upon memory. The delusive memory, we have to admit, conflicts with some other of our memories, even clearer and firmer. Or it conflicts with a consensus of other people's memories, we having satisfied ourselves that these other people have as good memories as we have on the ground that their recollections of events that we and they have witnessed together coincide, in the main, with our own, but are fuller or better because they remind us of details we had forgotten but recollect when they tell us about them. Or the delusive memory conflicts with the written records, that is to say, with the notes made by ourselves or other people when the memory of the events recorded was fresh.

In other words, we all trust our memories to a greater extent than we commonly notice. Indeed, we may say that the world, regarded as an epidoxaston, or epistemological substance, is based, in the main, upon anamnesta rather than upon æstheta, although these individual anamnesta are themselves based upon æstheta. On the other hand, and paradoxically enough, we decline to claim infallibility for any particular memory, or for any particular species of memory, just because we trust our memories so thoroughly. By comparisons principally within the sphere of memory we learn that, speaking broadly, our clearer memories are more trustworthy than our vaguer ones, but we also learn that *some* very clear memories are delusive, and that we have no sufficient ground for holding that any assignable degree of clearness in a memory is an absolute guarantee of its correctness. Similarly, by comparisons of a memorial kind, we learn that our more recent memories, in the main, are more accurate than our more remote memories. But recency, once again, is not a perfect title to certainty. To take a third point, we generally remember the better if, when we notice anything, we notice with intent to remember; but this precaution also does not ensure perfect accuracy. The same principle also applies to a semi-conscious intent to remember. Without any appreciable conscious endeavor, we all tend to note for memorial purposes what is likely to be serviceable to us in our subsequent experience. Thus we forget our dreams with amazing rapidity, because they would be an encumbrance rather than a help in waking life, and are usually of no advantage to subsequent dreaming, even the pleasantest. And we remember small incidents that have a way of being useful. But there is nothing infallible about such memories.

It is sometimes maintained that there is no such thing as a *general* faculty of "memory," and hence that, if we are speaking accurately, we should always speak of "memories" in the plural and not of "memory" in the singular. Apart from the technical point that the word "faculty" is only the classification of a capacity—and this is a criticism that applies to specialized as well as to general "faculties"—there is something of substance in this contention. We all know of "memories" that seem to us singular and abnormal, simply because we falsely assume that any one capable of remembering some particular sort of thing should be equally capable of remembering any conceivable sort of thing. For example, a very competent mathematician of my acquaintance has to consult his lecture notes even for the simplest mathematical formulæ, but remembers (i.e. can repeat with accuracy) an amazing quantity of humorous verse, even if twenty years have elapsed between his first reading of the verses and his first repetition of them. I know of other people who remember the plot and many of the incidents in hundreds of detective stories, but cannot put a name to any of the characters; and of college porters who have marvellous memories for faces and for names, but otherwise do not seem to remember particularly well. And every one can supplement these examples from his own experience.

On the other hand, despite this notorious specialization of "memory," it seems pointless to deny that the word "memory" does stand for a general, and not for a special, classification.

§ 7. Some Remarks Concerning History

Mnemic facts, as we saw, are facts concerning the growth and development of experience. They may therefore be said to include man's historical consciousness, and the circumstance invites attention to the larger pages of what we call history and historical evidence.

There has been much dispute concerning what history is, and it has become the fashion to distinguish history pretty sharply from historiography. "The word 'history' has two meanings," Mr. Shotwell says. "It may mean either the record of events or events themselves. We call Cromwell a 'maker of history' although he never wrote a line of it. We even say that the historian merely records the history which kings and statesmen produce. History in such instances is obviously not the narrative but the thing that awaits narration. The same name is given to both the object of the study and to the study itself."[22]

The need for Mr. Shotwell's comment may, however, be questioned. A "maker of history" surely is quite simply one whose deeds are worth recording in the historical way. There are not two usages, but one. On the other hand, history must plainly have a theme, and it may not be a simple matter to decide what a historical theme is.

According to Sir Charles Firth, "History is not easy to define; but to me it seems to mean the record of the life of societies of men, of the changes which those societies have gone through, of the ideas which have determined the actions of those societies,

[22] *Introduction to the Study of History*, pp. 2 sq.

and of the material conditions which have helped or hindered their development.[23] "On the whole, this may be taken to be an accurate description of what we usually mean when we speak of "history" *sans phrase,* or include the subject in a university curriculum. It should be remembered, however, that Fielding, who was a master of English, wrote *The History of Tom Jones, A Foundling,* and that "histories" of philosophy, of the arts, of the drama, of dogma, and so forth, while they have a cultural or social reference, may keep that reference subordinate. It might be simpler, indeed, to say that a "history" is the story of the development of *anything,* although historians, for the most part, are humanists whose endeavor is to narrate the story of the development, or decline, of some human society.

This being premised, it seems clear that any authentic account of any such social development must be an account of what actually happened, or else not be history. In this sense, Ranke's statement that the historian "has only to show what it was that actually happened" [24] is indisputable, except for the little word "only." Historians can not (and should not) deal with anything and everything that actually happened. They have to deal (we may say) with some large-scale process of social development, and are concerned, not with every event in this development, but essentially with the events that are salient in the development. And this qualification, in its turn, is insufficient without a further qualification. There has been a tendency on the part of Comtian positivists, and others concerned with the "science" of man, to misconceive history and to transform it into sociology. And plainly history is not *any* sort of selection and correlation of the salient elements in human societies. It is restricted to continuous and connected development in time and can not deal directly with any other species of general sociological correlation.

Any one who accepts these qualifications, however, must admit that there is very signal difficulty in deciding, according to any rational principle, what is "salient" or "important" in any social development. If the life of a people were simply an appendage

[23] *A Plea for the Historical Teaching of History,* pp. 6 *sq.*
[24] Quoted by Teggart, *Theory of History,* p. 52.

to the deeds of governments and of dynasties, it would be reasonable to regard history as, in the main, the record of wars, treason, and ship-money. But the presuppositions of this view of history are plainly untenable. A better suggestion would be that history is principally concerned with large-scale crises and great mutations in the life of a people, such crises being due, say, to the marked intrusion, from whatever cause, of a foreign culture; to inventions that altered the entire human geography and way of living of some social group; to acute pressure from over-population or from undersupply of customary food; and so forth. The people that has no history, is, in the main, the people that has no such crises to record or experience. Without these crises there is little development in any ordinary sense. Instead, there is stagnation or marking time.

Nevertheless, gradual change *is* a development, although it may not be a spectacular development or charged with heroic emotion; and therefore crises, however significant, can not exhaust the historian's theme.

A third suggestion, appropriate to theologies or "philosophies" of history, is that human society, wittingly or unwittingly, has the definite and single purpose of reaching the millennium, or some City of God, or the final development of ideal spirituality. In this case, the best historians would be those who applied their knowledge of this theological or philosophical world-plan to the selection of incidents that illustrated it in some striking way. Infidels and agnostics might then take heed.

Let us return, however, to the historian's task.

As we have seen, historians have to give a continuous and connected account (in a selective fashion) of what actually happened. As Lord Balfour has said, "Fact has an interest, because it is fact; because it actually happened; because actual people who really lived and really suffered and really rejoiced caused it to happen, or were affected by its happening. And on this interest the charm of history essentially depends."[25]

How, then, are historians to know what actually happened?

A part of their business, pretty clearly, concerns the interpretation of records. The distinction between what is historical and

[25] *Theism and Humanism*, p. 83.

what is prehistoric, we say, is the distinction between the presence and the absence of written evidence, not because pottery, arrow-heads, and the drawings of cave-men are other than evidence, but because conjectures from such evidence are enormously more nebulous than inferences from charters, scripts, and annals.

This interpretation of records and sources, this *Quellen-kritik*, is a science (or art) in itself. Chronicles, laws, diplomatic and private correspondence, and the rest can not be marked, verified, and digested by any random, wayfaring man. Philology, paleography, heraldic and numismatic lore have to be pressed into the service of historical hermeneutics. It is no marvel, then, that some should hold that a historian's occupation comes to an end when he has extracted what can be extracted from his "documents."

Clearly, however, unless these "documents" themselves are histories proper, the work of the historian may be said to begin, rather than to end, with this "proving" of the documents. Such evidence is the source from which the narrative of continuous development should be drawn. And even the work of annalists or logographers (supposing it could be shown to be accurate) would not, in this sense, be properly a historical narrative. It would not envisage a process of development, but would only supply the materials for a historical *vue d'ensemble*. In other words, to revert to Greek etymology, a historian is an "inquirer"[26] and not a logographer.

Here a mistake is commonly made. A connected historical narrative is plainly quite different from a string of annals or a tabulated catalogue of sources. Hence it is inferred, quite falsely, that the "science" of history concerns the former—"every historian being his own Dr. Dryasdust"—and that the latter is an affair of *literary* art. Obviously, however, if history and annals are different, they really are different, and the presence or absence of literary art is a different question altogether. There is no sufficient reason why annalists should not employ, and show proficiency in, literary art, of a kind; and some of them have done so. And a connected historical narrative (*not a*

---

[26] The original meaning of ἱστορία

set of annals) *might* be presented with very indifferent literary art. It might even be possible to cite examples of such indifferently artistic narratives.

To be sure, even a pedestrian history may require considerable literary art; from which it would follow that history must always be a branch of literature. That, however, is another story; and it is impossible to infer very much concerning the meaning and office of history from the circumstance that so much great history has also been very great literature. The greatness of the theme that inspired Herodotus to tell how Xerxes failed to subdue the Athenians and how the Athenian empire rose, or that led Gibbon "at an awful distance" [27] to contemplate the decline and fall of Rome, are surely sufficient to evoke great literature —from a Herodotus or from a Gibbon. This ample stage, this dramatic unity, these heights and these depths of human grandeur seem imperatively to demand all that a great writer's great art can give them. It was only necessary that there should *be* great writers to respond to such themes.

It seems unnecessary to maintain, however, that the sole office of history is to tell a great story greatly. A Gibbon, to be sure, could not be satisfied with anything less. When he thought of narrating, not the history of declining Rome, but the achievements of the Swiss in their triumphant guardianship of freedom and of peace, he remarked, "My judgment, as well as my enthusiasm was satisfied with the glorious theme." [28] Such enthusiasm, however, can hardly be said to be a *requisite* of all history. When Mr. Trevelyan suggests that it is part of the business of a historian to give an "exposition of facts and opinions *in their full emotional and intellectual value* to a wide public by the difficult art of literature," [29] he is suggesting something that may always be true of the kind of history best worth writing but that can hardly be essential to *any* history. And if the full emotional value of the past be its grandeur and its inspiration to *present* patriotic fervor, the dangers of so regarding history (if history seeks the truth) are too manifest to need more than the mention.

Certainly, since the life of a people is largely an emotional

[27] *Autobiography.*   [28] *Ibid.*   [29] *Clio: A Muse,* p. 5.

life, there could be no full or adequate account of its life that did not penetrate into the emotions of the people. In this sense, Clio, like her sisters, must be not only an imaginative Muse, but must be instinct with sympathetic understanding. This, as we shall see, may well be the deepest trait in her character. But for the same reason, it is eminently desirable, that our historical enthusiasm should not be imitative, parochial, or conventional, responding only to what is "glorious" in some accepted sense, or fanning the somewhat artificial flames of our own national hearths.

This account of the nature of history, although very condensed, has perhaps been over-long for its purpose. As a result of it, however, there should now be no great difficulty in putting the essential question with which we are here concerned. That is the question whether social tradition and the records of history supplement our personal memories in any distinctive way, and whether this historical evidence can lay claim to certainty.

In an interesting passage quoted by Mr. Teggart, Sir Ian Hamilton says: "On the actual day of battle naked truths may be picked up for the asking; by the following morning they have already begun to get into their uniforms." [30] This statement obviously casts a slur upon the reliability of tradition, and no one, I suppose, would be eager to defend tradition as a good depositary of literal truth. "Official" histories, however, are scarcely in a different plight. Frontenelle's *mot* "L'histoire n'est qu'une fable convenue" is not a pointless gibe, and history as a "mirror for magistrates," that is to say, as an agreed narrative for the use of the governing classes, is not unknown. Truths in uniform, to be brief, are, at the best, truths in disguise.

So far as the interpretation of documents goes, it may be said that while a great deal of sound historical evidence is thereby available, such evidence, from the nature of the case, is frequently less stringent than would be acceptable in a court of law, and immeasurably less stringent than anything a philosopher in search of indefectible certainty could accept. And since historical narratives, however great their literary art, must be based

[30] *A Staff Officer's Scrap-book during the Russo-Japanese War*, I, v.

upon such records, it is permissible to doubt whether these literary streams are capable of rising higher than their sources.
Precisely at this point, however, a *caveat* may be entered.
Granting that the objective truth of history is placed where
we have said it is placed, may not historical insight and historical imaginative sympathy, in their subjective aspect, be
capable of penetrating the veil and of discovering, not so much
what actually happened, or how some great thing (in detail)
came about and why, but the spirit of the past itself? Speaking
of the chapter "The Steeples at Midnight" in Carlyle's *French
Revolution*, Mr. Trevelyan says, "Whether or not it is entirely
accurate in detail, it is true in effect: the spirit of that long dead
hour rises on us from the night of time past." [31] And again, he
says that history "can mould the mind itself into the capability
of understanding great affairs and sympathising with other
men." [32]

Many historians have believed that, instead of guessing old-
world motives, they could gage and penetrate the characters of
the men they studied and, as it were, live and converse with
Cromwell or Mazarin in such a fashion as to obtain an insight
into the past far more secure than any contemporary insight
that comes from flurried, rapid intercourse with our next-door
neighbors. If this be a dream, it may nevertheless be a dream
well dreamt. For time may efface what is petty and confusing,
and the still shadows of history may be appareled, not in official uniforms, but in their proper essence.

It would be unwise to deny that historians who have this
assurance may conceivably have it on rational grounds in some
favored places that they visit, or that, if they can not impart
the certainty of their insight to their readers, they may, nevertheless, possess the insight. But it would be equally unwise to
assert that such insight undoubtedly occurs; and it has to be
confessed that any axioms historians rely upon, in connection
with this insight into the past of humanity, are singularly unplausible in their appearance. "The deep and well-grounded
certainty, attested by general experience, of the analogy between

[31] *Op. cit.*, p. 17.
[32] *Ibid.*, p. 19.

one man's feelings, perceptions and will and another man's, or
of the identity of human nature," Bernheim says," is the fundamental axiom of all historical knowledge." [33] Let us hope that
it is not relied on to excess.

[33] *Lehrbuch der Historischen Methode,* Fourth Edition, p. 170.

Chapter XIV

OF INTROSPECTIVE CERTAINTY

§ 1. HISTORICAL

Before the theory of Behaviorism came into fashion, the authenticity of introspection, in some sense, was seldom seriously denied—Hume always excepted. On the other hand, there was much dispute concerning what the introspective process actually was.

Thus Locke regarded introspection (or, as he called it "reflection") as an "internal sense." "Though it be not sense," he said, "as having nothing to do with external objects, yet it is very like it."[1] And he explained the character of this "reflection" quite simply by saying that the mind "turns its view inwards upon itself, and observes its own actions about those ideas it has."[2]

Even in Locke's day, however, this simple-minded theory was by no means universally accepted, as may be seen in the following excerpt from Peter Browne's *Procedure, Extent and Limits of the Human Understanding*, published in 1728. "The Eye of the Mind," Browne says, "as I said before, cannot take a view either of its own Substance or Essence, or of its own Properties or Qualities by any *Reflex* Act; it doth not come to the knowledge of its own Faculties by any such unnatural *Squint*, or distorted *Turn* upon itself; but by an immediate *Consciousness* of the several different ways of its own working upon those Ideas of Sensation lodged in the Imagination."[3]

In the later eighteenth century, as is very generally known, Kant's account of the "internal sense" is so obscure as to be pronounced unintelligible on all hands. "I am conscious to myself of myself," Kant says, "—this is a thought which contains a twofold I, the I as subject and the I as object. How it should be possible that I, the I that thinks, should be an object . . . to

<hr>

[1] Essay II, i, § 4. [2] *Ibid.*, II, vi. [3] Pp. 96 *sq.*

myself, and so should be able to distinguish myself from myself, it is altogether impossible to explain." What Kant thought he could explain was that the self that might be said to be perceptible by the internal sense was not the thinking subject, but only a phenomenal or apparent subject. Yet Kant goes on to say of this "I" that thinks (in regard to its capacity for being an object to itself): "It is, however, an undoubted fact . . . and has as a consequence the complete distinguishing of us off from the whole animal kingdom, since we have no ground for ascribing to animals the power to say I to themselves." [4]

At a later date, indeed, Comte argued that "this pretended direct contemplation of the mind by itself is a pure illusion. . . . The thinker cannot divide himself into two, of whom one reasons while the other observes him reason. The organ observed and the organ observing being, in this case, identical, how could observation take place? Our descendants will doubtless see such pretensions some day ridiculed upon the stage. The results of so strange a proceeding harmonize entirely with its principle. For all the two thousand years during which metaphysicians have thus cultivated psychology, they are not agreed about one intelligible and established proposition. 'Internal observation' gives almost as many divergent results as there are individuals who think they practise it." [5]

This seems explicit enough. It moved Comte's readers, however, to protest that there must be something wrong with Comte's argument. He had discovered a puzzle, they thought, but he could not conceivably have discovered an insoluble puzzle. Perhaps, they suggested, we can thus divide ourselves in memory. In any case, the experience of every moment refutes Comte's doctrine. "M. Comte," Mill says, "would scarcely have affirmed that we are not aware of our own intellectual operations. We know of our observings and our reasonings, either at the very time or by memory the moment after: in either case, by direct knowledge, and not (like things done by us in a state of somnambulism) merely by their results. This simple fact destroys

---

[4] As quoted in Kemp Smith's *Commentary*, Introduction, p. li note.
[5] As quoted by James, *Principles*, Vol. I, p. 188.

the whole of M. Comte's argument. Whatever we are directly aware of, we can directly observe."[6]

In short, according to Mill as well as according to Locke, there can be no doubt at all about the reality of self-observation or introspection. There is no question, even, of an "unnatural squint."

§ 2. Division of This Discussion

I propose to discuss the following questions *seriatim:*

(1). Is there an "inner" or "internal" sense, and, if so, what are its "objects"?

(2). Have we any capacity which, although it be not a sense, yet is "very like" an inner sense?

(3). Have we any capacity, for example the capacity that Mr. Alexander calls "enjoyment," which, although quite different from a "sense," nevertheless yields direct acquaintance with our individual minds and consciousness?

(4). Does introspection, regarded in any of these ways, or in any other way, yield certainty?

(5). What is the relation of introspection to self-cognition, i.e. to our knowledge, if we have such knowledge, of any continuing Ego or Self?

(6). Has each of us quite certain knowledge of the existence of his Ego?

§ 3. Endosomatic Sensa

The obvious literal meaning of "introspection" is "inward looking"; and introspection is therefore opposed to extrospection, or outward looking. Here the word "looking," of course, must be held to include any sort of sensory apprehension. It is not restricted to vision. The terms "inward" and "outward," however, conceal a great number of metaphysical pitfalls. As we have seen, it is commonly held (although not universally, and, very likely, wrongly) that *all* sensa are "inner" phenomena, being either cerebral or mental. If so, all sensory inspection would be introspection, and extrospection (so called) would be

[6] As quoted, *ibid.,* p. 189.

only a kind of meaning or significance rightly or wrongly attached to introspective sensa.

This, indeed, is one of the commoner stock ambiguities in the psychological treatment of introspection. We are all, it is said, confronted with a "subjective" or "private" inner circle of sensation, and psychology is a distinctive science precisely because it concerns itself expressly with this inner circle of presentations, while other sciences either neglect the privacy of the inner circle or proceed, rashly and hypothetically, to deal with an "outer" circle of fact, supposedly "public" and "objective."

If so, there is no necessary distinction in principle between sensa and introspecta, although there may be certain "subjective" æstheta that are not sensa—for example, images, attention, and pleasure-pain of certain kinds. On the other hand, as we have seen, it may be disputed whether many sensa are either private, or mental, or subjective. And if they were private merely in the sense that we happen to have an exclusive private view of them, it would not follow that they are "inward," or cerebral, or mental.

Accordingly, if introspective certainty raises problems quite distinct from the problems of sensitive certainty, introspecta must either be wholly distinct from sensa or must at least be a quite special class of sensa. Let us consider, therefore, whether it is possible to define the "inner sense" in such a way as to make this distinction plain.

One obvious distinction is between æstheta that appear to be "outward (e.g. color, sounds, and other such sensa) and æstheta that appear to be "inward" (e.g. kinæsthetic sensa, or organic sensa like toothache). The boundary here is the epidermis as we see it. Any æstheton that appears to be external to our bodies is the direct object of extrospection as thus defined, and any æstheton that appears to be internal to our bodies is the direct object of introspection. One further explanation must be made, however. In certain cases, it is possible for a man to look inwards (into his body) by means of his external senses. If he were under a local anesthetic, for example, he might perceive, by vision, the regions inside him where a surgeon is operating. "Internal" sensa, in other words, may occasionally be sensed by one of the "external" senses; and therefore it is necessary to explain that the objects of the inner sense, according to this account of it, are not merely apparently inside the body, but are also not apprehensible by any one of the "external" senses.

To mark this distinction, I shall call the immediate objects of the "external" senses *exosomatic* æstheta, and I shall call the immediate objects of the "internal" senses *endosomatic* æstheta. There is, of course, no particular virtue in using Greek terms instead of Latin terms, but the terms "external" and "internal" have been very much abused, especially by metaphorical extensions of their meaning, and it is also important to show that "external" sensa, in this sense, are sensibly external to the sensible *body* and that "internal" sensa, similarly, are sensibly inside the sensible body.

Our first question, therefore, is whether there is anything singular in the epistemological status of endosomatic æstheta in comparison with exosomatic sensa, and, if so, whether this difference has any logical bearing upon the problem of their certainty.

It is argued that the status of the two must be different, because exosomatic sensa might conceivably be included in physical fact while endosomatic æstheta could not be so included. This argument, however, is itself most disputable. Even if the "physical" world were defined by properties either similar to, or possibly identical with, the spatio-temporal properties of exosomatic sensa (i.e. if the physical world were composed of what are called the "primary" qualities), it is not true, in fact, that endosomatic sense-qualities are either spaceless or timeless. On the contrary, they are ostensibly voluminous and also ostensibly changing. Indeed, this distinction seems to rest on the ground that the exosomatic senses acquaint us immediately with a public physical world, while the endosomatic ones acquaint us immediately with a private physical world, and with this only. Manifestly, however, the public character of exosomatic sensa, in any direct and ostensible sense, is highly questionable. Again, since the physical world includes our own bodies, there is no inconsistency in believing that we are capable of perceiving certain conditions inside our bodies that other people are incapable of perceiving. In short, we seem to have the same reason (and therefore as good reason) for believing that there is pain in our gums as that there is red on our cheeks or on somebody's else cheeks. Mistakes are possible in both cases—in the former case, for example, when "transferred" pain is felt in the upper jaw although the inflammation is in the lower; in the latter case, in various kinds of sensory illusion. Such errors, therefore, do not nonsuit only one of the parties.

It is further argued that endosomatic æstheta have a peculiarly close and intimate relation to the self, and that this close relation is absent from exosomatic æstheta. For the self, we are told, is, psychologically at any rate, an *embodied self;* and endosomatic æstheta reveal our bodies to us in so far as our bodies are sensible. Indeed, our endosomatic sensa are just what the Germans call *Erlebnisse,* that is to say, they are, quite precisely, what we live through with consciousness of our vitality. It may plausibly be maintained, therefore, that these sensa *are* the embodied self so far as it can be sensed at any time.

This union between endosomatic sensa and the self (if it exists) would not seem to prove that the epistemological status of these æstheta is different from the epistemological status of other æstheta. It proves just what it purports to prove, viz. that relatively constant endosomatic sensa are continually present to our minds, and that exosomatic sensa, although some of them are always present, are individually highly variable. Our environment, in detail, changes more than our organic sensations. There is no logical passage from this contention, however, to the profoundly different theory that endosomatic æstheta must be apprehended in an entirely different way from exosomatic ones, and by a new and distinctive faculty of introspection.

I seem to find a certain confirmation of this opinion even among the arguments of notable opponents. Mr. Stout, as I apprehend, disputes the opinion,[7] but his argument, in the main, concerns the distinction between what he calls the "sense-factor"

[7] See e.g. the new (fourth) edition of his *Manual of Psychology,* pp. 408 *sqq.*

and the "activity-factor" in all our perceptual experience. Organic sensa, however, like other sensa, are instances of the sense-factor, not of the activity-factor, and any arguments that concern our acquaintance with our own activity, whether "embodied" or "mental," can *not* be based upon the relevant *sensa*.

I think we should conclude, therefore, that there is no sufficient reason for holding that endosomatic sensa have a different epistemological status from that of exosomatic sensa. And since the status of sensa has already been discussed, there is, accordingly, no occasion for a separate discussion of the status of *these* sensa. If all sensa are apprehended with certainty, these sensa must also be so apprehended. If not, they might belong to the more or to the less certain class of sensa. In one sense, they seem often to be vague and not informative. In another sense, they are very convincing indeed. The pain that we feel when we stub our toes seems to most of us a pretty definite reality. But, as we have seen, it is illegitimate to infer that we *must* have certainty regarding the character and the existence of the pain simply because, if it exists, it is ours, or again, because, if it exists, it must be very "near" our minds—whatever that may mean.

It is to be remarked, however, that the mere possibility of the existence of toothache and of other organic sensa is a complete refutation of behaviorism. Behaviorism as a policy eschews introspective methods and relies upon exosomatic measurements; and this policy, in the present situation of psychology, may pay very well. Behaviorism as a creed, on the other hand, maintains that there are no facts except the facts that can thus be measured. And endosomatic sensa can not so be measured. Inflammation, for example, may be measured in this way, but not pain. Writhings and grimaces may similarly be measured, but, again, they are not pain. Even if inflammation always diminishes when we are asleep and do not feel it, this diminution is not the same thing as the absence of pain.

The existence of any toothache, therefore, refutes behaviorism; and, while it may be rash to assert, in opposition to behaviorists and to Christian Scientists, that it is absolutely certain that there has been such a thing as toothache, I mean, in effect, to make this very assertion. In other words, I do not intend to discuss behaviorism (as a creed) in this connection at all.

§ 4. IDIOPSYCHIC EXPERIENCE

According to traditional psychology, the essential aim of psychological science is to deal with personal experience, and with objects only in so far as they are expressly conditioned by personal experience. Psychology is therefore individualistic and in that sense subjective. Within the territory thus demarcated as individualistic, however, there are usually said to be different kinds of "subjectivity." On the one hand, we are told, there are presentations, i.e. sensa, their echoes in imagery, and (perhaps) intellectual presentations. On the other hand, there is the attitude, activity, and conscious life-history of the subject, or experiencing individual, himself. These latter are "subjective" in a deeper and more accurate sense than the former. They *are* the (empirical or apparent) psychological individual, and are not merely related to him in some specially intimate way.

As we have seen, the psychological treatment of sensa does not require any particular theory of introspection, and may not even be an instance of introspection at all; and the same observation applies to "presentations" generally.

For the remainder of this discussion, therefore, we may neglect presentations, and consider only what may be considered "subjective" in the deeper sense of psychical individuality. In the last chapter, this deeper sense of "subjective" was called idiopsychic, and it seems convenient to retain the name.

According to Dr. Ward, who has given, on the whole, the most systematic account, in English, of the traditional psychological view, the idiopsychic department of psychology (to call it by my name and not by his) consists of Attention and Feeling. Attention, according to Ward, is a general name for the subject's activity. It includes "remembering, perceiving, inferring, desiring, striving,"[8] and so forth. In other words, it includes both cognitive and other activities. Feeling, on the other hand, is pleasure-pain.[9]

[8] *Psychological Principles,* p. 60.   [9] *Ibid.,* p. 41 *sqq.*

This general scheme is usually modified in certain particulars, at any rate by those who do not go all the way with Dr. Ward. In view of the differences between cognitive and other idiopsychic activities, it is usual to distinguish between cognitive attention and the other activities of "conation." It is generally agreed, also, that it is inadvisable to restrict "feeling" to pleasure-pain, and advisable to regard it in a wider sense as a dimension of tension or excitement. It has also to be explained that such feeling is not an organic sensum (like toothache), since that is probably a sense-presentation, but what would commonly be called the "mental" discomfort, vague or acute, that may be an unpleasant accompaniment of certain organic sensa, and also occurs when we are vexed at an intellectual discrepancy, or distressed at a friend's lack of candor, or otherwise experience some psychic uneasiness.

Our question, then, is whether we have an inner sense for idiopsychic phenomena as thus defined, or, if not, whether we have any faculty "very like" an inner sense. Dr. Ward and many others strenuously deny that we have either the one or the other. They argue:

(1). That there is no sense-organ for this inner sense. Since this, however, is a physiological, not a psychological, argument, and since our answer to it must be doubtful in view of the present condition of our physiological knowledge, it seems inexpedient to set any considerable store by this contention.

(2). That our senses acquaint us with presentations, and that attention, conation, and feeling are not presentations. This argument is further developed as follows:

(3). That attention and conation are activities, and that the active element in any experience is always fundamentally distinct from the passive or sense element. Hence, *ex vi terminorum*, there can be no *sense* whose object is activity.

(4). That although feeling *is* passive (indeed more plainly passive than sense), nevertheless what is felt is not inspected or contemplated, and therefore is not a sense. "Feeling," in the phrases "I feel assured," "I feel confident," "I feel excited," and the like, as well as in the phrase, "I feel pleasure," always expresses a species of *passive* impression, but not, it is said, an impression of a sensory kind.

Whatever may be thought of the logical relations between arguments (3) and (4), the principal argument of all is said to be:

(5). That whatever is sensed is sensed *as an object,* that what is subject, properly speaking, can not be object, and hence that what is strictly subjective (or idiopsychic) can not be sensed, since, if it were, it would become an object.

This argument, taken in conjunction with the foregoing, is probably sufficient to show that any one who believes in an "inner sense" believes in a species of introspective sensation so thoroughly different from other species of sensation that little except confusion can be expected from his use of the same word "sense" in both sets of instances.

On the other hand, if he maintains only (with Locke) that introspection of the idiopsychic is "very like" sense, in the fundamental respect that it is inspection of what is ostensibly actual, he would appear to be saying something which, despite these arguments, may very well be true. The root idea in all these arguments is that if a subject inspected itself, it would convert itself into an object, which, by definition, is impossible if subject and object are always distinct. This interpretation, however, seems unnecessary. Subject and object, in terms of this contrast, express an epistemological relation; and, although there may be entities that are always objects and never subjects, it is quite illegitimate to infer that whatever is the object-term in some particular epistemological relation can never, at any time and in any other context, be the subject-term in some other particular epistemological relation, whether of the same or of a different kind. Putting the point otherwise, we might say that there is no difference between inspecting anything and inspecting it "as an object." (If this were not true, there would be something *inspectible* that was *not* an object.) Therefore, the question is simply whether or not direct inspection of the idiopsychic is possible. There is no contradiction in supposing that such inspection *might* occur, although, of course, it is quite another question whether such inspection *does* occur.

§ 5. The Nature of "Enjoyment"

Mr. Alexander adopts a different view which has found favor in many quarters. Choosing the perception of a tree as his example, he says, "The act of mind is the experiencing, the appearance, tree, is that upon which it is directed, that of which it is aware. The word 'of' indicates the relation between these two relatively distinct existences. The difference between the two ways in which the terms are experienced is expressed in language by the difference between the cognate and the objective accusative. I am aware of my awareness as I strike a stroke or wave a farewell. My awareness and my being aware of it are identical. I experience the tree as I strike a man or wave a flag. I am my mind and am conscious of the object. Consciousness is another general name for acts of mind, which, in their relation to other existences, are said to be conscious of them as objects of consciousness. For convenience of description I am accustomed to say the mind enjoys itself and contemplates its objects. The act of mind is an enjoyment; the object is contemplated."[10]

Unfortunately for this theory, it is not true that "my awareness and my being aware of *it* are identical," (i.e. that my awareness and my awareness of my awareness are identical). If they were identical, there could never be any difference between them, and plainly there is the difference that, rightly or wrongly we describe as the difference between express introspection and the absence of express introspection. Not improbably, whenever we are aware of anything, we have also a concomitant acquaintance with our own mental attitude. We may call this awareness subreflective, on analogy with Locke's term "reflection," and when we attend, as we say introspectively, to this subreflective awareness, we may be endeavoring, in a memorial way, to discern what was (subreflectively) always present. Nevertheless, in doing so, we are plainly adopting a fresh attitude, and concentrating our attention upon a part only of our original total experience. We *were* aware of X and only subreflectively aware of our awareness of X. In what is called introspection, we try to attend expressly to our awareness of X, and have relatively

[20] *Space, Time and Deity,* Vol. I, p. 12.

little interest in X itself. This difference, even in our intentions, would be utterly inexplicable if our awareness and our awareness of our awareness were literally identical.

It would appear, therefore, that this doctrine of "enjoyment," if it is capable of righting itself, has to contend that, although our idiopsychic processes (or at least those that are called "awareness") are non-inspectible, nevertheless they carry with them, in fact, a species of self-acquaintance, not of the order of inspection, that may be explicit in various degrees (as in the difference between subreflective self-awareness and attempts at express self-cognition) but is never entirely absent. This doctrine may, of course, be consistently advocated; but it can not be said to have the certainty that results from an identical proposition.

§ 6. The Reality of Introspecta

While it is difficult to deny either that we attempt introspection or that we attain some measure of success in our attempts, it is quite another thing persuasively to defend the traditional interpretation of introspection and to show that we have direct acquaintance with what is idiopsychic. Indeed, the fashionable opinion at the present moment is quite definitely opposed to the spirit of Mill's reply to Comte. A great many writers nowadays do deny that we are "aware of our own intellectual operations," either by introspective inspection or by enjoyment. They have looked, they say, or "enjoyed" with calculated deliberation, and yet they have not found anything idiopsychic at all. This pretended "awareness of our own operations" they say (as Southey said of all psychology), is altogether in the babblative case.

In discussing these contentions we should, I think, initially distinguish the major subdivisions in the traditional psychological account of what is idiopsychic, viz. cognitive awareness, conation, and feeling. For it is not clear that the same difficulties, and the same arguments, apply to all of these alike.

First, then, let us consider cognitive awareness.

When we attempt to examine cognitive attitudes of the same kind, e.g. the seeing of blue and the seeing of red, very few would maintain that they can observe any qualitative difference in the two "seeings," although they can readily discern the difference in the sensa, or objects, "blue" and "red." Proceeding on these lines, it may plausibly be maintained that there is no observable difference between the awareness of red and the awareness of sour, although red and sour are distinct and although the kinæsthetic and other organic sensa accompanying seeing and tasting, respectively, are manifestly different. An inch having thus been obtained, it may seem reasonable to take an ell. May it not be correct to deny that *any* cognitive process can either be inspected or enjoyed? Need there be any difference except in the objects that become apparent? Admittedly, our failure to distinguish any qualitative difference between the seeing of blue and the seeing of red is not a convincing proof that there *is* no qualitative difference between them. On the other hand, that is a possible conclusion. And if, extending the range of our observations, we still find no difference, it becomes (does it not?) more and more reasonable to hold that there is no such difference.

When we compare the processes, say, of perceiving, on the one hand, and of remembering, on the other hand, there manifestly is a difference in the objects. Hence, it might seem an unnecessary luxury to maintain that there is *also* an idiopsychic difference; and in that case, sensible men, who pride themselves on being economical of their hypotheses, naturally will not waste their time in looking for something that is not there. *Per contra*, however, it seems clear that we may have different mental attitudes towards precisely the same object or objects. For example, it seems plain that we may (although perhaps at different times) question, suppose, and believe the same identical proposition. In such cases, the object is the same, and yet there is a difference, viz. the difference between questioning, supposing, and believing. What is this difference except an idiopsychic difference, and how can we conceivably be acquainted with the difference except by inspection or by "enjoyment"?

It would seem, then, that certain differences of this kind are introspectively observable, and it may reasonably be suggested that those who have looked for other such differences and have not found them may not have looked hard enough or long enough. It need not, however, be contended that a qualitative idiopsychic difference can be observed in *all* instances of awareness, or that the awareness of different objects may not frequently be identical in its quality.

Secondly, the same argument may be applied to the difference between cognitive awareness, on the one hand, and conation or feeling, on the other. A man may doubt whether he can observe any difference between the sensing of blue and the sensing of sour. But he is singularly constituted if he can doubt that there is a manifest difference between the sensing of blue and the feeling of discomfort. Pleasure is different from pain, striving is different from renouncing, pleasure is different from striving. If we are not acquainted with these differences in immediate experience, how in the world do we learn of them? Are they simply inferred, to quote Mill's parenthesis, "like things done by us in a state of somnambulism," or are they deduced from some difference in "objects" *après coup?* It is surely inconceivable that they should be. Cognitive awareness, conation, and feeling may all, indeed, be members of some general class called "consciousness," but in that case there are visibly different modes of "consciousness." And the difference must be apparent to some sort of introspection.

§ 7. The Certainty of Introspective Experience

If Mr. Alexander's contentions could be sustained, "enjoyment" would be not only certain in many instances, but wholly infallible in all instances. For we are aware of this or of that very frequently indeed, and, if in "enjoyment" the awareness and the awareness of the awareness are identical, there is no room for any error, or appearance of error, in "enjoyment." We have seen, however, that this part of Mr. Alexander's view is not tenable, and it is not evident on what other premises the infallibility of enjoyment could be based.

If, on the other hand, introspection is a species of inspection of idiopsychic phenomena, it has no better claim to infallibility than any other species of inspection, say, the inspection of sensa. To be sure, although fallible, it might sometimes yield certainty, but how could we tell when the indubitable cases arise?

Psychologists frequently inform us that delicate and accurate introspection is a very difficult art, confined to the very few who have a rare and discriminating insight into human nature, but that rough introspection into the more elementary psychic differences is the commonest, as well as one of the surest, exercises of human apprehension.

This opinion may very well be correct; but it is opposed, in psychological literature, by the odd and confused notion that introspection, despite its signal difficulties, must be infallible. There is some point, then, in examining the superstition; but the principles on which it rests have already been considered so frequently (in other connections) in the present book that an elaborate examination is needless.

The superstition is based upon the argument from the nature of appearances, supplemented by the "inner" character of idiopsychic appearances. The first of these arguments states that introspecta, being apparitions or psychical seemings, must be precisely what they seem, and, as we have argued in Chapter XII, § 4, and elsewhere, this supposed consequence does not follow. (In reality, it is very difficult indeed to be quite certain of the precise character of the "look" of anything, even if that thing be ourselves.) The second argument is also quite worthless. It relies partly on some doctrine to the effect that what is outer is superficial and that what is inner is penetrating, and partly upon the mistaken spatial metaphor that what is "inner" (or perhaps "innermost") is so very near to our minds that our minds have no space in which to maneuver disastrously. Its proximity, as Dilthey said, "shuts us in with a unity that is intelligible from the inside." "Wir wissen, verstehen hier zuerst," he continued, "um allmählich zu erkennen." [11] In other words, all science is relatively "outer" and superficial. We pass to it, more or less tentatively, from an "inner" comprehension and certainty; and this is the ultimate difference between *knowledge* and mere science.

There is no occasion for thus confusing between proximity and understanding.

[11] *Einleitung in die Geisteswissenschaften,* Vol. I, p. 109.

§ 8. Introspection and the Ego

It is natural to suppose that introspection is a species of self-cognition, yielding knowledge of the Ego to each of us; and it would be pedantic, as well as unusual, to describe introspection, when nothing turns upon this special point, in language wholly destitute of this implication. It is now our business, however, to examine the point closely.

Introspection, we may now agree, whether it be inspection or enjoyment, is esthetic, or of the order of a sense, in at least one crucial aspect. For it is limited to rapid and relatively detached glances at, and glimpses of, idiopsychic phenomena. Introspection, strictly speaking, resembles perception or sensing inasmuch as it deals with the visible present; and retrospection, in such affairs, is of the same order as the memory of events.

The Ego, on the other hand, is a continuant, at any rate during waking life. Even if, by a lavish use of the conception of subreflective acquaintance with the psyche, we could be said in some vague way to be acquainted with the whole of our present personality at any moment in time, it would be contrary to all experience to maintain that, at any moment, we are acquainted (by introspection and by retrospection combined) with the whole of our past existence. It is conceivable that the Ego itself is intermittent, and that, as Berkeley said, "in sleep and trances the mind *exists not*." [12] In that case, its continuity would be limited to waking life and to the half-awake condition that we call dreaming. This limitation being granted for argument's sake, however, no one could plausibly maintain that the whole of our psychical lives can ever be present to us as a single æstheton.

The continuing Ego, therefore, is at least an epidoxaston, not a simple æstheton, and various theories, all of them possible and none of them certain, may be propounded concerning what sort of epidoxaston it is. It may be held with James (suitable allowance being made for the presence of conation and of feeling) that "the passing thought is the Thinker," [13] or, in other

---

[12] *Works,* Fraser's edition, Vol. i, p. 34.
[13] *Principles of Psychology,* Vol. i, p. 342.

words, that the Ego contains nothing at any moment of which we are not at least subreflectively aware at that moment; that psychical continuity exists only at this level and should not be a borrower from dubious theories concerning the sub- or unconscious or from a hypothetical connection with the brain; and that our retrospections are confined to that of which we were formerly aware, either introspectively or subreflectively. Many, on the other hand, would maintain that the epidoxaston we call the Ego is richer by far than James's theory suggests, and that we must attribute to psychical continuants permanent or semi-permanent dispositions and tendencies that can never be supposed to be introspectible or apparent to express retrospection. The Ego, according to such theories, is an inferred or constructed thing, rather than a perceived thing. And some would maintain that Ego is so different from other things that it is not a thing at all.

In Chapter XII, § 5, we described an epidoxaston as something that *required* æstheta as part of the evidence for its existence, although not itself a simple æstheton. We have now to consider whether the Ego can be correctly described as an epidoxaston in this sense.

The argument, in detail, would run as follows. Each of us is acquainted by introspection with certain introspecta which form a continuous unity during waking life. Without such introspecta, there would be no evidence for the existence of *any* self. With them, there is such evidence, and our belief in the self, or our knowledge of it, is therefore based upon introspecta, although we may be forced to conclude that the Ego is very much more than simply a series or procession of introspecta. Furthermore, each of us is acquainted with *his own* introspecta, and with these only. Hence, each of us has a source of evidence regarding the existence of *himself* that he does not have regarding the existence of any other self. Our self-acquaintance is based upon the visible unity of *our* introspecta, and need not be supposed to be based upon anything else.

These contentions have much in their favor. We do have very good introspective and retrospective evidence of our continuance during our waking lives. There may be a gap when Peter is asleep, but when he awakes he is the same old Peter; and he is not Paul. Memory itself, being restricted to *our own* past, is similarly evidence of our continuance in some profound and important sense. Again, a most significant degree of personal continuance can be inferred with enormously high probability from the essential characteristics of many of our passing thoughts and swift experiences. We are disappointed; that is to say, *we* have previously entertained expectations. We should not be disappointed if the event were contrary to somebody else's expectations. Again, we draw conclusions from certain premises. It is necessary, then, that *we* should hold premises and conclusion *together* in our minds. If I know only that Smith was on board some particular vessel and if you know only that the vessel sunk with all hands, neither of us can infer that Smith is dead.

In other words, Hume's celebrated contention that the self, so far as our observation goes (that is to say, for Hume, the self *simpliciter*), is only "a bundle or collection of different perceptions, which succeed each other with an inconceivable rapidity, and are in a perpetual flux or movement," [14] is a palpable misdescription of the visible appearances. The flux of our experiences is sensibly continuous and is manifestly connected in a way that we describe broadly as "personal." It is not a disconnected "bundle."

On the other hand, we should rightly have to anticipate a chorus of protest if we maintained that visible introspective (or retrospective) continuity is an absolutely perfect proof even of what we call personal identity in ordinary life. Such a proof might indeed be called "cast-iron." For cast-iron is brittle. But it is not better than cast-iron. "The permanance of the soul," Kant said, "can only be proved [empirically] where everybody grants it, during the life of man." [15] It is not, however, accurate or just to assert that everybody does grant the proof from visible psychological continuity, or should grant it, during the life of man. Setting aside the difficulties that arise in connection with fugues, loss of memory, "multiple personality," and other cases that are called "abnormal," it is evident, from normal and every-

[14] *Treatise*, p. 252.   [15] *Prolegomena*, Mahaffy's translation, pp. 98 *sq.*

day experience, that our conviction that we were the same selves ten years ago as we are to-day might have an awkward time under cross-examination, however strong the conviction might remain. The sense, even, in which our bodies are the "same" from the cradle to the coffin permits of much discussion, and is hardly fitted to be a paradigm of metaphysical certainty; and the psychical continuity and identity of our "selves" is considerably feebler than our bodily continuity, when tested and attested in the ordinary way. Unless we know in advance that any experience *must* belong to a single self, and that there can not be more than one self "in" one body, we are not in a strong position to defend our assurance of personal psychic identity against a resolute and skilful skeptic.

Accordingly, it is maintained, I do not say with certainty, but with very high probability, that the visible continuity of what we call ourselves is visibly insufficient to be *all* that we mean by a self, and hence that, if the self is an epidoxaston, it must contain much more than introspecta in any ordinary sense. It might, however, be contended that there is a visible self in each of us additional to introspecta in the ordinary sense, and Dr. McTaggart, for instance, maintained that there was. "There is a quality," he argued, "the one which we have called selfness—which can only be perceived by me, in present experience, when I am self-conscious, since, in present experience, I can only perceive it in myself, but which is a quality which can exist without self-consciousness. This quality wants a name, and it seems best to appropriate the name of selfness to it." [16]

Of this I can only say that such "selfness" does not seem to me to be visible, and that, if selfness must be distinguished from introspectible continuity, the quality of selfness is definitely *metaesthetic*, that is to say, definitely imperceptible, although possibly to be reached by inference or other intellectual reflection.

Very frequently a distinction is drawn between the "empirical self," or the "Me," and the "pure," "noumenal," or metaesthetic self, the "I"; and sometimes this distinction is treated as if it were absolute. The distinction itself, however, bears traces of

[16] *The Nature of Existence,* Vol. ii, p. 81.

cross-purposes. Sometimes the assumption is that the Ego *must* be metaesthetic; and in that case the most plausible interpretation would be that the "empirical" (or æsthetic) Ego is either a continuous series of introspecta or an epidoxaston based upon these. At other times, however, the Ego is regarded as the "owner" of its "states" and as the substance in which these states inhere. This is a metaphysical theory of substance, and does not properly yield the conclusion that a "substance" is ultimately distinct from its states. When the theory is supposed to yield this conclusion, however, we obtain the result that the "empirical ego" is a succession, or perhaps a bundle, of "states," and that the Ego itself is a metempirical and metaesthetic "substance" that "owns" or "possesses" the "states." Finally, and by a third interpretation, it is maintained that the "empirical ego" consists of certain objects or presentations which have a peculiarly close relation to the self. The ego itself, on this view, is not an object of empirical experience (perhaps because it is active, not sensory) but the objects in which we are interested, e.g. our children, our friends, our bank accounts, and the like, are said to be parts of our "empirical selves." [17]

All these accounts of the "empirical self" are different, and each of them implies a different relation between the empirical and the metempirical "self." It is confusing to find the same name applied to such different relations and arguments, but conceivable that all the three accounts, in different ways, might be true. On the other hand, he would be a very rash man who could claim that he knows for certain how far what he calls himself is empirical and how far it is metempirical, or what, precisely, the relation between the empirical and the metempirical part of him is. We rely very largely upon sensible personal continuity; but when we begin to ask how far such continuity is psychical and how far due to the "warmth and intimacy" [18] of our bodies; how far it is introspectible and how far an inference from objects in which our interests reside; how far it is logical and an expression for the sort of unity implied in coherent, or semi-coherent, thinking; we are either singularly fortunate or

[17] *Cf.* James, *Principles of Psychology,* Vol. i, pp. 291 *sqq.*
[18] *Ibid.,* p. 333.

singularly blind if the prospect of certainty in these affairs does not rapidly recede.

§ 9. THE METEMPIRICAL OR METAESTHETIC EGO

The following arguments may be noted. They are mainly, although not quite exclusively, metempirical.

(1) Dr. Ward, whose system of metaphysics had a noticeably egocentric basis—"we find *again* without us," he says, "the permanence and individuality, the efficiency, and the adaptation we have found *first of all* within" [19]—maintains that "pure Ego" is an "inexpugnable assumption," [20] and further explains that "by pure Ego or Subject it is proposed to denote here the simple fact that everything experienced is referred to a self experiencing." [21]

According to his analysis, the Ego attends and feels. Whatever is known must be an "object" or "presentation"; and the Ego, its attention, and its feeling are not objects at all. Neither the Ego, nor its feelings, nor its attention, therefore, can ever be known immediately in themselves. They are only known mediately and through their effects.[22]

Since this statement implies that our pleasure and pain are not known immediately, but only by inference from "their" effects, there seems plainly to be something wrong with it, or at the least, a misleading and undesirable restriction of the term "knowledge." We do have immediate acquaintance in our experience with our pleasure and pain (to say nothing of other introspecta) ; and if this acquaintance is not to be called "knowledge," it is at any rate immediate and non-inferential.

If it be granted (in accordance with § 6 of the present chapter) that we may be immediately acquainted with our attention and our feeling, or, in other words, with what Ward calls "subjective being," whether or not such immediate acquaintance is to be called "knowledge," the question at once arises whether this continuum of attention and feeling *is* the "pure Ego" or whether the pure Ego is additional to the continuum. To this question, so far as I can see, Dr. Ward gives no decided answer. He says

[19] *Psychological Principles*, p. 335.   [21] *Ibid.*
[20] *Ibid.*, p. 35.   [22] *Ibid.*, p. 58.

that the Ego is "active and affectible," [23] but he also says that "we know *intellectually* what we are as experients; into the empty 'form of consciousness' our being fits"; [24] that the "pure subject or Ego which we reach in our analysis of experience at its rational level stands for an abstraction so long as we are content to distinguish it without attempting to separate it from its objective complement, the non-Ego"; [25] and that "this concept of the pure Ego, or I, is the limit to which the empirical Ego points." [26]

These latter statements are all to the effect that presentations can not be self-sufficient but logically imply something, not itself a presentation, *to* which the presentations are presented. If so, the "Ego" is simply a complementary term to presentation, and is inferred from the admitted fact that there are presentations. The relation of this complementary term to introspection and to "enjoyment" therefore remains obscure. And there are further notable obscurities. If the argument be that any presentation is only one term, the term immediately known, in what Ward calls the "subject-object" duality (the subject-term, while indubitable, being only inferred), how can we infer with certainty that there is only *one* subject for *many* presentations, that there is greater or lesser unity in "the" subject than in the fluctuating, although pretty evident, unity of the empirical "me"? Indeed, how can we form any indubitable inferences of this kind?

The inevitability of the subject-object duality in all experience may also be disputed. As we have argued on various occasions, the admission that "something is presented" does not entail the consequence that there exists a distinctive entity called a presentation. It may similarly be denied that the admission entails the consequence that there is a distinctive *subjective* entity. The main point, however, is whether we can infer with certainty that such subjective entities, supposing them to exist, are parts of the life history of a single continuant.

(2) It is sometimes argued that processes of attention do not attend, processes of perceiving do not perceive, and so forth.

[23] *Psychological Principles*, p. 24. [25] *Ibid.*, p. 379.
[24] *Ibid.*, p. 381. [26] *Ibid.*, p. 377.

The least that can be said with accuracy is that *I* attend, *I* perceive, and the like.

This statement is in conformity with common language, but would not seem opposed in principle to the possibility that "I" may be the continuum of perceiving, remembering, and other processes of "attention" and of "feeling," provided that this continuum has the kind of unity we call "personal." If the statement is so opposed, the opposition rests upon a certain conception of "substance" according to which *operari sequitur esse.* In other words, perceiving presupposes something that perceives, walking presupposes something that walks, and so *ad infinitum.* In opposition to this view of substance, many would maintain that the history of anything is simply the history of its performances, that nothing but prejudice prevents us from saying that the thing *is* its performances, and that the thing's unity and continuity are the unity and continuity of these performances.

I do not wish to contend that this account of substance is certainly true, but I think it would be over-bold to assert that the account is certainly false.

(3) Dr. McTaggart says, "I believe that there cannot be experience which is not experienced by a self, because that proposition seems to me evident, not as a part of the meaning of the term experience, but as a synthetic truth about experience. This truth is, I think, ultimate. I do not know how to defend it against attacks. But it seems to me to be beyond doubt. The more clearly I realize—or seem to myself to realize—the nature of experience in general, or of knowledge, volition, or emotion, in particular, the more clearly does it appear to me that any of them are impossible except as the experience of a self." [27]

If the "self" here means a *continuing* self, Dr. McTaggart's statement implies that a so-called "floating" experience, or a "little thought of *q*" can never occur. Such an experience, according to him, would not be self-contradictory, but would be impossible in fact. And it is true that any examples we can give of experiences that come near to "floating," in delirium, in twilight sleep, or in so-called dissociations of personality, have

[27] *The Nature of Existence,* Vol. II, p. 82.

a certain self-like continuity and may be held, without any considerable strain, to be really, although not very visibly, parts of a "self" in a more ordinary sense of selfhood. On the other hand, Dr. McTaggart's "synthetic truth" seems to be rather an extension of our subreflective experience of self-like continuity, than a metempirical proposition for which general or axiomatic self-evidence can reasonably be claimed.

(4) Dr. McTaggart also argues that acquaintance with the Ego is implied in the *significance,* irrespective of the *truth,* of the statement "I am aware of *this* awareness." [28] This statement, true or false, is clearly significant, he says; it implies that the person who is aware of the awareness is the person who makes the judgment; and if we had only an indirect or descriptive apprehension of "the" person who makes the judgment, we could not know that this person is also aware of the awareness.

If, however, the "I" meant a unity of awarenesses and of other experiences that was possibly self-conscious, it might surely be argued that the "I" would count itself twice over if it counted the Self as one entity and the unity of "its" personal experiences as another entity.

[28] *Ibid.,* pp. 63 *sqq.*

Chapter XV

THE KNOWLEDGE OF OTHER MINDS

§ 1. General

EVERY human being believes that other human beings exist, and also that these other human beings have minds in the same sense as he himself has. Every writer on the principles of human knowledge, again, uses language which implies that there *are* human knowers other than himself. And solipsism (which is the theory that I know my own existence for certain but can not be said to know for certain that anything other than myself, whether person or thing, exists) is commonly employed as a sort of dialectical bogy, or awful example of the way in which sane men may involve themselves in radically insane theories.

This bogy, in all probability, is partly the product of confusion. It is one thing for a man to *believe* that he alone (ipse solus) exists, quite another thing for him to believe or suspect that he has much better evidence for his own existence than for the existence of anything else. Schopenhauer said, "Shut them up in a madhouse" of solipsists, (of the first type) if there were any; but he himself used arguments that implied solipsism (of the second type). Indeed, it is the usual philosophical opinion that each of us has *better* evidence for believing in the existence of his own mind or self than for believing in the existence of other minds or selves. And since certainty has no degrees, whatever is certain being completely so, it follows that all who accept this difference in the conclusiveness of the evidence are bound in consistency to maintain that none of us *knows* that other minds exist whether or not each of us *knows* that his own mind exists.

§ 2. Some Common Arguments

It is generally held that a man has sources of evidence regarding the existence of himself that he does not have regarding the existence of other selves. In so far as the self is an embodied self, the man has, in his own case, direct acquaintance with endosomatic æstheta but has only a roundabout acquaintance with another man's toothache or nausea. In so far, again, as the self is either a continuum of introspecta or an epidoxaston logically based upon introspecta, a man's acquaintance with the minds of his fellows (it is commonly held) *must* be indirect, or even inferential, in comparison with his acquaintance with his own mind. For it is generally agreed that no one can either directly inspect or personally enjoy the introspecta of other people. What is more, the same conclusion would follow if we held with Dr. McTaggart that each of us can perceive a "quality of selfness" in himself. For Dr. McTaggart does not maintain that we can perceive this quality in any one else.[1]

To be sure, we might have *certain,* although *indirect,* apprehension of the existence of other selves, but in the stock arguments on this subject the indirect evidence looks decidedly shaky. The stock argument rests upon analogy and is developed as follows. I know that I exist and am a mental being. I also know that I have a body that expresses and corresponds to my mentality. When I feel ashamed, for instance, there is a blush on my countenance. I also know that other human bodies exist in the world and are very similar to mine. When, therefore, I observe in them a condition similar to that which in my own case expresses or corresponds to a condition of my mind, I am entitled to conclude that they have minds like mine.

As we have seen, this presumed *knowledge* of our own minds and of physical bodies (including our own) has itself to withstand criticism, and it is notorious both that the correlation of "mind" with "body" and the constraining character of analogical arguments are very seriously disputable. Setting these perplexities aside, however, we can surely observe genuine difficulties of detail in the analogy here set forth. In general, these expressive bodily gestures (with the important exception of speech) are much clearer to others than they are to ourselves. It is other people who notice our mannerisms and tell-tale gestures, and like to have us sit in a good light when they suspect we have some-

[1] *The Nature of Existence,* Vol. ii, pp. 81 *sq.*

thing to conceal. Even in the case of speech we are not well acquainted with the sound and inflections of our own voices as these are heard by other people. In short, in this correlation between our private feelings (F) and the public expressive bodily movements (B), there are manifest gaps on one side or on the other. *We* may be well-acquainted with F, but we are relatively ill-acquainted with B; and *other people*—so it is argued—are pretty well acquainted with B, but not at all with F. (i.e. with *our* personal feelings and experiences). I do not say that the argument, despite these flaws in it, is bad; but it is absurd to claim utter certainty for it in this form.

Again, the above argument, if it is at all plausible, can be propounded only as a sophisticated *justification* of any man's belief in other selves, and not as an account of the way in which we all come by this belief. There is no reason to doubt that very young children do believe in the existence of other selves, although, no doubt, they are even less capable than the rest of us of formulating the belief or of defining precisely what is meant by a self; and, as we shall see, it is impossible to suppose that they reach the belief by an analogical argument of the type supposed. Admittedly, origin and validity are essentially distinct. On the other hand, it is clear that if the belief in other selves is not "innate" or "instinctive," but arises in each of us through a genetic psychological process, it would be the worst kind of dogmatism to assert in advance that this genetic process is unreasonable or illogical. On the contrary, even if it does not conform to the etiquette of the schools, it may very well be predominantly reasonable.

Therefore, unless we are compelled, we should not hold that a sophisticated argument, relatively (although not entirely) remote from the genetic process in which this belief in the existence of other selves is normally reached, is likely to be the sole or the proper justification of the belief in their existence. It is much more likely that part, at least, of the evidence for the belief is contained in the species of unsophisticated logic that may reasonably be supposed to be present and operative throughout the genetic process. Accordingly, we should endeavor to find out what this unsophisticated logic probably is.

§ 3. The Origin of the Belief

Without being guilty of presumptuousness in any considerable degree we may assert, with some confidence, that what occurs is of the following order. The human infant, as soon as it begins to notice anything—and it becomes a smiling, responsive, and almost a conversable animal in a very few weeks—must be assumed to discover a very marked difference in its surroundings according as these (as *we* should say) do or do not respond to its wishes. (Kittens may be supposed to make the same discovery.) Some things, to speak half-sophisticatedly, seem to divine the infant's wants and to respond to these, clumsily, it may be, but, on the whole, effectively. Other things are unresponsive, although, to be sure, there may be doubts about the boundaries in these matters, as when the kitten's ball of string appears to the kitten to be at least partly responsive.

The infant can not *say* all this, or any of it, but he feels and sees the force of it pretty soon. And in the large, his development is rather of the type "I am (more or less) as these responsive things are," than of the type "They are as I am." In other words, this development is fundamentally non-solipsistic. Self-consciousness, so far from being prior to other-consciousness, is for the most part posterior. Moreover, there is no question, at this stage, of an Ego versus an unresponsive world. The infant is confronted with a world that is partly responsive and partly not responsive. He is, on the whole, more concerned with the former than with the latter, and he gradually discovers his place as a participant in the former from its familiar characteristics and not from the analogy between it and his prior knowledge of himself.

This genetic process, which might readily be corroborated by anthropological investigations into the mentality of primitive peoples, should not be supposed to be fundamentally illogical. These distinctions between what is responsive and unresponsive in the infant's environment (with further distinctions, within the responsive environment, between the responses of parents, nurses, brothers, strangers, dogs, and cats) are genuine distinctions that any sensible infant must be supposed to notice rapidly if vaguely.

If what I have called the "stock" argument is to be accepted at all, it must be reached within the ambit of this responsive and social situation.

Let us then consider the relation between the stock argument and this one.

§ 4. THE CONJOINT FORCE OF THESE ARGUMENTS

Taking the genetic and the analogical arguments together, we obtain some such result as the following.

(1) *A priori*, anything may be anything.

(2) The distinction between a responsive and an unresponsive environment must be noticeable at a very early stage in the life-history of human infants, and of kittens, puppies, and other young animals.

(3) This distinction should not be assumed, at this stage, to be necessarily and solely a distinction between observable physical movements, or between responsive and unresponsive physical bodies. On the contrary, it should be assumed to include all that we call fellow-feeling and sympathetic understanding. (It is a question for further and quite philosophical argument whether this fellow-feeling and sympathetic understanding must ultimately be inferred from or suggested by living "matter," in accordance, perhaps, with an original or instinctive belief, or with an original and unacquired "suggestion.")

(4) The human infant participates in this responsive life, and itself responds to other human beings, and to animals.

(5) The human infant need not be supposed, however, to be originally self-conscious in any clear or distinctive sense; and when it begins to be reflectively self-conscious, the probabilities are that it arrives at self-consciousness by comparison with, and (in part at least) in logical dependence on, other-consciousness.

At this point philosophers commonly intervene, and it is convenient for purposes of clearness to consider initially those philosophers whose views besides being conventional, are very clipped and precise. Let us call them dogmatic philosophers.

The dogmatic philosopher argues, then,

(6) That in fact minds and physical bodies are utterly distinct.

(7) That in fact any given mind may know itself directly but can not have direct knowledge of any other mind.

(8) That minds may perceive matter.

(9) That minds may communicate through matter, but not otherwise; and therefore

(10) That whatever erroneous ideas may be present to infantile or other developing (but as yet undeveloped) minds, the "responsive" environment can not, in reality and ultimately, be known in any other way than is consistent with, and logically (although not necessarily psychologically) dependent on, these analogical arguments from (6) to (9) inclusive.

Since it is conceivable that arguments (1) to (5), and again arguments (6) to (9), are all true, this conclusion can not be said to be a logical *impasse,* but it is not a promising attempt either to prove that we have *certain* knowledge of other minds or to account for the assurance we all feel in the existence of other minds. On the latter point, all that can be urged on these lines is that the massive and cumulative effect of our experience of responsive behavior, in infancy and afterwards, predisposes us to accept the analogical argument with eager hospitality. On the former point, it has to be admitted, as we saw in § 2, that the analogical argument is very far from being demonstrative. To hold, as some do, that *because* the analogical argument is weak, and *because* we all have overwhelming assurance in the existence of other minds, *therefore* this belief must be "instinctive," is but to abandon the attempt to maintain that we have knowledge, certainty, or sufficient evidence in the matter. It is simply a statement that we do believe because we do believe. And it is hard to suppose that there is no greater rationality in this belief.

Accordingly, it would seem more promising to be less dogmatic than the dogmatic philosopher. On the other hand, a vague and sapient qualification of some of his arguments seems insufficient. To say that we should speak of mind-bodies rather than of minds *and* bodies, that mind and matter may be rather like one another, that it is doubtful whether mind does perceive itself, and also doubtful whether it perceives matter, may alleviate the difficulty in some degree, but remains a vague and wide solution unless these suggestions become more precise. When they do become more precise, however, they also become uncertain. For although the propositions asserted by our dogmatic philosopher are, for the most part, visibly uncertain, any specific alternative philosophy is not less uncertain.

On the whole, I think, most alternative suggestions in this matter *are* pretty vague. They amount to saying that we may have some sort of immediate acquaintance either with other minds or with a social "atmosphere," although we do not have the same sort of acquaintance with these as with our own loves and hates and other personal experiences. Or else they endeavor to diffuse a general uncertainty by denying that our vaunted acquaintance with ourselves is of much account, by refusing to admit that a society consists of individual psychic centers, and by other such denials. This general uncertainty concerning "mind" and our knowledge of it, however, should not appreciably affect the *contrast* between our acquaintance with ourselves and our acquaintance with others.

Perhaps, however, the most significant point in this matter is that many philosophers profess themselves far more certain of the existence of Mind writ large, than of any private personal existence, including their own. The great certainty, they argue, is the certainty of "significant structures" [2] of language, history, commerce, and art, and not the certainty of personal existence. On such a view it need not, indeed, be denied that Corporate Mind and its manifestations rest upon, and might not exist without, the existence of personal experients, but it seems to be held that individual minds, even if their existence be not doubtful, can not be understood in detail with any considerable degree of rational comprehension; and that Corporate Mind, *per contra*, is thus comprehensible.

Or is the claim only that individual minds are rather uninteresting?

§ 5. FURTHER ON THE SAME

According to sociologists and anthropologists, particularly of the Durkheim school, the conception of personal psychic individuality, whether of a man's own self or of the selves of others

[2] *Cf.* G. P. Adams, *Idealism and the Modern Age*, especially Ch. vi.

in his society, does not emerge at all among primitive peoples in any sense that approaches ours. Instead, the primitive interprets his responsive social environment fundamentally, if not quite exclusively, in communal terms.

It is hard to believe this theory in its entirety. Even the least reflective of savages, one must suppose, to some extent distinguishes himself from his wife, and distinguishes *his* wife or wives from other people's. It is also to be supposed that the savage sees some importance in the point. Again, it seems most unreasonable to deny that there is something psychological in these primitive distinctions.

On the other hand, it may fairly be asked, in view of this anthropological evidence, how far such conceptions of personality and of psychical individuality as were asserted by the "dogmatic philosopher" of our previous section are the result of inevitable inference from the immitigable fact of the restriction of all direct acquaintance with mind to self-consciousness, and how far they are the result of a long theological and juristic development according to which each soul must work out its own salvation, each punishable person be personally responsible for his own guilt, and society itself be regarded as composed of distinct and, so to say, impervious personalities. May not the dogmatic philosopher's theory be built up, in part at least, *après coup,* and be, in that measure, an attempt to justify a foregone legal or priestly conclusion, instead of being the inexpugnable basis of all such legal or theological views? These juristic and theological conceptions, to be sure, are not empty dogmas based upon nothing at all, or mere social conveniences that might just as well have been conceived in some wholly different spirit. To choose the simplest ground, the heart has *some* acquaintance with its *own* bitterness, and is aware that it does not intermeddle in the same way with the bitterness or with the joys of a stranger; and, although Aristotle's assertion that the doer of a deed can not be ignorant concerning him who has done it—"for how can he not know himself?" [3]—may not be so entirely evident as Aristotle supposed, there is clearly an impressive truth contained in the assertion.

[3] *Ethics,* 1111a.

On the other hand, it seems at least possible, as many philosophers assert, that whatever is true on these simple grounds is hardened into exaggeration and falsity in the dogmas we have endeavored to consider. If so, our certainty in these matters would seem either to reside in a fluid region which can hardly be distinguished with satisfying accuracy, or else to apply to "mental structures" rather than to individual minds. In other words, we should either submerge our thoughts, at some risk of suffocation, below the apparently pellucid distinction between "self" and "others," or else we should transcend this distinction.

Without attempting to pursue this question still further, I should like to conclude this brief chapter with a quotation from John Grote's *Exploratio Philosophica*. In this passage, perhaps, certainties are claimed rather recklessly, and I might myself be disposed to be more cautious, even if I were not engaged in my present task of considering whether *utter* certainty of a knowledgeable sort can anywhere be proved to be impervious to grounded (not fantastic) criticism. I have thought for a long time, however, that there is more of truth in this passage from Grote than in any other of the many hundreds of pages upon the present topic with which I can claim acquaintance. The passage runs:

"Were we solitary beings in the universe, *immediateness* would be in its nature the same. We should or we might have our eyes and ears open, and fact and we would meet each other as well in solitude as in company. Nor would there, perhaps, be wanting some impulses to reflection, or to the vivifying, by our intelligence, of this meeting of us and fact. But the *great* impulse to reflection would be wanting, namely the impulse to communication. Intelligence is really *co-intelligence*. . . . In fact we have here *another* of our primary experiences, which places us not only in an universe of things to be known, but in an universe of *fellow-knowers*. The universe of what is to be known surrounds not only *us*, but a number of intelligences like us: and our *knowing* has the second character of being not only a mirroring of the universe or of fact, but of being a sympathy with other intelligences. There is a large portion of our thought, in regard of which its being individual or peculiar to ourselves is wrong: and thus we arrive at a second criterion of trueness, besides the derivation from individual immediateness. Thought, if it is to be true, must be not only derived from fact, but must satisfy, or be thought good for, other intelligences as well as our own." [*]

[*] Vol. II, pp. 212 *sq.*

Chapter XVI

OF EMOTIONAL CERTAINTY

§ 1. Introductory

EMOTION, it is generally agreed, is not evidence. On the contrary, it suborns the witnesses and seduces the jury. Geometers, physicists, and engineers are fortunate because they can easily prevent emotional prepossessions from clouding their calculations. Students of the human sciences, on the other hand, have to fight an incessant battle with emotional bias. And this is often a losing battle.

Per contra, as we saw in Chapter V, § 5, emotion, pretty clearly, is evidence of *something;* and it might conceivably be evidence of much. It is not evidence of lines or angles, of Boyle's Law or of Gresham's Law. It is, however, evidence of *itself,* and if there is such a thing as emotional significance, it may signify, and therefore be evidence of, a great deal.

According to many philosophers, art-critics, moralists, and theologians, our emotions signify, and are evidence of, *values.* If so, this emotional evidence may be good evidence, and perhaps even conclusive; and if our emotions, sentiments, and "approval" yielded conclusive evidence of values, such evidence would be a "certainty," although a certainty different in type from the "certainties" we have considered hitherto. We must therefore examine this claim.

I do not say that emotional theories of value are the only possible theories concerning value. On the contrary, as we saw at the conclusion of Chapter XI, they are not. They are, however, a very usual, probably the most usual, type of value-theory, especially in the great departments of esthetics, morals, and religion.

§ 2. Mr. Sturge Moore's Esthetic Theories

In the sphere of esthetics, the arguments of Mr. Sturge Moore's recent *Armour for Aphrodite* are so exceedingly pat to my purpose that I may be excused for confining my attention to them.

"The world of taste," Mr. Sturge Moore says, "appears confused: people, willing to expend on art money, intelligence and sensibility in far greater measure than the average educated person, yet disagree completely, not only as to the objects which they chiefly admire, but as to the standards by which they appraise them." [1] His endeavor is to remove or to diminish this confusion.

One of the confusions, he says, is that beauty can be other than objective. "Beauty," we read, "is a real value just as truth is, and quite unaffected by human error in regard to it. We make mistakes about it, just as we do about all experience; but the truth about it awaits discovery all the time." [2] Again, we read: "Beauty is a fact, not an emotion or opinion, and is as inseparable a part of the universe as we ourselves; and though all men became totally blind to it, would patiently await rediscovery in the proportions and arrangements of complex wholes of frequent recurrence or of great permanence." [3]

The question, therefore, is what is the relation of this objective beauty to our taste and admiration.

Objective beauty, he says, is "the quality we ascribe to admired sensuous wholes." [3] suitable allowance being made for an extension of the "sensuous" to imagination and to thought. [4] What, then, he asks, is the nature of admiration, and what evidence does admiration give us concerning beauty?

Mr. Sturge Moore denies, as most serious inquirers are compelled to deny, that there is any single esthetic emotion. "There is no distinctively esthetic emotion," he says. "The thrill of pleasure caused by a work of art cannot be distinguished from that due to a flower or sunset save by this difference of source." [5]

[1] *Armour for Aphrodite*, p. 1.
[2] *Ibid.*, p. 55.
[3] *Ibid.*, p. 28.
[4] *Ibid.*, p. 20.
[5] *Ibid.*, p. 54.

Nevertheless, his theory of admiration is essentially emotional, for it is based upon *liking.*

This is asserted time and again. "Beauty," he tells us, "names the value to each of us of things we like to gaze at, repeat or listen to." [6] "The value of the work of art is never that it is faithful to a mental picture, but always that it is able to move us." [7] "What avails it to discriminate good from less good, if you do not like it better?" [8] "To value is to prefer." [9] "The only fact behind taste is enjoyment—delight in certain proportions and harmonies." [10]

For this reason, our author firstly lays the strongest emphasis upon the requirement that our liking must be *genuine,* and secondly, firmly asserts the total distinction between admiration and logic or reason.

On the first of these points we read: "No genuine liking is bad, for it must always be sounder than simulated taste." [11] "The authority of evident enjoyment is the authority of life itself. To admire is to live fully." [12] "Man can never be sure that any object is beautiful by which he has not been profoundly moved, nor on the other hand sure that it is not beautiful and apt to move a finer soul." [13] And other such statements.

On the second we read: "Perhaps the most difficult task of an aesthete to-day is to subordinate the intellectual part of an experience." [14] "There are no reasons for beauty." [15] "Taste grows by the experimental process as knowledge does, only its criterion is beauty, not truth, and demands admiration, not comprehension." [16] "Knowledge is discovered only by those who probe, beauty only by those who admire.' [17]

Plainly, then, the essential question is how far genuine liking is good evidence (I do not say *logical* evidence) of the presence of objective beauty; and here, so far as I can see, Mr. Sturge Moore has little to say that could possibly be regarded as effective. He does not pretend that *every* liking reveals the goddess Aphrodite; for much of our liking has nothing to do with taste or esthetic admiration. He does not claim, either, that

[6] *Armour for Aphrodite,* p. 31. [10] *Ibid.,* p. 140. [14] *Ibid.,* p. 102.
[7] *Ibid.,* p. 89. [11] *Ibid.,* p. 47. [15] *Ibid.,* p. 149.
[8] *Ibid.,* p. 98. [12] *Ibid.,* p. 140. [16] *Ibid.,* p. 131.
[9] *Ibid.,* p. 131. [13] *Ibid.,* p. 105. [17] *Ibid.*

every liking for a sensuous whole that is speciously proportionate can be regarded as an authentic revelation of beauty; for in that case there would be no distinction at all between good taste and bad. There would only be a distinction between simulated liking and genuine liking. "Tolerate all genuine pleasure," he says, "as a stage on the road to perfect appreciations." [18] Yes; but where is the standard of appraisal (additional to the *sine qua non* of genuine liking) that is clearly implied in this statement? "Emotion," he says again, "is prized according to the company it keeps." [19] Yes; but how are we to prize its company?

When Mr. Sturge Moore (who is himself a craftsman) squarely faces this problem, he answers it in the craftsman's way. "Neither fidelity to the outward world (realism) nor fidelity to an impression, is the *sine qua non* of art," he says, "but integrity within the work, coherence, harmony like the unity of living organisms." [20] We agree, because we must agree. But what is the relation of this craftsman's standard of integrity and coherence to the *other* standard of genuine liking? The likings of those people who like a revue and dislike grand opera are not less genuine than the likings of those who like grand opera and dislike revues. Grand opera, it is true, may itself be lacking in "integrity"; for it may be an unnatural alliance of two distinct arts that refuse to amalgamate. On any theory, however, it is enormously better integrated than a music-hall revue.

In short, these two standards of integrity and of personal enjoyment seem essentially distinct; and Mr. Sturge Moore does not seem even to attempt to unite them except for his vague suggestion that our enjoyment of any sensuous "whole" is, for the time being, a function of our entire "life," and that the integrity within a work of art resembles the coherence of a living organism.

It is no accident, I suggest, that this wide and deep hiatus appears in Mr. Sturge Moore's theory. There is bound to be a similar hiatus in every claim similar to Abt Vogler's in Browning's poem, viz. that "we musicians *know*" in the peculiar way of "knowing" (or of final and self-certifying admiration) that is based upon pleasure, rapture, or delight, If there were, as in

[18] *Ibid.*, p. 149 *sq.*   [19] *Ibid.*, p. 57.   [20] *Ibid.*, p. 92.

fact there is not, either a peculiar esthetic emotion for all species
of beauty, or a series of peculiar esthetic emotions having a one-
one correspondence with all the various beauties of poetry, sculp-
ture, painting, and all the other arts and natural beauties, the
vagaries of taste and of fashion among the critics, as well as
among the laity, would forbid us to speak with any considerable confidence of the possibility of certainty in the way of
penetrative admiring insight. And the difficulty is all the greater
when we admit, as we should admit, that there is no such specific
emotion or set of emotions.

Indeed, I have lingered so long upon Mr. Sturge Moore's
delightful argument precisely because I wished to show, in some
detail, how considerable and how inevitable this hiatus is when
any one reflects seriously upon these matters.[21]

I hasten, however, to add that Mr. Sturge Moore himself carefully avoids anything more than a modulated aspiration after
certainty. "A great docility," he says, "is needed to foresee that
the present feeling of rightness is necessarily as illusive as any
other, is but one rung on the ladder that can only be mounted by
leaving it behind. The ladder implies its top, and so do conscience, taste and inquiry imply their several goals. To this degree there is evidence of the absolute; so much is part of the
meaning of the words goodness, beauty, truth. But obviously,
by creatures so limited as human beings at present are, ultimate
degrees must remain for long unattained." [22]

"Very little is known," we read in another passage, "and
nothing is so simple as the positive mind supposes; our certainties are approximate and rare, and there are practical incon-
veniences in supposing them to be more numerous and better con-
solidated than in truth they are." [23]

[21] The reader may consider the implications of the following lines from
the late Poet Laureate's *Testament of Beauty:*
  "What is Beauty?" saith my sufferings then—I answer
  the lover and the poet in my loose alexandrines:
  Beauty is the highest of all these occult influences,
  the quality of appearances that thro' the sense
  awakeneth spiritual emotion in the mind of man,
  And Art as it createth new forms of beauty
  awakeneth new ideas that advance the spirit
  in the life of Reason to the wisdom of God."
Op. cit., p. 119.   [23] *Ibid.,* p. 93.

§ 3. Lætitia Spiritualis

The wider contention that some finely-tempered spiritual joy (lætitia spiritualis) or some heaven-born clarity of loving yields non-intellectual but profoundly evidenced certainty concerning all that is noble or excellent has been made, in some form, in every considerable period of the history of philosophy.

Thus in Plato's *Symposium* the thing was said in parable by Diotima, a wise woman of Mantineia. Her discourse was firstly of the lesser mysteries of love, and secondly of the greater mysteries. In the lesser mysteries, Socrates made her say, love is not knowledge. Love at this stage is a thing of concupiscence, unsatisfied and seeking satisfaction. At the best it is but right opinion, something bent upon the truth and not inapprehensive of the truth, but without knowing it. This lesser type of loving is attracted by sensible beauty, not by beauty in itself, and by some specious appearance of eternity, such as the simulated perpetuity of offspring, or the semi-permanence of the written word in literature. The true object of love, however, is beauty eternal, and the love of the greater mysteries is of this second and profounder order. It culminates in the perfect vision of beauty as beauty is in itself, naked, true, and eternal. In the lesser mysteries, love, although it does not see clearly, nevertheless proceeds aright. As love's ascent goes on, the mists lift.

Psychological classification, as it was made by Plato's pen, was a classification of attitudes or levels of the entire soul, rather than a division of specialized aptitudes or faculties within the soul. It would be a mistake, therefore, to interpret this parable of Diotima's as a veiled way of saying that *intellectual* insight into eternal beauty *supervenes* upon the obscure attractions of emotional loving. The spiritual love of the greater mysteries is not indeed non-intellectual. On the contrary, it is an attitude of soul in which reason and intellect are most abundantly manifest. But love is also present in this attitude, and in so far as true knowledge is regarded (as Plato always regards it) as the *possession* of the true and eternal by the soul, or as an identity between the soul and the eternal, the quest for *union*, so characteristic of loving, may be said to be more authentically prefigured in the experience of attraction and human affection than in many kinds of "right opinion."

Neoplatonism, and particularly the Neoplatonism of Plotinus, is commonly held to tell the same story, although it may not be altogether clear what the Neoplatonic story was. According to Proclus, "Faith gives all things a solid foundation in the Good. Truth reveals knowledge in all real existence. Love leads all things to the nature of the Beautiful." [24] According to Plotinus, "The natural love which the soul feels proves that the Good is there; that is why paintings and myths make Psyche the bride of Cupid. . . . But Yonder is the true object of our love, which it is possible to grasp and live with and truly to possess. It knows what I say, that the soul then has another life, when it comes to God and, having come, possesses him, and knows, when in that state, that it is in the presence of the dispenser of the true life, and that it needs nothing further." [25] Again, he says that "love is an activity of the soul desiring the Good"; [26] and he holds that it knows when it attains its desire.

§ 4. PASCAL'S RAISONS DE COEUR

Among modern (or less ancient) authors, Pascal is most frequently quoted in this connection. Indeed, his famous apothegm that "the heart hath its reasons that the Reason knoweth not" [27] is commonly regarded as one of the clearest enunciations in history of the principle that there may be emotional certainty as well as intellectual, and that the former, in its own peculiar way, is as authentic and as well-grounded as the former. There are advantages, therefore, in considering Pascal's views on this subject in some detail, more particularly because his opinions have an intimate connection with much that has to be discussed in our fourth and concluding Book.

In the first place, then, it is to be noted that the "heart," according to Pascal's *Pensées*, is a remarkably distended organ. Arguing in support of his thesis that the heart must be conjoined with reason in our knowledge of truth, Pascal says that first principles are apprehended by the heart and not by Reason, and

[24] As quoted by Inge, *The Philosophy of Plotinus*, Vol. II, pp. 76 *sq.*
[25] See Inge, *op. cit.*, pp. 138 *sq.*   [26] *Ibid.*, p. 187.   [27] *Pensées*, § 277.

he cites space, time, movement, and numbers as instances of these "first principles." [28] It is in this sense that, according to him "les principes se sentent, les propositions se concluent," and it is surely plain that space, time, and numbers are not emotional. In short, the "heart," according to Pascal, is the organ of sensitive and instinctive certainty in general, and in one sense, is exclusively the organ of emotion or of emotional divination.

As M. Brunschvicq points out,[29] there is a close connection between these views concerning the "heart" and another of Pascal's distinctions, viz. his distinction between "l'esprit de géometrie" and "l'esprit de finesse." [30] The distinction here, however, is between the power of grasping recondite and austerely abstract principles firmly, and the power of grasping the concrete in a single total impression which may nevertheless be accurate and delicate. "Les géomètres," in short, are the abstract reasoners, "les fins" are the impressionists who sense the niceties of fact in a wide cast of perception.

Here, again, the contrast is not properly between emotion and cogitative insight, but between what is sensitive and what is abstract—although it may be true that what we call tact similarly implies an emotional sensitivity to the niceties of a human and social atmosphere. It is unfortunate that the term "sentiment" allowed Pascal to vacillate within the same ambiguity as his other term the "heart." It refers to custom and habit as well as to emotion.

Secondly, we should note that "reason" in much of Pascal's argument is narrowly circumscribed to the function of *reasoning*, and therefore is denied any intellectual insight into the principles from which we infer by the logical processes of reasoning. This restriction is apparent in Pascal's distinction (already noted) between our apprehension of first principles and our ratiocinations from them. And no sane philosopher ever maintained that the whole of rational or intellectual insight could conceivably be contained in mere ratiocination. In this sense of reason, therefore, it is universally agreed that, as Pascal says, "nothing

[28] *Ibid.*, § 282.   [30] *Pensées,* Sec. 1.
[29] In his edition of the *Pensées,* p. 457 n.

is so conformable to reason as this disavowal of reason"; [31] for the disavowal in question is only the disavowal of the omni-competence of ratiocination with regard to the premises of ratio-cination. This admission, however, does not in any way involve the consequence that either reason or reasoning is obliged to submit to "sentiment." [32] In drawing this conclusion, therefore, and still more in his famous assertion that "il faut s'abêtir" and throb with animal sensitivity, Pascal was inferring what should not have been inferred.

In view of the peculiar terms in which Pascal states his argu-ments, we are less surprised than we might otherwise be at the contradictory statements he makes concerning emotion and value. On the one hand, he tells us that "reason may protest as it will; it cannot put a price upon things" [33]—or stamp them with value and worth. This superb power and persuasiveness, he says, be-longs to imagination, the enemy of reason and not at all to reason. It creates a second nature in mankind, and incidentally makes man doubt and deny his reason as well as believe it.[34]

On the other hand, in a passage still more celebrated, Pascal says: "It was maladroit to filch the title of reason from love. There is no proper foundation for opposition between them. For love and reason are the same thing. Love is a precipitation of our thought that exists in one aspect without any wide or scrupu-lous examination of truth. It is always, however, a *reason*. We should and could not wish it to be otherwise, for then we would be very unattractive machines. Therefore we should not drive reason out of love. For they are inseparable. The poets were wrong in depicting love as something blind. Let us strip the bandages from its eyes, and give it back the joy of them." [35]

§ 5. Approval and Prizing

Among the more considerable and the more pertinacious phil-osophical attempts to show that emotion and sentiment have evidential significance, the analysis of "approval" on the part of the British Moralists of the eighteenth century, and the analysis

[31] *Pensées*, § 272.   [33] *Ibid.*, § 82.
[32] *Ibid.*, § 274.   [34] *Ibid.*
[35] *Opuscules*, Brunschvicq's edition, p. 133.

of "prizing" (*Werthaltung*) associated with the names of C. von Ehrenfels and A. Meinong in the late nineteenth and early twentieth centuries, deserve special mention.

The first of these movements began with Shaftesbury, who claimed, *inter alia,* to prove the existence of a moral sense. This "sense," being direct and immediate, had, like other senses, a *prima facie* claim to certainty; and the claim to certainty might be said to be supported by the contentions (1) that this "sense" was "natural" and therefore an original and unacquired admonition of nature, and (2) that it included the moral conscience (whose certainty, in many quarters, was accepted as an article of faith). While the moral sense, according to most of its expositors, was rather of the nature of perception than, strictly speaking, of the nature of emotion, it had strong affinities with emotion, particularly with the emotion of shame when the moral sense is offended.

The range of the moral sense (so interpreted), on the other hand, was enormous. It included not only a biblical or puritan conscience, but taste and good breeding in all their departments. According to Hutcheson, it "diffuses itself through all conditions of life, and every part of it, and insinuates itself into all the more humane amusements and entertainments of mankind." [36] To believe in its certainty, therefore, would be to believe in a lot; and Shaftesbury and his immediate followers (e.g. Hutcheson) busied themselves about its reality rather than about its certainty. "However false or corrupt it be within itself," Shaftesbury said, "it finds the difference, as to beauty or comeliness, between one heart and another, one turn of affection, one behavior, one sentiment and another; and accordingly, in all disinterested cases, must approve in some measure of what is natural and honest, and disapprove what is dishonest and corrupt." [37]

Indeed, the main philosophical problem, according to the later members of the school, and particularly according to Hume and Adam Smith, was how these "disinterested cases" could occur and yet be evidenced by our feelings and sentiments.

---

[36] *Introduction to Moral Philosophy,* p. 20.
[37] *Characteristiks,* Vol. II (1723), p. 30.

"When a man denominates another his *enemy*, his *rival*, his *antago-nist*, his *adversary* [Hume said] he is understood to speak the language of self-love, and to express sentiments, peculiar to himself, and arising from his particular circumstances and situation. But when he be-stows on any man the epithets of *vicious* or *odious* or *depraved*, he then speaks another language, and expresses sentiments, in which he expects all his audience are to concur with him. He must here, therefore, de-part from his private and particular situation, and must choose a point of view, common to him with others; he must move some universal principle of the human frame, and touch a spring to which all man-kind have an accord and sympathy." [38]

In short, according to Hume, the transition from private feel-ing or emotion to disinterested approval is the fundamental cir-cumstance to be explained. The "different language" that we speak when we speak of virtue, on the one hand, and of our pleasure, liking, or preference, on the other hand, corresponds, he admits, to a genuine difference of fact. Therefore, our emo-tions, in some sense, must be capable of yielding evidence beyond their private selves. Instead of accepting this situation, however, Hume attempts, in effect, to evade it, and asserts, without any stringent empirical evidence, that the distinction is between what we *all* like, on the one hand, and what some of us like and others dislike, on the other hand. Anything which, on ·reflection, stirs everybody's liking is "approved," and everything that arouses universal dislike, or is inseparable from what is universally dis-liked, is "condemned." In any other case, we correctly speak the language of private feeling. In other words, according to Hume, emotion is *not* evidence of anything except individual feeling; but some individual feelings are prevalent or even uni-versal in certain situations, and others are variable. From this foundation the language of approval may, up to a point, be justified.

Adam Smith's *Theory of the Moral Sentiments* was developed along the same lines. For him, disinterestedness meant agree-ment, and he endeavored to show how our private feelings may come to agree with those of our fellows by restraining our anger or resentment, on the one hand, to the pitch that others not specially concerned may feel when any occasion for anger arises, and, on the other hand, by cultivating our more placid sym-

[38] *Enquiries,* Selby-Bigge's edition, p. 272.

pathies with our neighbors until these sympathies attain an amiable condition. It is evident that a development of this sort could not, at the best, reach a level higher than that of respectability and camaraderie, and that the standards of respectability and of "good mixing" would vary from group to group and from age to age. There could be no question of anything certain or absolute in such emotional "evidence," if, indeed, this social agreement could be said to be "evidence" at all.

Brentano, in the next century, held that value or worth is the object of a *right* kind of loving, just as truth is the object of a right kind of thinking.[39] He did not, however, develop this suggestion in any considerable detail, and it may be doubted whether Messrs. Meinong and von Ehrenfels (although they both owed much to Brentano) succeeded in showing that emotion is evidence of worth or value in any more stringent sense than that of Hume or of Adam Smith.

Von Ehrenfels,[40] indeed, maintained that Brentano was defending a prejudice and that value expressed the relation between objects and personal desire (or individual capacity in the way of desiring). According to this view, desire would indeed be evidence of something, and might be said to afford *certain* evidence if we knew for certain what we wanted. Since it is obvious, however, that frequently we do not know what will satisfy us, and that we sometimes do not know what we are striving to attain, it has to be confessed that we may not "know what we want"; and consequently that the evidence of desire, even regarding values in von Ehrenfels's sense, must be held to be suspect in many particulars.

It is more difficult to deny (although, as we have seen in our inquiries into introspection, it is not impossible to deny) that we know what we like when we like it. Accordingly, Meinong's theory of "personal" valuing and prizing (which is based upon liking and not, in the main, on desire) is in some respects better fitted to claim certainty than von Ehrenfels's. And Meinong, in the final chapter of his *Grundlegung*,[41] advocates a theory of

---

[39] *The Origin of the Knowledge of Right and Wrong*, English translation, p. 20.
[40] *System der Wert-theorie*, Vol. I, p. 43.
[41] *Zur Grundlegung der allgemeinen Wert-theorie.*

"dignity" which, although broadly similar to the analysis of the British Moralists, endeavors to supply a firmer basis to emotional evidence, strictly interpreted.

Meinong consistently holds that while value implies, and is based upon, appreciative emotional experience, it never *is* the state of appreciating, since the very meaning of appreciating is to signify or refer to something beyond itself. And he concludes, eventually, that while *absolute* worth is a vulgar error, the greatest goods need not vary from person to person but may have complete objective validity in the sense that all such goods ought to be the same for every one.

§ 6. Ritschl's Theory of Value

Among Protestant theologians of the nineteenth century, Albrecht Ritschl of Göttingen stands preëminent in his emphasis upon the authenticity of value-judgments (based on feeling) in the domain of morals and of religion. While admitting that "value" entered, as a concomitant aspect into scientific and positivistic judgments, and even that the scientist's quest for system and totality is in a sense "religious," he also and strenuously maintained that *independent* value-judgments were the basis both of morals and of religion, and that they gave evidence of a clear and certain truth from which science, perforce, had to stand aloof. "All perceptions of moral ends or moral hindrances," he argued, "are independent value-judgments, in so far as they excite moral pleasure and pain, or, it may be, set the will in motion to appropriate what is good or repel the opposite." [42] Here the basis of the independent value-judgment is a certain feeling, or pleasure and pain, which is so far forth spiritualized as to have a social, although secular, message, and in this sense to be evidence of ethical truth.

Religions, however, may exist without possessing any moral character, as in orgiastic nature-worships. Therefore, religious value-judgments are distinct, in principle, from moral value-judgments, although, in the higher religions, the two come together. Accordingly, Ritschl holds that religious knowledge

[42] *Justification and Reconciliation*, English translation, p. 205.

"moves in independent value-judgments, which relate to man's attitude to the world, and call forth feelings of pleasure or pain, in which man either enjoys the dominion over the world vouchsafed him by God or feels grievously the lack of God's help to that end."[43]

"In Christanity" [he continues] "we can distinguish between the religion functions which relate to our attitude towards God and the world, and the moral functions which point directly to men, and only indirectly to God, whose end in the world we fulfil by moral service in the Kingdom of God. In Christianity, the religious motive of ethical action lies here, that the Kingdom of God, which it is our task to realise, represents also the highest good which God destines for us as our supramundane goal. For here there emerges the value-judgment that our blessedness consists in that elevation above the world in the Kingdom of God which accords with our true destiny."[44]

Here love is the clarifying conception. "The conception of love," Ritschl says, "is the only adequate conception of God, for it enables us, both to understand the revelation which comes through Christ to His community, and at the same time to solve the problem of the world."[45]

"The truth is [he further says] that only through the special attribute of love is it possible to derive the world from God; this quality of love therefore, serves in general to discover to us in God the ground of the unity of nature and spirit, and the law of their co-existence."[46]

This is a claim, one might suggest, to faith rather than to anything certainly evidenced; and we seem bound to conclude that even if emotions are in some sort evidential, they can hardly yield conclusive evidence according to any wholly defensible standard. In particular, if the intellect fails us, emotion can not justifiably supplant it.

There is no ineffable or numinous way of superseding the usual certainties. Religious experience, as Dr. Otto contends,[47] may indeed express an attitude appropriate to the presence of the "numinous," that is to say, appropriate to the presence of a great and fascinating mystery, possessed of a majesty far tran-

[43] *Ibid.*
[44] *Ibid.*, pp. 205 *sq.*
[45] *Ibid.*, p. 274.
[46] *Ibid.*, p. 276.
[47] *The Idea of the Holy*, especially Chapters I-VII.

scending our creaturehood. This is no proof, however, that we have, in fact, some supereminent faculty of apprehending a peculiar "category" or pervasive essence called the "numinous."

With this reflection, we may close the present book.

Book IV

PRESUMPTION, FAITH, AND PROBABILITY

CHAPTER XVII

OF PROBABILITY

§ 1. BELIEF, CERTAINTY, AND PROBABILITY

IN the traditional treatment of probability, and particularly in the traditional treatment of it in British philosophy, belief and probability were supposed to go hand in hand.

The reason for this was principally negative. On the assumption, common to Descartes and to Hume, that *knowledge* or *scientia* deals exclusively with what is either intuitively or demonstratively certain, every other species of cogitation, sensitive, experimental, or whatsoever its kind, is, with reference to our apprehension, unscientific, uncertain, and contingent. In this sphere there may be persuasion, and with persuasion, full belief. There may be faith, and with it belief and full assurance. There may be conjectures that incline our assent without necessitating it. There may be guesswork that, because it is known to be only guesswork, never generates full belief but arouses, at the best, a species of half-belief that may induce us to act with some approach towards grounded confidence.

Since "belief," in the ordinary use of language, although incompletely evidenced, connotes complete psychological assurance or conviction, and since what is apprehended *only* as probable, or *only* as likely, plainly excludes such conviction or assurance, it is, upon the whole, unfortunate that belief and probability should have been so closely united in the traditional treatment of them. Even if we adopted the disputable attitude of this tradition, holding that the fundamental contrast in epistemology is between utter certainty, stringently and completely evidenced, on the one hand, and what is less stringently evidenced, or not evidenced at all, on the other hand, and, furthermore, maintaining that philosophy is primarily concerned with certainties, and only casually and incidentally with anything not certain, we should still find it necessary to distinguish between what is authentically believed, and what no one pretends to be other than guesswork. There are, in fact, two principles of contrast that should never be confounded, and should not be put in danger of being confounded. On the one hand, there is the contrast between what is completely and what is incompletely evidenced, between *knowledge* and surmise, between conclusive evidence and evidence that, although relevant, is inconclusive, between reasons that necessitate and reasons that ought *only* to incline, although they *should* incline. On the other hand, there is the contrast between assurance or conviction, on the one hand, and the absence of such assurance, on the other hand. We may reach this assurance in spite of logic, and in the absence of anything approaching the clear apprehension of relevant and sufficient evidence. And yet we may be very sure indeed.

Looking at this matter from a slightly different angle, we may surely hold that it is a fundamental error to assert that what is rational and what is evidenced with complete certainty are one and the same, with the consequence that anything not thus completely certified is wholly irrational or at least non-rational. For surely there *may* be good, that is to say, logically relevant evidence, which, nevertheless, is not completely conclusive. It is not certain that I shall meet a dog or a cat if I walk up the street in a Scottish town, and it is also not certain that I shall not meet an Indo-Malayan dragon; but it is preposterous to maintain that I have *no* rational evidence to support the statement that I am more likely to meet a dog or a cat than this saurian beast belonging to the *Agamidœ*.

According to Thomas Reid, who was an honorable exception to the eighteenth century tendency to confuse good but inconclusive evidence with irrational or non-rational persuasiveness, "it is evident that, as there are some first principles that yield conclusions of absolute certainty, so there are others that can only yield probable conclusions; and that the lowest degree of probability must be grounded on first principles as well as absolute certainty." [1]

This is the type of problem with which we shall be concerned

[1] *Intellectual Powers*, Hamilton's edition, p. 436.

in the remainder of our discussion. Our question is: Can there be rational presumption, rational faith, rational probability? And if there can, what are the principles of this important species of rational evidence?

Even if it should happen that we should be forced to conclude that the *principles* of probability must themselves be certain, not probable (although the *conclusions* are but probable), and yet that we must confess to some perplexity concerning what these principles precisely are, we should not be dismayed. For we are in the same plight here as elsewhere. It is a contradiction to say that we are certain that we know nothing for certain, and yet, as we saw in Book III, we may have the utmost difficulty in pointing to anything that we *know* with utter certainty.

What holds of probability in this matter holds also of presumption. Perhaps, even, it may hold of "faith."

§ 2. Objective Contingency

In ancient times (e.g. in Aristotle's) it was held that there was a realm of objective contingency, in which whatever occurred occurred really at random, and in which events were not merely apparently but actually disconnected. Regarding this realm, the most we could say (having reason on our side) was that a certain type of event had occurred, for the most part (ὡς ἐπὶ τό πολύ) in some department of the contingent realm. This realm of the objectively contingent was contrasted by Aristotle (1) with the realm of regular motion (e.g. with the movements of the spheres in astronomy), and (2) with what is invariable (e.g. with mathematical relationships that might be demonstrated in pure science or that were axiomatic).[2]

On these assumptions, it would be alogical and non-rational to expect that what had prevailed in the past had any tendency to prevail in the future. For tendencies imply connections; and if the realm of the contingent is, ontologically as well as epistemically, the realm of the disconnected, there would be no factual connection tending towards the continuance of a pattern of events that had been prevalent.

I do not want to maintain that it is quite certain that objec-

[2] E.g. *De Interpretatione,* 18a; *Metaphysics,* 1027b.

tive contingency is a myth, but it is not the point of view from which these matters are commonly regarded in modern or in semi-modern times. On the contrary, it is usual to accept, in some form, the general principle enunciated by Roger Bacon (himself half-mediæval and half-modern) that "a particular nature is obedient naturally and not by violence to universal nature." [3]

In other words, we commonly believe (although there are more doubters in the twentieth century [4] than there were in the eighteenth or nineteenth centuries) in the species of determinism sometimes called "experimental determinism." This is the view, not merely that all the facts in nature are interconnected, but that they are interconnected in a special way. They are so interconnected, according to the theory, that we are entitled to assume, for experimental purposes, that identifiable events are uniquely determined by their identifiable natures taken in conjunction with the relevant identifiable influences to which they may be discovered to be subject. This general presumption is not self-evident, and its opposite, plainly, does not involve a contradiction. But we commonly believe it, unless, perhaps, in the instance of psychological experiments concerning the human "will," [5] in which case many believe that certain events happen for no reason at all, and that human history need not repeat itself—again for no reason.

---

[3] *Cf.* A. G. Little, "Roger Bacon," p. 3 (*Proceedings of the British Academy,* 1928).

[4] *Cf.,* Schrödinger's "Principle of Indeterminacy," and *e.g.,* G. P. Thomson's *The Atom,* p. 242.

"If the position of a particle is very accurately determined, its momentum is very uncertain, and conversely. The product of two uncertainties is always round about "*h.*" Now "*h*" is very small, and this restriction is only noticeable on an atomic, or indeed electronic, scale, but there it matters a great deal. This cuts the bottom from under the argument for determinism."

[5] Mr. Thomson (*op. cit.*) and some others appear to argue that the indeterminism of atoms or electrons = "randomness" and also = "free will." They also maintain that the human mind and will is characterized by "order" and not by "randomness." Hence the conclusion ought to be that the human mind and will is the least "free" thing in nature. But they seem oblivious of this consequence. In other words, their arguments appear to show the ambiguity of "freedom" in an acute form. "Randomness" is the apparently arbitrary behavior of the "will;" but "freedom is also the *necessitas boni,* or, in other words, a different (and spiritual) type of necessitation from physical causality.

It is important, then, to examine the implications of this experimental determinism, not because such determinism is necessarily metaphysically ultimate, but because it is expedient to pursue the analysis of probability without assuming that there either is, or could be, objective contingency in the sense of complete factual disconnection.

Determinism should be distinguished from inferable determinism. The former theory states simply that any particular fact in nature is uniquely determined by its own properties together with the other influences that affect it. Inferable determinism implies, in addition, that this unique determination is such that a calculating demon, having, it may be, fuller data than an ordinary man of science, but no intellectual faculties of a different order from those of ordinary men of science, could infer this unique determination according to a relatively small number of general laws.

The possibility of prediction is an instance of inferable determinism, and is obviously a special case, although a striking case. It is a special case because the same principles that enable us to *pre*dict also enable us to *post*dict. We can infer the former visibility of Halley's comet, at particular times in the past, by the same principles as (we think) enable us to infer its visibility at particular future times, whether or not there are historical records of its appearance (not belonging to the data on which the inference is based). The possibility, however, that events, although uniquely determined, may nevertheless be such that prediction concerning them is impossible, is sufficient to illustrate, with clearness, the pronounced distinction between determinism and inferable determinism.

And this possibility is very frequently exploited in modern scientific theories—for example, in all theories of emergent evolution. In this latter theory, to choose its simplest example, it is held that the properties of the compound water (e.g. its property of expanding as it approaches freezing-point) could not *all* be inferred from the properties of its constitutent elements, hydrogen and oxygen, although certain of its properties (e.g. its weight) could be so inferred. What is maintained, therefore, is determinism (for it is agreed that water is uniquely determined

by the combination of hydrogen and oxygen in certain proportions) but not inferable determinism (with regard to what are
called the "genuine novelties" in the properties of the compound).

§ 3. Inferences From These Considerations

The principal relations of these considerations to the theory
of probability are the following:

(1) Probability does not necessarily imply objective contingency. It only implies contingency relative to our knowledge.
What, relatively to our knowledge, is "contingent" (e.g. the
distribution in a well-shuffled pack of cards) may nevertheless
always be uniquely determined.

(2) Probable inference may occur and may be justifiable, not
only in cases in which determinism may be supposed, but also in
instances in which inferable determinism may be supposed. For
although, according to the theory of inferable determinism,
every property of every particular thing could be inferred with
certainty from *other* facts sufficiently ascertained, *we*, at any
given time, may have ascertained only some of the relevant
data and not all. From this partial knowledge we could not
infer more than a probability; and yet (as we shall see) we
might infer a probability.

(3) Such probable inferences might very well be logical, provided that they were based upon real connections in nature. It
is quite another question, however, whether, if any part of
nature were wholly disconnected (as it would be according to the
theory of objective contingency in the full sense), there could be
any reason or any logic in such inferences.

§ 4. The Probability of Events and of Propositions

For the most part, we are accustomed to speak of the probability of events. The explanations of § 3 of this chapter, however,
have shown that we need not be dealing, in probable inferences,
with objectively contingent events; but that we seem to deal,
instead, with what is probable relatively to our imperfect knowledge. Indeed, we have suggested that nothing, and therefore no

event, is either probable or improbable in itself, but only in relation to connected, but insufficient evidence.

Judged from this standpoint, probability is an evidential relation, i.e. it never expresses less than the probability-of-p-as-evidenced-by-q. For this reason, probability is very often held to apply strictly to propositions and not to events, thus coming into line with other logical evidence. As we shall see, however, many of the "frequentists" reject any such view.

Since a probable proposition is neither, on the one hand, completely certain, nor, on the other hand, utterly impossible (or certainly false), it is usually said to lie between the limits of certainty and impossibility.

§ 5. PROBABILITY AND "QUANTITY OF BELIEF"

We may now proceed to consider the principal theories of the nature of probability.

One of the oldest of these is the theory that probability is concerned with a certain "quantity of belief" or degree of conviction falling somewhere between the limits of full conviction, on the one hand, and total disbelief, on the other hand. We may consider this theory in the form in which De Morgan upheld it.

In his *Essay on Probabilities*, De Morgan argued as follows. Our impressions of certainty (which are feelings in our minds) plainly permit of degrees. Between the limits of full certainty and of utter disbelief we have impressions of likelihood in all the degrees of favorableness and of unfavorableness. Accordingly (De Morgan says), we should accept the following axiom: "Let it be granted that the impression of probability is one which admits perceptibly of the gradations of more and less, according to the circumstances under which an event is to happen." Thereafter, we proceed straightway to another axiom: "Let it be granted that when one out of a certain number of events must happen, and these events are entirely independent of one another, the probability of a certain number of events happening must be made up of the probabilities of the several events happening." [6]

These axioms, De Morgan says, "contain *all the theory* I shall be obliged to use; grant this, and you can be constrained, by

[6] *An Essay on Probabilities*, p. 9.

demonstration, to admit all the rest as simple logical consequences."[7] In other words, if you object, "Speak now, or ever after hold your tongue."[8]

It seems necessary, therefore, to speak now.

The first axiom makes it plain that De Morgan meant to refer to degrees of assurance actually felt. While it must be granted that there are degrees of psychological assurance, it is much more doubtful, as we shall see, whether probability is concerned with, and measures, these psychological quantities. De Morgan's view was that probability must either be subjective, and so a feeling of the mind, or else objective, and so "the inherent property of a set of circumstances."[9] As it is not the latter, it must, he thought, be the former; and many would agree with this opinion to-day. We shall see, however, that the alternative is not exclusive.

De Morgan himself admitted that "some discussion" might be excited by his second axiom.[10] "But we must observe," he continued, "that it is the uniform practice of mankind to act upon it, which is a sufficient justification; for what are we doing but endeavouring to represent that which actually exists"?[10]

The point, however, is not by any means so simple. In the first place, the axiom, as De Morgan stated it, applies only to alternatives *known* to be severally independent, mutually exclusive, and conjointly exhaustive. Assuming that our "knowledge" is not interpreted too narrowly or too pedantically, we may be said to "know" that these conditions are fulfilled in the throwing of dice, the use of playing cards duly shuffled, and in other such cases. The die must fall on one of its six sides and on one only; and one throw of the die does not affect the next throw. It is absurd to maintain, however, that the probabilities on which we are accustomed to *act* are *known* to fulfil these conditions. On the contrary, we act on alternatives that *seem* to be exclusive and independent. In other words, we count as independent what we do not know to be dependent. And that is quite another story.

Again, it is necessary to consider the sense in which De

[7] *An Essay on Probabilities*, p. 11.   [9] *Ibid.*, p. 7.
[8] *Ibid.*, p. 12.   [10] *Ibid.*, p. 9.

Morgan understood his axioms. His theory, in essentials, was that a total "impression of certainty" (in a favorable sense) was compounded of its several favorable constituent impressions in such a way that it is precisely and numerically the sum of the several favorable impressions. The total force of our impressions of certainty he therefore supposed to be simply calculable from the particular impressions of certainty that correspond to what we call each favorable scrap of evidence. The elaborate mathematics employed in the calculation of probabilities, De Morgan affirmed, has this simple foundation; for mathematics, however elaborate it be, is only "the abbreviation of long numerical operations." [11]

Of this theory (which, incidentally, was also Hume's) [12] it has to be said that there is no good psychological evidence that our "impressions of certainty" *are* compounded in this way from small favorable sub-impressions, or that, if they were so compounded, the total "impression of certainty" would be the sum of these tiny favorable indications. The theory might apply to a logical gambler whose impressions tallied precisely with what would usually be called the odds. It would not apply, however, to the vast majority of actual gamblers who traffic irrationally in their luck. *Their* subjective "impressions of certainty" do not, in general, correspond with any precision to the logical force of the probable evidence.

This point (which is a cardinal point) was handsomely, although unintentionally, conceded by De Morgan himself in his *Formal Logic,* Chapter IX. Nominally, indeed, he there retained the view of the *Essay,* affirming that " 'It is more probable than improbable' means in this chapter 'I believe that it will happen more than I believe that it will not happen.' " [13] In the very next sentence, however, he effectively annulled this assertion; for he went on to say, "Or rather 'I ought to believe, &c': for it may happen that the state of mind which *is,* is not the state of mind which should be. D'Alembert believed that it was *two* to *one* that the first head which the throw of a halfpenny was to give would occur before the third throw: a juster view of the mode

[11] *Ibid.,* p. 12.   [13] *Formal Logic,* p. 173.
[12] *Treatise,* pp. 124 *sqq.*

of applying the theory would have taught him that it was *three to one*. But he *believed* it, and thought he could show reason for his belief: to him the probability *was* two to one. But I shall say, for all that, that the probability *is* three to one: meaning that in the universal opinion of those who examine the subject, the state of mind to which a person *ought* to be able to bring himself is to look three times as confidently upon the arrival as upon the non-arrival."

The correction is quite fundamental. What is now said to be probable and to be measured is not the quantity of psychological conviction but the amount or force of the evidence, not the degree of belief but the degree of justification a given proposition may have (relative to its grounds). This is not simply a subjective feeling, or "impression of certainty." Indeed, it is not subjective at all, unless in the sense that one man may have evidence that another man may not have. And this last is true of a man's knowledge, also. Some explanation may indeed be required if we say, "The probability, *whether you know it or not,* is so and so"; [14] but the explanation, in terms of De Morgan's correction of his original theory, should be only "The probability, relative to certain data, is so and so, whether you, or any other people, know it or not." These data may be all the data that you individually possess; and in that case probability may be very important for you. But there is no theoretical reason why *you* should not estimate the probabilities relative to some piece of information that is less than your total information (as when, in the *post mortem* examination of a hand at bridge, you estimate the "chances" of a finesse on the assumption that you do not know precisely how the cards lay, although, in the *post mortem*, you do know this). And similarly there is no sufficient reason why probabilities *might* not be estimated on the basis of "available evidence to any one," or of "commonly accepted evidence," or, generally, upon evidence that is not any one's private belief in any distinctive sense.

A modification of De Morgan's theory that I have heard suggested is to the effect that probability *does* deal with subjective impressions of certainty which are divisible into separate plausi-

[14] *Formal Logic,* p. 172.

ble items, *but* that the reckoning of the chances may reveal certain latent contradictions in these subjective plausibilities. To illustrate. At a recent cricket match I overheard a spectator betting both that Mr. Holmes would make 300 runs, and that Yorkshire, his side, would not make 500. As Yorkshire's score, at that time, was 478 and Mr. Holmes's score 271, there was some inadvertence in this betting. Yet it dealt with uncertainties.

I can not see, however, that this explanation alleviates the difficulty. Setting probabilities aside altogether, it is clear that we may all inadvertently hold beliefs that imply a contradiction. In this case, however, the standard is set by the objective laws of logic. And if reasoning concerning the "chances" may similarly reveal a contradiction, the reason again must be the objectivity of these inferences concerning the "chances."

I am aware, however, that very different opinions are held by competent persons on this matter, and therefore that some competent readers may not be convinced by De Morgan's self-refutation. To such readers I would commend the arguments in Dr. Venn's *Logic of Chance*, the fifth chapter.

The salient points in Dr. Venn's admirable piece of reasoning in this connection are the following:

(1) Any strong emotion or passion may play the strangest tricks with "quantity of belief." "A deep interest in the matter at stake, whether it excites hope or fear, plays great havoc with the belief-meter." [15]

(2) Our beliefs rest usually upon very complex evidence, and at any given moment belief "is one of the most fugitive and variable things possible." [16] "To borrow a striking illustration from Abraham Tucker, the substructure of our convictions is not so much to be compared to the solid foundations of an ordinary building, as to the piles of the houses of Rotterdam which rest somehow in a deep bed of soft mud. They bear their weight securely enough, but it would not be easy to point out accurately the dependence of the different parts upon one another." [17]

(3) The very existence of lotteries should be sufficient to

[15] *The Logic of Chance*, Second edition, pp. 107 sq.
[16] *Ibid.*, p. 108.   [17] *Ibid.*, p. 109.

demonstrate the striking difference between psychological credulity and logical credence. Even if we say that the fever for lotteries is due to the smallness of the stake and to the magnitude of the possible prize, rather than to any strict probability of receiving value for one's money, this consideration works against De Morgan and not in his favor. For people who cheerfully buy one or two tickets do not normally care to adventure one hundred or one thousand times the price of them in such lotteries. On De Morgan's principles, provided that people have the money, there would be no reason why they should hesitate over a large sum, and part so briskly with a small sum.

(4) "Granted that we have an instinct of credence, why should it be assumed that it must be just of that intensity which subsequent experience will justify"? [18] Instincts may be more or less prophetic, but this instinct would be quite amazingly so.

§ 6. The Frequentist Theory of Probability

Dr. Venn himself was a notable exponent of the Frequentist or Class Frequency view of probability. According to this view, probability-statements are statements of proportions in very large series. As Mr. Eddington has recently said, "When numbers are large, chance is the best warrant for certainty." [19]

This view is often held, but there are very few expositions of it (and, particularly, very few recent expositions) at all comparable to Venn's in point of serious philosophical elaboration. Granting, therefore, that Venn's view might be, and to some extent has been, modified in such a way as to diminish the force of certain fundamental objections, it is nevertheless expedient to begin by examining the view in the form in which Venn set it forth.

Essentially, then, Dr. Venn's theory was that, "in the long run" or in very large series, individual differences cancel out and become insignificant. In their stead, certain broad proportions become manifest, and what is called "probability" is in reality the statement of these proportions in large aggregates.

---

[18] *The Logic of Chance*, p. 111.
[19] *The Nature of the Physical World*, p. 72.

It is a statement of statistical frequency, and it is "objective" because large aggregates, as our statistics show, really do manifest these proportions.

An obvious objection is that where there are no statistics there can be no room for a theory of probability. This severe restriction of probability is contrary to a great mass of firm opinion.

In a recent work of Auction Bridge,[20] for example, we are informed (in the section entitled "Mathematics that Matter") that a hand containing six trumps will win the following number of tricks in 100 games: three or more in 77 percent, four or more in 48 percent, five or more in 26 percent; and that a hand containing nine trumps will similarly win six or more tricks in 98 percent, seven or more in 82 percent, eight or more in 26 percent of the cases.

Although there are card players who are accustomed to keep rather elaborate records of their performances, it is absurd to suppose that these percentages describe the proportions in actual available statistics. Such statistics, if they were relevant and available, would have to be based upon the performances of bridge-players all of whom made no mistake in any game but invariably extracted the last ounce out of each of their hands. There are no such bridge-players, and, in any case, no statistics of their performances are available.

Accordingly, we must maintain either that these probabilities depend upon a non-frequentist theory of probability, or else that frequentists can deduce them, in some indirect fashion, from available statistics.

The general type of the frequentist's reply is somewhat as follows: We know in advance that there are fifty-two cards in a pack, each pack being subdivided into four suits, and each suit into thirteen individual cards. We also know (from statistics?) that "in the long run" each card is dealt to a given hand (*A's* or *B's*, *X's* or *Y's* in the usual conventional description) an approximately equal number of times. The rest of the argument is based upon the logical character of these subdivisions, but it is said to depend ultimately upon our experience,

[20] A. E. Manning Foster, *Auction Bridge for All.*

in long series, of the proportions of aggregate distribution of the cards in the pack.

Even in this statement there are strong grounds for supposing that use is being made surreptitiously of a conception of probability widely removed from the frequentist's. Could we not make similar deductions on mere presumption, given the premise that there are fifty-two cards in every pack, each card having a separate value, but so constructed that their individual differences are unknown to the dealers of the cards, and independent in the sense that the values of the individual cards do not affect the way in which they are distributed? Is not the inference really *a priori*, viz. that because there are precisely so many alternatives subdivided in such and such ways, therefore it is probable that the percentages will be such and such?

A second point emerges here. Speaking of the game of whist, Dr. Venn says,

"At the commencement of the game our sole appeal is rightfully made to the theory of probability. All the rules upon which each player acts, and therefore upon which he infers that the others will act, rest upon the observed frequency (*or rather upon the frequency which calculation assures us will be observed*) with which such and such combinations of cards are found to occur. . . . But as the play progresses all this is changed, and towards its conclusion there is but little reliance upon any rules which either we or others could trace up to statistical frequency of occurrence, observed or inferred. A multitude of other considerations have come in; we begin to be influenced partly by our knowledge of the character and practice of our partner and opponents, etc." [21]

The second point concerns the parenthesis that I have put in italics. *Does* calculation assure us that a certain frequency *will be observed?* Pretty clearly, this is not, in reality, Dr. Venn's theory at all. On the contrary, his theory is that our experience of these large aggregates assures us that in the long run individual differences (such as the "character and practice of our partner and opponents") cancel out, and therefore that certain broad mathematical proportions hold without qualification of large aggregates.

The individual game, however, is *not* a large aggregate, and because it is not a large aggregate two critical questions emerge.

[21] *The Logic of Chance*, p. 426 (italics mine).

Firstly, what justification has Dr. Venn for saying that at the beginning of the game each player *"rightfully"* appeals solely to proportions in large aggregates when he is dealing with something that is not a large aggregate? The fact surely is that at the beginning of the game, knowing nothing of the personal peculiarities in the play of his partner or opponents, he is thrown back, because of his ignorance on these points, upon his general knowledge that he is about to play a game of whist and upon this knowledge only. Assuming, for argument's sake, that his general knowledge of the proper play is what the frequentist says it is, the question arises how this frequentist knowledge of aggregate proportions is to be applied to a particular game which is not an aggregate. Dr. Venn appears to maintain that the reasoning is as follows. "I know that the general proportions in the class "games of whist" is such and such, and having no knowledge except that I am concerned in a game of whist, I therefore rightfully assume that this particular game will correspond to these general proportions." This argument, however, would be quite shockingly bad. Individual games, as Dr. Venn admits, do differ very often from the general type (where individual differences cancel out). Therefore, it would seem, he ought to say, in any "rightful" inference, that it is *probable* that the individual game will (more or less) conform to the general proportions of the type, and that if we have no other relevant data we are "rightfully" entitled to guide our play according to this general probability. This explanation, however, would bring Dr. Venn's entire theory to ruin. For the "probable" application of the general frequency to the individual case is a nonfrequentist probability. It is not a proportion "in the long run."

Secondly, what of the inferences that, according to Dr. Venn, are made (and, one supposes, "rightfully" made) when the game is in progress, and each player has learned something about the character and practice of his opponents, etc? If *these* inferences are not probable inferences, what in the world are they? If a player, observing, as he thinks, that an opponent is over-cautious, "takes a chance" accordingly, what can his action, rationally speaking, be based upon *except* probable inference? Yet Dr. Venn, as we have seen, himself asserts that these "other considerations" concerning character, etc., can not be based, with any considerable degree of reliance, "upon any rules which either we or others could trace up to statistical frequency of occurrence, observed or inferred."

In short, we certainly do apply the conception of probability to the individual case; and any theory that is forced to deny the legitimacy of this application of the conception is very ill-suited to maintain that probability guides those individual histories that are called our lives. This point seems absolutely fundamental. Although I have referred in some detail to a single sentence of Dr. Venn's, there is no question of a casual inadvertence, on Dr. Venn's part, in a single unfortunate sentence. This may be seen by considering another of his examples.

He supposes a man in a dense mist on Morecame Bay with the spring tide rapidly coming in. The man knows that he will be drowned if he stands still, and he hears a church bell in the distance, but does not know whether the church is on his side of the estuary or on the opposite side. In this case, Dr. Venn says, "probability cannot say a word" on the question whether safety should be sought by going towards the source of the sound or away from it. The decision "must be grounded on the desires, feelings and conscience of the agent." This is clear, he says, if there are two persons in the mist instead of one. "If they are husband and wife, they will probably prefer to remain together; if they are sole depositaries of an important state secret, they will decide to part." [22]

I do not know whether this little word "probably" in connection with husbands and wives is based upon statistics or not. But let us adapt the illustration slightly. Let us suppose that there is not complete certainty in either case—that the man who goes unwittingly towards destruction might conceivably be picked up by a boat or saved by a sudden lifting of the mist, and that the man who unwittingly goes towards safety might perish in a ditch or on a treacherous sand bank. In that case, the messengers who separate will not make certain of preserving the state secret by separating. But surely they are much more *likely* to

[22] *Ibid.*, p. 120.

preserve the secret if they separate than if they keep together. And there is no evidence that this type of likelihood is based upon statistics of class-frequency, or even upon a wide general experience that may be supposed to take the place of ascertained statistical knowledge.

The principle of this criticism of the frequency theory is not restricted to the individual case. It applies also to all "short run" series, and to all the proportions in what for any reason are special subclasses in a large aggregate. If our statistics concerning consumptives, for example, give certain "long run" statistics, how are we to pass from these "long-run" proportions to the comparatively short run proportions of the subclass of consumptives who winter in Davos? Is it seriously to be contended that *no* probable inferences can be made concerning any small subclass?

This leads to a third general criticism of the frequency view. The frequentist, replying to the last argument, may say that there are general long run propositions concerning the relations of subclasses to major groups, the proper coefficients of "error," etc. This may be true, but these general propositions are themselves only probable propositions—in a non-frequentist sense of probability. Indeed, the frequentist's view ought not to be that small individual differences *must* cancel out in large aggregates, but only that it is probable (in a non-frequentist sense) that they should cancel out. The proportions, in other words, only *tend* to be fulfilled in large aggregates, but are *more likely* to be fulfilled in large aggregates than in smaller groups.

A similar, but a very important, point arises in connection with induction. Suppose our statistics show certain very definite general proportions, say in European rates of mortality in peacetime over a considerable period. It is clear that war, or pestilence, or (contrariwise) better sanitation and better medical service might effectively alter these proportions in the future. And there may be unknown causes of the same general sort. The continuance of the proportions, therefore, is not itself a matter of statistical frequency, but a matter of probable induction; and *this* probability also is fundamentally non-frequentist.

§ 7. FURTHER ON THE SAME

It is more than sixty years since Dr. Venn's book first appeared, and modern frequentists, of whom there are several in Great Britain, although few on the continent, need not be expected to subscribe to all that Venn said. On the other hand, as a recent exponent of the frequency theory has said, "The general feature of all such attempts is that they make the probability of an event dependent on the frequency with which the event has happened in the past." [23] If this description is correct the fundamental criticisms to which Dr. Venn's theory is subject apply to all frequency theories without exception.

In general, then, we may confidently assert that probability-judgments are very often made which are not, in any intelligible sense, statements of class-frequency, and that, concerning these judgments, the frequentists have nothing more convincing to allege than that *somehow* all our judgments may be said to be tutored by former experience. It is another question, of course, what the justification, if any, of these probability-judgments is; but there should be no question at all concerning their distinctness from judgments of class-frequency.

This point seems to be conceded by Dr. N. R. Campbell, who has given the most serious and elaborate among the recent expositions of the frequentist theory.

"It is generally recognized [Campbell says] that there are two kinds of 'probability.' There is (1) the probability (of the happening) of events, and (2) the probability (of the truth) of propositions. Etymologically the term belongs more properly to the second kind of probability, and it will be confined to that kind in this paper. For the first kind, the term 'chance' often used in some connexions as a synonym of probability, is available. Accordingly we shall speak throughout of the chance of an event happening and of the probability of a proposition being true. . . . The conclusion towards which this paper is directed is that chance in the sense primarily important to physics, is a physical property measurable by ordinary physical measurement. . . . But the further view . . . that probability is always measurable in terms of chance . . . will not be upheld but . . . combated." [24]

[23] R. H. Nisbet in *Mind*, N.S. No. 137, p. 1.
[24] *Philosophical Magazine*, July 1922, pp. 67 *sq.*

In short, the suggestion is that class-frequency is the only possible basis for a tenable scientific theory of "chance," and that non-frequentist "probability" is so vague as to be useless. In his *Physics: The Elements,* Campbell endeavors, it is true, to give some explanation of the relations between frequentist and non-frequentist assertions. Addressing himself to the question (which he admits to be important) "why is it that the probability of an event, or the probability of a cause, is a measure of the degree of knowledge that the event will happen or that the cause is in operation," [25] he argues in effect "that when we think we have different knowledge about the happening of the particular event we are confusing such knowledge with the result of a long series of similar events." [26] We do not expect to be surprised by the particular event—that is to say, we think, not of it, but of its class. And when we ask, as we must ask, "Why should we assume, as we seem to do, that the result of the trial will be such as to spare us surprise and mental discomfort?" [27] Campbell, while admitting the legitimacy of the question, finds himself forced to reply that we have here a feeling very deeply rooted but incapable of any rational justification. We have only the discomfort, attendant on surprise, to guide us at all.

The frequentist account of "chance," on the other hand, is designed to extract the venom contained in Poincaré's gibe that nobody understands probability because mathematicians believe its foundations to be experimental while experimentalists believe its foundation to be mathematical. "Chance," Campbell maintains (i.e., the chance of an event happening), "is always a physical property of a system, measured by a process of derived measurement involving the two fundamental magnitudes—number of events and number of trials." Or, again, he maintains that "chance is applicable only to events which contain an element which is wholly and completely random to everybody." [28]

This property, he continues, is experimental in the same sense as any other experimental property in physics. It expresses the proportions in large aggregates that experiment determines; and

---

[25] *Physics: The Elements,* p. 192.   [26] *Ibid.,* p. 193.   [27] *Ibid.,* p. 198.
[28] *Philosophical Magazine, loc. cit.,* p. 67.

is no more mysterious than any other instance in which we have knowledge of an aggregate without having knowledge of its constituent parts. This experimental result, however, is amenable to mathematical measurement; and there is no other sense in which "probability" is thus amenable. "For after all what we really want to say and what we really do assume in the mathematical development of the science of probability is that equally probable events are those which happen equally often in an infinite series of trials" [29] It is possible by suitable explanations (he argues) to apply this conception to a finite number of experimental trials, and so to give an experimental and objective account of what is "equally likely." It is further possible, without any serious theoretical obstacles, to elaborate the various mathematical abbreviations that depend upon the multiplication and addition of "probabilities."

Dr. Campbell himself seems to become involved in unnecessary difficulties when he regards "chance" as necessarily opposed to "law"; [30] and he is disposed to coquette with objective contingency (in the sense of § 2 of the present chapter) without raising the question whether, if nature were disconnected, there could be any reason whatsoever for believing that the proportions of aggregate experimental trials could have any tendency to be repeated. He also maintains that the "randomness" of experimentally observed "chances" is ultimately derived from our experience of arbitrary free-will,[31] although he admits that what we take to be chosen at random (e.g. "Think upon a number") may very well have unknown psychological causes (e.g. some Freudian reason why we should tend to select some particular numbers, although we believe ourselves to be choosing at random). These philosophically "ultimate" explanations, however, are unnecessary for his main thesis. *In physics*, "randomness" is ultimate; [32] and as Campbell says, "The typically random distribution is that of equally probable independent events." [33]

The fundamental experimental question, therefore, is whether any given extensive series of trials has or has not this typical

---

[29] *Physics: The Elements*, p. 170.
[30] *Ibid.*, pp. 161 *sq.*
[31] *Ibid.*, p. 205.
[32] *Ibid.*, p. 207.
[33] *Ibid.*, p. 208.

form. If it has, the question is whether Dr. Campbell's account of "equally probable" is adequate. And Dr. Campbell maintains emphatically that it is. "The principle of sufficient reason," he says, "may be reasonably held to decide that, in a perfectly shuffled pack of cards, the chance that the card next after a heart is another heart is equal to the chance that it is a club. But if enquiry is made what is meant by a perfectly shuffled pack, and how we are to know whether a pack is or is not perfectly shuffled, I can see no answer except that it is one in which a club occurs after a heart as often as another heart." [34]

§ 8. PROBABILITY AS AN INDEX OF DEGREE OF RELEVANCE

As we saw in § 1 of the present chapter, there may be good or relevant arguments that are nevertheless insufficient to demonstrate the certainty of a conclusion. Such arguments, we have suggested (and now maintain), demonstrate the probability of a conclusion in the conventional sense of "probability" which includes all gradations between impossibility, on the one hand, and complete certainty, upon the other hand.

Obviously, the relation here described actually does exist. Suppose, for example, that any one is to be accounted a Scotsman if (1) he himself has been born in Scotland, and (2) if his parents and grandparents have also been born in Scotland. In this case, seven points would have to be established in order to prove the man a Scotsman, viz. his own birth in Scotland, and the birth in Scotland of his two parents and of his four grandparents. It is clear that proof of each of these seven items is relevant evidence in the case, and it is also clear that a demonstration of six or of any lesser number of these items is *not* a complete proof that the man is a Scotsman. It is a requirement of general logic, therefore, that there should be some way of describing the extent to which relevant but inconclusive arguments bear upon the conclusion towards which they point. In the above instance, the proof of six of these items would have a greater bearing upon the conclusion than the proof of five, or of four, or of three of them.

If "probability" were, by definition, the index of this relation,

[34] *Philosophical Magazine, loc. cit.,* p. 74.

there should be no dispute concerning its meaning and legitimacy. The question may be raised, however, whether an index of relevance in this sense *is* what is either usually or legitimately meant by probability, or whether the proper meaning of probability must necessarily be more subtle.

Clearly, there is a difficulty. For if we hold that whatever is "probable" is not impossible, it may very well happen that the conclusion in question *is* impossible. Consider the instance of the alleged Scotsman once again. He could not be a Scotsman, in the sense required, if one of his maternal grandparents was in fact an Englishwoman. In that case, proof of his Scottish descent in the other six relevant particulars would establish no probability of his being a Scotsman, for the thing would be impossible.

In other words, as soon as we begin to examine these questions with any care, we speedily run upon the cardinal distinction between what, on the one hand, is *known* to be possible (if, indeed, there is any such thing that is not also known to be certain) and what, on the other hand, is not known to be impossible. These are very different indeed. For the first, if it could occur, would be a piece of knowledge; and the second (which does occur) is a piece of ignorance.

Accordingly, the suspicion is readily aroused that probable inferences and calculations are an attempt to extract knowledge out of ignorance. And here the frequentist appears to triumph. He agrees, indeed, that we do, and must, form probable inferences when we are, in large measure, ignorant. "It is impossible to prove that any events are independent," Dr. Campbell says, "but . . . we only require to be unable to discover that they are not independent." [35] Dr. Campbell has, however, the simple explanation to offer that many series whose members appear to have this "random" independence turn out, after repeated trials, to be characterized by the proportions of "randomness." Thus, *he* is not extracting knowledge out of ignorance. But he strongly suspects that his opponents are doing that very thing.

Before examining this question in greater detail, I should like to make some general remarks upon the situation as it now presents itself.

[35] *Physics: The Elements,* p. 209.

Firstly, then, it has to be said that probability is an epistemic matter and is not simply ontological. Statements concerning probability are always subject to the express or implied qualification "so far as we know." And this qualification, I think, should be understood fundamentally in a personal sense, and not merely in the general sense that probability is relevant to "evidence." For evidence may exist whether we know it or not. There may very well be unexamined registers about the grandparents of "Scotsmen" in the terms of our illustration; and therefore there might *be* conclusive counter-evidence regarding conclusions that we call probable. There are cases, indeed (as we have seen), in which we use the language of probability although we have convincing counter-evidence (e. g. in the *post mortem* examination of a hand at bridge). In these instances, however, the accurate statement is that such and such a result *would be* probable *if* we had this or that piece of information *and no more.*

Secondly, if I am right in asserting that all probability inferences are in this way hypothetical, there is a sensible diminution of the difficulty we are now considering. The difficulty is that we frequently speak of the "probability" of conclusions that in fact are impossible. But even if we were dealing with conclusive, and not merely with probable hypothetical inference, the same thing might occur. For a conclusion that follows demonstrably from false hypotheses may be false in fact, and yet be the necessary consequence of its premises. The greater part of the alleged difficulty is due to our forgetting that we are dealing with a probable conclusion *relatively to the evidence that is known.*

§ 9. The Principle of Indifference

The design of most theories of probability is not merely to give an account of the nature of probable reasoning but to supply a satisfactory basis for the calculation and measurement of probabilities. Attention is therefore concentrated upon equiprobability, that is to say, upon the measurement of probabilities that are equal.

It must be confessed that the principle of these attempts (on non-frequentist lines) has been unfortunately named. Sometimes a Principle of Non-Sufficient Reason is invoked, and any such principle, nominally at least, would seem to attempt to extract knowledge out of ignorance. Mr. Keynes proposes another title. We should speak, he thinks, of the Principle of Indifference (in a modified form). It may be doubted, however, whether the negative implications of this alternative title are much less noxious than in the case of its predecessor.

"The Principle of Indifference," Mr. Keynes says, "asserts that if there is no *known* reason for predicating of our subject one rather than another of several alternatives, then relatively to such knowledge the assertions of each of these alternatives have an *equal* probability." [36]

This principle might be expressed more positively (but hypothetically) and then would run: "If we have favorable relevant evidence regarding any conclusion which, so far as we know, is not impossible, then it is reasonable to conclude that this conclusion, so far as we know, is probable in some degree. And if such relevant evidence includes alternatives any one of which, so far as we know, is possible, it is reasonable for us to assume, provisionally, that these alternatives have the *same* degree of probability if they *seem* to have it, that is to say, if they seem to be equally relevant."

This principle appears to me self-evident; and I submit with confidence that it is intelligible. It also provides a certain indication of the possibility of measuring such alternatives, although it is, of course, a further question whether it provides a sufficient basis for the special inferences regarding the measurement of probabilities that mathematicians are accustomed to draw.

Mr. Keynes, commenting upon the Principle of Indifference, in the form in which he has stated it, concludes (following Von Kries) that it requires modification in view of certain unnecessarily paradoxical implications. I have therefore to show that the principle (at any rate in its more positive form) may be freed from these objections.

The type of difficulty is roughly as follows. Given the information that X is a European, and that the Dordogne is somewhere in Europe, then, if this is *all* we know, we should conclude that the chance of X's belonging to the Dordogne is $\frac{1}{2}$. For we have

[36] *A Treatise on Probability,* p. 42.

no reason for discriminating between the Dordogne and the rest of Europe in this matter. Suppose, however, we reflect that the Dordogne is a part of France, and that France is a part of Europe, what then? We may still, in one sense, have no reason for discriminating between the Dordogne and the rest of Europe (assuming, that is, that we know nothing about the size of the Dordogne relatively to the rest of Europe and nothing about the incidence of population). But we might also say that the chance of X's being a Frenchman was ½, and that, since the Dordogne is part of France, the chance of a *Frenchman's* belonging to the Dordogne is also ½. On these grounds, however, the chance of X's belonging to the Dordogne would be ½ of ½, i.e. ¼.

Similarly, given that Mrs. Green's hat has some color, we might argue that it has ½ chance of being red. For there is no reason for discriminating between red and not-red in this matter. The same argument might, however, be applied to the probability of the hat's being blue, or pink; and so, in the result, we should contradict ourselves.

These objections seem to me to be mistaken. In the instance of the color, the supposed difficulty arises because we know that there are several colors. If we know this, the chance of the hat's being red is less than ½, because we know that there are more than two possibilities, all, so far as we know, equally probable. We can not combine the probabilities of the hat's being blue or pink and of its being red without admitting this greater number of alternatives.

In other words, the paradox only illustrates the extreme difficulty of supposing ourselves to know much less than we really do know. And the same comment must be made about X and the Dordogne. If we could think ourselves into the required condition of nescience, there is, so far as I can see, no paradox. If our information is only that X must have been born somewhere in Europe, and that the Dordogne is a part of Europe, then, provided that we have no information about the size of the Dordogne in relation to Europe, the "chance" of X's belonging to the Dordogne *is* ½. If, however, we are given the *additional* information, that the Dordogne is a part of France which is a part of Europe, then, arguing simply upon the basis of partition, the "chance" given this additional premise, *is* $\frac{1}{4}$. (It is not $\frac{1}{3}$, i.e., divisible into the Dordogne, the rest of France, and the rest of Europe outside France; for the basis of the argument is the relevance of partition to the conclusion and therefore a part of a part is in a different position, relatively to the basis of the argument, from any unpartitioned residue).

Mr. Keynes himself claims, in view of these alleged paradoxes, that equiprobability can only be said to occur when the alternatives are ultimate, that is to say, not further divisible.[37] If so, we should have to face the question whether we *knew* them to be indivisible, or merely do not see any sufficient reason for regarding them as divisible. If the former condition were requisite, we should have to have a precison of knowledge regarding probability-units much more rigorous than is needed for ordinary arithmetic. And this would be a serious restriction of arguments in probability.

On the whole, however, we may perhaps conclude that difficulties of this species corroborate the prudence of employing a positive, instead of a negative, formula for the principle of probability and of interpreting the principle fundamentally as a legitimate hypothetical assumption in view of what *seems* equally probable. To be sure, the two statements that x and y seem equally probable, and that there is no visible reason for distinguishing between the likelihood of either, might themselves be held to be precisely equivalent. On the other hand, unless the evidence is very clear indeed, we might suspect a difference where we did not know of one, and might quite reasonably doubt whether alternatives *are* precisely equal (according to our lights) even in cases in which we are unable to produce any definite positive reason for regarding them as unequal. The phrase "no *known* difference," in other words, does not seem to describe the situation quite comprehensively.

It is further to be remarked that, if we start in this way with what *seems* to be equally probable, there is nothing to prevent us from sifting and refining these apparently equal probabilities, any more than in any other argument in which we start,

[37] *A Treatise on Probability,* pp. 59 *sqq.*

as we must start so often, from what appears to be true. Thus, like the frequentists, we might prefer to argue in terms of apparently equal probabilities which do not merely have this appearance initially, but continue to have the appearance after a prolonged series of trials. Or, again, like certain other authors, we might prefer to deal with events like the throwing of dice or the shuffling of cards, in which care has been expended with the object of producing an artificial equiprobability. For dice are constructed in order to produce an equiprobable result. And thirdly, without experiment, but *a priori* or by purely logical analysis, we might endeavor to test what *seems* equiprobable with the object of showing that on general logical grounds at least, it *is* equiprobable.

The last of these attempts, I think, is quite precisely what underlies the so-called "orthodox" mathematical view of probability; but the two former expedients are not quite on the same footing. For causal inferences concerning the behavior of dice and coins and cards are themselves probable inferences, as we shall see when we come to treat of induction; and we noted at the conclusion of § 6 of this chapter that frequency arguments concerning the probable continuance of a statistical proportion imply at some point, a non-frequentist interpretation of probability. On the other hand, there can be no reasonable objection to an *internal* progressive verification of a probability hypothesis, or to modifications of the original appearance of the hypothesis on such internal grounds. And fresh subsequent evidence (very often of a statistical kind) may, of course, rightly induce us to abandon our preliminary hypothesis concerning apparent equiprobability.

I shall suggest, indeed, that some sort of reconciliation between the rival theories of probability may be sought along these lines with some small prospect of success.

§ 10. Further Concerning the Measurement of Probabilities

In the common sense view of this matter (which is endorsed by Mr. Keynes), some probabilities do not, in practice, permit of accurate numerical measurement, and need not be supposed to permit of it theoretically. Even when figures are assigned, as in

the damages for probable injury awarded by the rough justice
of the law courts,[38] it is often unnecessary, Mr. Keynes says, to
suppose that the figures are other than arbitrary; and when we
have evidence that the sky looks clear but that the barometer is
low, there is no reason to suppose, apart from arbitrary conventions, that these counter-claims in the way of probable evidence
could, even in theory, be measured with any refinement of numerical precision.[39]

These contentions are manifestly consonant with the view we
have suggested. When we perceive that two pieces of relevant
but inconclusive evidence have a bearing upon some conclusion,
it is only in special cases that we are inclined to adventure the
opinion that they *seem* to indicate an equal probability. For the
most part, we are doubtful on the point. Even when we are
clearly of opinion that one piece of evidence has a greater bearing upon the conclusion than some other, we need not be prepared, and frequently should not be prepared, to attempt to express in figures how much greater its bearing is. And when two
pieces of evidence do *not* seem unequal we require, and we should
welcome, further evidence of their equality.

On the other hand, Mr. Keynes claims that in certain types
of argument complete numerical precision may be obtained in
probability calculations. Broadly speaking, these are the cases
in which one or other of a definite set of exclusive alternatives
must be true, and in which each alternative is equiprobable.
Reckoning certainty as 1 and impossibility as O, it follows that,
if there are n equiprobable exclusive alternatives, the probability
of each such alternative is $1/n$.

Some such claim is commonly made in the "orthodox" mathematical treatment of probability, but Mr. Keynes's critics (in the
frequentist camp) complain that the relations between these calculations and the degree of relevant evidence that bears logically upon a probable conclusion are much more arbitrary than
Mr. Keynes supposes, and that he has no logical right to maintain that he can multiply probabilities (or degrees of logical

[38] *Keynes, op. cit.,* pp. 25 *sqq.*
[39] *Ibid.,* p. 30.

relevance) together, although he can obviously multiply the numerical values he assigns to such evidence.[40]

On the technical point at issue, these critics seem to me to be correct. The main question, however, is whether this initial assignment of numerical values is or is not justifiable. It is a minor point whether the addition, multiplication, and division of relevant evidence is addition, multiplication, and division in quite the same sense as in arithmetic. If the foundations of this mathematical treatment are secure, there will be an intelligible correspondence in the results; and there are few kinds of measurement in which a lesser degree of convention is reasonably to be expected.

Let us keep, then, to a simple instance, and consider the logical justification of these numerical estimates. When we say that the odds are three to one against two successive heads in the tossing of a penny, what is the logical justification for assigning precisely these figures?

The assumptions are (1) that the penny must fall either on one side or the other. It cannot fall on both sides, or be suspended in some intermediate position. (In the alternative, we might say that if the latter event happened we should not count the throw). Again, it is assumed (2) that "heads" and "tails" are equiprobable.

These assumptions being made, we proceed, in effect, to develop the logical alternatives, or to assign the logical pigeonholes implied in the assumptions. Calling the result "heads" H, and the result "tails" T, we can see, a priori, that there are four alternatives, viz. HH (i.e., "heads" succeeded by "heads"), HT, TH, and TT. The specific alternative HH, therefore, is but one alternative out of four, and its probability is said to be one to four, the equiprobability of the alternatives being assumed. The probability of the three other alternatives conjointly is similarly three to four, and the ratio of HT or TH or TT to HH is therefore three to one.

It is evident that the numbers here employed have a perfectly definite meaning. They are not at all arbitrary, apart from

[40] Cf. R. H. Nisbet, *Mind*, N.S., No. 137, pp. 6 *sq.*

the convention of reckoning certainty as one. No other numerical ratio could conceivably express the ratio in question; and these numbers do express it.

On the other hand, it seems equally evident that this numerical reckoning is not, strictly speaking, a measuring of probabilities at all. It is a precise enumeration of what is *certain*, not probable, viz. a precise enumeration of the alternatives, followed by a statement concerning the proportions of these alternatives. It is, in short, the aforesaid counting of the logical pigeonholes in the case: and the probability, strictly speaking, is an *inference* from the logical structure and divisions of the alternatives *to the particular case.* This inference is that the "chances" or the "probabilities" are against some particular succession *HH*, *because* there is the ratio of three to one against in the structural proportions of the alternatives.

We should therefore conclude that much that is commonly called "probability" is not probability at all, although it may supply a logical basis from which the probability of the happening of some particular event may be inferred.

§ 11. Concluding Remarks

In view of the above conclusion, we may, I think, approach the task of mediating between the three current theories of probability with some faint degree of hope, anticipating as much harmony as is reasonably to be expected from a *ménage à trois,* and we may say

(1). That what is called *a priori* "probability" is really a certainty, since it is an enumeration of the logical structure and proportions of alternatives *quâ* alternatives.

(2). That it is always legitimate to argue *hypothetically* on this assumption, and to draw the probable inferences (to particular cases) which depend upon this *a priori* or structural proportion of the alternatives.

(3). That if the alternatives seem equal, independent, exclusive, and collectively exhaustive, it is legitimate to claim that probable inferences of the above species are not *merely* hypothetical but have a certain claim to be asserted as probable, i.e., to *be* probable But

(4). That this appearance of equiprobability may very well be subjected by reasonable people to further tests.

In common life we do form probable inferences of this kind with regard to alternatives which seem equiprobable and exhaustive (or, roughly speaking, where we perceive no reason for deciding one way or the other). This is a non-frequentist employment of probability, and may be applied both to novel and to singular instances in which there is no question of statistical evidence or even of previous experience. It is further to be remarked that frequentist theories themselves require a non-frequentist interpretation of probability in addition to any frequentist interpretation. This is seen in the application of statistical proportions to individual cases, to inductive and analogical inferences from former statistics, and in other such ways.

This being admitted, however, it is unreasonable to object to the following opinion, viz:

(5). That normally we are not content with what merely *seems* equiprobable but endeavor to investigate its equiprobability further; and that, in general, we do this by making (when we can) a series of trials with the object of discovering whether the proportions that result in the trials are probably (in a non-frequentist sense) of the type that physicists hold to be objective and describe as "random."

Ultimately, the function of empirical statistical evidence, is, like other empirical evidence, to limit the *a priori* logical possibilities. What is actual or empirical is narrower than what is abstractly possible (in the merely logical sense that, *a priori*, anything might conceivably be anything). Statistics yield empirical evidence of proportions and tendencies other than the *a priori* proportions and tendencies, although probably conforming (again according to a non-frequentist interpretation of probability) to the general structural proportions of large aggregates.

Per contra, equiprobability does not *mean* "happening in approximately equal proportions in the long run," although statisticians, and others who make extensive use of mathematical calculation concerning probability, may justifiably prefer to deal, so far as they can, with large series that have shown this proportion, or with coins, dice, etc., regarding which it may plausibly be inferred (inductively) that the proportions will (probably) turn out to be "random," and although this is one of the usual ways in which we endeavor to sift and to clarify what initially *seems* equiprobable.

These remarks concern the relation between probability as an inference from relevant but inconclusive evidence, on the one hand, and the frequentist theory of probability, on the other hand. Regarding theories of De Morgan's type we have to say

(6). That probability does not deal with, and does not attempt to measure, capricious actual psychological "feelings" or "impressions of certainty." Instead, it has to do with impressions of relevance falling short of conclusiveness, and is therefore, from the start, at least semilogical. Again

(7). It does not attempt to divide a (normally indivisible) "impression of certainty" into a small collection of subimpressions of certainty (as De Morgan held); but it endeavors instead to analyze the relevant yet incomplete evidence, paying special attention to the logical structure of the alternatives and to their logical proportions.

Chapter XVIII

OF CATEGORIAL PRECONNECTIONS

§ 1. Rational Presumption

An integral part of the design of the present volume has
been to inquire into the answers philosophers might be disposed
to give to-day to the questions set by the great epistemologists
of the eighteenth century, and particularly by the great British
epistemologists Locke and Hume. If these questions, in their
essential features, had been wrongly put, this same defect would
permeate our entire discussion. And perhaps it has done so.
Being of opinion, however, that Locke and Hume asked what, in
the large, were the right (or among the right) epistemological
questions, I have ventured to discuss these matters in the same
general spirit as these authors, and propose to continue to do
so. This general agreement in the standpoint of the present work
as compared with the eighteenth century attitude, however, need
not, and should not, be understood to impose a rigid and unwavering acceptance of the precise terms in which Locke and
Hume put their fundamental questions.

In particular, as we have seen at many points in the foregoing
discussion, the assumption that complete certainty, or demonstratively conclusive evidence (including self-evidence), on the
one hand, and cogitations or evidence in some degree uncertain
or inconclusive, on the other hand, are *toto cœlo* distinct is
dangerous and misleading, however plausible it may be. To be
sure the importance of this distinction, both practical and theoretical, is not in dispute. However hard *real* certainty may be to
come by, it implies a standard both distinctive and highly important. Any reasonable claim to certainty deserves the most
scrupulous examination, and nothing is shoddier in any argument
than to be cozened into accepting as a certainty what in fact is
only problematical. On the other hand, it is illegitimate to as-

397

sume, and, in the event, it may be quite unwarrantable to maintain, that, epistemologically speaking, whatever is not of *knowledge* (or of completely evidenced certainty) must be held to be of sin, and, in the last analysis, tainted, invertebrate, unreasonable, and corrupt. The possible rationality of evidence that can not be supposed to yield utter and invincible certainty should at least be inquired into. For it is not absurd to suggest that presumptions and probabilities may themselves be rational. Logic and reason, in other words, may be wider than demonstration and self-evidence. If they are wider, the sphere of the uncertain must include *something*, be it little or much, that is not non-rational and that is not alogical.

In the British tradition, the terms commonly employed to mark this (very possibly exaggerated) contrast were *knowledge*, on the one hand, and *probability*, on the other. The term probability, however (for reasons sufficiently shown in the last chapter), has tended to become rather narrowly specialized; and it is desirable to use a more general designation. Let us inquire, therefore, into the general domain of what may be called presumption, remembering always that presumptions need not be prejudices, and that, if they are prejudices, they should be shown to be so. Accordingly, our fundamental topic now is whether there may be reasonable presumptions for which utter certainty should not be claimed.

Here, for obvious reasons, we should begin at the top and consider major or governing presumptions—in Reid's phrase, the "first principles" of presumption. The inferences from such governing presumptions may fairly be regarded as the domestic concern of formal logic and of the numerical or non-numerical estimation of "chances."

In other words, we should consider certain of the "categories," viz. those categories that are not self-evident. The term "category," it is true, like so many other philosophical terms that have had a long history, has been put to many uses, some of them unusual and some of them confused and not to be commended. On the whole, however, we shall be following tradition and at the same time shall be designating what is worthy of notice, if, with

Mr. Alexander, we call the *pervasive* features of things their categorial features.[1] I do not, indeed, propose to go all the way with Mr. Alexander in this matter. According to him, what is strictly categorial must pervade all existents without exception, and is contrasted with what, in the strict sense, is empirical or contingent, that is to say, with what is a property of some things only, and is not a property of other things in any form at all. This usage seems to me inconvenient. I do not think we should scruple to call *pervasive* properties "categorial" in cases in which we do not know, and could not prove, that they are, strictly speaking, *all-pervasive*. And I do not think that Mr. Alexander's use of the term "empirical" is at all convenient. By "empirical" evidence, in the customary philosophical sense, we mean a certain *type* of evidence, viz. the type that, in the language of some of our earlier discussions, is, in part at least, based upon, or that logically requires, an æstheton or a number of æstheta. And it is generally held that many (perhaps all) of the existential pervasive properties of things are in this sense quite strictly "empirical."

Such questions, to some extent, are verbal, and so have only the importance (not inconsiderable) that attaches to the use of words. Moreover, Mr. Alexander himself admits that "the boundaries of the categorial and the empirical are from the nature of the case, hard to draw and may seem indistinct and fluid." [2] On the other hand, more than the mere question of words is usually at stake in such seemingly verbal debates; and something more than verbalism is pertinent to the present instance. According to Mr. Alexander, "the *a priori* and the empirical are distinguished within experience itself. Both are experiential or in a general sense empirical." [3] He therefore, in effect, substitutes the distinction between what is strictly all-pervasive and what is not all-pervasive for the traditional distinction between what is *a priori* and what is empirical.

I do not wish to assume that Mr. Alexander's view is false, but also I do not wish to assume that the traditional view is

[1] *Space, Time and Deity,* Vol. i, pp. 183 *sqq.*
[2] *Op. cit.,* Vol. I, p. 343.   [3] *Ibid.*

false. On the contrary, I wish to leave the possibility open that there may be noëtic evidence that is wholly non-æsthetic and therefore metæsthetic.

The point has some importance in another way. For the most part, and particularly in discussions that follow the British tradition, the most important and the most interesting questions which are concerned with governing presumptions that are uncertain in some degree have to do with such presumptions concerning the general character of the existent, or, so to say, of the make-up of Nature herself. The discussion gravitates towards what Dr. Ward called the "real categories," [4] such as substance, or cause, or end; and the essential question is whether the whole of our evidence in such matters is contained in sensory, mnemic, and other æstheta, on the one hand, and in general logical inference, on the other hand; or whether it is necessary further to maintain that what we regard as our "knowledge" of nature, whether based upon experimental science or on the cruder experiments of daily life, would be quite ludicrously inept and unconvincing if it were not governed by certain general presumptions that are neither definitely a priori (in the traditional sense) nor definitely part of the strict and proper "testimony" of sensa and other æstheta.

In the latter case, if such general presumptions are rational, our "experimental knowledge" (to use Locke's phrase) may be rational even when it is general and far removed from the immediate testimony of the senses, or from logical conclusions demonstrably to be inferred with certainty from this immediate testimony. If, on the contrary, such categorial presumptions are definitely non-rational, all "experimental knowledge" of a general kind is, as Hume said it was, non-rational also.

§ 2. ANTHROPOLOGICAL EVIDENCE IN THIS MATTER

I have borrowed the term "preconnection" from M. Lévy-Bruhl's Lowell Lectures on "Primitive Mentality," and shall approach the problems of presumption from this anthropological angle. The reason for adopting this course is that the nature of such pervasive presumptions is more readily perceived when we

[4] *Psychological Principles*, pp. 334 *sqq.*

are disposed to differ from the presumptions than when we ourselves take them for granted. Familiarity breeds obtuseness. M. Lévy-Bruhl's thesis is described in a way very nearly adequate in a quotation with which his book opens. This quotation is from a Jesuit missionary to the Indians of North America, and runs as follows: "Although there are minds among them quite as capable of scientific thought as those of Europeans, yet their upbringing, and their need to hunt for a living, has reduced them to a state in which their reasoning power does not go beyond what pertains to their bodily health, their success in hunting and fishing, their trading and their welfare; and all these things are like so many principles from which they draw all their conclusions, not only as regards their homes, their occupations and their way of life, but also their superstitions and their deities." [5]

The qualification needed in this statement, according to M. Lévy-Bruhl, is simply that the minds of primitives have a different orientation from our own. The primitive mind, he informs us, "is both complex and developed in its own way." [6] It can reason as well as observe. It has a mystical dimension in addition to its preoccupation with tools, needs, and immediate environment. But it is not *positivistic*, if we define positivism in terms of our natural and experimental science; and in this sense it is pre-scientific or even pre-logical regarding the course of nature and of human life.

Let us consider some examples.

The missionary Bentley, speaking of the natives of the Congo, averred that these natives "never recognised any similarity between their own trading and the coast factory. They considered that when the white man wanted cloth he opened a bale and got it. Whence the bales came, and why, and how—that they never thought of. Everyone said that the cloth was made by dead men under the sea." "The whole thing," Bentley went on, "was hopelessly mixed with the magic and occult" [7]—in proof of which he related the following incident. At the trading station the custom was for the agent who received the native produce to scribble

[5] *Primitive Mentality,* English translation, p. 22.
[6] *Ibid.,* p. 33.   [7] As quoted, *ibid.,* p. 28.

the amount due to any native on a piece of paper which was duly honored at the counter. The natives, however, imbued with their magical and occult notions, regarded the paper itself as a fetish, and attempted to obtain payment, without bringing goods, by themselves forging a similar paper fetish.

It seems obvious that there is something wrong with the reverend gentleman's account of this matter. Even civilized mankind has been known to treat bank-notes as fetishes, and to consider that the forging of such fetishes, if it could be accomplished, gives a prospect of easy money. Again, it would surely need quite inordinate powers of imagination on a savage's part to conjecture the nature, or even the existence, of cotton looms in Manchester. To him the trader does seem to get as many bales as he wants from across the sea, and to do nothing in particular in order to obtain them. Any hypothesis concerning the magic of this supply might well seem as rational as any other hypothesis. In short, the native mind should not be supposed to be working illogically in this instance. It is only working along the lines of certain preconnections that are different from ours, because *we* know what the trader meant by his writing and the native does not. *We* have also a certain acquaintance with the way in which cotton bales are produced and exported to the Congo.

At the same time, these preconnections in the native mind, that is to say, the structure or drift of argument along which the native mind proceeds, is not what we call positive science. Indeed, there is a great deal of evidence that the causes we consider primary are regarded as definitely secondary by the majority of primitives. And this, in effect, is M. Lévy-Bruhl's principal contention.

Take, for instance, illness and death. "Whitehead saw one of his men sitting in the cold wind on a rainy day. He advised his going home and changing his wet cloth for a dry one, but he said 'It does not matter. People do not die of a cold wind; people only get ill and die by means of witchcraft.'"[8] And similarly in a host of other instances. In New Guinea "a tree falls; it is a witch who caused it to do so, although the tree may be quite rotten, or a gust of wind may break it off. A man meets

[8] *Primitive Mentality*, p. 37.

with an accident; it is the action of *werabana*." [9] "I was at the Ambrizette when three Cabinda women had been to the river with their pots for water; all three were filling them from the stream together, when the middle one was snapped up by an alligator, and instantly carried away under the surface of the water, and of course drowned. The relatives of the poor woman at once accused the other two of bewitching her, and causing the alligator to take her out of their midst. When I remonstrated with them and attempted to show them the utter absurdity of the charge, their answer was 'Why did not the alligator take one of the end ones then, and not the one in the middle '" [10]

In substance, then, M. Lévy-Bruhl's argument is that in all matters of tribal importance (and the native mind can scarcely be expected to revolve round anything else) the fundamental causes, according to primitive conceptions, are, as we should say, magical, and only the secondary causes are positive or scientific. Very naturally, then, the native employs his reason mainly in the elucidation of these primary or magical causes. "All the natives believe that *muai* (ordeal by poison) is infallible, while they know very well that the testimony of their countrymen is not so." [11] Omens, on these hypotheses, are the best sort of experimental evidence. Dreams, spontaneous or induced, are the really reliable medical textbooks. "The powers must not be offended. In this country, when a rule has been broken, men do penance, because the dead have unlimited power." [12]

On these premises the natives may argue quite logically and quite acutely, as they did about the alligator's selection of a particular victim. Why *should* the one woman have been taken and the others left?

No doubt, perplexities may arise on the magical as well as upon any other system of presumptions. A Mr. Grubb relates that an Indian journeyed a hundred and fifty miles in order to demand compensation for some pumpkins he had dreamed Mr. Grubb had stolen.[13] When Mr. Grubb proved his alibi, the Indian admitted that Mr. Grubb could not have stolen the pumpkins, but nevertheless persisted in his claim for compensation.

[9] *Ibid.*, p. 45.   [11] *Ibid.*, p. 220.   [13] *Ibid.*, pp. 106 *sq.*
[10] *Ibid.*, p. 49.   [12] *Ibid.*, p. 265.

Here, according to our notions, there is certainly a discrepancy, and the case may have presented some little difficulty to the candid and persistent native as well as to Mr. Grubb. Even if Mr. Grubb's dream body had made this felonious excursion, it could only have stolen dream pumpkins after all. The visible pumpkins were visibly in the Indian's garden when the Indian set out to claim compensation for the loss of them. It may be true, as M. Lévy-Bruhl argues, that the native idea of time contains nothing approaching the definiteness of our ideas concerning time; but, even so, the Indian seems to have grasped the essentials of Mr. Grubb's alibi so far as the point of time was concerned. Apparently, the Indian regarded the pumpkins as doomed, Mr. Grubb being the culprit; and, from that point of view, the presence or absence of the pumpkins at any given time was naturally immaterial. The pumpkins were no longer a secure possession, and Mr. Grubb, in the Indian's view, ought to pay compensation for this change in their status.

There are perplexities in detail on any system of preconnections, but I can not see why the native should have been more inclined to forgo *his* common sense than Mr. Grubb was inclined to forgo his own positivism.

§ 3. COMMENTS ON THE ANTHROPOLOGICAL EVIDENCE

The conclusion that is generally supposed to emerge from evidence of this type is that the *inferences* of primitive people are at least semi-logical and of the same order as the inferences of the people we call civilized, but that the structural preconnections, explicit or unavowed, from and according to which the inferences are drawn, are widely different, the primitive tradition of preconnection being, in our eyes, irrelevant because magical or superstitious, and our system of traditional preconnections being "scientific," that is to say, of the same order as experimental science, although, doubtless, among the laity, very crude. What *we* regard as the *only* rational type of explanation the savage regards as "secondary," although relevant so far as it goes. And we reject all his primary preconnections as merely magical and superstitious.

This contrast, in all probability, is overdrawn. It is not the savage but the anthropologist who draws this rigid distinction between the primary magical preconnections and the "secondary" preconnections in which positivism puts its trust. For the savage, dreams, omens, and the rest *are* evidence; and they are *not* evidence for sophisticated positivists who pride themselves upon being hard-headed. In the primitive preconnections, in other words, the two types of evidence are mixed, and the product, to us, seems amazing. It is a brew to which we are not accustomed. There is no sufficient evidence, however, that the magical always preponderates over the non-magical in the savage mind, however good the evidence may be that it frequently does so. In order to help us to understand that the savage's cogitative orientation is not sheer, wild unreason and utter madness, the anthropologist imports from the outside a distinction between magical and positivistic that is entirely foreign to the savage's point of view. This is a legitimate artifice, but it can not be a final explanation.

Again, it is not unreasonable to maintain that the sacrosanctity of positivism is itself a superstition, and that there may be a faint glimmer of reason and intelligence among those who are not hard-shell positivists. Most of us, indeed, are pretty confident that there is no such thing as magic; for magic is a term of abuse applied to what is regarded as impossible as well as disreputable. We are not, however, agreed as to what *is* magic— whether, e.g., "second sight" and "telepathy" be magic or no. And similarly over a wide range of debatable territory.

A competition in magic like that recorded between Moses and the rival wizards of Egypt does not, I suppose, impress many of us. A monopoly of magic, as when Elijah in the narrative proved that the priests of Baal had no magic at all, although Jehovah was capable of conferring very definite magic upon His prophet, does not impress us either. Unlike Paley in *The Evidences of Christianity*, we do not any longer look upon miracles as the main authentic proof of the truth of the Christian faith, either when these miracles are recorded in the Scriptures, or when they are recorded of St. Columba or of other holy men. There are too many miracles of this species in too many religions; and the record of miracles in the Christian story is to our minds an encumbrance and not a help.

Assuming, however, that "science" means "positivism," many of our contemporaries would deny with the utmost vehemence that positivistic explanation is the only possible explanation of everything, or that positivism in itself should supply the whole of our intellectual orientation. At the moment, indeed, it is the fashion to deny that there is any important discrepancy between science and Christianity. The lion is licking the lamb, and the lamb is snuggling against the lion's mane. Hence, if it be granted that "science" deals with natural uniformities, a "miracle," in the sense of an unnatural hiatus, is either denied or kept very sedulously in the background. The Spirit, it is agreed, does not work by violent occasional interference with the established natural order; and, in the result, scientific causes *are* secondary, but they may legitimately be treated as primary for all the usual purposes of ordinary life and also in all scientific explanations. They are secondary, in any ultimate analysis, because Nature as a whole is deiform, and because our ultimate orientations should therefore be Godwards, not timewards. But they are primary as regards any particular explanation of any particular event. On this point, it is held, there is no possible conflict between science and Christianity. On the contrary, all is amity. Positivism is mistaken only when it regards itself as all-sufficient. In that case it is the bigotry of half-educated science, admirably trained along its own narrow lines, but miserably inadequate when regarded from the standpoint of cosmic interpretation or in connection with the discernment of spiritual values.

Such, in general, is the argument, and, for the moment, I am setting it forth without any attempt at commentary. Our present interest in it is wholly restricted to the logic of categorial preconnections. And here the conclusion, I should suppose, is sufficiently obvious. Even if positivism were the final truth in all such matters, it could not be inferred that the preconnections of primitive peoples and of their traditional orientation were utterly absurd and unreasonable. The immitigable truth of positivism (if positivism were quite certain) would compel us, indeed, to hold that much of the evidence on which primitive peoples rely can not withstand reasonable criticism, and also that the prolonged attempt on the part of Christian teachers to allegorize Nature (personification being parsonification) and to discover particular symbols of deiformity within Nature, were mistaken in their principle. This, however, would be a very different thing from being compelled to assume that there was no *prima facie* case for any such interpretations, or that they must be moonshine (relatively to every conceivable species of evidence), and incapable of blending with the light of day.

There is no sufficient justification for this interpretation, and the mere fact, if fact it were, that much *prima facie* evidence must eventually be discarded because it is not good evidence is surely no proof that the entire structure of such preconnections is fundamentally illogical. Let us take M. Lévy-Bruhl's argument at his own valuation. He asserts that what primitive peoples regard as secondary causes are the only genuine causes, and so that their preconnections are frankly superstitious because what they regard as primary causes are what we know to be magical. Be it so; and we have still to admit that in that case (which is the worst conceivable) a certain common structure of preconnection remains between savage and civilized preconnections. Both agree that there *are* causes. Both agree in accepting certain causes. Both agree, at least to a certain and most appreciable extent, in the tests by which causes may be distinguished. It may be superstition on the part of primitives to conclude that the coming of a few strangers in a ship is the cause of a pestilence, although I do not think our doctors would agree. (*They* would speak, however, of streptococci and not of magic.) But whether the strangers do or do not disseminate magic, and whether the magic may or may not be exorcised by incantations, it is at least common ground that what logicians call the Method of Difference should be applied, and that the special characteristics of subsequent events should be explained in terms of some special and peculiar antecedent.

A word of explanation concerning the meaning of the prefix in the term "*pre*connection" (or, for that matter, in the term *pre*sumption or even in the term *pre*judice) may conveniently be given at this point.

Very frequently, especially when we are thinking of origins, we interpret this prefix as signifying temporal priority. It is what comes first in the mind before it is applied, or before its *prima facie* appearance is submitted to some further test. And it is natural to think of origins when we are examining the ideas of primitive peoples; for we consider that our forefathers must have passed through a stage similar to theirs, although the primitive peoples with which we now come into contact are as ancient as we are.

On the whole, however, it is logical, not temporal, priority that is properly in question here, especially if, as we have argued, the general structure of the preconnections of primitive and of civilized peoples concerning their respective environments is fundamentally the same, although the form and, to some extent, the manner of its application vary. In general, indeed, especially among primitive peoples and among the lay majority (i.e. among the laity, philosophically speaking) of civilized men and women, the ultimate preconnections of their *Weltanschauung* (or world-view) are not explicitly formulated at all, and therefore do not come before their minds in any ostensible way, late or early. It is philosophers, and experts in analysis, who make these formulations, and when they do so they attempt to describe the general, unacknowledged, and even unnoticed principles according to which common sense, either at a primitive or at a civilized level, deems any argument concerning Man or Nature reasonable. This, although it is only implicit logic, is a logical rather than a temporal sense of priority. It is what should be stated first when it is the premise of a defensible logical argument—the major or governing premise of such an argument that should be stated first because our attention should be attracted to its primary logical importance. It need not be that with which our minds, in their confused, groping way, normally begin. Indeed, in general, what is logically first *in ordine ad universum,* is temporally last *in ordine ad nos,* that is to say, in the temporal order of our discovery of it.

§ 4. THE LOGIC OF PRESUMPTION

We are born to be participants in a social tradition, in our thoughts as much as in our arts, and crafts, and literature. Into these structures (which need not be quite rigid) all our ideas fall. The lazier we are, the more we follow the tradition passively. The more active we are, the more we sustain its vitality, and help it to put forth new buds and shoots. In so far as we reform, transform, or innovate, we do so by contrast with, and in marked dependence upon, the tradition in which we have participated.

These platitudes hold of "common sense" and of experimental or scientific preconnections quite as clearly as they hold of sonnet-writing or of the cinema. (In the last instance, it does not take long to establish a tradition.) The question then is, what is the logic of this circumstance as regards either positivistic or other preconnections in our "natural" and in our "human" outlook and sciences. For up to the present, in this chapter, we have been content to point out that there *are* such preconnections both among primitive and among sophisticated men and women, and that these preconnections may be justifiable. We have said nothing directly to justify them at the bar of logic.

Let us, then, consider various representative opinions on this matter.

(1). Some would say that the thing is only an affair of fashion. There are, *de facto*, certain climates of opinion which, when they alter, may evince causes for the alteration, but seldom or never sufficient reasons for it. If we knew more about this meteorology of opinion we might be able to ascertain more of the causes of such alterations, but would still fail, and fail signally, to discover justifying reasons for them. Ways of thinking come into fashion, and anon go out of fashion, for no apparent reason, just as women, at various recurrent epochs in recorded history, have endeavored to do what men do in politics, literature, sport, and in the tourney, and at other periods have set their thoughts upon being very manifestly feminine. We say vaguely that we grow tired of one fashion of ideas, and that we like a spice of novelty. In general, we neither say nor think that the new (or the newly recurrent) ideas are *better* than the old, even if, sometimes, they happen to be better. In the main, we can say only that, for the time being, they seem more interesting or more promising. And we may revert to the older ideas from similar causes. It is a question of intellectual repletion (is it not?) rather than of anything else. The rule is temporary satiety consequent upon a certain type of continued intellectual diet; and return to the old diet when, in due time, we are sated with the new.

This view is skeptical in its essence. To be sure, it may avoid complete skepticism by asserting that the diet in question is always a diet of partial truth, that a temporary surfeit (with consequent exhaustion) gives some sort of reason for a change in intellectual policy, and that within the limits of any *cadre* of opinion we may, in general, argue reasonably and logically enough. If, however, our principal preconnections vary for no sufficient reason, the variation itself, and a great part of its outcome, belong to illogic and not to reason.

(2). In order to avoid this fundamental skepticism, many philosophers maintain (or, should I say, used to maintain?) that we have to distinguish between the admittedly capricious climate of certain opinions and the stable currents of "natural" opinion. The constitution of human nature is such that there are certain invariable preconnections of natural belief. These preconnections (apart from wilful paradox and a few insignificant exceptions) are universal in the species, and may well be original (or unacquired in individual experience). This, in effect, was Thomas Reid's view.

Apart from the extreme difficulty of discerning where "nature" is to be distinguished from "nurture" or from artifice; of renouncing nurture and artifice, although "nature" survives through assimilating "nurture" and mankind takes pride in being an inventive species; and, finally, of discovering definite preconnections that can be shown to be universal in the species, the great difficulty in this alternative to skepticism is that skeptics might consistently accept it. Our constitution and its fundamental instincts are not wholly rational, and, if we had congenital belief-instincts, or the seeds of them, of a certain type, it would still be an open question whether these belief-instincts are rational at all. They might only be something that we *must* believe without anything that could properly be called sufficient evidence. There is not much point in arguing about our "constitution" in general, if the problem concerns the *rational part* of this constitution.

(3). To say that such preconnections belong to our constitution *as rational beings* is to say that these preconnections are not only conformable and amenable to rational reflection, but that they are somehow justified by rational evidence. Can this be seriously maintained, and, if so, in what sense or senses? Let us note some of the principal views.

(a). If the assertion is that nothing is reasonable except *certa e certis*, it follows that all such preconnections are either self-evident or deduced from what is self-evident. They would, in Kantian language, be synthetic propositions *a priori*, synthetic because they could be denied without direct and flagrant self-contradiction, and *a priori* because they would be logically prior to all our experience and experiments.

(b). It is conceivable that such preconnections should be *probable a priori*, i.e. that without ever being fitted to yield certainty, they might evince inevitable logical relevance. Kant usually denied the possibility of this alternative because he thought that mathematics and physics would be stultified if they attempted to prove anything less than certainty. In his account of the "Ideas of Reason," however, he might be said to have approached some such view; for he held that as rational beings we were compelled to employ the idea (or ideal) of a complete system of nature *heuristically*, or as a guiding thread, although we could not expect finality in any such enterprise.

(This we observed in the concluding sections of Chapter II.)

(c). It is frequently argued that there must be sufficient inductive evidence for all preconnections, or else that such preconnections must ultimately be regarded as prejudices. Thus, J. S. Mill endeavored to prove that the Uniformity of Nature could be proved by a (particular and, in many ways, by a rather special) type of induction, and that, when the Uniformity of

Nature was accepted as the major premise of all experimental inquiry into Nature, it was possible to prove all the more special results of experiment by means of what Mill called the Experimental Methods.

As we shall see in the next chapter, observation and experiment may suggest our structural preconnections, and, to some extent confirm them. It is a further question, however, whether these empirical and experimental pieces of evidence can be regarded as satisfactory rational proof, and indeed whether inductive experiments would have any high degree of plausibility if there were not certain initial and quite definite presumptions in their favor. The question, therefore, is whether inductive generalizations based on experiment and observation make the preconnections of natural science intelligible; or whether, contrariwise, it is these preconnections that render the evidence of inductive experimental observations at all cogent.

(d). A variation of the above argument is that what we have called "preconnections" are initially mere assumptions or arbitrary hypotheses when judged from any strict logical standpoint, but that those "preconnections" which are progressively confirmed by experience become entitled to a considerable measure of rational belief. This is a suggestion in terms of induction by the hypothetical method, instead of, as in the former argument, in terms of induction by means of the method of enumerating instances. The logical questions at issue, however, are fundamentally the same.

(e). It is sometimes asserted that the whole question is one of "coherence," preconnections being but impressions or descriptions, *ex post facto,* of the tendencies and general outlines of a cohesive system of nature, and being worthy of serious attention only if we can say, "This or nothing."

According to this view, something more than mere logical consistency is requisite. What is required is the maximum extent of a special kind of logical harmony. Since it is admitted, however, that certain kinds of non-logical harmony may be found in experience, e.g. an emotional harmony, or the kind of harmony that results from the sedulous neglect of inconvenient types of evidence, and since it is also admitted that, in the imperfect condition of actual human knowledge, complete coherence is an unattainable dream, and partial coherence seriously liable to error (despite its coherence when it builds upon a mistake), it may be questioned whether this criterion is either workable or adequate in principle, and, if it is, whether it is not itself a single, immense preconnection of the same logical type as the minor preconnections it is designed to supersede.

I do not say that these alternatives exhaust the possibilities, or even the admissible plausibilities, in this enormous subject. They are among the main alternatives, however, and they give us a good deal about which to think.

§ 5. ILLUSTRATIONS OF PRECONNECTIONS ACCEPTED AS SUCH BY PHILOSOPHERS AND BY PSYCHOLOGISTS

It is possible to regard nearly all, if not quite all, of "the usual certainties" we discussed in Book III of the present volume as rational presumptions rather than as certainties completely evidenced. Those who regard them in this light usually admit, indeed, that *something* must be accepted as certain, if these presumptions have the office that is imputed to them. It must be certain, they admit, that the presumptions really are rational presumptions, that is to say, that they do give genuine evidence genuinely favorable to the conclusions towards which they are said to point; and they also admit, in general, that the inferential implications of these presumptions must be held to be necessarily implied, that is to say, that the principles of *inference* are not themselves problematic.

In so far as Reid's appeal to the "constitution of human nature" is really an appeal to man's *rational* constitution, his account of the "first principles of contingent truths" is of the above order. Reid held it to be certain, indeed, that all knowledge got by reasoning must be built upon first principles,[14] that the inferential relations discovered by correct reasoning are certainly what they are discovered to be, and that some "first principles" (e.g. mathematical axioms, in the sense of "axiom" accepted in Reid's day) are wholly self-evident.[15] Other first principles, however (he said), are of the nature of rational pre-

[14] *Intellectual Powers,* Hamilton's Edition, p. 435.   [15] *Ibid.*

sumptions. In their case, indeed, "There is no searching for evidence, no weighing of arguments; the proposition is not deduced or inferred from another; it has the light of truth in itself, and has no occasion to borrow it from another." [16] But they do not yield certainty. Thus he says, "In a matter of testimony, it is self-evident that the testimony of two is better than that of one, supposing them equal in character and in their means of knowledge, yet the simple testimony may be true, and that which is preferred to it may be false." (Here, I suppose, the two witnesses are independent.) And he goes on: "When an experiment has succeeded in several trials, and the circumstances have been marked with care, there is a self-evident probability of its succeeding in a new trial; but there is no certainty." [17]

Reid himself was very well aware that his enumeration of these governing rational presumptions might be defective. "If the enumeration should appear to some redundant," he says, "to others deficient, and to others both—if things which I conceive to be first principles, should to others appear to be vulgar errors, or to be truths which derive their evidence from other truths, and therefore not first principles . . . I shall rejoice to see an enumeration more perfect in any or in all of those respects." [18] Nevertheless, and greatly daring, he proceeded to give his enumeration, and set forth the following rational presumptions: (1) the existence of everything of which I am conscious (i.e. of pleasures, pains, etc. introspectively evidenced); (2) the principle that *my* thoughts, etc., belong to *my* Ego; (3) the testimony of distinct memory; (4) our own personal identity as evidenced by memory; (5) the doctrine "that those things do really exist which we distinctly perceive by our senses, and are what we perceive them to be;" (6) the principle that we have some degree of power over our actions; (7) the truth "that the natural faculties, by which we distinguish truth from error, are not fallacious" (i.e. are not fallacious inveterately or in principle); (8) the existence of life and intelligence in other men; (9) the possibility of inference to other minds from gestures, etc.; (10) some degree of reliability in human testimony; (11)

---

[16] *Intellectual Powers*, Hamilton's Edition, p. 434.
[17] *Ibid.*, p. 435.   [18] *Ibid.*, p. 441.

some justifiable reliance upon the actions of our fellow-men in society; (12) the doctrine "that, in the phenomena of nature, what is to be, will probably be like to what has been in similar circumstances." [19]

On the whole, a classification of this kind could not be expected to withstand the charges of redundancy and of deficiency that, as Reid anticipated, could be brought against it. In a sense, for example, Reid's seventh principle included all the others, and, apart from that, his other eleven principles are not independent. Judged from this standpoint, the modern procedure of the *Gestalt* psychologists is simpler in its principle and should also be much less pretentious. If we endeavor, as these psychologists attempt, to present broad patterns or schemata of our integrated thought-processes, paying special attention to their character at the level of reflection, and noting their interrelations and logical subordinations, together with any peculiarities in their special type or special application, we may reasonably hope to avoid many of Reid's difficulties. On the other hand, there is necessarily a certain vagueness in this tracing of involved and interrelated patterns, and also, at the psychological level of discussion, a certain blurring of the essential distinction between what is logically justified in the patterns and what need not be regarded as more than an inveterate human interpretation of the pattern. For this reason, it is important to consider some expressly philosophical theories of this general type, and I shall select the views of Mr. Stout for particular discussion.

Examining the relatively special, but highly important, instance of the rational interpretation to be put upon the testimony of the senses, Mr. Stout maintains that "what is primary in our knowledge of physical objects through sense-experiences is not merely "direct apprehension" of sensa but also direct knowledge that these sensa are connected with existence beyond themselves." [20] The original reference is to the whole source indiscriminately." [21] In the light of this governing principle he attempts to examine "the general head of what Hume would

[19] *Ibid.*, pp. 441 *sqq.*
[20] *Proceedings of the Aristotelian Society*, 1913-1914, p. 382.
[21] *Ibid.*, p. 383.

call knowledge of matter of fact which anticipates experience, and what Kant would call knowledge of synthetic propositions *a priori*." [22] A mere appeal to the constitution of the human mind, he concedes, settles nothing. On the other hand, "no more ultimate reason can be given for the possibility of anything being known than that it has being and that a mind is there to know it." [23]

In accordance with the principle we have already discussed in Chapter III, § 6, Mr. Stout infers from the last of these statements that, since knowledge is in principle unlimited, "we must take account also of the fundamental principle of empirical philosophy, the principle that knowledge is throughout limited by experience." [24] And in this general way, he asserts, we may reasonably expect to solve, or at least to obtain clear light upon, the problem how our partial and momentary sense-data nevertheless carry us, with high probability, if not with complete certainty, to the apprehension of a physical world with definite and pervasive physical features. Here the fundamental point is that "the original unreflective act of referring an existentially present sensum to a correlated existence beyond it, is itself the immediate knowledge of the sensible as incomplete." [25] "The primitive mind, we suppose, directly apprehends a primary sensum and in so doing refers it to a source. But there are no motives or conditions which could lead it to make any distinction or reservation in this reference to a source. In particular, there is nothing which could lead it to single out one part of the source from others and refer distinctively to this. The reference will be to the source in general. But in ordinary perception the reference is only to part of the source; it is limited to this by the way in which different sensa are correlated with each other as having a common source." [26]

In general, therefore, according to Mr. Stout, we are entitled to put the matter thus: Experience is always *special* experience, and limits the undiscriminating reference to a single "source" (i.e. to all reality) that is all that "knowledge" could be apart

[22] *Proceedings of the Aristotelian Society*, 1913-1914, p. 389.
[23] *Ibid.*   [24] *Ibid.*, p. 390.   [25] *Ibid.*   [26] *Ibid.*, p. 395.

from special experience. Special experience, however, is always subject to the general implications of this "reference to a source" and, since all experience is "rational" in the sense of being amenable to critical interpretation, the problem is to discriminate progressively, within the "source," between what, on the basis of special experience, have rationally to be regarded as its distinctive pervasive features, and its highly special and particularized details as presented, say, in some given sensum. The whole process is an instance of the critical articulation of a pattern through logical reflection upon the restrictions indicated by "experience." And it is suggested that the categorial properties of existence, such as a definite spatial or temporal order, thinghood, causality, and the like, may thus become articulate through a rational process of discrimination.

In its principle, this metaphysical theory is capable of assimilating both psychological and physical schemata, or patterns, with at least a plausible show of rationality, and it is not subject to the whole brunt of the objections which, as we shall see in the next chapter, appear to be fatal to extreme "empiricism" of the traditional type. On the other hand, there seem to be grave doubts concerning the cogency of its logic. The "source" is so very general, and "experience," for the most part, is so very narrow. If, a priori, an infinity of patterns is possible, why should the restriction of our experience to a few narrow and highly specialized patterns give us any great confidence in concluding that these patterns and no others pervade the whole of existence? Mr. Stout would presumably say, "Produce, if you please, some good reason why they should not. If you can not produce such a reason, you are entitled to presume that they are strictly categorial. For at least you have a categorial reference to the "source," firstly, lastly, and all the time." These same arguments would apply, however, to the experience of cats or of fish, if cats or fish could reflect upon the way in which the "source" was limited by *their* experience; and, if our human categories were not better evidenced than such feline or piscine categories, we might not have very satisfactory evidence of the rationality of our presumptions concerning the world-order.

§ 6. Concerning Kant

Kant's philosophy, at any rate according to some of his accounts of it, is very definitely a philosophy of preconnections, although these preconnections, on the one hand, are, in his view, not mere presumptions (since they may entail complete certainty), and although, on the other hand, they are decidedly anthropomorphic (since they govern *human* phenomena, and these only). Indeed, all the four groups of fundamental principle which, according to Kant, are implied in our understanding of natural science are preconnections of a definite type. These four groups are: the axioms of intuition, the anticipations of perception, the analogies of experience, and the postulates of empirical thought.

For Kant, space and time, regarded as the objects of pure mathematics, are forms of intuition, axiomatic in their evidence. and are sometimes said to be temporally as well as logically prior to any act of perception. Spaceless and timeless sensa, Kant seems to have held, are in one sense given to us through the influence of (unknown) physical things, but these mental sensory effects are caught up into vast mental receptacles, or preconnective *cadres;* and these receptacles are the forms of space and time. The phrase "anticipations of perception," again, is quite literally a doctrine of preconnections. It is an assurance *a priori* that sensa differ in degree, and that space must be filled in a quantitative fashion. The analogies of experience, once again, are *a priori* connections in terms of which the logical conceptions of subject, and of ground and consequent, are applied to scientific experience and yield the scientific conceptions of substance and of cause.

According to Kant, we are dealing in all scientific experience with what is "empirically real" but "transcendentally ideal." In other words, the properties that we discover by scientific thought are not properties of things in themselves, and are thus metaphysically or transcendentally ideal, being thought-constructed. They are also said, however, to be necessary properties of all human phenomena scientifically ascertained, that is to say, properties of natural stimuli as assimilated by human faculty, and therefore to be empirically real, i.e. to be in no sense illusory.

Human faculty, Kant further maintains, in so far as it deals with (phenomenal) nature evinces the conjoint operation of passive sense and of active or spontaneous understanding. The business of sense is to intuit, and the business of the understanding is to think. Thinking, when employed about physical nature, is an activity that transforms passive sense by active construction and interpretation. Without the passive element, it would be endeavoring to make bricks without either straw or clay. On the other hand, clayey sense could never spontaneously become the manufactured article which is natural science.

In the result (at any rate in one of its aspects, and in the aspect upon which Kant usually laid most stress), we are presented with a certain theory of scientific construction and integration. Ultimately, Kant held, the controlling preconnection is the unity of self-consciousness itself, and this is interpreted not personally or individually, but as *Bewusstsein überhaupt* or as consciousness in general. In short, we *must* think in certain determinate ways, and these determinate ways are what logical thought fashions out of sensory stimulation. According to Kant, no question should arise whether such integration corresponds to, or is like, non-phenomenal nature. The only relevant question is whether these scientific constructions are internally coherent and at the same time are the necessary results of a logical or rational *modus operandi*.

This aspect of Kantianism (and, initially at least, it is the dominant aspect of the discussion in the *Critique of Pure Reason*) is, we may say, quite precisely opposed to Mr. Stout's contention. Instead of natural knowledge dealing from the outset and all the time with a "source" other than itself and progressively discovering the articulations within this "source," as on Mr. Stout's view, natural knowledge, according to Kant, elaborates crude and passive mental sensation. Kant asserts, indeed, that such sensations are the result of the action of extra-mental things upon our mental senses; but, on his own principles, he has no right to assume this or even to conjecture it. For, he says, it is nonsense to ask whether our mentally constructed scientific world corresponds in whole or in part to any extra-mental world that is transcendentally, not merely empirically, real.[27] The question for science is always one of subtle and elaborate domestic unity. From the nature of the case it can not be concerned with anything out of doors. And therefore, if Kant had been consistent, there would never be a suggestion in his pages of Mr. Stout's "source" so far as natural knowledge is concerned. (As we saw in Chapter II, the question, for Kant, of our intellectual habitation in a realm of pure reason is quite another story.)

Setting this aspect of the affair aside for the moment, however, let us consider the nature of Kantian preconnections in a general way.

The ultimate status of the forms of space and time in Kant's philosophy seems particularly puzzling. On the one hand, they are said to be forms of sensibility, i.e. of man's sensory consti-tution, and are therefore human or animal or at any rate not Godlike or applicable to things in themselves. On the other hand, they are said to be "pure," i.e. inevitably such as to yield the ideal certainty that Kant (like his contemporaries) assigned to geometry. Since it may be easily shown that neither sight-space nor touch-space nor any other spatial expanse that is directly sensed in the normal way by human percipients has the purity of this geometrical form, the natural conclusion, if not, as many think, the inevitable conclusion, is that geometrical space is distinct from anything we see or touch and is either inferred from, or suggested by, sensory perception. If so, it would appear that there is no psychological stage at which the understanding can truly be said to construct the objects of pure geometry.

Kant's "anticipations of perception," again, appear to yield, in a condensed form that is not over-clear, two sets of precon-nections, viz. (1) a doctrine of the filling of space and time, and (2) a doctrine of continuity.

The axioms of intuition inform us (he holds) that every nat-ural fact must be perceived both as spatial and as temporal. Merely empty space and time, however, would contain nothing real. Therefore we may anticipate that anything perceptible is

[27] E.g. *Prolegomena,* Conclusion of Remark, II, § 13.

filled space or time, not empty space or time. It is not clear, however, what precisely is thus to be anticipated. For example, it is commonly held that the sensation of blackness or darkness is due to the absence of any physical optical stimulus. Black is therefore an illusory physical quality, giving the appearance of a spatial filling that is not a scientific fact. Does Kant's principle, then, tell us *both* that space always *looks* filled, and that it (scientifically considered) always *is* filled?

In the former case, there would always be perceptible continuity in sensible nature, although such continuity might sometimes be an inevitable illusion. In the latter case, there would necessarily be continuity in a "filling" that is not merely spatial or temporal. Accepting the former, however, must we also accept the latter, and hold that it would be a plain logical absurdity to suppose that any space or time was unfilled even in its minutest part?

It seems sufficient to remark that many physicists deny that there is any absurdity in the supposition, and that, in any case, Kant's argument is a flagrant begging of the question. For if space and time are real, empty space and time, although empty, would nevertheless be real.

The analogies of experience are by universal admission the crux of Kant's doctrine of the necessary logical preconnections in any tenable theory of natural knowledge. Let us consider, therefore, whether Kant's view of the chief of them (i.e. of substance and cause) is undeniable or even tenable.

It is generally agreed that Kant's deduction of phenomenal substance is thoroughly unsatisfactory. As Mr. Kemp Smith remarks, "Kant offers no sufficient deduction or explanation of the category of substance and attribute, and . . . is unable to account for its use in experience, or at least to reconcile it in any adequate fashion with the principle of causality." [28] These hard words may readily be justified in detail, and therefore we have to ask, not whether Kant's explanation of (phenomenal) substance should be accepted *au pied de la lettre,* but whether his arguments prove anything at all regarding the principle of substance.

[28] *A Commentary on Kant's Critique of Pure Reason* (First Edition), p. 363.

In general, the nerve of Kant's argument has to do with change. Our representations change, he argues, but scientific experience can not be regarded as a mere psychological procession of vanishing successive sensa. On the contrary, they have their place in an *order* of time, and are so apprehended. Change, as we experience it, is change *in* time, not simply change *of* private psychological tempo.

From this it may be stringently inferred that our apprehension of time implies, implicitly or explicitly, a reference to an orderly and objective time series; and it is good scientific argument, although it is not unchallengeable metaphysics, to infer further that the objective time-order must be expressed and understood in terms of the regular motions of physical bodies, e.g. in the approximate regularities of the seasons or of an hourglass, and in the more precise regularities of sidereal or instrumental clock-time. Kant, however, appears to give the fantastic explanation that the objective time-order must be a *permanent* (i.e. unchanging) phenomenon having unalterable properties at every time, and further to identify this unchanging phenomenon with a fixed numerical quantum of "substance" perpetually occupying space. It is not surprising, therefore, that he failed to reconcile the unchanging with the changing. His argument ought to prove a fixed and determinate *order* in what changes. Instead, he gave a parody of his argument by interpreting this fixed order as somehow a permanent and unalterable substance.

Granting that a substance is a continuant (i.e. something that endures continuously in time), it is impossible to account for change as the consequence of the unchanging; and change is left inexplicable if it is regarded as something supervening upon, and quite distinct from, the unchanging. The principle of Kant's analogies, we must therefore say, in opposition to Kant, is that the solution should be sought, not in the impossible notion of unchanging existence somehow blending with changing existence, but in a fixed intelligible order of changeable existence. This, it would seem, is Kant's principle of causality, which should not therefore be distinguished from his principle of substance. As Mr. Kemp Smith says, "To be conscious of change we must be conscious of an *event*, that is, of something as happening at a particular point in time. The change, in other words, requires to be dated, and as we are not conscious of time in general, it must be dated by reference to other events, in contrast to which it is apprehended as *change*. But according to the results of what constitutes objective experience, it can be fixed in its position in objective time only if it be conceived as related to the preceding events according to a necessary law; and the law of necessary connection in time is the law of causality." [29]

This argument, I think, obviously deserves great respect. It is possible, indeed, that there might *be* an objective time-series although our sensory and other experiences, like those of a man in delirium, were chaotic and whirling. In that case, however, it is not apparent how we could either know or conjecture that there was an objective time-series, and, since we do conjecture this when we are not delirious, it seems plain that, having no separate experience of "empty" time (if there is such a thing), we must draw our conclusions concerning time from a basis of relatively well-attested regularities in our experience. On the other hand, it would also appear that approximate regularities might suffice to give us our cue in this matter, and hence that absolute necessity need not be presumed in order to make our experience even colorably what it is. To be sure, if scientific physics implies this demonstrable necessity, demonstrable necessity there must be—or else, farewell to scientific physics. But modern theories of physics do not make this assumption, and I can see no convincing metaphysical reason why they should be held to be wrong in refusing to make it.

In so far as "cause" and "substance" go together, it may similarly be argued that continuants having an appreciable degree of endurance are all that is required to supply a tangible basis of regularity in our experience. The existence of everlasting and indestructible substances can not be proved in this way.

§ 7. FURTHER ON THIS TOPIC

Much of Kant's philosophy of Nature may be summed up in the statement that the Newtonian world-scheme may be demonstrated, with certainty, in its outlines, provided that we remem-

* *Op. cit.*, p. 369.

ber always that we are dealing with a rational or scientific integration of our own experience, and not with an extra-mental reality. Thus, space and time are *mental* forms or receptacles, not extramental *receptacula*, and they permit of free construction having the characteristics of pure geometry. Our sensible representations, according to this doctrine, may be *supplied* from without, but it is their impact within us that is *given*, and our logical interpretation of them is an inner and mental construction, although, being a construction according to the *common* principles of reason, it is not a private and individual affair. Intellectual anticipation is, so to say, coanticipation.

Kant's preoccupation with *scientific* experience (and particularly with mathematics and physics) led him to pay too little attention to other sciences, and also to unscientific experience. Those "other sciences" he evidently regarded as pseudo-sciences, although, as we have seen in Chapter II, he was prepared to make certain grudging admissions regarding teleology in biology and elsewhere. Kant also seems frequently to be prepared to concede that *unscientific* experience might be what Hume said all experience was, an affair of association and habit.

It is natural, therefore, that subsequent investigators who to some extent shared Kant's views should have endeavored to extend the scope of Kant's use of the term "science," even at the cost of depriving "science" of some of its mathematical and ostensibly demonstrable character. M. Bergson, for example, is a notable exponent of this broader, and at the same time vaguer, point of view. What is still more fundamental, from the epistemological standpoint, however, is the contention that there could be *no* experience at all without those principles of intelligent anticipation that are the basis of Kant's doctrine of science. If our unscientific experience could not advance a step without these preconnections ("science" being but a refinement and elaboration of them), Kant's position, in its essentials, would be enormously firmer than, in most of his expositions of it, it appears to be. For, in that case, even the simplest recognitions and statements of fact on which Hume and others relied would themselves be permeated by, and be unintelligible without, those governing preconnections that, at another level, manifest themselves at the foundations of physics.

It seems essential, therefore, to consider whether it is possible to give a freer and less dogmatic statement of such preconnections than Kant did. This attempt is the more likely to be successful if the magical potency that Kant ascribed to the office of "reason" in its scientific use is discarded, and if the mentalism (whether private or embracing all humanity) of his point of view is also discarded.

These explanations being premised we seem to have:

(1). Preconnections of continuity.

What is here presupposed is the extensive continuity of space-time. The actual infinity of space, or of time, or of space-time need not, however, be implied in this preconnection. Space might be finite, as in Riemann's theory; and Lamarck may have exaggerated the truth when he said that "for Nature time is nothing. It is never a difficulty, she always has it at her disposal."[30] On the other hand, there is always enough time or space or space-time for science and for common life to draw upon— enough and something to spare. They are never defeated by a paucity of time or space, and they argue in terms of this preconnection.

The preconnection holds either on the absolutist view of time and space or on the relativist view of these (including the "theory of relativity," according to which "time" and "space" are necessarily interrelative in "space-time"). Even on the absolutist view, however, continuity in the "filling" of space and time is not precisely upon the same footing as the continuity of space and time. Action at a distance in space, or (mnemic) action at a distance in time,[31] should not be regarded as totally and necessarily excluded by the preconnection. On the other hand, the legitimacy of demanding a continuous history in any of the processes of nature is something we are very loth to abandon.

It should further be noted that "continuity in space and time or in space-time" is an abbreviated statement of what, in the

---

[30] As quoted by Teggart, *Theory of History*, p. 131.
[31] As in Mr. Russell's *Analysis of Mind*, p. 209 and *passim*.

long, may be much more complicated. For there may be several, perhaps an indefinitely large number of, relatively independent time-systems or space-systems. If so, however, this preconnection implies that such times and spaces are correlated according to some intelligible principle. The formula of such correlation need not itself be space, or time, or space-time. It may be only a formula. But it does express a correlation.

(2). Preconnections of stability.

This is the traditional doctrine of "substance"; and contemporary opinion regarding "substance" is so very fluid and so much at cross-purposes that a certain arbitrariness must attach to any specific interpretation of the preconnection. Without excessive dogmatism, however, it seems possible to say (a) that the logical distinction between that which has attributes and its attributes seems, in some form, unavoidable; and (b) that although it is a long step from this logical distinction to "substances" which are the permanent bearers of characteristic attributes, and a longer and probably unjustifiable step to *indestructible* substances, there is nevertheless an important empirical, and also an important theoretical, meaning to be attached to continuants sustaining themselves with characteristic individuality for a prolonged period, and, similarly, to the self-maintenance of the whole of Nature. Further, the transeunt action of continuants upon other continuants in what Mr. Stout calls the "executive order of the world" is a preconnection that in some form or other seems very hard, if not impossible, to abandon.

This preconnection includes the identification of continuants. If we could not single *out* some of these continuants and follow their individual histories and interactions with other continuants, we could not apply the preconnection either empirically or more scientifically.

An allied question that we shall encounter in the next chapter is that of "natural kinds," that is to say, of the striking fact that most natural continuants may be classified into stable analogous *sets* of individuals, as the chemical elements, or as cabbages, and mice, and men.

(3). Preconnections of natural regularity.

This is the preconnection that nature shows recurrent or persistent regularities, and so that we can argue (say with the frequentists in the theory of probability) that we are entitled to infer from a past regularity (particularly in large aggregates) to a similar future regularity, unless we have reason to suspect that conditions have altered, in which case we argue to another regularity expressive of the changed conditions.

This is the preconnection at the basis of the induction of causal uniformities, and falls for consideration in the next chapter. It should be noted that "uniformity" and "causation" need not be identical notions. For if "cause" meant "agency," as it frequently does in popular explanations, it would be quite conceivable that some or many natural agencies should be capricious and not uniform.

(4). Preconnections of system.

Here it may be sufficient to cite Roger Bacon's aphorism once again. "A particular nature is obedient naturally and not by violence to universal nature."

In other words, all existence is somehow one, and our knowledge of it proceeds according to the preconnection of a systematic totality. The sense, if any, in which this preconnection implies any of the major historical monistic philosophies is quite another question. Indeed, the great majority, if not all, of the attempts to determine the specific fashion in which the "many" are united in the "one" may be gravely and greatly suspect. And this remark extends, retroactively, to pluralisms as well as to monisms. On the other hand, the vague but inspiring admonition to seek for a unity that must somehow be present in and pervade the universe seems to be more than a dream, whether or not it is an attainable goal.

Chapter XIX

INDUCTION IN RELATION TO BELIEF AND PROBABILITY

§ 1. Philosophical Empiricism and Induction

Kant's entire doctrine of natural knowledge (i.e. of the science of nature) is in one of its aspects a sustained polemic against what is usually called Empiricism.

Empiricism, in its essentials, denies the necessity for preconnections in natural knowledge and in natural conjecture. Instead, it maintains that there can be neither knowledge nor belief unless such knowledge or belief is either sensory observation (including the observation of the results of controlled experiments) or derived from the same. This derivation may either, as in Hume's theory, be utterly animal and non-logical, that is to say, it may evince nothing except custom, habit, and association, or it may be held to be a logically legitimate inference of the type commonly known as inductive. In either case, no preconnections are officially supposed to be required or desired. Observation with consequent association, in the one case, and inductive generalization, in the other case, are held by empiricists to be sufficient to explain, or to justify, all that is explicable, or justifiable, in this important affair.

Induction, to be sure, might conceivably be demonstrative. If we knew in advance that our instances were absolutely typical of some general property, we might proceed to generalize these typical properties in the typical instances, and this procedure, being a process that, in a sense, starts from particular instances, might technically be called induction, and would be logically legitimate precisely to the extent to which the instances were known to be typical. This, as I understand Mr. Johnson, is the process he calls "intuitive induction";[1] and although I can not

[1] *Logic,* Part II, Ch. VIII. (*Cf.* further Chs. IX, X, and XI.)

personally assent to all that Mr. Johnson says on this subject, I have no wish to deny that there is such intuitive induction. "Mathematical induction," again, in which, say, a property belonging to some given member of a series is shown to belong to the nth and $n + 1$th member of the series, i.e. to *any* member of the series, is held to be demonstrative proof. And I have no desire to deny that it is.

What is meant, according to the theory of empiricism, however, is not these species of induction, but induction of the type commonly known as "problematical" and in which there is said to be no question of antecedent (preconnected) knowledge of what is typical, but the simple observation of brute and, for all we know at the beginning, isolated facts. There is also (empiricists hold) no question of including the rigorous requirements of mathematical induction.

The classical example of this Empirical Logic is, of course, J. S. Mill's; and, although empiricists may avoid or palliate many of Mill's special difficulties, they have all to answer the same general objections as Mill's theory has to answer. It is therefore important to consider Mill's particular theory of empiricism at the outset of this discussion.

Mill's *System of Logic,* indeed, is even more empirical than Hume's *Treatise;* for Mill maintained that all geometrical and other "axioms" (including much of the exiguous territory that Hume was prepared to admit as "knowledge" and not as "probability") are ultimately established by problematical induction. Speaking, for example, of the "axiom" that two straight lines can not enclose a space, Mill says, "Experimental proof crowds in upon us in such endless profusion, and without one instance in which there can be even a suspicion of an exception to the rule, that we should soon have stronger ground for believing the axiom, even as an experimental truth, than we have for almost any of the general truths which we confessedly learn from the evidence of our senses. Independently of *a priori* evidence we should certainly believe it with an intensity of conviction far greater than we accord to any ordinary physical truth. ... Where then is the necessity for assuming that our recognition of these truths has a different origin from the rest of our knowledge when its existence is perfectly accounted for by supposing its origin to be the same?"[2] Similarly, he informs us that the fundamental truths of arithmetic all rest on the evidence of sense[3]—a proposition that Hume himself did not maintain—and any one who looks for a superior and quite special brand of *certainty* was advised by Mill "to study the general laws of association." For Mill was "convinced that nothing more is requisite than a moderate familiarity with those laws to dispel the illusion which ascribes a peculiar necessity to our earliest inductions from experience, and measures the possibilities of things in themselves by the human capacity of conceiving them."[4]

§ 2. MILL'S ACCOUNT OF THE PRINCIPLE OF PARALLEL CASES

Mill's doctrine is that causes can be proved to be operative by one or other of the Experimental Methods of induction—Agreement, Difference, Concomitant Variations, and Residues—or by some combination of these, although in the present state of our knowledge we have sometimes to rely (with much less confidence) upon the guesswork of hypotheses or upon some other less satisfactory and more indirect procedure. Causes, he holds, are uniformities of sequence, and the essence of experiment is to discover the operative causes by elimination of the irrelevant conditions. (Mill admits that a philosophy of Nature has to take account of uniformities of coexistence as well as of uniformities of sequence, but he spends most of his labor upon causes.)

When we ask how causes, or uniformities of sequence, can be proved, he informs us that the proof is dependent upon the Uniformity of Nature, or, more particularly, upon the Law of Universal Causation, that is to say, upon the governing principle that every event in Nature is an instance of some regularity of sequence. (The problem of experiment, therefore, is to single out the appropriate uniformity of sequence in a particular case or class of cases.) Mill denies, however, that this governing principle is ultimately a preconnection; for he says that it can itself be proved by induction of a special sort.

When he examines the ground of induction, Mill asserts: "We

[2] *System of Logic,* Book II, Ch. v, § 4.   [4] *Ibid.,* Book II, Ch. v, § 6.
[3] *Ibid.,* Book II, Ch. vi, § 2.

must first observe that there is a principle implied in the very statement of what induction is; an assumption with regard to the course of nature and the order of the universe; namely, that there are such things in nature as parallel cases; that what happens once will, under a sufficient degree of similarity of circumstances, happen again, and not only again, but as often as the same circumstances occur. This, I say, is an assumption involved in every case of induction. And if we consult the actual course of nature, we find that the assumption is warranted. The universe, so far as known to us, is so constituted, that whatever is true in any one case, is true in all cases of a certain description; the only difficulty is, to find what description." [5]

Oddly enough, this statement regarding the existence of parallel cases is, verbally at least, very similar indeed to the foundations of a view of induction widely different from Mill's. According to Mr. J. M. Keynes, for example, "Hume rightly maintains that some degree of resemblance must always exist between the various instances upon which a generalisation is based. For they must have this, at least, in common, that they are instances of the proposition which generalises them. Some element of analogy must, therefore, lie at the base of every inductive argument." [6] Mill says the same thing. "Induction," he informs us, "properly so called . . . may be summarily defined as Generalisation from Experience. It consists in inferring from some individual instances in which a phenomenon is observed to occur, that it occurs in all instances of a certain class; namely, in all which *resemble* the former in what are regarded as the material circumstances." [7]

Yet Mill and Mr. Keynes put widely different interpretations upon this principle of analogy or of parallel cases.

Broadly speaking, the difference between them is that Mill, having spoken in general of parallel cases, proceeds very promptly to interpret this parallelism in a peculiarly narrow sense and that Mr. Keynes does not. This parallelism, Mill seemed to think, is solely an affair of causal uniformities of the type "Every dose of five grains of strychnine is a lethal dose,"

[5] *Ibid.*, Book III, Ch. iii, § 1.   [7] Mill, *loc. cit.*
[6] *A Treatise on Probability*, p. 222.

and in so far as he argued on these lines he ruthlessly disregarded the broader aspects of pattern, analogy, system, and interconnection in Nature. "Between the phenomena . . . which exist at any instant," he says, "and the phenomena which exist at the succeeding instant, there is an invariable order of succession; and, as we said in speaking of the general uniformity of the course of nature, this web is composed of separate fibres; this collective order is made up of particular sequences, obtaining invariably among the separate parts." [8] It is true that Mill was prepared to admit that there *might* be other applications of the principle of parallel cases. He held, however, that very few of the other applications "have any, even apparent, pretension to rigorous indefeasibility," and that the Law of Universal Causation was "of these few the only one capable of completely sustaining it." [9] He therefore neglected the others, with the solitary exception of "Uniformities of Coexistence not dependent on Causation," to which he devoted a solitary chapter.

§ 3. MILL'S PROOF OF THE LAW OF UNIVERSAL CAUSATION

Firstly, then, let us consider Mill's attempt to prove the governing principle of experimental induction by (another type of) induction "with rigorous indefeasibility."

To begin with, it is to be observed that Mill, by his own confession, does *not* prove it. "I am convinced," he says, "that any one accustomed to abstraction and analysis, who will fairly exert his faculties for the purpose, will, when his imagination has once learnt to entertain the notion, find no difficulty in conceiving that in some one, for instance, of the many firmaments into which sidereal astronomy now divides the universe, events may succeed one another at random without any fixed law; nor can anything in our experience or in our mental nature, constitute a sufficient, or indeed any, reason for believing that this is nowhere the case." [10]

In short, the rigorous indefeasibility of Mill's proof is supposed (by himself) to be limited to terrestrial events and to their astronomical neighborhood. Indeed, it is not clear what Mill

[8] Mill, *op. cit.* Book III, Ch. v, § 2.   [10] *Ibid.*, Book III, Ch. xxi, § 1.
[9] *Ibid.*, § 1.

would say regarding the whole of this astronomical neighborhood. According to a distinguished modern astronomer, for instance, "The type of conjecture which presents itself, somewhat insistently, is that the centres of the nebulae are of the nature of 'singular points,' at which matter is poured into our universe from some other, and entirely extraneous, spatial dimension, so that, to a denizen of our universe, they appear as points at which matter is being continuously created." [11] How could Mill's "proof" deny such speculative (or empirical?) possibilities?

Did Mill, however, prove the principle for "our" universe, whatever "our" may mean? In other words, did he prove it "within the range of our means of sure observation," [12] as he professed to do?

His argument is as follows. *Inductio per enumerationem simplicem*, where there are no negative instances, is a "valid" process, although it is fallible, and its precariousness is "in an inverse ratio to the largeness of the generalization. The process is delusive and insufficient, exactly in proportion as the subject-matter of the observation is special and limited in extent. As the sphere widens, this unscientific method becomes less and less liable to mislead; and the most universal class of truths, the law of causation for instance, and the principles of number and geometry, are duly and satisfactorily proved by that method alone, nor are they susceptible of any other proof. . . . If we suppose, then, the subject-matter of any generalization to be so widely diffused that there is no time, no place, and no combination of circumstances, but must afford an example either of its truth or of its falsity, and if it be never found otherwise than true, its truth cannot be contingent on any collocations, unless such as exist at all times and places; nor can it be frustrated by any counteracting agencies, unless by such as never actually occur. It is, therefore, an empirical law co-extensive with all human experience, at which point the distinction between empirical laws and laws of nature vanishes, and the proposition takes its place among the most firmly established as well as largest truths accessible to science." [13]

[11] Sir J. H. Jeans, *Astronomy and Cosmogony*, p. 352.
[12] Mill, *loc. cit.*, § 4.   [13] *Ibid.*, § 3.

Even so, however, the proof is not "indefeasible." "In matters of evidence, as in all other human things," Mill says, "we neither require, nor can attain, the absolute."[14] All we are entitled to say is that "whatever has been found true in innumerable instances and never found to be false after due examination in any, we are safe in acting on as universal provisionally, until an undoubted exception appears; provided the nature of the case be such that a real exception could scarcely have escaped notice."[15]

It is one thing, however, to say that every observed fact, up to the present moment, has clearly been an instance of some uniformity of sequence, and quite another thing to make the much more moderate assertion that, "after due examination," no observed historical fact has been conclusively shown to be an exception to the law of universal causation. The latter and more moderate claim is the only claim that Mill, "after due reflection," finds himself able to make, and plainly it is the only claim he is entitled to make. There can be no doubt whatsoever that, while much in our experience suggests regularity of sequence, much suggests irregularity also. Unsupported apples fall regularly to the ground; but some sparks fly upwards. The seasons come and go in a stately, inevitable succession, but the wind (even now) appears to blow whither it lists. The *prima facie* evidence is therefore conflicting; and even if our reflective reëxaminations of the evidence tends markedly to support the hypothesis of universal regularity, and progressively to diminish the region of apparently obvious irregularity, it is a daring leap, and not a sober advance, to claim that we know of *necessary* regularity in any single instance, that it is absurd to suppose that some aggregate regularities are compounded of, or permit of, individual irregularities, or even that we know for certain that, in the past at least, there has been no goodish evidence whatsoever for the belief in natural irregularities at any time or place.

In short, Mill does not seem to have noticed how much he had to prove. What he had to prove, on the basis of past experience, was that all the past sequences in nature have been regular se-

[14] Mill, *loc. cit.*, § 4.   [15] *Ibid.*

quences, not merely in the large, but in the minutest detail. What he shows, at the most, is that, in the past and in the neighborhood of the observer, instances that have been carefully examined are compatible with the hypothesis of universal regularities of sequence, and show, over a very wide range, an approximate regularity of sequence.

Even so, he was not entitled to claim the unanimous testimony of all past experience in his favor. He was only entitled to claim the plausibility, or general reasonableness, of a modern positivistic interpretation of recorded facts that had been widely differently interpreted, very often, by the eye-witnesses of former times. If the sun had really stood still during Joshua's campaign, the regularities of astronomy would have to be modified in a way not contemplated by positivistic science. Therefore, the positivists have to deny the evidence of miracles of this type. I do not say that such denials weaken their theory, but I have to point out that any one who argues on Mill's lines has to "cook" the evidence of historical testimony concerning fact as well as the primitive interpretation of such evidence, and that he is bound to confess, if he is challenged, that a smallish quantity of modern scientific evidence is not only incomparably better evidence than cartloads of ancient records, but is sufficient to justify us in neglecting all recorded evidence (doubtless of a vaguer kind) that is clearly inconsistent with it. If this is so, the evidence on which Mill relies is not universal experience at all, and is not coextensive with the testimony of history and common sense. On the contrary, it is the testimony of a small selection of recently examined facts whose examination has been conducted on scientific principles. The rest of our evidence is said to support the positivistic explanation based upon this smallish but well-attested range of evidence, and is quietly ignored if it does not support it.

According to Mill himself, early observers "never thought of assuming that this uniformity was a principle pervading all nature; their generalizations did not imply that there was uniformity in everything, but only that as much uniformity as existed within their observation, existed also beyond it. The induction *Fire burns* does not require for its validity that all nature should observe uniform laws, but only that there should be uniformity in one particular class of natural phenomena: the effects of fire on the senses and on combustible substances. And uniformity to this extent was not assumed, anterior to the experience, but proved by the experience. The same observed instances which proved the narrower truth, proved as much of the wider one as corresponded to it." [16]

The design of these very just reflections of Mill's was to obliterate the myth that causation, in the sense of necessary uniformity in the sequence of events, was an *a priori* preconnection inevitably held and followed by humanity at every time and place. The justice and pertinence of his reflection, however, should have made Mill himself pause. For in what respect can Mill claim that the logic of the evidence for *uniformity* in nature is different, in any respect, from the logic he here attributes to "early observers"? We have evidence, to be sure, for uniformity in a great many "particular classes of phenomena" that early observers could not be expected to regard in the same light as the convincing uniformities they knew of, such as that Fire burns, and that Water drowns; and it is much more reasonable for us to assume that every sequence in nature is uniform, despite the surface objections of a good deal in our experience, than it would have been for them. In both cases, however, we are outrunning the evidence when we assume universal uniformity of sequence in nature. We should outrun it in any case, when we passed from the uniform effect of fire upon combustible substances in the narrow domain of the recorded past to its similar action in the future and in the unrecorded past; or when we inferred that a prevalent and uncontradicted uniformity must be held to be a *necessary* uniformity. But we outrun it in the most significant way when we generalize from attested uniformities of a particular class to necessary uniformity in every class. In a way, what Mill *means* by induction is a species of outrunning the evidence. For him, induction *is* generalization, presumably by the association of similars; but he also admits that logical generalization is the control of this general propensity by the relevant evidence. And this control, I

[16] Mill, Book III, Ch. xxi, § 2, footnote.

suggest, plainly includes what Mill ascribes to the "early observers."

In another passage Mill says that "we arrive at this universal law from many laws of inferior generality. We should never have had the notion of causation (in the philosophical meaning of the term) as a condition of all phenomena, unless many cases of causation, or, in other words, many partial uniformities of sequence, had previously become familiar. The more obvious of the particular uniformities suggest, and give evidence of, the general uniformity, and the general uniformity, once established, enables us to prove the remainder of the particular uniformities of which it is made up." [17] Here the reasoning is manifestly a *petitio principii*. The particular uniformities may indeed suggest and give *some* evidence in favor of the general uniformity, but they do not *prove* it; and the "remainder" (it is a huge remainder even if it is diminishing day by day) can not surely be *proved* by the *unproved* "suggestion."

§ 4. Experimental "Proofs" Derived from the Law

We have next to ask whether, if Mill *had* established the Law of Universal Causation, his account, or any similar account, of inductive "proofs" derived from the law could be accepted as satisfactory. This type of question, it may be remarked incidentally, is very important for Mill himself. When we examine Mill's theory of our (inductive) apprehension of nature, we find that it logically requires, not only the Law of Universal Causation, but also the possibility of distinguishing "primeval" or fundamental causes from derivative ones.

Take, for example, the argument of Chapter XIX in Book III of his *Logic*. Discussing the sequence of day and night (which, in any ordinary sense, is one of the most striking examples of the uniformity of nature in our planet and in its neighborhood), Mill argues that this sequence is a uniform sequence dependent on causation, not itself an instance of primeval causality (or uniform sequence), since it is caused by the emission of light from the sun upon uniformly rotating bodies. Given the "collocation" of the sun and the planets in the solar system, we

[17] *Ibid.*, Book III, Ch. xxi, § 2.

can recognize (Mill says) the derivative character of the sequence of day and night, and can infer, *with a very high degree of probability*, that day and night will continue to succeed one another in the proportions specifically laid down in our almanacs and pocket diaries—at any rate in the near future.

At the same time, Mill also argues that these derivative inductive inferences are inferior in certainty to our definite experimental knowledge of fundamental or "primeval" causal laws. They depend upon a definite "collocation," and it is quite possible that causes may be in existence that (either gradually or suddenly) disturb the collocation. If there are, for example, slight but persistent causes altering the collocation, it is unlikely that any appreciable change will occur within the next few years or within the next few centuries; but 20,000 years hence (Mill says) there might easily be a different story. And in that case day and night would not succeed one another in the way we now expect. There is also the possibility of a new intruding cause (e.g. in an astronomical collision); but Mill does not separately discuss this possibility, being inclined to hold that the chance of such a collision is very slight.

It follows from these admissions that if we knew (1) that all events in nature are instances of *some* uniform sequence, and (2) that some particular type of sequence has been without exception uniform throughout a prolonged series of observations, we should still be unable to infer with certainty that this particular type of sequence would be uniform to all eternity. This result might even be said to be improbable, although the uniformity of the sequence in the proximate future might be very probable indeed. To prove an inevitable uniformity for all time, according to Mill's express assertions, we should have to be quite certain that we were dealing with a "primeval" and not with a derived causal sequence.

Could we, then, have any certainty, in experience or in experiment, that this crucial condition was fulfilled? According to Mill, we should have this assurance in one case, and in one case only, viz. in the case in which we had rigorously applied the Method of Difference, and had eliminated all the possible causes, save one, in some *experimentum crucis*, or "crucial experiment." But how could we ever be certain that we had eliminated all possible causes except the one "primeval" cause? What happens in any ordinary *experimentum crucis* is that, conceiving ourselves to have narrowed down the likely causes to a few alternatives, we endeavor to show the extreme improbability of some one of them. We do not pretend that we have forestalled all subsequent scientific conjectures, much less all that might be conjecturable on the part of investigators better skilled than we can hope to be. In short, our confidence is relative to certain patterns of explanation for which, in general, we think there is pretty good evidence. Assuming nature to be specified in this general way, we can proceed to eliminate certain types of conceivable sub-specification that experience, thus tutored, rejects. Greater certainty we do not look for, even when we apply the Method of Difference.

In a well-known parody of Mill's Method of Difference, a bibulous logician is said to have declared that soda-water gave him headaches every morning because it was the only common constitutent in the brandy-and-soda, whisky-and-soda, etc., with which he had experimented every night. The parody is not very effective since this logician had presumably never tried soda-water by itself, and did not recognize that brandy, whisky, and the rest contain the common constituent of alcohol. Elimination in these circumstances is not impracticable. In a more general way, however, there is point in the parody. Suppose that we apply a much more scrupulous chemistry than this bibulous logician, and eventually reach the chemical elements. Can we *then* be quite certain, or is it even probable, that these elements are not themselves composite? And if they are composite, how can we know whether some part or parts of them, on the one hand, or the whole of them taken together, on the other hand, is the effective cause in question? Again, if the relevant effect is the effect upon a complicated structure (like the effect of alcohol upon the nervous system), how can we know what the primeval sequences are and what the derivative?

Even if we could draw these inferences with certainty in cases in which we could apply the Method of Difference, we should still be left with a great deal of uncertainty concerning most of the particular uniformities in nature. For often we can not isolate the factors in question, or eliminate the irrelevant in detail. The more important point, however, is that we can not, in general, employ Mill's Method of Difference under the ideal conditions that he took to be natural and usual.

§ 5. Mill's Account of Uniformities of Coexistence

Mill's general doctrine "that there are parallel cases in nature" would be far too vague if it yielded no effective information concerning something more than uniformities of sequence. Even it we could legitimately infer from "this sample of arsenious weed-killer is poisonous" to "any sample of arsenious weed-killer is poisonous," that is to say, if we could pass without question from the behavior of some particular thing to the precisely similar behavior of any other thing of the same kind, we should still be very far from exhausting the degree of parallelism we all ascribe to nature both in the physical sciences and in common life. For the latter purpose we should need some reasonable expectation that waves of sound are parallel to waves of light; that if peonies do not suffer transplanting gladly, some other occupants of our herbaceous borders may also be affected by transplantation; and the like. It is not simply a question, as in Mill's metaphor, of the separate strands of the web of nature running true to type. It is also a question of a comparatively small number of patterns appearing in the web, and of the separate strands being governed by such patterns. Whether or not there is one great pattern pervading the whole web is a problem for monists and pluralists to wrangle over. But even our pluralists in science, or in philosophy, or in common life habitually employ the preconnection that there is an extensive set of interrelated patterns of this general type.

To a certain extent, Mill admitted this circumstance, and debated the place of uniformities of coexistence not dependent on causation. Broadly speaking, his contentions were as follows:

Many coexistences, he says, are themselves effects. They might, for instance, be joint results of the same set of causes. Thus "high water at any point on the earth's surface, and high water at the point diametrically opposite to it, are effects uniformly simultaneous, resulting from the direction in which the combined attractions of the sun and moon act upon the waters of the ocean." [18] Nevertheless, there must be ultimate properties of coexistence which can not depend upon causation. There are, in fact (according to Mill), extensive systems of these ultimate connected properties in what are commonly called Natural Kinds. In a minor and tentative way, Mill continues, we might regard the woolly hair of negroes or the yellowness of gold as ultimate, underivative uniformities of coexistence, and in these applications of the principle we might easily be wrong. The gaseous form of oxygen, for example, might readily appear to be an ultimate property of that substance. But Faraday showed that it was due, in part, to the causal operation of latent heat. Indeed, in all substances which are compound "there is considerable reason to presume that the specific properties of the compound are consequent, as effects, on some of the properties of the elements." [19] On the other hand, when we come to the chemical elements themselves, the position is wholly altered. These "elementary natural agents are the only ones, any of whose properties can with certainty be considered ultimate; and of these the ultimate properties are probably much more numerous than we at present recognise, since every successful instance of the resolution of the properties of their compounds into simpler laws generally leads to the recognition of properties in the elements distinct from any previously known." [20]

Mill goes on to say (1) that there is no general "axiom" similar to the Law of Universal Causation in these instances of Uniformity of Sequence. ("We have no previous certainty," he says, "that the property of blackness in crows must have something which constantly co-exists with it—must have an invariable co-existent in the same manner as an event must have an invariable antecedent").[21] Again, he remarks (2) that there is no room for elimination among these stubborn coexistences. Because they go together we can not force them to march separately.[22] And therefore (3) he concludes that "we are thrown

[18] *System of Logic*, Book III, Ch. xxii, § 1.
[19] *Ibid.*, § 2.   [21] *Ibid.*, § 4.
[20] *Ibid.*   [22] *Ibid.*

back upon the unscientific induction of the ancients, *per enume-rationem simplicem ubi non reperitur instantia contradictoria*. The reason we have for believing that all crows are black is simply that we have seen and heard of many black crows, and never one of any other colour."[23] We have only empirical laws and can not have experimental proofs.

Despite this, Mill also affirms that the principles of induction operate similarly in coexistence and in causal sequences. "There is a point of generality," he affirms, "at which empirical laws become as certain as laws of nature, or rather, at which there is no longer any distinction between empirical laws and laws of nature. As empirical laws approach this point, in other words, as they rise in their degree of generality, they become more certain; their universality may be more strongly relied on."[24] Furthermore, we are not limited to unique singularities in each particular natural kind. "There is a sort of parallelism in the properties of different Kinds, and their degree of unlikeness in one respect bears some proportion to their unlikeness in others. We see this parallelism in the properties of the different metals . . . in the natural orders of plants and animals, etc. But there are innumerable anomalies and exceptions to this sort of conformity; if indeed the conformity itself be anything but an anomaly and an exception in nature."[25]

§ 6. The Preconnections of Inductive Argument Concerning Nature

Mill's contention, in general, was that there are no preconnections in induction other than those that induction itself can supply. Our objections to his argument may be briefly recounted as follows.

(1). He admits that an induction is a *generalization* from observed facts and he does not seriously examine a contention like Hume's according to which there is no logical bridge from "These observed S's are P's" to "Therefore other S's are P's," and *a fortiori*, no logical bridge from "These observed S's are P's" to "All S's (observed or unobserved) must be P's." In so far as

---

[23] *System of Logic*, Book III, Ch. xxii § 4.
[24] *Ibid.*, § 8.   [25] *Ibid.*, § 9.

Mill explains the process of generalization itself by the "laws of association," his explanation, like Hume's, would seem to be psychological and even non-logical. The entire affair might be, as Hume said it was, a matter of subjective expectation. *We* might construct an associative connection in our own minds, without any sound logical reason for believing that there was any corresponding connection in nature. For the most part, however, Mill argued as if there could be no doubt that inductive generalizations are logical, and are evidenced by the objective characteristics of the facts we observe.

(2). In certain passages, Mill seems to admit that *one* preconnection is always employed in induction, viz. the "little small one" that there are parallel instances in nature. Moreover, in his account of ultimate "collocations" or uniformities of coexistence and of *their* parallelism (despite its anomalies and exceptions), he goes some little way towards admitting the existence of general patterns in nature in addition to the uniform action of separate causes. As we shall see, however, his account of this important matter is not even approximately adequate.

(3). He admits that causal inductions rest upon the "prior certainty" of the Law of Universal Causation, but argues (a) that this prior certainty is itself proved by induction, and (b) that, given the "prior certainty," particular causal laws may be inferred with certainty by the use of the experimental methods.

Neither of these contentions can be sustained. Mill's "proof" of the Law of Universal Causation is fallacious, and his experimental inferences from it are also fallacious. Even the Method of Difference does not yield certainty on Mill's assumptions; for, to mention no other reason, we cannot assume that the isolated action of some substance experimentally observed may not be allotropic.

(4). While Mill speaks, for the most part, of the *certainty* of such inductive inferences, he seems to have meant, not absolute certainty (which he regarded as an unattainable dream), but a degree of conviction partially evidenced and subjectively indistinguishable from certainty—in other words, a very high degree of probability—and to have restricted this high probability to events in the neighborhood of our planet and not very remote in time. This limitation of Mill's argument diminishes the force of some of the objections brought against the "proofs" which he sometimes described as "rigorously indefeasible." As we shall see, however, it does not suffice to save them.

On the whole, therefore, we must conclude that Mill's account of the preconnections of experimental inferences concerning nature is palpably insufficient, and that his account of their rationality is also ambiguous and insufficient. In view of this, it is scarcely surprising that his views concerning either the rational certainty or the rational probability of inferences drawn in terms of these (by him unexamined) preconnections should also be defective. We must therefore reëxamine the entire situation.

§ 7. Back to Hume

The celebrated argument by which Hume endeavored to demonstrate the non-rationality of causal inductions is in substance as follows.[26] All observed facts are in themselves loose and separate. In our observations of any sequence, therefore, we simply observe one distinct fact A followed by another distinct fact B. We observe no connecting bond between them. And from a single instance of succession (unless the instance is assimilated in advance into a presumed causal system, as in so-called crucial experiment[27] we never dream of inferring causal connection. When, however, we find B repeatedly following A, and nothing except B following it, we do infer causal connection, and we come to expect B in the unobserved future whenever we observe A in the present. Our expectation that the entire unobserved future will resemble the past, and that, although the past be unrecorded, everything that has a beginning must have had a cause, instead of being a preconnection of our expectations, is but a massive tendency engendered by our expectations of uniformity in particular instances,[28] doubtful or contradictory evidence being ignored for the time being.

Such inductive "inferences" must, in the end, be non-rational expectations. For how, Hume asks, can *repetition* have logical

---

[26] The best summary of Hume's views is to be found in his *Treatise,* Book I, Part III, Sec. xiv.

[27] *Treatise,* p. 104.   [28] See especially *Treatise,* p. 82.

cogency? In any strict logical proof (as we see in mathematics) repetition is redundancy. One instance suffices. If the repetition *altered* the observed facts, and either *produced* or *discovered* anything new in them, it might logically affect the situation. But it does not.[29] The A's and the B's that we observe in the tenth, or in the hundredth, or in the nth instance, must, *ex hypothesi*, be the same identical A's and B's. If they were not, we should have *another* set of causes and effects to deal with. Hence, logic and reason must be inoperative. And this conclusion, Hume argues, is confirmed by the reflection that the denial of causation in nature implies no contradiction whatsoever. Water has been in the habit of drowning human beings in the past, but, if we really do exclude the assumption of uniform causes, there is no contradiction involved in supposing that water might change its habits as a woman changes her mind.

In short, repetition is not logical evidence, and there is nothing but repetition to distinguish the sequences we call causal from the sequences we regard as casual. What happens when there is repetition is that there is a difference *in us*. These repeated A's and B's become familiar in their sequence. They are sequentially associated, and we cheerfully embrace the illusion that they are consequentially connected. The sole "impression" from which the "idea" of causal connection can be derived is this distinctive psychological impression of familiarity. This "impression of reflection" [30] is the nursing mother of our inveterate habit of ascribing necessary causal connections to Nature.

A volume could easily be written concerning this celebrated argument, but I must here treat it summarily. In the few reflections I shall make, I shall begin with minor points and pass to more considerable ones.

(1). If Hume had said that the feeling of familiarity *causes* us to expect, he would have admitted the existence of certain causes, viz. psychological ones, and so would have contradicted himself. Although his language is frequently careless in this particular, however, he could have avoided the fallacy by simply stating that, up to the present, men have expected when they had the feeling of familiarity; and by leaving the matter there.

[29] *Ibid.,* pp. 163 *sq.*   [30] *Ibid.,* p. 165.

(2). According to Hume himself, there are no objects of human knowledge other than our perceptions (i.e. our "impressions" and our "ideas"), and it is therefore illegitimate to discriminate between observed facts and impressions in the mind. This being granted, Hume is surely wrong in maintaining that there is *no* difference, either produced or discovered, between the hundredth impression of *A* followed by *B*, and the first impression of the sequence so described. The feeling of familiarity is not a separate impression lying side by side in the mind with the impression of *B*'s sequence upon *A*. What happens, on the contrary, is that the entire hundredth impression feels different from the first, because it feels familiar. Psychologically, there *is* a difference between the hundredth impression and the first.

In this instance, Hume might have replied that, for the time being, he was allowing himself to use the language of his opponents. They asserted that there were objective causes. He showed them that, if they did distinguish in this way between objective and subjective, the only relevant difference between the hundredth impression and the first was a subjective difference.

But is it so? Let us grant that the *A*'s and *B*'s that are observed to follow one another for the hundredth time are "objectively" indistinguishable from the *A* and the *B* observed on the first occasion in which the sequence was noticed, and we have still to remark that *epistemically* they are not the same. The evidence *about* them is different. In the one case, we have a hundred uncontradicted instances of *A*'s being followed invariably by *B*. In the other case, we have only one instance of the sequence. But, *ex hypothesi*, causation *means* uniform sequence. Is it, then, at all reasonable to maintain that we have *no* better evidence for *uniform* sequences when we have a hundred uncontradicted instances of *B*'s following *A* than when we have only one instance? If we had any reason, even the smallest, to suspect in the first instance that *A* might be regularly succeeded by *B*, we should surely have somewhat better evidence with the hundred uncontradicted instances before us than with one only.

(3) This leads to a point of still greater importance. Hume's doctrine is that "impressions" (and therefore Nature is so far as it is experienced by us) are always and utterly "loose and

separate," so that there is never any connection between observed events, and never any occasion for reasonable suspicion, whether by way of preconnection or otherwise, that there is such a connection. This doctrine is in itself a denial of the possibility of causal or other connections in nature, and so we have to consider whether the doctrine itself is either reasonable or even plausible.

To begin with, can we accept Hume's account of the evidence of observation?

Hume says that all we can observe is the sequence of two distinct events, A and B. Do we, then, never observe A *becoming* B, or *growing* into B? And if an "immanent" process of this kind is never *purely* immanent, may we not observe (or seem to observe) a certain continuity in the process whereby A responds to, or is influenced by, C and thereby becomes B in a continuous process? In any case, is not the continuity of the sequence as clearly a fact of (ostensible) observation as the sequence itself? If a hen lays an egg, it must be near its egg before, after clucking, it proudly wanders away, and we should not suspect the hen of performing this feat if we had eaten the hen at our Sunday dinner, and the egg had been laid on Monday morning.

Here we should have to anticipate the following type of reply. Regarding "influence" it might be said (and Hume, in fact, does say), that there may be the appearance of causation in some vulgar sense of cause,[31] but not in the scientific sense of unique determination through invariable uniformity of sequence. Even if, by a stretch of language, we could be said to see a plant growing, how could we possibly be said to observe that it *must* grow in the way in which it does grow, that a larkspur, for instance, must put forth its own type of flowers and not the type of flower we find put forth by a daisy? And if *this* larkspur were observed to put forth *this* flower, how could we be said to observe that every larkspur must put forth a similar flower?

Regarding continuity, again, Hume might (and incidentally does)[32] admit that the sequences he has in mind are, as we say, continuous sequences, but would deny that proximity and juxta-

---

[31] E.g. in his account of the animal *nisus* of "power," *Enquiry*, p. 67 note.
[32] *Treatise*, p. 76.

position are logical evidence of causation. Action at a distance in space, he might have argued, is not inconceivable, and the same might be said of action at a distance in time (as recently in Mr. Russell's hypothesis of mnemic causation).

These replies are manifestly pertinent, but are they conclusive?

Concerning the first of them, it has to be remarked that it is doubtful whether causation, even in science, *does* mean uniform sequence and nothing more. Indeed, many philosophers are disposed to believe that uniformity is an inference from causation and not the same thing as causation. For, in the first place, a uniformity *might* be casual, and, in the second place, uniformity would be a legitimate (or, at any rate, an approximately legitimate) inference from the vulgar non-uniform conception of causal "influence" if we found that only *one* influence were operative, in scientific causation, upon elements that, except for this influence, remained the same, and that this single influence, in vulgar language, "exerted all its force" whenever it operates. (If it did not do so, we might go on to ask what caused it to be so restrained.) Accordingly, if "activity" in some vulgar sense is observable either in ourselves or in nature, it should not be inferred that such observed "influence" is irrelevant even to the scientific conception of causation, although the further and more logical investigation of such observed facts might well be a tedious and intricate affair.

Concerning the second reply (i.e. concerning the point of continuity) it may surely be suggested that, although it be not certain that causal connection implies spatio-temporal continuity, it is outrageous to deny that such continuity may have some logical bearing upon the problem of causation, and that what has been said about the hen and its eggs has nothing to do with the question.

On the whole, therefore, we should conclude that Hume's account of the *facts* of observation, in this matter, is not indisputably adequate. Indeed, it might be suggested, with at least equal probability, that all observed facts visibly suggest causal connectedness at the beginning and all the time, and that the logician's problem is to restrain and purify these suggestions of connectedness rather than to manufacture them by inference. If these suggestions of connectedness were themselves alogical or merely instinctive, the admission of their existence would not, of course, imply any reasonableness in our beliefs concerning causes. But it is begging the question to say that such suggestions are illogical, or that the supposed refining and purifying of them is arbitrary and unreasonable.

Nevertheless, if continuous brute sequence were the fundamental fact of natural observation, all else being hopelessly vague if not completely negligible, Hume's position would be very strong indeed. It is necessary, therefore, to examine this matter still more carefully.

(4) The essential point that now falls for consideration is the same as confronted us at the conclusion of Chapter XVIII. What right has Hume to assert, as he does with such supreme confidence, that we can observe what he calls "conjunction" with precision (i.e. spatio-temporal position including juxtaposition), but can not possibly observe "connection"?

It may be manifest, indeed, that all that we observe has a certain specious endurance, and that most that is observed has a certain specious extension or spread-out-ness, if not voluminousness. That, however, is not the point. Hume is plainly presupposing a definite single order of time and space in which we can place and date the facts we observe, and the question is whether anything approaching this spatio-temporal order could even be dreamed of, if the facts we observe (including their specious durations and extensions) were loose and separate.

Are we supposed to observe these spatio-temporal positions in Newtonian or "absolute" time, and "absolute" space? The answer plainly is "No," since absolute time and absolute space are separately imperceptible, and since there is no way of assigning perceptible positions except relatively to other perceptible positions. Alternatively, if Newtonian space and time exist and are the theater in which events occur, we cannot be acquainted by immediate perception with this theater. Indeed, the only plausible suggestion is that the theater itself, and even its general character, is either suggested by, or inferred from, certain uniformities of motion, or, in other words, by natural connections that are not mere spatio-temporal conjunctions.

Or do we take the relative view of these affairs? In that case, we certainly attempt to elaborate our spatio-temporal order from perceived distances and from perceived endurances. Such perceived distances and endurances, however, are relations within perceptible facts that have other properties than those of space or of time. And in their case, just as clearly as on the absolutist hypothesis, any recognizable fixed order of space or of time is excogitated from the interrelated regularities that are partly perceived in, and partly suggested by or inferred from, observed related facts presumed to be connected in other ways than spatio-temporal.

Hence, several consequences follow. For instance, it follows that the assignment of spatio-temporal position is not an affair of direct observation, but an affair of thought and reflection based in part, upon such observation. Hume might legitimately argue that a certain space-like connection and that a certain time-like connection are perceptible, but he is not entitled to argue that definite spatio-temporal order is perceptible. Moreover, he would find it hard to say with any confidence how far thought and reflection do or do not enter into the spatio-temporal perceptions of adults or even of young children. He might still, of course, deny that *any* cause-like connections can be observed, although space-like and time-like connections are observed. As we have seen, however, it is unlikely that he would be correct in such denials. What he shows is that *necessity* (implying causal uniformity) is imperceptible. But if necessity has to be thought, not seen, so have space and time (or space-time), regarded as a general world-order, themselves. And if what is "seen" includes the spontaneous interpretations that we read into our perceptions, there is little plausibility in maintaining that space and time are exempt from such interpretations, or that other connections, particularly causal ones, are, or could be, strangers to normal percipience.

But, it may be said, surely there *are* conjunctions in Hume's sense, that is to say, sequences that appear to be disconnected rather than connected. *Post hoc, ergo propter hoc,* after all, *is* a plain fallacy.

This must be admitted; but if *post* itself logically depends upon *propter,* the distinction, however manifest, is not prior to all induction (so that *propter* has to be superinduced, by violence, upon *post*) but, on the contrary, any *post* gives evidence of *some propter,* and the problem is to distinguish between the indirect connections that we are inclined to consider casual and the more direct connections that we consider to be *propter* as well as *post.*

It may fairly be claimed, then (I think), that Hume's assumptions do not tally with the general situation within which our inductions concerning causes and concerning substances take place, and that the natural connections which are elaborated (and restrained) in the reasonings both of science and of common life may be much more rational and much less arbitrary than Hume's assumptions would permit them to be. On the other hand, it is necessary to consider a further circumstance that *prima facie* might be thought to support Hume's contention.

According to Mr. Keynes, "the law of the Uniformity of Nature . . . involves" (and essentially is) "the assertion of a generalised judgment of irrelevance, namely, of the irrelevance of mere position in time and space to generalisations which have no reference to particular positions in time and space," "two total causes being regarded as the *same* if they only differ in their positions in time and space." [33] As Mr. Keynes himself hints, these statements might require modification if we accepted the "local times" and the "local places," the Theory of Relativity.[34] Apart from any such qualification, however, we certainly do hold some such doctrine, and, if time and space, as such, are irrelevant to causal arguments, would it not appear that Hume, after all, was right, and that, upon reflection, we deny the causal relevance of *mere* sequence in the very sequences upon which our causal inferences are based?

Obviously, this is an overstatement. What is meant by Uniformity, as interpreted by Mr. Keynes, is not the irrelevance of

[33] *A Treatise on Probability,* p. 226.
[34] *Ibid.,* p. 248 *note.*

spatio-temporal configurations to causation within a causal process, but the homogeneity of such configurations throughout Nature. When a kettle is boiled in Scotland, the size of the kettle, the pressure of the surrounding atmosphere, the rate of the rise of temperature, and other spatio-temporal features of the situation are not irrelevant. On the contrary, the causal process is a temporal sequence within a spatial configuration. The meaning of "Uniformity" in this connection is only that the same, or a precisely similar, kettle with the same atmospheric pressure will behave in the same way in Scotland, China, or Peru.

Such homogeneity is part of the meaning of absolute space, and, on the relative theory, *might* be an intellectual intuition concerning the ultimate implications of what is presupposed in ordinary spatial measurement, viz. that yardsticks and other measuring instruments may be moved about freely in space without *thereby* suffering any deformation. On the whole, however, the prevailing trend of current opinion in physics is towards the view that we need not accept the rigid homogeneity of older theories of physics (as Hume, in this instance, assumed like his contemporaries), although there is no occasion for modifying the preconnection appreciably except over a range much wider than the terrestrial. Ultimately (as we saw in Chapter X, § 6), this is an assertion that geometry and chronometry are derivative from physics. (And exception may reasonably be taken to any such view on the ground that if "physics" is dependent upon the pointer-readings of actual measuring instruments, it is rash to conclude that we cannot have any better insight into geometry and chronometry than the skill of our instrument-manufacturers permits at any given time.) In so far, however, as this trend of modern opinion should be upheld, the modern doctrine is a plain assertion that temporal sequence, so far from being the only connection ultimately to be found in Nature, is, on the contrary, less important than, and ultimately derivative from, other natural connections. And, in any case, if the complete uniformity of space and time everywhere *were* a fundamental verity comprehended by intellectual (not by sensory) insight, or even a well-grounded "construction" by "extensive abstraction," [35] it would not follow that such insight or extensive abstraction jettisons any other, and interrelated, categorial connections in Nature.

These considerations have an important bearing upon what Hume manifestly regarded as the clearest point in his general contention, viz. that there *can not* be sufficient logical evidence for maintaining that the future must resemble the past. For if time itself is either derived from, or an expression for, certain pervasive characteristics of a more general connectedness in Nature, future time, as well as past or present time, is included in the scope of this derivation of special characterization. In other words, if time is an inseparable feature of the connectedness of Nature, and if future time is a necessary part of time, the question is not at all what Hume said it was. For time would not have that aloofness from events in time that is implied in Hume's doctrine that events at one time, for no reason at all, might quite easily be utterly different at some other time.

§ 8. Repetition and Induction

As we saw, Hume maintained that the repetition of favorable evidence is the foundation of inductive inference, and that induction must be non-rational because repetition is logically irrelevant to any strict proof.

To this it may be replied that, while the number of instances is irrelevant to any demonstration of the *certainty* of a conclusion (unless, indeed, the number is exhaustive, as when we prove that each apostle was a Jew and therefore that all were Jews), it may be logically relevant to the *probability* of a conclusion. Thus, repeated confirmations of a hypothesis may increase the probability that the hypothesis is one of the few tenable explanations. And the accumulation of favorable instances is, so far as it goes, additional testimony to the probability that because all observed S's are P's therefore all S's must be P's. (In this statement, it is assumed, of course, that there are no negative instances, i.e. no known cases of S not being P. If there were such a negative in-

[35] *Cf.* Whitehead, *The Principles of Natural Knowledge, passim.*

stance, known for certain to be negative, we should have a demonstration of the falsity of the view that S *must* be P, although we might still have evidence for the probability that most S's are P's.)

On these grounds, it might be maintained that an enormous accumulation of favorable evidence, together with the complete absence, so far as we know, of any unfavorable evidence, might reach an enormously high degree of probability, and even a degree of probability approaching certainty without limit. This, in effect, is what Mill tried to prove in the arguments we examined in § 2 of the present chapter.

Obviously, however, if we argued in this way, what we should need to know in order to prove a degree of probability very near to certainty would be, not merely that there was consilience of a great mass of evidence, with no known contradictory evidence, but also that most of the evidence had been examined. If there was a large proportion of unexamined evidence, there could be no question of a high degree of probability, logically grounded.

Clearly, this question of the proportion of the known evidence (supposing it to be favorable to some particular conclusion) to the total possible evidence is of the greatest moment in scientific theory. The facts analyzed in laboratories (or otherwise observed with precision) form an insignificantly small proportion of the total events in the universe, and even when the known favorable evidence is supplemented by the probability that evidence definitely unfavorable would not have escaped our notice, or our deliberate scientific observation, if it had occurred, there is still an enormous disproportion between the evidence that may be said in this way to be known, directly or indirectly, and the whole of nature in the unrecorded past and in the immensities of the future.

Indeed, we proceed according to quite another plan. The ordinary scientific view is that we have a certain reliable insight into what may be called the ground-plan of Nature, and that in terms of this insight we can obtain "fair" samples of events which are typical of the trend and constitution of nature everywhere and at every time. If the samples really were "fair" and if the atypical in Nature were either non-existent or negligible, we might dispense with the repetition of instances; and we regard the accumulation of evidence by mere addition of enumerated instances as something radically unscientific. The scientific importance of repetition, we say, is fundamentally a *precaution* enjoined by the theory of probability.

Thus, a certain number of repetitions of what we call "the same" experiment or "the same" observation may be prudent in order to guard against "probable" errors due to slight variations of attention on the part of the observer, and similar precautions should be taken regarding the "personal equation" in observation. Here we endeavor to eliminate the "chance" of an "error" not likely to be repeated by the same person, or, if likely to be repeated by the same person, not likely to be repeated by different observers of the same event. And even here we proceed in terms of the ground-plan of continuants in Nature, since, strictly, all these "events" are different.

This precaution being admitted, we say that mere repetition of the performance of the same continuants is not evidence regarding the performance of other continuants of the same kind, not to speak of the performance of other continuants of a different kind. When different continuants are in question, however, each gives *independent* confirmation of that to which they conform; and such uncontradicted accumulations of independent evidence do increase the probability of a hypothesis or *prima facie* explanation.

Obviously, however, the essential question concerns what it is that is being confirmed. To chose a trivial but sufficient example, the accumulation of evidence towards a proof that mice are fond of cheese would not go far towards proving that all animals are fond of cheese. Each individual mouse, to be sure, would be an independent witness; and each mouse is an animal. But extensive inquiries into the behavior of mice in this matter would have little relevance to the general question; and even regarding mice we should have better evidence if we examined a few specimens of different mousy families than if we examined a much larger number of mice of the same family.

Undoubtedly, in this particular instance, we *have* evidence that many other animals have no pronounced partiality for cheese, but the point is that if we have reason to suspect that our observations, however numerous, refer to a restricted class, then, even if all such instances are "independent," we do not think the evidence good evidence regarding anything more extensive than the restricted class in question.

In other words, we endeavor to obtain variety rather than mere independence of instances. Mere numerical difference (if things ever do differ merely numerically) might have *some* bearing upon these arguments in probability; but, in the main, what we call a "mere" numerical difference (as between one individual mouse and another individual mouse in the foregoing illustration) seems to be important because the units are slightly different, not simply because they are members of the same class. And, however that may be, it is plain that evidence drawn from widely different, rather than from narrowly similar, types of instance is strengthened on account of this thoroughgoing variety far more than by any other strengthening.

On the other hand, any merely general statement concerning "similarity" and "variety" of instances is manifestly also insufficient. We never proceed on any simple basis of similarity and of variety. On the contrary, we work within some ground-plan or general system, and discriminate between the kind of variety that, as we say, ought to *count* most significantly in terms of the effective character of the system. We are, for instance, not greatly concerned with the question whether rust, breathing, and flame are superficially similar or dissimilar. The question is whether these different modes of oxygenation are effective manifestations of the same fundamental chemical action and yet also evince the kind of difference that chemical theory demands.

§ 9. INDUCTION AND NATURAL KINDS

Mr. Broad, in a very candid and searching examination of these questions,[36] suggests that induction in conjunction with the principle of Natural Kinds might yield a degree of probability not palpably insufficient to justify the reliance we actually do place upon simple generalizations such as that water drowns, and also upon the more subtle and precise generalizations of the natural

[36] *Mind*, N.S., Nos. 108 and 113, particularly the latter.

sciences. His view, in a sense, might be said to resemble Mill's in this particular, with the important exceptions, firstly, that Mill did his best to diminish the rôle of Natural Kinds in the explanation of Nature, and to exalt the rôle of causal induction, while Broad's view is that such inductions are almost worthless *unless* they are inductions concerning Kinds; and secondly, that Mill seems prepared to jettison the visible Kinds of common sense (e.g. the species of animals) in favor of the ultimate chemical elements, whereas Broad, with greater precision, explains that the visible stability of certain chemical compounds (e.g. silver chloride) may be much greater than the stability of the elemental constituent silver, although the simpler or "first-order" Kind called silver may be of deeper chemical importance when the regularities of its mode of combining with chlorine and other substances are understood.

Without attempting to pursue this intricate question into greater detail, I may quote Mr. Broad's conclusion as an admirable and admirably fair general statement of the condition in which experimental science and common sense actually find themselves. "What we actually assume," Mr. Broad says, "is that Nature consists of a comparatively few kinds of permanent substances, that their changes are all subject to laws, and that the variety of Nature is due to varying combinations of the few elementary substances. These assumptions are neither self-evident nor mutually independent nor are they capable of complete proof or disproof by experience. . . . The upshot of the matter is that whenever we make a particular induction we have this general view about Nature at the back of our minds. . . . The kind of evidence is that this plan is suggested to us in a rough form by crude experience, and that, as we investigate Nature more and more thoroughly, experience itself *suggests* ways in which we can state this plan with greater and greater definiteness and rigour, and, at the same time, Nature is found to *accord* with the more rigorous and definite plan far better than it did with the first crude suggestion of a plan. For example, we believe we have got very near to the ground-plan of the material world in the theory of chemical elements, in the laws of mechanics, and in Maxwell's equations, and it is relative to these beliefs that particular inductions in chemistry, electricity etc. are practically certain. The certainty of the most certain inductions is thus relative or hypothetical, and the probability of the hypothesis is not of a kind that can be stated numerically." [37]

§ 10. REASON AND UNREASON IN THESE AFFAIRS

I do not see how this account of Mr. Broad's could be bettered or abbreviated, and therefore I have quoted it at such length. What, then, is the inference concerning the place of reason and of unreason in such matters?

However great our confidence in this "ground-plan" of induction may be at any given time, we must always hold ourselves in readiness to entertain the possibility of a revolution in it; and also must admit that philosophies in the grand manner may be successful in putting a wider, perhaps a "spiritual" interpretation upon the mechanical or other aspects of the ground-plan. The natural sciences adopt the policy of pursuing a ground-plan suggested in experience so long as success, that is to say empirical confirmation, seems probable. This policy is a very different thing from any final belief in the omnicompetence of "mechanical," "materialistic," or even "spiritual" and "idealistic" interpretations of the universe; and the policy should not be confounded with any such creed. The essential philosophical question is whether our provisional and tentative confidence in such policies is rational at all, or whether, as Hume held, it has no logical justification whatsoever.

Part of my design in the present chapter was to explain in some detail why induction, unless it is governed by certain tacit or avowed preconnections and presumptions, could not yield a satisfactory logical proof of anything remotely resembling the beliefs of common life or the conclusions of the experimental sciences in this important matter. This conclusion, in general, I suppose, would nowadays be accepted by all competent persons who have given prolonged attention to the question. None would claim certainty for *mere* induction in this field, and few would claim high probability.

The problem, then, is whether induction, when it is governed

[37] *Mind*, N.S., No. 118, pp. 42 *sqq.*

by preconnections of this order, yields appreciable or high probability in terms of such preconnections; and if, as I have argued, the answer to this question is in the affirmative, the onus of discussion falls upon the rationality of the preconnections themselves. Induction is a logical process; but if the logic of it is governed by mere "postulates" or by assumptions utterly arbitrary, the unreason and caprice in the preconnections extends to the logical inferences drawn from them, whether such inferences are deductive or inductive.

I have therefore endeavored to show, as the main part of my contention, that these preconnections, both in the general form of the connectedness of Nature, and in more special forms that come nearer to a "ground-plan" of Nature, are not arbitrary and capricious, but are, on the contrary, rational presumptions such that, if they were denied, much more would have to be surrendered than Hume or other such philosophers ever thought of relinquishing. In other words, I have endeavored to vindicate the line of argument roughly sketched at the close of Chapter XVIII, in and through the process of commenting on the very different contentions of Mill, and on the intransigent denial of the connectedness of Nature that is the basis of Hume's "naturalism" in his account of the belief in causes.

Such an argument has been, of necessity, tortuous, sinuous, and involuted; and I do not say that it is the best way of debating these affairs. It is, however, a possible way of treating them.

In general, I do not think that, if it were an entirely open question whether or not there is connectedness in Nature, the empirical suggestions and partial confirmations of such connectedness, and of special ground-plans in the connectedness, could be held to be a proper logical justification of our beliefs or even of our policies in this matter. In some way, therefore, the connectedness of Nature must be shown to be a rational presumption (I do not think we can here speak of certainty) in all apprehension of Nature and of her ways. I have therefore tried to show (following humbly in the wake of much distinguished authority) that the visible continuities and stabilities of Nature would be not merely unintelligible without the rational presumption of the connectedness of Nature, but prove, on examination, to imply such connectedness, or, in Kantian language, that they would not be *possible* in the absence of the connectedness. And by *possibility*, in this, sense, I mean, not what Kant seems often content to mean, that without these pre-connections *exact science* would be impossible, but that the very recognition of partial continuities and stabilities, even of the humblest and most commonsensical kind, would be impossible.

Chapter XX

FAITH

§ 1. Introductory

Some discussion of the nature of faith has been inevitable in the preceding pages. To many thinkers, it is true, the conception of faith, supposing that there is such a conception, seems a barbaric intruder into the classic and orderly polity of gnostic cogitation. In their eyes, faith pertains to piety, not to philosophy, and they suspect some incompatibility of temperament when piety and philosophy try to live together. This, however, is only one out of many possible opinions, and an alliance between faith and cogitation is eagerly sought in more directions than is easy to enumerate. Sometimes faith is regarded as a supplement, sometimes as a complement, sometimes as an alternative to cogitation, and, in particular, to the intellect. Sometimes it is held to be the beginning, and sometimes the culmination of knowledgeable process. More frequently still, it is said to be a total, massive attitude and orientation of the soul within which thought and intellection dart and intermittently apprehend.

Again, when faith is assigned any of these offices, it is interpreted, in detail, in a great variety of ways, these interpretations ranging from an animal *nisus* to the purest spirituality in faith's hunger and thirst. In a general way, it is true, the conception of faith that the writer of the Epistle to the Hebrews made so magnificently unforgettable dominates most of these interpretations. Faith is the substance of invincible aspiration whose nature and reality at any time cannot be effectively described except in terms of that which it is determined to become. This general (not universal) agreement among faith's advocates, however, is rather an opportunity for diversity in their descriptions of faith than a uniform determinate message. The

461

natural man, according to many of these doctrines, lives by his natural faith; yet, as St. Paul said, faith in the things that are spiritually discerned is foolishness to the natural man.[1] So much in all these accounts of faith and of its function has, intentionally or unintentionally, been borrowed or adapted from the Christian tradition that it seems essential to begin this chapter with an examination of the Christian conception, or conceptions, of faith, even if such a discussion must necessarily be too brief to be thorough. Similar conceptions might indeed be quarried from other mines, but there is no parallel, outside Christian literature, to the care and fidelity with which the character of faith has been analyzed and illustrated by Christian writers.

§ 2. The Conception of Faith in Early Christianity

As we have already seen, especially in Chapter I, § 9, it has always to be remembered that the doctrine of faith in the Christian tradition is governed by the fundamental implications of that tradition itself. Faith, in this story, takes its place as an integral part of *the* faith, and the story is unintelligible otherwise. To treat of faith by itself, as an attitude of the soul that might be found in other religions or in no religion at all, an attitude that might readily grow and flourish among atheists, or secular scientists, or natural men, however reasonable such treatment of it may seem to us, is simply not to discuss what Paul, or the writer of the fourth gospel, or the writer of the Epistle to the Hebrews, or Augustine, or Aquinas, or Luther meant by their faith.

For them, *the* faith was a faith unto salvation, something that attested a transformation spiritual in its character but also having dominion over the world and over death. It was faith unto the remission of sins, unto the overcoming of the world, unto the frustration of demons. It was faith consubstantial with Christ or with God, in the sense at least that through faith men became partakers in life eternal. *The* faith was stronger than sin, and death, and all their powers; and "faith," in the large, was a

[1] I *Cor.* 2.14.

partial description of the force and vitality of those who had laid hold upon eternal life.

This being understood, it is readily apparent that most references to faith and to its province in the Scriptures and in the earlier Church tradition are concerned to lay emphasis upon various striking aspects of the way in which Christ possesses and inspires the faithful, and not at all to draw distinctions between faith and other stages or elements in the way of salvation. What are described are moods of enthralled piety, impressions of a vehement experience interpreted as the impact of God upon our souls. There is no attempt to count the rungs in the ladder of redemption.

One aspect, and the simplest aspect, of faith so regarded was trust and submissive obedience, and this aspect seems to be the only one expressly to be found in the sparse references to faith in the Old Testament.[2] Here faith is of the heart, and is compounded of loyalty and of reverence. It includes moral earnestness, but is not a moralism of a secular cast. For it is obedience to God's commands.

In the gospel narrative of Christ's life and teaching, the same simple conception of faith is deepened rather than transformed. Christ's intense reliance on his Father was the expression of perennial communion between them. From his disciples and from his other followers, Christ expected trust and reverence in the power and goodness of God. Such trust was also trust in God's power over the world, and in the dominion over sin that worked through the Master. "Why are ye so fearful? How is it that ye have no faith?"[3] Jesus said to the disciples when he rebuked the storm; and in the account of the cure of the man sick of the palsy, the narrative states, "The son of man hath power on earth to forgive sins" and to remit the natural penalty of sin in disease. "Arise, take up they bed, and go into thine house. And he arose and departed to his house."[4]

[2] E.g. *Heb.* 2.4. There are, however, many references in the Old Testament to "the faithful in Israel" and to "faithfulness towards God and man."

[3] *Mark* 4.40.   [4] *Matt.* 9.2-7.

In the Epistles of St. Paul we have, no doubt, something much liker a psychology, philosophy, and theology of faith. Nevertheless, as Deissmann says, "Paul is not so much the great *Christologos* as the great *Christophoros*." [5] Paul's epistles are not theological tracts, or compendia of doctrine, but pastoral letters from the greatest of missionaries. He spoke of faith (πίστις) to the faithful, or to those whom he besought to remain faithful (οἱ πιστεύοντες). Faith for him *was* the spiritual fact, power and experience of salvation and communion in Christ coming from above and descending upon the church of Christ that was, so to say, Christ's body on the earth.

It is therefore unhistorical to regard Paul as the preacher, say, of an evangelical, or purely inward and personal faith, as opposed to any sort of Catholicism or sacerdotalism; as a Doctor Sanctæ Theologiæ intent to show the precise relations between faith, on the one hand, and justification, adoption, or sanctification, on the other hand; as a philosopher who could not but distinguish between gnostic intellection of things invisible and the mystic unity through which our souls dwell in Christ and Christ abides in our souls; or even as one who was definitely opposed to a doctrine like St. James's regarding the relation of faith and works. Paul was indeed the apostle of a new revelation that abolished the Law, and he inveighed against a spirit that can still be found in the Talmud. His temperament was predominantly evangelical, and he was possessed with the desire to reveal the secrets of his own personal and mystic experience at Damascus and ever thereafter. He was not, however, laying down a canon of theology or a system of religious philosophy; and therefore we have to accept his diverse and numerous references to faith in the spirit in which they were written, that is to say, as documentary evidence of the flashes of illumination that were kindled, in divers manners, by the exaltation of Paul's piety, and not as a piece of cool and careful theorizing. Faith, for Paul, came from the Spirit, and, being received by the human soul, gave that soul access to Christ, made the soul firm and steadfast (indeed *alive*) in Him. It supplied the soul with a shield and breastplate. Militant,

⁵ *The Religion of Jesus and the Faith of Paul*, p. 189.

it was also joyful; and its fruits were love, peace, hope, confidence, forgiveness, victory. The children of faith walk in the light and walk in the Spirit. Yet faith, for Paul, was but one manifestation of the Spirit that gave to one man wisdom, to another knowledge, to another the gifts of healing; and all these manifestations were the work of one and the self-same Spirit dividing to every man severally as he will.[6]

In the fourth gospel, the dominant note resounds in the statement that a man sent from God whose name was John came to bear witness of the Light, that all men through him might believe.[7] Near the close of this gospel, however, the writer tells how Thomas, the doubter, was bidden thrust his hand into the Master's side. And the Master's comment was, "Thomas, because thou hast seen me thou hast believed; blessed are they that have not seen and yet have believed."[8] Yet, speaking generally, it seems clear that the writer of the fourth gospel held that faith of any relatively blind species had to be supplemented by knowledge, obedience, and inward fellowship with God, before it could attain its goal and culmination in the life eternal.

All competent modern commentators seem to agree that the conception of faith in the Epistle to the Hebrews shows marked differences from St. Paul's conception of the condition. While Paul regarded faith from the standpoint of receptive mysticism, the writer of Hebrews regarded it as the inspiration of all high and heroic deeds in the old dispensation as well as in the new. There is, indeed, a certain resemblance between Paul's account of the faith of Abraham in the fifth chapter of the Epistle to the Romans, and the long catalogue of the ancient heroes of the faith in the eleventh chapter of the Hebrews; but there is a clear distinction between the receptive faith of Paul and the active, adventuring prospicience described by the writer of the Epistle to the Hebrews. There are also certain other notable differences. With Paul, the emphasis was upon the new revelation, the putting off of the old man. In the Epistle to the Hebrews, the emphasis is upon the continuity of the heroic history

---

[6] *I Cor.* 12, 9-11.   [7] *John* 1. 6 and 7.   [8] *John* 20, 27-29.

of the faithful, Abel, Enoch, Gideon, Barak, Samuel. Indeed, in the Epistle to the Hebrews, the note of continuity recurs so forcibly that the marvels of the new dispensation tend, in a measure, to be dimmed, and we have to be careful to note that these ancient heroes, according to the writer's narration of the inspired tradition, had to wait *for us*, that is to say, until Christ's coming (or perhaps until Christ's return with power) in order *through us* to become perfect. Abel, being dead, yet speaketh.[9] These all, having obtained a good report through faith, obtained not the promise.[10]

Another difference (at least of emphasis) between Paul's account of faith and the account given in the Epistle to the Hebrews, turns upon the celebrated definition of faith in the latter account "as the substance of things hoped for, and the proof of things invisible."[11] In this connection, it is generally held that the Epistle to the Hebrews owes much, directly or indirectly, to the philosophy of Philo the Jew. True, there are marked differences between Philo's conceptions and those of the writer to the Hebrews. In particular, there is an emphasis upon futurity and latter-day consummation in the latter account that is quite foreign to Philo, and an expressly epistemological doctrine of the relation of sense to intellect in Philo that is not to be found in the Epistle to the Hebrews.

Nevertheless, the resemblances are marked, as Dr. E. F. Scott's quotations from Philo show. "He who has in all sincerity believed God," Dr. Scott quotes,[12] "has by so doing received a disbelief in all things which are created and perishable, beginning with all things in himself which exalt themselves very highly, such as reason and outward sense. For reason, thinking that to it pertains the decision on things intelligible and unchanging, is frequently in error. But the man to whom it has been granted to lean and found himself on God alone, with unalterable and sure confidence, is truly happy and blessed." Or again, "For as men who are going along a slippery road stumble and fall, but they who proceed by a plain path journey without stumbling, so they who hasten towards God are guid-

---

[9] *Hebrews* 11, 4.   [10] *Ibid.*, 39.   [11] *Hebrews* 11, 1.
[12] *The Epistle to the Hebrews*, pp. 176 *sq.*

ing their souls in a safe and untroubled path. So that we may say with absolute truth that the man who trusts in the good things of the body disbelieves in God, and that he who distrusts them believes in Him." [13]

§ 3. THE "FAITH" OF THE CHURCH

According to St. Thomas Aquinas, faith (*fides*) is the substance and foundation of the entire spiritual edifice, the *principium spiritualis vitœ*, and *per se* the first of the virtues, although *per accidens* posterior to courage and to humility. So regarded, therefore, it is the animating principle of the Christian's life and the corner-stone of the Catholic Church, implying the consequence that anything approaching an adequate history of "faith" would touch upon, and would frequently penetrate, anything of moment in the Church's structure.

Since no such history can even be attempted in these pages, I shall adopt a different plan, and, after making some general remarks upon the historical situation of the developing Church concerning its conception of faith, I shall linger, for a somewhat greater space, upon St. Augustine's and upon St. Thomas Aquinas's conceptions of *fides*.

(1) On the general issue, we may say:

(a) That among the Fathers and among the hierarchy there was necessarily a divided attention towards (1) *fides qua creditur* and (2) *fides quae creditur*, that is to say, toward (1) faith regarded as the quickener and sustainer of the Christian's soul (whether such faith was God-given or half-humanly *won*) and (2) faith regarded as the tenets necessarily believed by every Christian. Considered from the latter standpoint, faith was, so to say, the articles of the Christian association, a sort of passport into the Christian community. Tertullian's interests were almost exclusively concerned with this aspect of the question, i.e. with the *regulae fidei;* and the ecclesiastical problem was very largely one of the *articuli fidei* or the creeds, that is to say, of the formulation of the quintessence of the Christian doctrine necessarily and literally to be accepted and professed by all Christians.

[13] *Ibid.*, p. 177.

(b) That, in connection with the above distinction, some differentiation between the faith of all believers and the faith of the more spiritually minded among the believers, or, again, between the faith of the relatively ignorant laity, on the one hand, and the faith of instructed priests or of monks who had dedicated their lives to devotion and to the study of the *arcana* of Christianity, on the other hand, had to be drawn. To some extent this differentiation was signalized by the technical terms, *fides implicita* or *informis* and *fides formata,* i.e. between latent and developed faith, although, as was natural, this same distinction was also applied to the first stirrings of faith in the believer's mind, on the one hand, and to its fuller growth in the believer, on the other hand. It is evident that some such differentiation *had* to intrude itself in any organized religious community that included saints but also included a large number of adherents who were not saints, and which distinguished bishops, monks, and priests from the laity. A similar distinction, for example, is also found in the Muslim community where *Iman fi taghid* means the faith of the unlearned in mere authority, *Iman fi ibn* means faith based on intelligence, and *Iman fi a'yan* means the intuition of the mystics. Muslim theologians seem even to hold that a man is a Muslim, and not a Kafir (or heathen), if he assents to the teaching of Muhammad, although such assent does not, in his case, bear its appropriate fruit in the practice of good works.[14]

(c) That many of the Fathers, particularly in the Eastern Church, were intent upon philosophizing the Christian faith, so far as they were able to do so without patently embracing Gnosticism. The accounts of faith in Origen or in Clement of Alexandria are deeply tinged with this ideal.

(d) That ritual, penance, and the problem whether the sacraments operated *ex opere operato* (i.e., as unsympathetic critics would say, by a kind of physical magic irrespective of the spiritual condition either of the dispenser of the sacraments or of those who received them) could not be effectively sundered from these matters; but

(e) That the testimony of piety, and of perfervid religious

[14] *Cf.* Article "Faith" in Hastings' *Encyclopædia of Religion and Ethics.*

devotion and insight, was also a vital part of this entire churchly tradition.

Among these perfervid spirits, Augustine's was one of the greatest in the history of the world. Essentially he was a reformer of piety, whose principal aim was to expel fear from the heart of man, and to make men secure in their union with God. Nevertheless, Augustine was also one of the most earnest defenders of the authority of the church, and in one passage he even states that he would not believe in the gospel itself, unless the authority of the Catholic Church joined in moving him to do so.[15] As Harnack says, "The Church guaranteed the truth of the faith, where the individual could not perceive it. . . . Acts of faith were at the same time acts of obedience."[16]

In much of his thought, Augustine regarded faith principally as the beginning of a new possession, in which the loss and infirmity (rather than the guilt) of sin were done away. From this point of view, the order of spiritual life is to begin with faith and to be perfected through sight (*inchoari fide, perfici specie*).[17] Thus authority preceded reason, and our natural reason was further held to be too weak to put us in possession of the living truth.[18]

On the other hand, no one in the world's history had a greater thirst after truth or a greater impatience of doubt than Augustine; and Augustine never supposed that the living truth imparted by Christ, the Scriptures, and the Church was other than rational. As he says, "Authority puts its seal on faith, and prepares man for reason. Reason leads men to intelligence and to knowledge. On the other side, reason is never completely separated from authority. For we give heed to what ought to be believed; and when a truth is known as something evident it exercises sovereign authority over us."[19]

Such faith is manifestly conceived as being the reverse of credulity; and Augustine in other passages explains that faith is a purification of the soul, without which the truth could not become visible. "In order to obtain wisdom," he says, "it is

[15] *Contra Epist. Manich.,* v.
[16] *History of Dogma,* English translation, Vol. V, p. 80.
[17] *Enchir.* 5.   [18] E.g. *Conf.* vi. 5.   [19] *De Utilitate Credendi,* xvi.

necessary to stand firm in the truth, and this is impossible for
a soul that is soiled. . . . Accordingly, to wish to behold the
truth, in order to purify the soul, when the soul must first
be purified in order to behold the truth, is contrary to sound
sense and is a contradiction." From this point of view, intellect is the reward of faith, and we should believe in order
to understand. ("Intellectus merces est fidei. Ergo noli quaerere
intelligere ut credas; sed crede ut intelligas.")[20]

(2) Turning now to St. Thomas of Aquino, I shall try to give
a brief account (a) of his views concerning the psychology of
faith, (b) of his account of the kinds or species of faith, (c)
of what he says concerning faith's fruits, (d) of his position
regarding the relations between faith and certainty, (e) of his
doctrine concerning the connection and contrast between faith
and reason.

(a) According to St. Thomas, faith belongs primarily to the
speculative intellect and only subordinately to the practical
intellect.[21] It is essentially the assent of the intellect, through
election, to that which is believed with certainty. It may,
however, be greater in one man than in another, in respect of
assurance, devotion, confidence, and detailed understanding, although there is always the same object of faith.[22] The object of
faith is, of course, revealed by God,[23] but faith may suffer
some doubt and disturbance (motum dubitationis) owing to the
fact that assent is not given to the clear evidence of what is
believed (this being absent from faith) but results from an
injunction of the will.[24] The ultimate essence of faith is a true
knowledge of God, and of the mystery of the incarnation.[25]

(b) Faith is an intermediate condition, according to St.
Thomas, since the angels and the blessed do not have it,[26]
they having fuller understanding. The beginnings of faith, however, are widely disseminated, for men in a state of innocence
(he said) have rudimentary faith (fides informis) in the incarnation.[27] The faith of the ancients and of the moderns is an

---

[20] In Joh. Evan. Tractatus, xxix, 6.
[21] Summa Theologiæ (The Turin Edition, 1927, being consulted), 1 2
q.56 etc.
[22] Ibid., 2 2 q.5.4.   [24] Ibid., 1 q.1.5 etc.   [26] Ibid., 1 2 q.67.3.5.
[23] Ibid., 1 q.1.3.   [25] Ibid., 2 2 q.174.6.   [27] Ibid., 2 2 q.2.7 etc.

instance, therefore, of one and the same principle.[28] Nevertheless, the development of faith in love and the attainment of a
mature faith (*fides formata*) are a great part of the essence of
the Christian's life. For a servile fear is the effect of *fides
informis*, but filial respect is the effect of *fides formata*.[29]

(c) More generally, *fides formata* carries with it purity of
heart,[30] together with emancipation from sin,[31] and is succeeded
by the vision of the blessed.[32] It is also allied with *fiducia*,[33]
that is to say, with the hope of future assistance from above,
and with *robur spei*[34] or robustness of hope. In many respects,
fiducia is said by St. Thomas to be the Christian counterpart
of what the pagans called magnanimity.[35]

(d) St. Thomas consistently maintained that, in our faith, we
gave our assent to the firmest truth (*prima veritas*).[36] Faith
could therefore assent to nothing that was false[37] and (since,
according to St. Thomas, natural reason could not traffic in
falsity) faith could not assent to anything contrary to natural
reason.[38] The object of faith was objectively certain,[39] and the
enigmas and mysteries contained in this certain truth were *not*
what caused us to believe. Faith, however, could never be sight.[40]
It was an acquaintance with divine invisible things, and these
had to be apprehended by a more exalted faculty (*altiori modo*)[41]
than natural reason. Faith has a nobler object than the objects of
science, i.e. than any secular object. It was, however, a less
noble and indeed an imperfect way of knowing.[42]

(e) According to St. Thomas, metaphysics or *prima philosophia* has the knowledge of God for its ultimate aim and may
therefore be called *scientia divina*.[43] Nevertheless, so much that
pertains to our knowledge of God was, in his view, above
natural science that he was also able to say that it was impossible
for faith and (natural) science to deal with the same thing.[44]
Since he believed that natural knowledge was not, in principle,

[28] *Ibid.*, 1 2 q.103, 4c etc.   [33] *Ibid.*, 1 q.12.7 etc.   [38] *Ibid.*, 1 q.1.8.
[29] *Ibid.*, 2 2 q.7.   [34] *Ibid.*, 2 2 q.129.6 c.   [39] *Ibid.*, 2 2 q.171.5.
[30] *Ibid.*, 2 2 q.7.2.   [35] *Ibid.*, 2 2 q.128 c.   [40] *Ibid.*, 1 2 q.67.3 etc.
[31] *Ibid.*, III q.52.5 etc.   [36] *Ibid.*, 1 2 q.67.3 etc.   [41] *Ibid.*, 2 2 q.2.
[32] *Ibid.*, 2 2 q.129.6.   [37] *Ibid.*, 1 q.1.8 c. etc.   [42] *Ibid.*, 1 2 q.76.
[43] *Summa Contra Gentiles*, 1.1 and III, 25. *Cf.* Gilson, *Le Thomisme*,
p. 25.
[44] *Qu. disp. de Veritate*, q.XIV art. 9 *ad Resp. Cf.* Gilson, *op. cit.*, p. 26.

corrupt and that its intuitive or demonstrable verities were
authentic verities, he set himself, in consequence, to give human
or unrevealed science its proper place in the total fabric that,
as a whole, was grounded in, and inspired by, God.

Part of St. Thomas's contention was that reason, strictly, is
demonstration from premises, and is, therefore, so far subordinate. It is indeed a defect (St. Thomas maintained) to be
compelled to reason.[45] If our intellects were finer we should
ascertain all intelligible truth by direct intellectual insight,
as God does, and not by labored demonstrations. (This defect,
however, does not in any way imply the falsity of reason in
the sense of inferred conclusions. Reason is only laborious and
cumbrous.)

Much that pertains to faith is therefore *indemonstrable*. But,
since reason and intellect, according to St. Thomas, are in principle the same (however cumbrous the former may be), there
is (he maintains) no opposition in principle between intellectual
insight (such as God's) and clumsy human proofs. Again, our
natural reason is frequently able to proceed from, and in the end
must rely upon, the simple intellectual intuition of principles.[46]

The natural light of intellect, therefore, is a natural perfection,[47] and it has a very high office. On the other hand, not
all that is revealed can thus be apprehended by the natural
light or inferred syllogistically from what is so apprehended. For
the most part, therefore, although reasons against the faith
are nonsensical and derisory,[48] the natural intellect frequently
yields only an obumbration of divine truth, and is to be regarded
as an obedient schoolmaster in theology, although it may speak
with authority concerning the things that are connatural with
its natural office. Faith directs our aims regarding ultimate
ends and the light of nature directs us regarding human ends.[49]
Again (although this is by an extrinsic persuasion), natural
inquiries may increase and nourish our knowledge of the truth
revealed in faith.[50] For example, the reasons that the saints
have marshalled in defense of faith, although they are not

[45] *Summa Theologiæ*, 2 2 q.49.5.
[46] *Ibid.*, 1 q.79.8 etc.   [48] *Ibid.*, 1 q.1.8.   [50] *Ibid.*, 1 q.1, 2.
[47] *Ibid.*, 1 2 q.68.2.   [49] *Ibid.*, 2 2 q.10.4.

demonstrative, nevertheless are sufficient to yield the persuasion that the things we believe through the faith are not impossible.[51]

§ 4. FAITH AS EVANGELICALLY INTERPRETED

On the seventeenth of July, 1505, a young and talented Master of Arts renounced the world and entered the monastery of the Augustinian Eremites at Erfurt. Martin Luther (for that was the novice's name) tells us in his Table Talk that he vowed to become a monk in a moment of abject terror, when, on the second of July he was prostrated by lightning during a terrific thunderstorm. His experience on that occasion, however, did not equal that of St. Paul; for Luther, unlike St. Paul at Damascus, was still left groping after salvation. Later, while still a monk, he discovered the meaning of salvation (as he thought) in the great spiritual reality called "justification by faith," in the evangelical and personal sense which he believed to have been intended by St. Paul.

The first connected account that Luther gave of this discovery is to be found in his *Lectures on the Psalms* (1513). These lectures show traces of scholastic philosophy and of the Neoplatonism to be found in Augustine. Luther still speaks of a hidden wisdom too high for mere philosophy to unveil. In the main, however, intellectual and speculative questions occupy a very small place in Luther's mind. What he is concerned to show is the overwhelming efficacy of trust and of confidence in God's mercy in Christ, and in contrast to this efficacy the utter worthlessness of the natural man and his fleshly concupiscence. While Luther did not claim complete personal assurance of salvation, his trust in the justification of faith drove out fear.

In a very short time, the note thus sounded became clearer and fuller in Luther's *Lectures on the Epistle to the Romans*— lectures which, according to most Protestant theologians,[52] reveal Luther as the greatest of Paul's disciples, a disciple who had

[51] *Ibid.*, 1 q.1, 8.
[52] See Mackinnon, *Luther and the Reformation,* Vol. 1, p. 171. The quotations that follow are in Dr. Mackinnon's translation from Luther's Latin, and the very condensed account I am presenting of Luther's conception of justification by faith is intended to be, in essentials, an epitome of the full and admirably clear analysis of Luther's principal works on the subject which Dr. Mackinnon has given us in this standard work.

emancipated himself from legalism much as Paul had done, and, like Paul, was concerned not primarily to theologize, but to give expression to the piety that burned within him.

Luther's argument in these Lectures starts from man's absolute impotence and on his absolute dependence upon God for salvation. The natural man is guilty, a creature of the flesh, inheriting the mortal disease of Adam. "Thus as the ancient fathers have rightly said," Luther exclaims, "original sin is the *fomes,* the law of the flesh, the law of the members, the languor of our nature, the original disease." The taint of it, according to Luther, clung to the whole natural man and to all his works. It shows itself in self-love and in self-righteousness, as well as in what is usually called concupiscence, and extends also to the "reason" in which some men vainly take pride. (In other places Luther calls reason a whore, because she could so easily be put to uses not spiritual.) Luther expressly denied the existence of any synteresis or remnant of good will that (in the general opinion) might be efficacious if accompanied by rational intellectual discernment. "God," he said, "laughs our righteousness to scorn." [53] And he declared, without reservation or qualification, that salvation is God's gift to the elect, that is to say, to those who are made righteous by Him through faith in the gospel.

Luther admitted, indeed, that faith implied a certain apprehension and even a certain understanding of the divine plan of salvation. This apprehension, however, he further maintained was purely passive among the elect. And in the main, the emphasis of Luther's account of faith is vehemently directed towards showing the emotional and moral aspects of this engrossing conviction. As he said, faith was life and the living word abbreviated. Whatever knowledge was in question was knowledge of the ineffable which had to penetrate into the dark recesses of the soul before it could become efficacious.

Such faith, Luther held, begets confidence and trust as well as hope.[54] It is God's work of redemption within our hearts—for the human soul is *justificandus,* not *justus.* Luther denied, indeed, that a man could ever know from personal experience that he was

<hr/>

[53] As quoted, *ibid.,* p. 188.   [54] See references, *ibid.,* p. 197.

justified. For him, there was not this kind of gnostic security in the experience of faith. Yet there was, so to say, imperturbable filial assurance. Our faith should be such as to counsel us to accept damnation cheerfully if our damnation were the will of God. Yet where God is there is no hell.

At a later date, in *The Liberty of a Christian Man*, Luther gave a simple exposition of his doctrine of faith, which may be summarized somewhat as follows.[55] (1) God alone commands and God alone fulfils; (2) faith, therefore, is an inward thing expressing God's work of salvation; (3) it leads us from the law to the gospel; (4) it unites the soul to God, and honors God as true and righteous. The conclusion is (5) that "man is inwardly, according to the spirit, amply justified by faith . . . nevertheless he remains in this mortal life upon earth in which it is necessary to rule his own body and have converse with other men. Here, then, works begin."

Mere antinomianism was therefore very far from being Luther's intention, just as it was very far from being St. Paul's. Of works Luther says generally, "Bonum si in fide, malum si in infidelitate."

While the evangelical or Protestant tradition was not, of course, bound by Luther's words (perhaps, indeed, we should not speak as if there was or ever had been a single undeviating Protestant tradition), the resemblances between Luther's conception of justification by faith and the conceptions of other great Protestant teachers have, in the main, been very close indeed. This may readily be seen from a brief account of the doctrines of Calvin, Schleiermacher, and Ritschl on this subject.

In Calvin's *Commentary on the Epistle to the Romans*, we read: "Since there remains nothing for men, as to themselves, but to perish, being smitten by the just judgment of God, they are to be justified freely by His mercy. God's mercy is the efficient cause, Christ with his blood is the meritorious cause, the formal or instrumental cause is faith in the word, the final cause is the glory of the divine justice and goodness." [56]

Expanded, this doctrine implies, as Calvin explains in his

[55] See Mackinnon, Vol. ii, pp. 263 *sqq.*
[56] English translation, p. 141.

Institutes,[57] (1) that the breaking of the law deserves eternal death, (2) that we can have no hope in ourselves (i.e. as natural men) of *not* breaking the law, and therefore (3) that we have to rely entirely upon God's mercy after Christ had sacrificed Himself in order to atone for man's sins. Accordingly, "when God bids us work out our own salvation with fear and trembling, all He requires is that we accustom ourselves to think very meanly of our own strength, and confide in the strength of the Lord." [58] Calvin, indeed, agreed with St. Bernard, whom he quotes as saying: "The testimony of conscience which Paul calls the rejoicing of believers, I believe to consist in three things. It is necessary first of all to believe that you cannot have remission of sins except by the indulgence of God; secondly, that you cannot have any good work at all unless He also give it; lastly that you cannot by any works merit eternal life unless it also be freely given." [59]

Faith, therefore, receives all from God and brings nothing except a humble confession of want. It is contented with the assurance that however poor we may be in regard to present comforts, God will never fail us.[60]

Calvin admitted that faith might be accompanied by error; for Rebekah, although divinely informed of the election of her son Jacob, nevertheless procured the blessing for him by a wicked stratagem. Essentially, however, faith (Calvin maintained) is a belief in, and, in a certain way, a knowledge of, the living truth. It was a pernicious doctrine (of the schoolman) Calvin declared, as we saw in Chapter I, § 5, that there is no stronger evidence of faith than moral conjecture.[61] But, although faith in this way be knowledge, its knowledge is not comprehension in any ordinary sense, much less the kind of comprehension that is yielded by the senses. "What our mind embraces by faith is in every way infinite" and can not be a demonstration of reason. Is the admission of such "knowledge" rash and presumptuous? "I would grant this," Calvin says, "did we hold that we were able to subject the incomprehensible counsel of God to our feeble intel-

---

[57] English translation, Vol. II, p. 95.
[58] *Ibid.*, p. 123.
[59] *Ibid.*, p. 145.
[60] *Commentary on Romans*, p. 148.
[61] *Institutes*, Vol. ii, p. 160.

lect." [62] But, of course, we can not do so and should not attempt to do so.

In Schleiermacher's theology, faith takes its place in the philosophy of piety. All theology, Schleiermacher declares, starts from, and ultimately expresses the implications of, the piety of souls in communion, i.e. in a Church. Piety includes knowing and doing, but is essentially a feeling. And pious feeling, in the last analysis, is rooted and grounded in the feeling of absolute dependence from which, according to Schleiermacher's courageous doctrine, all theology can be developed and shown to be true.[63] Piety may thus include certainty and (in its own way) may reach the firmest and best grounded knowledge. A man, however, may possess such knowledge and yet not be pious; and the doing of pious acts is not enough; for true piety must move us from within. Here faith has its province, faith being the fidelity to one's convictions, the life that is tutored by the intimations that arise from the feeling of absolute dependence.[64]

Schleiermacher further explains that certainty of redemption is a necessary condition for belonging to the Christian community, and that this certainty is just faith in Christ. "In the same sense," he says, "we spoke above of faith in God which was nothing but the certainty concerning the feeling of absolute dependence as such. . . . The faith of which we are now speaking, however, is a purely factual certainty, but a certainty of a fact which is entirely inward. That is to say, it cannot exist in an individual until, through an impression which he has received from Christ, there is found in him a beginning—perhaps quite infinitesimal, but yet a real premonition—of the process which will put an end to the state of needing redemption." [65]

In principle, Schleiermacher accepted the doctrines of the great Protestant confessions. Like these Confessions, he was speaking of a faith *viva et vivificans*, which was called "alive" on account of Christ Whom it embraced (Twesten). He also did not dissent from Melanchthon's saying "Faith is fidelity in applying to ourselves the glorious gift of Christ . . . and fidelity

[62] *Ibid.*, p. 141.
[63] *The Christian Faith*, English translation, pp. 5 *sqq.*
[64] *Ibid.*, p. 10.   [65] *Ibid.*, p. 68.

is a movement in the will whereby the will acquiesces in Christ.
. . . This is the substance we are eager to retain whatever words
others may use." [66] On the other hand Schleiermacher held that
piety and the feeling of absolute dependence could and did attain
ultimate truth, and that faith was carried along this deep metaphysical current.

Ritschl's account of faith can hardly be denied to be more
subjective in conception than Schleiermacher's, and it is expressly
less voluntaristic than Melanchthon's. On the former point,
Ritschl's most definite statement appears to be the following:
"To believe in Christ implies that we accept the value of the
divine love, which is manifest in His work, for our reconciliation with God, with that trust which, directed to Him, subordinates itself to God as His and our Father, whereby we are
assured of eternal life and blessedness." [67] The emphasis here is
upon the *value* of Christ as we experience it, and Ritschl, intent
upon demonstrating the existence of a sphere of value in addition to the sphere of natural science, never adequately explained
how far and in what way our value-feelings, or the judgments
based upon them, can reasonably lay claim to truth and certainty of an intelligibly defensible kind. In the main, indeed,
Ritschl seems content to describe the reality and vivid impressiveness of a certain state of mind; for example, when he
says that "faith, which as related to the promise attached to
the work of Christ appropriates forgiveness, is to be understood
as trust in God and Christ characterised by peace of mind, inward satisfaction, and comfort." [68]

On the latter point, Ritschl definitely objected to the voluntarism of Calvin and of Melanchthon, declaring that faith was
not a thing of the will, but that it was "emotional conviction of
the harmony between the divine purposes and the most intimate
interests of men." [69]

Like Schleiermacher and (even) like Luther, Ritschl denied
that faith is purely individual, asocial, antinomian. "Religion,"
he declared, "is always social. . . . The individual believer, there-

[66] *The Christian Faith,* English translation, p. 481.
[67] *Justification and Reconciliation,* English translation, p. 591.
[68] *Ibid.,* p. 142.   [69] *Ibid.,* p. 101.

fore, can rightly understand his position relatively to God only
as meaning that he is reconciled by God through Christ in the
community founded by Christ. The fellowship with God through
Christ which is thus conditioned is the intelligible and valuable
content of the faith which is specifically conscious of itself."[70]

§ 5. TRANSITION TO A MORE GENERAL SURVEY

Before attempting to enter upon the specific problem of this
concluding chapter, viz. the relation of faith to epistemology
with special reference to faith's rationality, we may pause with
advantage to consider how far these careful analyses of the
significance of faith in Christian piety and in Christian theology
are likely to be instructive in a more general, if in a less richly
colored, inquiry of the type we call philosophical. Here we may
say

(1). that, despite the "modernists"[71] in theology, the Christian conception of the faith can not be separated from certain
historical matters. The historical record of Christ's life and
teaching, in short, is essential to the understanding of the
specifically Christian doctrine of redemption and salvation.
Without the acceptance of this historical record as the foundation of the tradition that has been built upon it, there might
indeed be trust and love and piety and devotion to all high
things in the universe, but there would not be Christianity.

In other words, Christianity is necessarily based, in part at
least, upon revelation. It is unfashionable, no doubt, to put
implicit reliance upon the simple-minded and rather old-fashioned distinction between natural and revealed religion, and we
may sympathize with the desire for a theistic unity that trans-
cends these ancient landmarks. Nevertheless, if we are dealing
with Christianity and not with theism in general (including
pantheism), we have to admit that the historicity of the Christian tradition is not less essential to Christianity than any general and philosophical reflections, and that matters of history
can not be established by general theistic and other such arguments. To prove, if it were possible to prove, that the universe
is deiform is not to prove that the God of the Old Testament

[70] *Ibid.*, p. 578.   [71] I.e. Loisy, Sabatier, Tyrrell, and others.

or the Christ of the New Testament ever existed, or that they are what Christians claim them to be. The story unfolded in the Scriptures and developed in the Christian tradition may indeed be amazingly and overwhelmingly congruent with the conclusions of general philosophical theism, but it could never be the same thing, and no good purpose could be served by pretending that it is the same thing or by forgetting that it is not.

(2). To put the question otherwise, we have to distinguish between historical and quite general revelation. All truth may be said to be revealed, and in any such statement nothing is said about the way in which the revelation comes about. Such revelation, therefore, may grow out of love and trust, devotion and piety, as well as out of the "natural" employment of our "natural" reason. It might also be an instruction from God. There is, however, a plain and an inescapable distinction between that which has the stamp of truth or of rational verisimilitude upon it when we come to perceive its essence by any means whatsoever, and that which, being matter of history, could only be established by definite historical evidence. It is only "revelation" of the former kind that could possibly be identified with philosophy.

(3). On the other hand, another old-fangled distinction, not disconnected with this question of "revelation," seems much more dubiously applicable. I am referring now to the distinction between natural and supernatural.

When St. Paul and others like him contrasted the new dispensation with anything that Abraham might have discovered and with anything that pagan philosophers might have discovered, they drew what seemed an obvious and an inevitable distinction. Philosophically speaking, however, it is hazardous to argue that the new covenant endowed men with supernatural faculties, or, again, that the best in this kind that had been achieved before the new covenant came was in fact the best that man's "natural" faculties could attain. As we have seen, if the new covenant, in the main, was to be regarded as a fresh historical fact which, like other historical facts, could not conceivably have been inferred from anything that preceded it, the distinction would inevitably be what St. Paul and the others said it was. On the other hand, if the essential message of the new covenant is general and non-historical, being an insight that penetrates into the essence of what always has been and always will be (if not, indeed, into what is non-temporal and so in a certain sense eternal), there could be no sufficient philosophical reason for asserting *ex cathedra* that such insight implies supernatural faculties.

To be sure, if we regard "nature" either in the traditional Christian way as that which may be observed by the senses, or in the modern way as that which is treated expressly by physics and other "natural" sciences and defined by the success that such sciences have achieved at any given date, it follows immediately that there is much in the universe that, in this sense, is non-natural. For plainly the senses do not exhaust the universe, and neither do the natural sciences at their present stage. Further, the "non-natural," in this sense, might be said to be supernatural if (a) it constituted a single order and were not an amorphous collection of all the things that are not sensed or have not been fully explained by the "natural" sciences, and if (b) this single order governed the "natural" order. In this sense, therefore, we could speak with some assurance of a supernatural order, and, if we were acquainted with it, of supernatural faculties by means of which we had the acquaintance. Obviously, however, all such boundaries are quite artificial, and are justified at the best by mere convenience on particular occasions. Any general interpretation of the universe must include what, in this sense, is "supernatural" as well as what is "natural." In interpreting the universe as a whole, we should employ all our powers, when these are relevant, and the distinction, if there is one, between natural and non-natural powers should be resolutely obliterated.

(4). A further point, however, needs to be raised. The Christian conceptions of faith, however notably these may have differed in detail, were essentially concerned with man's regeneration, redemption, and salvation. Hence, purity of character and single-mindedness of moral purpose (whether or not it was God that made the elect steadfast in their faith) was the very ichor of faith's body, and man's essential relation to God was filial and personal. Suppose, now, that the attempt is made, as frequently it has been made by philosophers and theologians, particularly by modern ones, to widen the basis of faith and to regard faith as the breath and living blood of all cogitative presumption as well as of all knowledge and belief. Is it possible, *then*, to transfer the Christian conception of personal, communal, filial trust to this wider realm, to regard cogitative presumptions concerning the universe as conceivably *in pari materia* with the pious experience of moral sonship, in short, to draw upon the Christian analyses of faith in this way without diluting them into something entirely colorless?

In this matter contemporary philosophy speaks with a divided voice. Some philosophers (e.g. the late Dr. Ward) seem, in the main, to ignore the problem. They perceive no essential difference between the faith of Abraham and the process of evolution that makes for "betterment." Others, like the Dean of St. Paul's, find the solution in the philosophy of values. Values, they say, must ultimately govern the universe, and piety, together with the beauty of holiness (although working in alliance with the intellect and not contemptuous of "science") are, in the last analysis, our tutors concerning values. Others, again, frankly confess that the traditional Christian orientation in these affairs was indefensibly anthropocentric and anthropomorphic. It could not survive Copernicus. And a fourth party, more vaguely, bid us, with Schweizer (and the ancient Stoics) endeavor to make our moral conceptions square with the order of the universe, or, like Mr. Sturge Moore, tell us not to forget "how impossible it is to imagine a man doing anything without the favour or connivance of the universe." [72]

For the moment, I propose to note this central question rather than to examine it. I hope, however, to keep it in mind in the few pages that follow. In these concluding pages, I shall offer some observations upon the principal respects in which faith has been contrasted with various species of cogitation.

§ 6. Faith and Sight

This is the oldest and, in many ways, the greatest of all the historical contrasts in this matter, and the contrast seems to

[72] *Armour for Aphrodite,* p. 80.

contain three principal parts or aspects. These are (1) that where sight exists there is, so far, no need for faith; (2) that faith reveals the insufficiency of sight and the subordination, *in ordine ad universum*, of things seen to things invisible; and (3) that faith, in due course, may bring a higher and supernal sight in which the invisible and ineffable may be apprehended, not as in a glass darkly, but face to face.

(1). Regarding the first of these points, the question should perhaps be raised whether the sufficiency of "sight" in its own province should be granted so readily. May not the truth rather be that it is necessary to have faith *in* sight, or, in other words, that trust in the senses is one of the chief lessons we ought to learn?

Epistemologically regarded, this, in its essentials, is the problem of the *testimony* of the senses. It should have been debated sufficiently in Chapter XII of the present work. If, on the other hand, we regard "sight" as a metaphorical expression for the entire secular view of the world, it is abundantly plain, as we have seen time and again, that the secular view of the world, whether or not this "secular" view is intended to include the whole panorama of the universe as unfolded by the "natural" sciences at any given time, is enormously more extensive than even the most cunningly selected patchwork of accurate sensory observation. The secular view should be based, in a part of it (and very likely in its principal part), upon what is *seen* or otherwise sensed. Nevertheless, if anything that goes beyond "sight" is "faith," our science, very largely, *must* be a thing of "faith," and materialism, considered from this angle needs "faith" as much as any other philosophy. Such materialism, in a word, is a great speculative hazard in which "sight" is exploited far beyond the boundaries of any possible sensory verification.

(2). The range of the intellect is so incomparably wider than the range of sense, and the intellect is so much more powerful than any other cogitative faculty, that we are accustomed to call a science the more "developed" in proportion as it is intellectualized. Even if the senses ultimately yield the material upon which all genuine science works, a science, regarded as a work of art, is essentially an intellectual integration, and in that sense subordinates the visible to the invisible. It would seem illegitimate to conclude from this circumstance, however, that there is a system of invisible or of supersensible "things" that governs and produces another system of sensible "things," or, in other words, to maintain that the intellect deals with one sphere of existence, the senses with another such sphere, and that the superior power of the intellect must be supposed to have an existential counterpart in the greater efficacy of this supersensible sphere.

It is not my purpose to consider here whether this interpretation ought to be put upon Plato's Forms, whether Plato, or Philo, or Plotinus argued that, because we can not understand, say, the meaning of justice except in terms of the conception of justice, therefore, in actual fact, this concept or Idea or Form of justice literally *produces* all that is just. All I need maintain is that, if and so far as this view has been held, it does not seem to be defensible. It is pictorial rather than reasoned, and it should be distinguished from, not assimilated with, the Christian's faith in what is invisible. Communion with God can not be said to belong to the sphere of ordinary sight, and if God is the Lord and Creator of the entire universe, visible or invisible, the natural world is certainly subordinate to the spiritual. There are, however, several distinct steps in this argument, and nothing but confusion can result from an indiscriminating allegiance to what, being unseen, is said to be Yonder, or in Heaven.

(3). The doctrine that faith may bring us, or enable us to fashion, spiritual eyes with which to discern the supersensible face to face, either at some later date when we are perfect and in Heaven, or in a mystic vision during which we may apprehend the supersensible at rare but precious moments in our present existence, is full of intricacy. In the present work, it has been consistently maintained that cogitation is *not* union or identity between knower and what is known, and that such union, if it did not abolish the possibility of cogitation, would at any rate put a barrier in the way of accurate cogitative apprehension. If so, the type of apprehension described as "face to face" must, as Paul's metaphor in its literal sense clearly suggests, be sharply

FAITH   485

distinguished from complete identity. In so far as faith is laying
hold upon and confiding in the supersensible, it may indeed be
regarded as achieving its proper goal (even if it thereby trans-
cends itself altogether) by accomplishing this literal and complete union. It would not follow, however, that perfect knowledge or even a "higher" vision would be an inevitable aspect
of this mystic achievement.

Putting the question otherwise, we may say that the relations
between the personal unity described in mystic piety, and any
sort of superior or ineffable insight of an intellectual or super-
intellectual order, remain obscure. God, theologically regarded,
may indeed, be the truth as well as the life; but the philosophy
of truth is, for the most part, differently orientated from the
devotional and largely emotional attitude of piety. It is difficult
to bring the two attitudes together, and it may be doubted
whether piety would suffer if they were sharply distinguished.
In any case, I can not help thinking that it is a false, not a
defensible, philosophy that attempts ultimately to unite philosophy with piety by asserting that knowledge is what I hold it
is not, viz. by asserting that knowledge is in its essence union,
or literal identity, between knower and known.

§ 7. FAITH AND BELIEF

In the Christian tradition, it became necessary to distinguish
carefully between the loyalty and devotion implied in faith, on
the one hand, and the assent of mere belief, on the other hand,
whether or not this assent was blind or evidenced. For, to repeat
what St. James said, "The devils also believe"; and St. Thomas
Aquinas was at pains to point out that this belief on the part
of the devils was coerced and not at all laudable. This distinction, again, became more, not less, important when acceptance
of the Christian creed no longer implied taking and making a
stand in the face of possible obloquy and persecution, but, instead, was a mark of respectability and not inconsistent with
worldly advancement.

In view of our previous analysis of belief, it is plain that
we also are disposed to distinguish between belief (or cogitative
assent) and the active or emotional attitude that commonly

goes along with belief. The pragmatists, and those who agree with the pragmatists in this matter, on the other hand, are anxious, in effect, to identify faith with belief.

Granting, however, that belief and faith are not the same, it may still be debated whether or not belief is to be regarded as an aspect or as the offspring of faith, in the sense that the cogitative assurance of belief is a subordinate thing which, whether we are aware of the circumstance or not, simply reports or attests what is sometimes called "practical" assurance, i.e. the fact, witted or unwitted, that the whole bent of our activity has a certain direction, unwavering and unperplexed. This question has the greater importance owing to the circumstance that most discussions of belief in British and in American philosophy are primarily concerned with the problem whether a particular species of belief (i.e. the belief that outruns the evidence of the senses in affairs of common life and of "practical" importance) is or is not evidenced in any rational way.

We may with advantage distinguish various points in this debate.

(1). According to the late Dr. James Ward in a striking passage, "the worst we can say of religious faith is that it leads us to a line of conduct that present facts do not warrant, that it is not rational in the sense of being clearly deducible from anything that we certainly know. Now I think if we glance at the past history of the organic world as Darwin and Spencer expressed it, we shall find that almost every forward step could be formulated in this way: it was an act of faith not warranted by aught within the ken of the savant at that point. There was little for example in all that the wisest fish could know to justify the belief that there was more scope for existence on the earth than in the water and that persistent attempts to live on land would issue in the transformation of his swim-bladder into lungs. . . . I know nothing more wonderful than this unscientific trustfulness that from the very beginning seems to have been ingrained in things, likening them to Abraham the type and father of the faithful who 'when he was called . . . obeyed and went out, not knowing whither he went'."[73]

[73] *Essays in Philosophy*, pp. 106 *sq.*

Here the analogy seems to limp. There is a general resemblance, it is true, between Abraham seeking a new country and a fish seeking a new habitat, but the analogy would be much less forcible if Abraham's action had been determined by economic pressure of the type familiar among nomadic communities, and if the faith made immortal by the writer of the Epistle to the Hebrews could only be said to occur if Abraham had divined the promise and set out to inherit it. Accordingly, it is the latter conception that is the crux of Dr. Ward's argument, and he appears to be begging the question when he implies that evolutionary process is the quest for *progress* or *betterment* and is dimly discerned to have this character when the pioneers of evolution have any tentative premonition of such a goal. In reality, the conception of efficient adaptation to circumstances, to the mortal peril of those who fall by the wayside, need not connote betterment, the more particularly if circumstances became more and more unfriendly. The last state of the organic world might, indeed, be the survival of lichens and of freshwater algæ.

(2). In a more general way, however, Dr. Ward was clearly justified in dissenting, say, from Clifford's emphatic statement that "it is wrong always, everywhere and for every one, to believe anything upon insufficient evidence."[74] Clifford, it is true, was speaking of the *ethics* of belief, that is to say, of the duty incumbent upon all thinkers and philosophers to submit their beliefs to the canons of evidence, and therefore should be acquitted of any greater misdemeanor than pardonable over-emphasis. On the other hand, if *belief* is regarded in Clifford's way, the explanation should be added that "belief," in the normal case, grows out of practical *faith*, that is to say, out of a general and largely preconscious reliance upon the practical employment that we call our lives and upon the feasibility of living. In this sense, faith undoubtedly precedes and may outrun anything properly to be called evidence, and, although it would be immoral for a philosopher (whose business is with evidence proper) to have faith of this kind without examining the evi-

[74] *Lectures and Essays*, p. 346. Quoted by Ward, *The Realm of Ends*, p. 413.

dence, this would not necessarily seem to be immoral for a *man*. *Credo ut intelligam* is a maxim greatly praised, because it is presumed that the sphere of belief is the sphere of evidence, and that such evidence is capable, in principle, of being clarified. On the other hand, comparatively few would praise the corresponding maxim *Vivo ut intelligam;* for this other maxim would imply that the *only* justification for living at all is to understand our lives, which is a gnostic, or ultra-gnostic, absurdity.

(3). *Per contra,* as we have seen, the contentions of voluntarism in this matter are much less defensible. In so far, indeed, as the "will" means a settled disposition towards action, it is, in the main, identical with the firmer tendencies of our vital existence; and a voluntarism of this species consequently does not differ seriously in its principle from the contention we have just examined. Of it, also, we may say that the total attitude of body and soul engaged in the business of living may be described as "faith," is reflected in cogitative or self-conscious "faith," and includes such beliefs as are not put to the proof in a logical sense.

Voluntarism in the ordinary sense, however, is quite another story. It represents faith and belief as acts of express volition, initiating some adventure in the absence, or even in spite of, evidence, and declaring "I will it to be so," when neither life nor logic decrees the conclusion. Since voluntarism of this species has, however, been sufficiently considered in Chapter VI of the present work, it need not be further considered now. (The extent to which preconnections may legitimately be considered as postulates will be examined later in the present chapter.)

(4). For similar reasons, it seems unnecessary in this place to repeat what has been said concerning the relations between belief and emotion. It should be sufficient to point out that faith, in Dr. Ward's sense, is something much wider than cogitative belief, evidenced or unevidenced; and that faith, regarded as a total vital attitude, may be touched (and indeed is commonly imbued) with emotion in so far as this total vital attitude attains the level of consciousness.

§ 8. Faith and Doubt

The Christian accounts of faith commonly assert or imply that faith, when it rises to the conscious level, includes belief (or at least the seeds of belief), although such belief does not exhaust the fulness of faith's attitude. Consequently (as we saw), the principal problem that had to be faced on these assumptions concerned the way in which faith may be retained in spite of relatively temporary perplexity and wavering.

The normal effect of belief (i.e. of unqualified assent) is complete security in action, so long as the belief prevails, and this normal effect would be inevitable if belief were the sole guide of action. If, on the other hand (as we have seen reason to conclude), active faith frequently precedes and also frequently outruns belief, we can no longer draw these inferences. In so far as faith is a step, or many steps, ahead of belief, there will be faith and action in accordance with faith, although there is not belief. In short, if faith be confidence in action, the opposite of faith is diffidence in action; and diffidence or faltering in action, although it may be the fruit of doubt, may also arise from other causes of a quite uncogitative kind.

By far the most interesting and the most important question in this connection is the relation between *intellectual* perplexity and faith. In so far as belief is evidenced, such intellectual perplexities are due to real or supposed counter-evidence, and all such counter-evidence, whether or not it is conclusive evidence, ought logically to put an obstacle in the way of belief. The question is not simply whether faith (and perhaps a species of belief) may anticipate proper evidence, or continue where evidence, either favorable or unfavorable, is totally absent, but whether faith is entitled to retain its confidence in spite of contrary evidence.

In this sense, it seems plain that faith is fully compatible with a considerable degree of intellectual doubt. The Christian's assurance of the promises is consistent with his admission that there seems to be counter-evidence whose relevance he can not clearly disown although he is certain that somehow these obstacles do not have the menace that they seem to have. In the sciences, similarly, it is common (and not necessarily irrational) to have confidence, almost implicitly, in the truth of some great hypothesis or scientific policy, while admitting that for the time being there are definite objections not yet overcome as well as mere gaps that time and industry should speedily fill. Finally, the attitude of certain professed skeptics is not psychologically impossible, that is to say, it is possible to hold that all our confident expectations in common life are ultimately irrational, and yet to retain a certain kind of assurance whatever the logical evidence may be. If and so far as "belief" is declared to be non-rational, these expectations might legitimately be styled "beliefs"; and there are no doubt certain points of view according to which such skeptics might be said to be without (a certain kind of) faith, although in possession of (another kind of) belief. At this point, however, all such discussions become unprofitably verbal.

§ 9. FAITH AND DEDUCTIVE RATIOCINATION

The historical contrast between faith and sight is not less important than the other principal historical contrast between faith and "reason"; and the discussion of both contrasts has suffered from ambiguity.

In the case of the second of these contrasts, as we saw when considering the views of St. Thomas Aquinas in the present chapter and those of Pascal in a former chapter, the important ambiguity is between "reason" regarded as the entire domain of relevant evidence, and "reason" interpreted much more narrowly as a species of ratiocination, that is to say, as syllogistic deduction from premises.

In the latter sense, it is readily apparent that not all evidence is deductive ratiocination; for, in this sense, all self-evident premises and all premises inductively established are unratiocinated, and may be said to be above reason or beyond the scope of reason (at any rate if there seems to be no hope of *deducing* the premises that are conclusions of an inductive process).

Hence, by an equivocation that should deceive nobody, certain authors falsely conclude, even to-day,[75] that what is unratiocinated must (in the wide and more usual sense of "reason" and "rational") be entirely indefensible from an evidential standpoint—as if a thing that proved itself in its translucent intelligibility, or even something inductively established, were logically on the same footing as something wholly unproved in the sense of being quite arbitrary and altogether irrational.

There should be no need to say more about this equivocation. What is unratiocinated need not be unevidenced. On the contrary, it may be quite perfectly evidenced. Therefore, in the wider sense of "reason" the unratiocinated need not require any faith additional to "reason," although "reason," both in its broader and in its narrower senses, may be said to imply an invincible faith in itself.

St. Thomas Aquinas, at least, did not fall into the error of confusing between evidence and ratiocination, although it is to be feared that Pascal did. On the contrary, Thomas held that "reason" in the sense of deductive ratiocination was an inferior exercise of our intellect, although necessary for humanity. In his view, as we saw, God and the angels would not reason because they would not need to do so. They would apprehend truth immediately by its own light, not indirectly by a chain of inferences.

So regarded, "reason," in the sense of ratiocination, is held to be defective, although not at all false, and something should be said of the conception of perfect knowledge that is implied in this derogatory, or partially derogatory, verdict concerning ratiocination.

The intellectual ideal implied is that everything that is true must either be true in its own light, or else that it should have so transparent a connection with other truths that the whole should be equally luminous in every part.

It is difficult to see why this ideal should be accepted. Why should truth be such that no truths are subordinate and consequential? And if any truths are subordinate and consequential, what need be more transparent, indeed what could be more trans-

---

[75] *Cf.* C. E. M. Joad, *Matter, Life and Value,* p. 114, for an egregious instance of this equivocation.

parent, than the several steps in a chain of logical deduction? We have seen, indeed, that the validity of deductive inference may be challenged, but so may the conceptions of axiomatic self-evidence and of all other intellectual evidence. The point is that there seems no sufficient ground for regarding deductive evidence as inferior to other intellectual evidence.

Speaking generally, indeed, there are serious objections to one of the commoner attempts to make room for faith, viz. the attempt to depict an impossible and unintelligible ideal of intelligibility, and therefore to invoke an intellectual faith that carries us beyond the province of ordinary intellectual processes.

§ 10. FAITH IN RELATION TO INDUCTIVE EVIDENCE

Turning now to inductive evidence, and more particularly to inductive inference from sense-observation and from the experimental questioning of Nature, we have only to recall the general conclusions of the last few chapters of this work in order to see the very close connection between such inductions and a species of scientific faith. Indeed, this connection is a commonplace of contemporary thought, and our endeavor should be, not to exploit this obvious analogy (for that would be a work of supererogation), but to restrict it to its proper domain. The greater part of natural science is based on induction, and such induction makes large drafts upon scientific faith. So much may be said to be established. It does not follow, however, that such faith is ultimately unreason, and therefore that we are at liberty to make *other* large drafts upon "faith" without troubling ourselves overmuch whether we have any "cover" for them in the way of ascertainable evidence.

What has been argued in the present volume is that the greater part of our natural science is based upon observation and experiment; that such sciences are instances of problematic, not of demonstrative or of intuitive, induction; and that our problematic inductions concerning Nature can not yield any high degree of rational probability unless they are governed by certain preconnections or proleptic obumbrations of a natural ground-plan which is not itself self-evident. If so, the *prima facie* inference seems unmistakable. These ground-plans of

Nature are scientific "postulates," scientific policy, scientific faith, and nothing else in the world.

We have also maintained, however, that such ground-plans are persistently and pervasively suggested by the course of Nature, and that they are persistently verified in an evidential way. Their probability, therefore, is not capricious or, in the most important sense of that adjective, downright irrational. And this further contention, I suggest, is essential to the whole situation. In view of it, theologians and philosophers are indeed entitled to argue that the deiformity of Nature is, like its scientific uniformity, suggested by experience and progressively verified in experience, or, again, that some spiritual ground-plan may have the same sort of evidence as, say, a physico-chemical ground-plan. What they have also to show, however, is that these spiritual or theological preconnections have been tested and confirmed with a scrupulous conscientiousness not less sedulous than the "natural" sciences have shown. (The tests, of course, need not be the same tests, but they should not be less exact, or the result more dubious.)

If this be granted (and we have proceeded too far with our exposition to examine the point *de novo*), it is entirely reasonable to notice how much in the natural sciences may properly be said to be matter of scientific faith. To be sure, it is not very much to say with the philosophical detective in the story-book, that "everything must be logical—if you look at it in the right way"; for, as we have seen, it is much harder to suppose that reality could conceivably contradict itself utterly than that it must always be logically consistent. If, however, we mean by this "logical" character the property of presenting no puzzles that are ultimately insoluble by human faculty, we are demanding a great deal of Nature when we insist upon this requirement. For we can not hope to do more intellectually than extend a very few simple principles with very great elaboration, and what, except faith, can assure us that methods of this sort can never be balked, and are everywhere sufficient, supposing, that is, that prejudice is out of the way? As has been frequently observed, the procedure of practicing physicists is most strictly comparable to the plain man's procedure when he tried to put the pieces of a jig-saw puzzle into position. But consider what this analogy implies. However pleasantly tantalizing our jig-saw puzzles may be, we are guided towards a solution by our prior knowledge that the pieces do fit, and that there is a single place for each of them. What right have we, however, to make the same assumptions regarding Nature? In this domain, is not our problem rather the problem of constructing an integrated pattern, although, for all we know, the greater part of the pieces may be missing? And if so, do we not need faith, and again faith, and faith yet again?

Similar considerations should attend the view that the principles, ground-plans, or preconnections of the natural sciences are properly to be regarded as postulates or statements of policy, rather than as statements purporting to be true. If, however, by a "postulate" is meant a *fiat* of the will, possibly capricious and irresponsible—a demand that Nature shall show herself in such and such a way, followed by the comment "So much the worse for Nature," if Nature does not respond—it should be plain that the sciences know nothing of postulates in this irresponsible sense. If, on the other hand, we mean by a "postulate" what Euclid seems to have meant by it (e.g. in his Fifth Postulate), that is to say, a policy of construction and of interpretation, not self-evident, but subject in all its employments to the most rigorous scrutiny and capable of being overthrown if it failed to perform its integrative and interpretative office, then, in that sense, it may well be admitted that the ground-plans of experimental science are as much postulates as premises. What is necessary, in short, is to strip the term "postulate" of misleading associations. Scientific "postulates" of this order are not volitional in any sense in which the practice and the policy of the sciences are not volitional. In particular, they are not "practical" in any sense in which "practice" is opposed to theory, speculation, or evidence. On the contrary, they are principles of procedure expressly speculative in type, pursuing the only defensible speculative policy, that is to say, the policy of interpreting, and conforming to, the evidence.

§ 11. Faith and Intellectual Insight

After so much spade-work and so many attempts to eliminate dead roots and obstructing rubble, it should now be possible for us to state the important relationships between faith and intellectual clarity quite tersely and compendiously.

Firstly, then, it seems clear that there is no essential antagonism between faith and intellectual insight. Faith may be blind and barbaric, but it need not be. Our trust and confidence and practical assurance might still remain, and *would* still remain, if knowledge were added to faith. In other words, although faith may but divine and dimly anticipate without prejudice to its trustfulness, it may also continue to be faith when clarity supervenes and takes the place of these misty divinations. Again, it is to be observed that we have faith in our intellects and in our cogitative faculties generally. This faith or trust is not, indeed, *mere* faith and trust, and it is sharply to be distinguished from a faith that is blind or merely rash, because it is evidenced faith (either self-certified or the conclusion of reasoned evidence) which mere faith is not. Nevertheless, it is wholly authentic faith.

While the possibility of a harmony on these lines, however, is entirely plain, it should be noted, in the second place, that the ideal of perfect science, or of utter intellectual transparency, may receive quite disproportionate importance in these arguments. Even in the mathematical sciences, as we have seen, there is a growing disinclination to maintain that the traditional "axioms," or pellucid, self-evident, self-certifying ultimate principles either exist to the extent that used to be supposed or are as essential to any genuinely intellectual fabric as was formerly maintained.[76] Assuming (as they did) that axiomatic clarity alone was perfect knowledge, medieval theologians were bound to maintain that God, whose ways were always perfect, had this type of knowledge about everything, and, therefore, that everything *could* be known in this perfect way, although, very likely, not by us. Suppose, however, that there could not be knowledge of this special type in regard to much that is nevertheless knowable, and the necessity disappears.

[76] *Cf.* Chap. X, § 6 above.

We have examined this point already in connection with the alleged defective character of deductive ratiocination.[77] A more important consideration, however, is the alleged opacity of the senses, with the consequent denial of anything approaching intellectual insight in the region of all that is empirical. Yet if the senses reveal fact, what right have we to call them opaque? We may say, if we choose, that such facts are "brute" facts, evincing no other reason for their existence than just that we perceive them to be so. But why should not the universe contain this sort of brutal factuality? If it did, it would not indeed be "intelligible" according to one ideal of intelligibility, but it might be understandable in the sense that the interconnections and the logical coherence of such empirical facts could be ascertained in a thorough and systematic way. In short, the opacity of the senses and of their testimony in an intellectual regard has all the appearance of a dogma. We need not hope to understand the universe, if we insist, without preliminary inquiry, that everything within it can only be understood in terms of a certain, quite special, intellectual pattern.

This leads to a third point of importance. I shall not attempt to examine the question whether or not there are truths "above" the intellect and too exalted for any faculty like the human. For aught I am about to say, our intellectual faculties are not, as Mr. Stout said they were, invincible [78]—and there *may* be ineffable truths known only by a super-logic too high for humanity, too eminent for the best-trained human intellect. Much, however, that is thus described in the traditional mystical vein seems to suffer from an initial failure to consider what intellectual comprehension should mean. In so far as these mysteries result from the attempt to describe an intense experience of personal communion in terms of an intellectual comprehension based upon a certain ideal of mathematical intelligibility, it is surely not surprising that they should be regarded as "above," or at least as "beside," the intellect. For personal relations are not of this mathematical order. On the contrary, they are of the order of personal empiricism, that is to say, they are spiritual (not

---

[77] Chap. IX, § 3 above.
[78] *Cf.* Chap. III, § 6 above.

"brute") facts whose only evidence is that they are apprehended for what they are. Their alleged opacity (in an intellectual regard) may well be the result of a false intellectual ideal.

§ 12. MORAL FAITH AND INTELLECTUAL PURIFICATION

St. Augustine's view that perseverance in righteousness is an indispensable preliminary to the clearer sort of intellectual insight is an interesting inversion of the traditional manner in which the close connection between philosophy, as a way of life, and philosophy, as an exercise of the intellect, was conceived. The more usual doctrine was that intellectual discipline purified the soul, making it thereby the apter to embrace the good. The alternative view is that moral faithfulness is the purifying agent, and that the soul thus purified inevitably shows an intellectual advance.

To-day we are much less confident concerning these matters, and are disposed to dispute the ancient doctrine of the essential unity of all the virtues as well as the essential unity between a clear head and a clean heart. We should all concede, it is true, that certain moral qualities, such as sincerity and perseverance, are requisite in any scientific or in any philosophical enterprise worthy of the name, but otherwise we are inclined to hold that great intellectual achievements are quite compatible with weakness, meanness, or even with definite corruptness in a man's moral nature. Indeed, we might even raise the question how far jealousy, rivalry, envy, and petty spite, these detestable private vices, may nevertheless have proved of public benefit in the history of science. These characteristics, we hope and believe, are less prevalent now than they were, say, in the notorious jealousies of scientists in the seventeenth century. We also know, however, that they still exist; and we do not think of scientists and of philosophers as unembittered sages miraculously forgetful of their *amour propre*.

Perhaps, however, we should distinguish in this affair. The pure in heart may not have greater sagacity concerning natural laws than other people, and yet may have much clearer insight than other people into the character of men and, in general, into what we describe as spiritual values. Furthermore, it is a question of perspective how far what we commonly call scientific insight should dominate our thoughts in this connection, and how far human, moral, esthetic, and theological insight should enter. It may well be maintained, although, I dare say, not without some moralistic prejudice and some trace of spiritual pride, that an adequate and synoptic apprehension of the general character of the universe will never arise and will never be able to put central things in the center without very definite and very persistent moral preparation.

§ 13. FAITH AND VALUE

Not infrequently we are told, at the present day, that the object of faith should be regarded as neither more nor less than "the" world of spiritual values, and that this world of values is a timeless and supersensible exemplar, dimly shadowed forth in the highest sensuous music or in the noblest moral aspiration yet also the governing citadel and productive source of all existence. In other words, this "world of values" is a newish name for what used to be called God, although more impersonal, less friendly, and very much vaguer.

It may be doubted whether the philosophy of this subject should be seriously affected by any such change in nomenclature.

Contrariwise, it is plausible to contend that these matters are best approached from the standpoint of *valuation*,[79] in one of the possible senses of that elusive term, and that the total personal attitude that we call "prizing," "setting store by," "setting our hearts upon" is the proper fulcrum of philosophy's lever in these affairs. This attitude of prizing, we are told, is compounded of love, and aspiration, and earnest seeking, sometimes vehement and almost ecstatic, more generally tranquil and profound; and our beliefs reflect, although they also mingle with, this general attitude. Again (it is said), the attitude of personal prizing and setting store is but one part of the story. The other part is the response of the universe to that which we hold sacred and try to lay hands upon. It is the "favor and connivance" of the universe, at the core of it, to our reverence, devotion, and aspiration. It is the quintessential and abiding substance which is

[79] *Cf.* Ch. XVI, § 5.

also the proof that the cries of man's spiritual hunger are not scattered and lost in a wilderness of neutral atoms, but are in some sense heeded and answered, if not individually yet in the large, in the governing metropolis of the cosmic process.

It seems evident that descriptions couched in these terms do, in large measure, actually describe the same facts as were described as "faith" in the Christian tradition. Whether or not the newer descriptions are also the better time only can show. Time may antiquate these novelties, and again it may not. We can scarcely forbear from remarking, however, that, in its widest sense, prizing or "setting store by" is a quite general characteristic of anything in the universe that exhibits any degree of tenacity in its existence. It is obviously a characteristic of all living things, and may well extend much more widely in nature. Accordingly, the essential question is not simply what human beings cling to or endeavor after, but whether humanity (or any other species) clings to and endeavors after what is fine, or noble, or excellent, and whether the universe, in any important sense, is also regulated in accordance with what is fine, or noble, or excellent.

It is impossible even to approach any intelligible examination of this question without thereby implying the possibility of *insight* into what is fine, or noble, or excellent, whether it is man that is adjudged to be potentially noble or whether what is so adjudged is the universe in which man has his being and from which man draws his life. Such insight may be tutored and kindled by much that is not cogitation, and by many forces that are more accurately described as love and loyalty and devotion. Nevertheless, our insight into what is noble or perfect or excellent must ultimately be of an intellectual order. Or so it would seem. For, although many alternatives have been suggested, none has hitherto been even approximately sustained.

In other words, it is neither prudent nor possible to abandon the traditional questions that have been raised for so many centuries concerning faith and knowledge.

SUGGESTIONS FOR READING

In a subject so vast as the present, it is impossible to present an adequate or fully representative bibliography and injudicious to compile a very extensive one. Accordingly, I shall not try to do more than indicate some few of the directions in which a serious student of the subject, not over-familiar with philosophical literature, may browse or study with profit in order to inform and to supplement such reflections as the text may evoke. In making this attempt, I am going to assume that the serious student aforesaid will himself consult the works to which I have referred in the course of my discussion, and that he will not be content simply to accept my accounts of them. And I shall restrict myself to works written in the English language, or translated into that tongue.

Chapter I

This chapter is a general introduction, whose object is to raise questions to be discussed in the sequel. Any relevant bibliography should therefore come later.

Chapter II

Here the intention is to make a plain historical statement, and the matter can be profitably considered in one way only—that is, by a careful study of the historical authors themselves. The perusal of commentaries or general histories of philosophy is, by itself, quite useless. On the other hand, commentaries and the like may usefully supplement the classical texts.

There are plenty of editions of Locke's *Essay*, and of his *Works* generally, as also in the case of Hume's *Treatise* and *Enquiries*. Regarding the latter, however, it should be remarked that the analytical index supplied by Sir L. A. Selby-Bigge in the Clarendon Press editions is particularly useful. Kant's principal works, especially the three *Critiques*, have all been translated with fair accuracy.

Mr. James Gibson's *Locke's Theory of Knowledge* is, in my judgment, by far the best commentary in English upon that author. (The Introduction to Green and Grose's edition of Hume is far too polemical in tone regarding both Locke and Hume.) I do not know of any English commentary upon Hume at all comparable in merit to Mr. Gibson's work upon Locke, but I should advise students to read Chapter I of Mr. Pringle-Pattison's *The Idea of God* in connection with Hume's *Dialogues concerning Natural Religion*. Mr. Kemp Smith's *A Commentary to Kant's Critique of Pure Reason* may be said to have superseded all former English commentaries upon that author, and might usefully be supplemented by reference to the work of R. Adamson, *The Philosophy of Kant* and *The Development of Modern Philosophy*, as well as by James Ward's *A Study of Kant*. (The last writer with special reference to the *Critique of Judgment*, and Symbolical Anthropomorphism). Mr. Whitehead's recent *Process and Reality* contains many valuable comments upon the position of Locke and of Hume.

CHAPTER III

The literature on the general subject of this chapter is too vast to permit any selection from it to be other than arbitrary. I shall content myself with saying that students should not omit the Introduction to Lotze's *Metaphysics* (English Translation, Volume I) and Chapter IV of *The Logic of Hegel* (in the late W. Wallace's translation).

Particular points in the discussion of the chapter should be supplemented by further reading. The student may find the nature of what I have called "contextual monism" more easy to understand if he consults Mr. Bosanquet's *The Principle of Individuality and Value*, Lectures I and II, and also reads Mr. Kemp Smith's paper "The Fruitfulness of the Abstract" (*Aristotelian Society Proceedings*, 1927-1928). On the debate concerning "internal" and "external" relations, Mr. B. Russell's essay on "The Monistic Theory of Truth" in that author's *Philosoph-*

ical Essays, and the ninth essay in Mr. G. E. Moore's *Philosophical Studies,* are perhaps outstanding. Concerning the realistic doctrine of perception, Mr. Hasan's recent *Realism* may be commended, and the most recent form of what I have called an "underhat" theory of perception is to be found in Mr. B. Russell's *An Outline of Philosophy.* Mr. Hoernlé's essay upon "Saving the Appearances," in his *Studies in Contemporary Metaphysics,* deals with an aspect of the general question very germane to the discussion in this chapter. On "Activity," Chapter VII in Mr. F. H. Bradley's *Appearance and Reality* seems to me of great importance. It should be read in connection with the relevant portions of Mr. Stout's *Analytic Psychology,* particularly Book II, Chapter 1.

CHAPTER IV

In this chapter, even more than in the others, an attempt has been made to allow the discussion itself to indicate a suitable bibliography.

I would suggest that the student supplement these indications (1) by making himself familiar with the Greek conception of ἐπιστήμη, and (2) by refreshing his memory concerning the history of Pragmatism. On the first of these, a judicious use of the information supplied by Mr. A. E. Taylor's *Plato: The Man and his Work* and by Mr. W. D. Ross's *Aristotle* should guide the reader to the most important passages in the Greek (translations are readily accessible). On the second point, the selections given in Mr. D. S. Robinson's *An Anthology of Recent Philosophy* seem to me to be admirable, and very well adapted for guidance in further study. Mr. C. I. Lewis's *Mind and the World-Order* gives recent and important expression to a point of view largely pragmatistic. It reached me after the present work had gone to the press; and the same (likewise to my regret) is true of Mr. Dewey's *The Quest for Certainty.* I need hardly say that I wish to lay emphasis on both these works in this short bibliography.

The question of "knowledge by acquaintance" should, I think, be followed up rather sedulously by a careful study of the portions of J. Grote's and of W. James's works that are referred to in the text. On the nature of "presentations," see Ward's *Psychological Principles*, Chapter IV. Mr. B. Russell's essay "On the Nature of Truth and Falsehood" (*Philosophical Essays;* also published in the *Proceedings of the Aristotelian Society,* 1909) develops the best known of his theories of judgment. It has been much discussed and remains important, although Mr. Russell has now abandoned it.

CHAPTER V

As in the case of its predecessor, this chapter has been designed to guide the student's reading. James Mill's account of Belief should be read in the edition of the *Analysis* edited by Bain and J. S. Mill. The account of Belief in Mr. Stout's *Analytic Psychology* (especially Book II, Chapter xi) is particularly valuable. Dr. F. C. S. Schiller's *Problems of Belief* should also be consulted.

On dreams, see S. Freud's *The Interpretation of Dreams* and Varendonck's *The Psychology of Day-dreaming.*

CHAPTER VI

In connection with the main topic of this chapter the reader should consider the problem of the limits of explanatory hypotheses concerning Nature (taking his start e.g. from Mill's *Logic*, Book III, Chapter XIV, the chapter on the artificiality of science in H. Poincaré's *The Value of Science*, or generally, the same author's *Science and Hypothesis*).

On "miracles," Mr. A. E. Taylor's recent Leslie Stephen Lecture on *David Hume and the Miraculous* is stimulating and important. On "meaning," *The Meaning of Meaning* by Messrs. Ogden and Richards has won deserved recognition. See also a symposium in the *Aristotelian Society Proceedings: Supplementary Volume VII*, and many works on symbolism, e.g. Mr. Whitehead's with that title.

CHAPTER VII

There is, of course, an immense literature on the relations between the sciences and philosophy. Among recent discussions, one of the best is Mr. C. D. Broad's in the Introduction to his *Scientific Thought.*

On the "Theory of Types" and its relation to the historical refutation of skepticism, see Russell and Whitehead, *Principia Mathematica,* Volume I, and B. Russell, *American Journal of Mathematics,* Volume XXX, No. 3.

The short Platonic Dialogue called the *Euthyphro* should be read in full as an example of Socratic method in definition.

The clear and admirably terse discussion in Mr. Whitehead's *Process and Reality,* Chapter I, may be specially mentioned in connection with the general questions dealt with in this chapter.

CHAPTER VIII

The concluding chapters of F. H. Bradley's *Logic* and the final chapter of B. Bosanquet's *Logic* are perhaps the most important pieces of reading in English on the main subject of this chapter.

In the age-long controversy on universals, Mr. Stout's recent paper "The Nature of Universals and Propositions" (*British Academy Proceedings,* Volume X) has perhaps broken fresh ground. *Cf. Aristotelian Society Proceedings: Supplementary Volume III* and N. K. Smith in *Mind,* Nos. 142, 143, and 144.

On Logic, and on Relations and their types, Lecture II in B. Russell's *Our Knowledge of the External World* should be carefully studied. The controversy between Messrs. Bradley and Russell in *Mind,* 1910 and 1911, is still of interest and importance. On the relation between primitive propositions and their certainty, see again *Principia Mathematica,* Volume I.

CHAPTER IX

Here the student should continue his studies in the principal English works on logic since Mill's time, viz. Bradley, Bosanquet, H. W. B. Joseph, B. Russell, Johnson, and Cook Wilson. The title of Mr. Joseph's book is *An Introduction to Logic.*

CHAPTER X

On the "logicizing" of arithmetic, see Mr. B. Russell's *Principles of Mathematics* as well as his *Introduction to Mathemat-*

ical Philosophy. In the text I have endeavored to explain the contrast between these views and the same author's opinions in his *Analysis of Matter,* and also to indicate the wide suggestions for reading made, e.g., by Mr. G. H. Hardy's article in *Mind,* No. 149. The work of Dr. H. M. Scheffer, Mr. F. P. Ramsey, and other contemporary authors in current mathematical journals are of special importance. On non-Euclidean geometry, Bonola's work with that title (English translation, Open Court, Chicago, 1912) is perhaps the most generally readable.

The reader who makes a beginning with these suggestions will soon perceive how tangled and extensive a country he has entered, and had better seek advice from practising mathematicians. Here it is only possible to suggest where he might start.

CHAPTER XI

Among the historical protagonists of intuitionism (of a rational cast) in British ethical philosophy, the following are perhaps the chief: Butler, *Sermons,* and the "Dissertation on Virtue" in the *Analogy of Religion;* R. Price, *Review of the Principal Questions and Difficulties in Morals;* T. Reid, *Essays on the Active Powers of Man,* Essay III, Part iii, Essay V, Chapter 1; W. Whewell, *The Elements of Morality,* Book II. (H, Sidgwick's account of Intuitionism in *The Methods of Ethics,* Part III, is classical. See also H. Rashdall, *The Theory of Good and Evil* Volume I, Chapters IV, V, and VI.)

Kant's *Fundamental Principles* and *Critique of Practical Reason* (which express his type of rational intuitionism) have been translated, e.g. by T. K. Abbott.

Among recent expositions (or indications towards an exposition) of rational intuitionism, Mr. H. A. Prichard's article "Does Moral Philosophy Rest on a Mistake?" (*Mind,* January 1912), and his Inaugural Lecture "Duty and Interest" (Oxford, 1928) should be mentioned, as also E. F. Carritt's recent *Theory of Morals* (especially Chapters VIII and XIV).

Mr. G. E. Moore's *Principia Ethica* expounds a "new" intuitionism with regard to "good" (not "right" as in traditional intuitionism).

Regarding the theory of value, see W. M. Urban, *Valuation; Its Nature and Laws* (the author has more recently published *The Intelligible World*); R. B. Perry, *General Theory of Value;* and *The Idea of Value* by the present writer.

CHAPTER XII

The term "sensum" seems to have come to stay, and to have supplanted its forerunners, such as sense-datum, sensible, and *sensibile*. The following reading concerning what may be called "the sensum theory" may be suggested. B. Russell, *Our Knowledge of the External World*, Lectures III and IV, and *Analysis of Mind*, passim; G. E. Moore, *Philosophical Studies*, Chapters II, V, and VII; S. Alexander, *Space, Time and Deity*, Volume II, pp. 158 *sqq.;* Berkeley, *The Principles of Human Knowledge;* C. D. Broad, *Scientific Thought*, Part II; G. F. Stout, *Manual of Psychology*, Book III, especially Part II.

On the special problem of the Specious Present, see James and McTaggart as referred to in the text, and Broad, *op.cit.*, pp. 348 *sqq.*

On the meanings or meaning of Idealism, R. F. A. Hoernlé's *Idealism* is useful and readable. J. Royce's *The Spirit of Modern Philosophy* and *Lectures on Modern Idealism* also supply a good general account. Naturally, these books are here referred to only as starting points for prolonged study. Idealism in some form is a description of the greater part of philosophy.

In the immense and rapidly growing literature on the relation of modern physics to the testimony of the senses the following reading may be suggested, again as a start. A. N. Whitehead, *The Principles of Natural Knowledge* and *Science and the Modern World;* B. Russell, *The Analysis of Matter;* A. S. Eddington, *The Nature of the Physical World;* and the works of C. D. Broad and of S. Alexander *ut supra*. Valuable comments on Eddington's book have been made by H. W. B. Joseph (*Hibbert Journal*, April, 1929). G. Dawes Hicks (*Aristotelian Society Proceedings*, 1928-1929) and R. B. Braithwaite (*Mind*, No. 152).

CHAPTER XIII

The subject of memory is discussed in all systematic works on psychology and in most accounts of what used to be called "the Philosophy of Mind." I have referred in particular to the works of Semon, James, Santayana, and Broad because of the special points raised. A good general account of historical views on the subject is given by Miss B. Edgell in her *Theories of Memory*. She discusses, *inter alia*, Samuel Butler's *Life and Habit*, Professor Watson's *Psychology from the Standpoint of a Behaviourist*, T. Hobbes's celebrated theory of memory as "decaying sense" in the *Leviathan* and elsewhere, the views of S. Alexander (*Space, Time and Deity*) and of B. Russell (*The Analysis of Mind*), together with M. Bergson's theories (*Matter and Memory*). Views similar to those I am expressing in this chapter are to be found in my *Study in Realism*, Chapter III.

Thomas Reid's account of memory (*Intellectual Powers*, Essay III) seems to me of permanent value.

With the exception of R. Flint's *History of the Philosophy of History*, elaborate or extensive works originally written in English concerning the philosophy of history or the general character of historical knowledge do not seem to be common. Thus, in the rather full bibliography in Mr. F. J. Teggart's *Prolegomena to History*, the preponderance of French or German works is very striking. The English-speaking reader might with advantage begin (I think) with Mr. Teggart's *Theory of History* and with Mr. Pringle-Pattison's lecture on *The Philosophy of History* (*British Academy Proceedings*, Volume xi).

CHAPTER XIV

On Introspection generally, reference may be made to C. D. Broad, *The Mind and its Place in Nature*, Chapter VI; Stout, *Manual of Psychology*, Introduction, Chapter II; B. Russell, *The Analysis of Mind*, Chapter I; W. James, *Essays in Radical Empiricism* ("Does Consciousness Exist?"); S. Alexander, *Space, Time and Deity*, Introduction, and *passim*; an article in *Mind*,

No. 112; and discussions in *Aristotelian Society Supplementary Volumes* VII, VIII, and IX (various writers).

On endosomatic or organic sensa, see Stout, *Manual of Psychology*, Book II, Chapter II; W. James, *Principles of Psychology*, Chapters IX, X, and XXV; and the present writer's *Problems of the Self*, Chapter III.

On Multiple Personality and kindred matters, see, e.g., Morton Prince's *The Dissociation of a Personality* and Janet's *The Major Symptoms of Hysteria*.

On the "pure" Ego," see Ward, *Psychological Principles*, Chapters II and XV, and *A Study of Kant;* Broad, *The Mind and its Place in Nature*, Chapter VI; H. J. Paton, "Self-Identity," *Mind*, No. 151; and J. M. E. McTaggart, article "Self" in Hastings' *Encyclopædia of Religion and Ethics*, also *The Nature of Existence*, Volume II, pp. 62 *sqq.*

CHAPTER XV

On the general problem of this chapter, reference may be made to A. E. Taylor, *Elements of Metaphysics*, Book I, Chapter iii, § 2; S. Alexander, *Space, Time and Deity*, Book III, Chapter I, Section B; C. D. Broad, *The Mind and its Place in Nature*, Chapter VII; and my *Problems of the Self*, pp. 24 *sqq.*

CHAPTER XVI

On the general esthetic question, such works as E. F. Carritt, *The Theory of Beauty;* R. Fry, *Transformations;* C. Bell, *Art;* B. Bosanquet, *History of Aesthetics*, and *Three Lectures on Aesthetics;* L. Abercrombie, *Towards a Theory of Art;* Croce, *Aesthetics;* and Ruskin, *Modern Painters*, Parts I, II, and III may be consulted.

On the wider issues, see A. Ritschl, *The Christian Doctrine of Justification and Reconciliation* (translated by H. R. Mackintosh and A. B. Macaulay), as well as Mr. C. C. J. Webb's *Pascal's Philosophy of Religion.*

The references previously given to works on the theory of value are here presupposed.

CHAPTER XVII

Among works on probability (written in or translated into English) other than those mentioned in the text, the following may be mentioned: J. Bentham, *Rationale of Judicial Evidence;* G. Boole, *Investigations of Laws of Thought on which are founded the Mathematical Theories of Logic and Probabilities;* G. Chrystal, *On some Fundamental Principles in the Theory of Probability;* A. De Moivre, *Doctrine of Chances* (1718); F. Y. Edgeworth, *Probability, (Encyclopædia Britannica,* Eleventh Edition); L. T. Hobhouse, *Theory of Knowledge,* Chapters x and xi; Laplace (translation), *A Philosophical Essay on Probabilities;* K. Pearson, *The Grammar of Science;* H. Poincaré (translation), *Science and Hypothesis;* A. Quetelet (translation), *Popular Instructions on the Calculation of Probabilities,* (1839); I. Todhunter, *A History of the Mathematical Theory of Probability from the Time of Pascal to that of Laplace;* W. A. Whitworth, *Choice and Chance* (Second Edition, Cambridge, 1878); G. U. Yule, *An Introduction to the Theory of Statistics.*

CHAPTER XVIII

In this chapter, the attempt is made to review the previous argument (especially the argument of Books II and III) from a fresh point of view, and to attempt a restatement of Reid's point of view (see especially *Intellectual Powers,* Essay VI), together with a wider formulation of certain apparent implications of Kant's position in the Analytic of the *Critique of Pure Reason.* The important point, therefore, is to study these authors in detail. Reference has already been made to Mr. Kemp Smith's Commentary on Kant. It is particularly valuable on the topics of the present chapter. Among commentaries on Reid, Mr. O. N. Jones's *Empiricism and Intuitionism in Reid's Common Sense Philosophy* is likely to be useful. Mr. A. D. Lindsay's *The Philosophy of Bergson* shows in an interesting general fashion how the problem of the preconnections of "science" have tended to be interpreted more widely since Kant's day.

The anthropological evidence referred to in the text is intended to be merely illustrative. Stress, therefore, need not be laid on the differences between this or the other anthropological school, e.g. between M. Durkheim's work and Sir James Frazer's in *The Golden Bough*, and its successors.

CHAPTER XIX

The emphasis laid in the text on the treatment of induction in Mr. J. M. Keynes's *A Treatise on Probability*, Part III and in Mr. C. D. Broad's articles in *Mind*, Nos. 108 and 113, is here reiterated. (*Cf.* Chapter XI of Mr. F. R. Tennant's *Philosophical Theology*, Volume I, and Mr. Broad's Presidential Address to the Aristotelian Society in 1927.) Venn's *Empirical Logic* is an admirable commentary on Mill's *Logic* (which, I am implying, is not yet and will never be out of date concerning the special problem of this chapter). The same must be said of the treatment of probability in relation to induction in Jevons' *The Principles of Science*.

On the general question of Analogy, see any standard work on Logic. On the principle of Extensive Abstraction, see Whitehead's *Principles of Natural Knowledge* and B. Russell's *Our Knowledge of the External World*.

CHAPTER XX

In addition to the works mentioned in the text, see A. J. Balfour, *The Foundations of Belief*, and *Humanism and Theism;* A. Caldecott, *Philosophy of Religion, Selections;* H. Scott Holland, *The Philosophy of Faith;* W. R. Inge, *Faith and its Psychology;* Martineau, *A Study of Religion;* W. R. Matthews, *Some Modern Problems of Faith;* J. B. Pratt, *Psychology of Religious Belief;* F. R. Tennant, *op. cit.*

INDEX

This index contains no reference; (a) to the governing terms "knowledge" "belief" and "opinion" or to the recurrent term "certainty", (b) to topics or proper names occurring in chapters or sections of chapters where such topics or proper names are mentioned in the titles of the chapters or sections, (c) to the bibliography, (d) to what the author considers incidental or episodic at any given place. The author hopes that his selection is not unduly arbitrary.

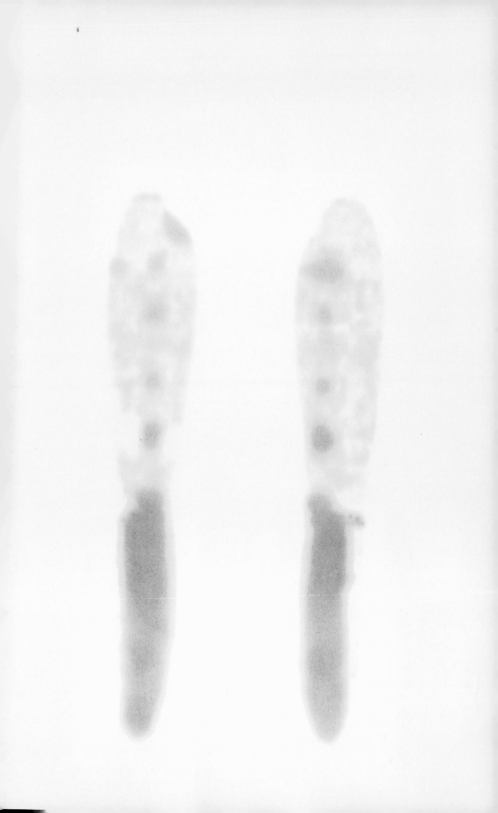

DATE DUE	
DEC 1 2 2005	

GAYLORD   PRINTED IN U.S.A.